THE SUBSTANCE OF CERVANTES

The substance of Cervantes

JOHN G. WEIGER

University of Vermont

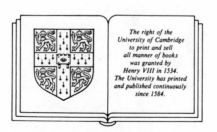

The right of the
University of Cambridge
to print and sell
all manner of books
was granted by
Henry VIII in 1534.
The University has printed
and published continuously
since 1584.

Cambridge University Press

Cambridge

London   New York   New Rochelle

Melbourne   Sydney

This book's dedication is for
LESLIE
for her dedication to this book

Published by the Press Syndicate of the University of Cambridge
The Pitt Building, Trumpington Street, Cambridge CB2 1RP
32 East 57th Street, New York, NY 10022, USA
10 Stamford Road, Oakleigh, Melbourne 3166, Australia

First published 1985

Printed in the United States of America

Library of Congress Cataloging in Publication Data
Weiger, John G.
The substance of Cervantes.
Bibliography: p.
Includes index.
1. Cervantes Saavedra, Miguel de, 1547–1616–
Criticism and interpretation.   I. Title.
PQ6351.W4   1985   863'.3   84–23264
ISBN 0 521 30516 0

Contents

Beware lest you lose the substance by grasping at the shadow.
                                    – Aesop, "The Dog and the Shadow"

                    ... for not in elegance
                    and manner of speech lies the foundation
                    and the principal substance
                    of truthful narration,
                    which in pure truth has its sustentation.
                        – Cervantes, *La Galatea*, Book III

Preface

The substance of Cervantes. Surely this phrase sounds presumptuous or platitudinous. But the substance of Cervantes that I seek to explore in this book is found not in an esoteric, exegetic interpretation but, rather, in an examination and revelation of what underlies his work. Generations of Cervantes' readers have moved from simple laughter through romantic idealization to mystical exegesis and, more recently, corrective textual scrutiny, but the point of departure for all readings must depend on the fundamental substance of the works. I take my title from the *OED* definition of "substance": "That which underlies or supports; a basis, foundation; a ground, cause... The vital part... That which gives a thing its character; that which constitutes the essence of a thing; the essential part, essence."

In order to come to grips with that substance, that essence, it is necessary to seek Cervantes' purpose. I do not claim to reveal that purpose, for such is beyond my capability. But I do bring to the fore how Cervantes portrayed his readers; how he depicted them as having misunderstood his intent; which elements he thought had been misinterpreted; how he saw himself and his writings in contrast to the views of those who presumed to understand and even enjoy those works; and how he saw the development of his and his nation's art during his lifetime. My first chapter takes up the matter of his purpose in *Don Quixote*; my sixth chapter examines his perception of Spanish literature during what we generally call Spain's Golden Age, now reduced ironically, in the minds of all too many, to Cervantes alone.

Don Quixote, confronted with the existence of his spurious namesake (the Avellaneda version), insisted that "no hay otro yo en el mundo" ("there is no other I in the world"). Although no one has claimed to be Cervantes other than the one we all know, that one we presume to know does not always turn out to be the same one after all. In Shakespeare's case, there is little uncertainty with respect to his having intended to write a history play or a comedy or a tragedy in, say, *Richard III, A Comedy of Errors*, or *Hamlet*, respectively. Yet with regard to Cervantes, the debate continues over whether his best-known work was intended to be a burlesque or a serious work. If it has been conclusively demonstrated that his contemporaries saw *Don Quixote* as a funny book, that evidence does not tell us that such was ipso facto the original intention of Cervantes himself. Chapter 1, which explores this matter, is a substantially expanded version of an article published in the *Bulletin of Hispanic Studies* in 1983.

What is meant by originality? Is it synonymous with newness? Is it a chronological matter – what comes first – or is it an aesthetic concern – what is best? Can originality displease? Is an imitation equal or even superior to its original, in whatever terms one may wish to use for considering such qualities in art? If Homer is better at epic poetry than those who preceded him, does the fact that others did precede him forbid us to speak of his originality?

A number of my publications deal with the problem of originality, particularly with reference to the theater of Cervantes' time – the *comedia nueva* championed by Lope de Vega – but it was not until 1978, when my good friend the noted Italian scholar Rinaldo Froldi invited me to lecture on the subject at the University of Bologna, that I first probed the nature of originality as Cervantes confronted it. Later that year, I presented a condensed version of that lecture at the first Congreso Internacional Sobre Cervantes in Madrid. Chapter 2 of this book is an outgrowth of those presentations.

The *OED* definition of "substance" – "that which gives a thing its character" – is particularly germane to Chapter 3. The question of illusion is patently characteristic of Cervantes' works. Episodes in which people mistake one object for another, situations in which identities are confused or concealed, conjurors who misrepresent reality, and ultimately the philosophical issue of appearance and reality – all these are readily associated with Cervantes' writings. But if this is part of the character, what is the "that" that provides it (to paraphrase the *OED*)? In a word, what is that character's substance?

The title of Chapter 3, "The Reality of Illusion," is plain: I seek not to interpret illusion but to demonstrate its real, physical basis. To see the windmills episode exclusively in a quixotic environment, which is to say, to read it only in the immediate context of Don Quixote's idiosyncrasy, or even to seek in the chivalric romances the source of the "giants," is to miss Cervantes' technique as he explores, not only there but in numerous episodes and in various works, the substance of illusion in a broad range of settings. It may seem a simplistic conclusion to reach, in Chapter 3, that the basis of illusion is, more often than not, reality. My purpose in that chapter, however, is not to elucidate the illusion but to study Cervantes' ways – and they are many – of presenting, rationalizing, scrutinizing, and revealing the phenomenon.

Chapter 4 presents the other side of the coin: "The Illusion of Reality." The premise is again the substance of the writer's art, namely, how to project to the reader's mind the images for which mere words must serve as the medium. It is one thing to narrate the effects of illusion on fictive characters; the challenge presented by the need to convey an illusion of reality without the resources of the dramatist (scenery, sounds, gestures, costumes, movement, distance, etc.) is measured by the writer's capacity for dealing with words. Moreover, the writer of fiction must have an understanding of the capacity of the reader for dealing with those same words. It is not enough to report that something happened or to construct a lively dialogue. The reader's inner eye must be able to visualize the setting and the action as graphically as though they were being witnessed directly. Cervantes' lifelong attraction to the stage serves him well as he attempts to convey the sights and sounds and the perspectives that distance, spatial relationships, and motion require – in short, the illusion that our minds are receiving, hence perceiving, the images that originally were in the author's mind alone. In Chapter 4 I have chosen examples primarily from Cervantes' first major work, *La Galatea*, published twenty years before *Don Quixote, Part I*, for it was in this pastoral novel that Cervantes experimented with these matters.

If Chapter 5 appears at first to take us into philosophical inquiry, a patient reading will reveal that we are still concerned with the underlying substance. The metaphorical representation of the soul as the triad of intellect, memory, and will is explored in that chapter not in exegetic terms but with the intention of showing how Cervantes can take a commonplace of his time and work significant portions of his plots around it. The reader of this chapter will find future perusals of Cervantes' works more fruitful, I daresay, as passages that invoke the so-called faculties of the soul reveal a carefully structured plot that otherwise might have been less evident.

In Chapter 5, I seek first to establish the frequency of the metaphor. We may tend to dismiss it nowadays as an inaccurate and threadbare apothegm, but this disregard for its significance is based either on philosophical reasoning or on the hackneyed nature of the cliché. Yet it is on the very triteness of its substance that we ought to focus. Precisely because it was a commonplace, readily recognized by Cervantes' contemporaries as a metaphorical description of the soul, the allusion to the three faculties served as a kind of shorthand. Cervantes used it not only for serious treatments of ethical issues but as well in sardonic, ironic, and even farcical contexts. If today the reader needs to be apprised of the metaphor's meaning, Cervantes could count on his contemporary readers' immediate recognition of the commonplace, which is to say that variations, distortions, and inversions would be noted and appreciated. The substance that I bring out in this chapter, accordingly, is not so much an analysis of the metaphor in question as a demonstration of how Cervantes used a cliché of this sort.

Chapter 6, as I have already remarked, reveals Cervantes' perception of the literature of his time and nation. An evident contrast emerges between the optimism of his younger years, a period during which he and others believed themselves to be engaged in daring experimentation, and the disappointment of his later years. That disappointment was animated not by a sense of failure on his own part but by the paucity of good poets in seventeenth-century Spain as he saw it. His sarcastic comment in the 1615 *Don Quixote* that there were then only three and a half poets was only one manifestation of this attitude. Little could he have known that centuries later it would be his own colossal stature that not only would continue to overshadow even such giants as Lope de Vega, Calderón, Quevedo, Góngora, Tirso de Molina – in short, what we call Spain's Golden Age – but would frequently provoke the question, "What else has Spain produced but Cervantes?" If that question reveals the ignorance of those who pose it, the irony lies in the fact that Cervantes, who foresaw the greatness of the Golden Age in his praises of the 1580s, found little to substantiate that greatness in the years when he produced the two parts of *Don Quixote*, his *Novelas ejemplares*, many of his dramatic works, and the posthumously published *Persiles y Sigismunda*.

The excursion into matters related to the Spanish national drama and several dramatists known primarily to specialists is not the digression it may at first appear to be. Inasmuch as the focus of Chapter 6 is on Cervantes' perception of the poetry and poets of his time, it is necessary to devote some attention to what the latter were about. Cervantes had several competitors (Mateo Alemán, for instance), but it is his rivalry with Lope de Vega that is central to a comprehension of the matters dealt with in this chapter. Although we tend to concentrate on Cervantes' prose fiction, it was in the theater that he aspired to success throughout his life. But to understand Cervantes' aspirations and frustrations, it is not enough to read his plays – and even some of these (*La entretenida*, for example) can be fully appreciated only against the background of the dominant Lopean formula.

Whether or not we today think highly of his theater, if it is our purpose to understand his dreams and dashed hopes in this regard, then we must understand the ambience in which, along with many poets of minor reputation, he labored. However much we may wish to applaud some of his dramas today, the fact remains that little applause was heard in the days when what was good was defined as *de Lope*. The frequent passages in Cervantes' works that deal with dramatic theory and success on the stage are invariably circumscribed by what others have done, from the days of his youth through the 1580s to the Lopean heyday. In order to understand Cervantes' posture, then, it is necessary to shed some light on what others like him were attempting to accomplish in the period just before Lope's dominance. The creation of a genre known as the *comedia* has been the subject of much of my research, the overriding conclusion of which is that, manuals of literary history to the contrary notwithstanding, the *comedia* was created not by one individual (Lope de Vega) but by a host of poets in the late 1570s and the 1580s who collectively contributed many of the ingredients that Lope later institutionalized as part of a virtually inviolable formula. Needless to say, most of these dramatists have been forgotten by all but specialists. Had Cervantes not written the prose works that make him unique, he too would be a footnote alongside the likes of Virués, Artieda, Tárrega, Cueva, and others. But all of these writers, among them Cervantes, believed themselves to be creating the kind of theater that would be appropriate for the Spain of their time. It was this belief, this feeling that they were daring to challenge dogmatic theory in the post-Lepanto and pre-Armada years, that animated the ambience that in turn informed Cervantes' perception of those times.

In recent years, scholars have shown that many episodes of *Don Quixote* were not written in the order in which they appear in the published version. Cervantists have been able to shed light on some textual inconsistencies, clarify confusing chapter headings, and reveal the author at work, so to speak. Clearly at issue is an intriguing aspect of the novel's substance.

It has long been held that Chapters 1–8 or, possibly, 1–7 constituted the extent of Cervantes' original plan (that is, a short story along the lines of his exemplary tales), and that the ultimate elaboration of the work into a full-length novel was a later development. But even within these early chapters there are inconsistencies and contradictions beyond those of a misplaced epigraph or a tardy division into chapters. In Chapter 7 of this book, I examine some of these discrepancies and postulate the existence of an early draft, one that included neither Chapters 1–3 and 8 nor certain parts of 4 and 7 but comprised only Chapters 5 and 6, plus portions of 4 and 7. Through acceptance of this proposition, for which I present much supporting evidence, a number of inconsistencies, ranging from the incidental to the substantive, are clarified.

Though less intricate, revision is found also in Part II of the novel. The matter of when Avellaneda's spurious continuation came to Cervantes' attention has long interested readers of *Don Quixote*, for there is speculation that Cervantes was influenced by Avellaneda's work long before it was officially acknowledged in Chapter 59 of Part II. But it is on a smaller scale that I examine revision in Part II. One of the three lawsuits brought to Sancho Panza's attention at Barataria interrupts the posing of a riddle. The evident relocation of this lawsuit has long been recognized. I close Chapter 7 with an examination of this episode, for

its interpretation leads us full circle in our understanding of *Don Quixote*
as a book that was received as a comedy and in our understanding that
such was not Cervantes' intention; in our understanding of Cervantes'
use of literary models for his refashioning and for accommodation to
new purposes; in short, in our understanding of his handling of the
substance of his works.

I have tried, as much as possible, to limit quotations to English renditions.
These are, unless otherwise noted, my own translations. Where helpful,
particularly to scholars, I have given the original in the notes. On some
occasions I have put the original Spanish in the text. In these cases my
reasoning has been that for English- and Spanish-speaking readers alike,
the immediate presence of the Spanish passage will be of help in making
clear the points I wish to bring out. The sections on *disparate* and the
faculties of the soul, in particular, reflect this practice. My procedure
may strike some readers as capricious, but my intention is pragmatic.
Rather than please those who prefer form to function, my aim is to serve
those who seek to follow my arguments. Accordingly, inasmuch as the
book is written in English and directed at those who read English, my
primary concern is to use English wherever possible. To follow each
and every quotation with the Spanish original – whether in the text or
in the notes – seems to me an infelicitous way of cluttering the pages
with material that is readily available to the Spanish-speaking reader. In
many cases, however – especially where works other than *Don Quixote*
are quoted – I have sensed that some readers might want to make immediate comparisons, and in these cases I have included the Spanish (in
the text for brief phrases, in the notes for lengthier passages). In some
instances what is at issue is not so much the meaning of a phrase or
sentence as the particular wording, sequence, verb form, or configuration. In these instances, I have placed the Spanish first, so that even the
reader without a knowledge of Spanish will focus first on those elements
(always followed by an English translation) in order to follow the thread
of my argument.

   Unless otherwise noted, quotations from *Don Quixote* are taken from
the edition of Martín de Riquer (Barcelona: Planeta, 1975); those from
La Galatea are taken from the edition of J. B. Avalle-Arce (Madrid:
Espasa-Calpe, 1961); those from *Persiles y Sigismunda* from Avalle-Arce's
edition (Madrid: Castalia, 1969); those from the *Entremeses* from Eugenio
Asensio's edition (Madrid: Castalia, 1970); and those from the remaining
works from Angel Valbuena Prat's edition of the *Obras completas* (Madrid:
Aguilar, 1956). Quotations from *Don Quixote* are identified by part and
chapter rather than by pagination, given the variety of editions to which
readers have access. I have similarly identified citations from the *Persiles*

(book and chapter), the *Viaje del Parnaso* (chapter), and *La Galatea* (book). Page references to the *Entremeses* refer to the Asensio edition, and references to other works, notably the *Novelas ejemplares,* are identified by the page on which the original may be found in the Valbuena Prat edition of the *Obras completas* (referred to as *Obras*). Although this last is an unreliable text for certain critical purposes, it is still the most accessible one-volume edition of Cervantes' complete works. I share my profession's reluctance to use this text but I agree with the recent remark of the Modern Language Association: "The advantage of this Aguilar publication is obvious, for it permits students to consult *La Galatea,* the exemplary novels, *Persiles y Sigismunda,* and Cervantes' lesser-known works" (Richard Bjornson, ed., *Approaches to Teaching Cervantes' "Don Quixote"* [New York: Modern Language Association of America, 1984], p. 8).

I have consistently spelled Don Quixote's name with the "x" that Cervantes used (the "j" of modern Spanish was not used with the title until the eighteenth century) because of the importance this detail assumes in the conclusions offered in Chapter 7. It might be argued that for consistency I should have used Pança instead of Panza, Rozinante instead of Rocinante, and spellings like *hazer* instead of *hacer.* My purpose, however, was not to reproduce a paleographic text but to concentrate on the implications of the pronunciation of the protagonist's name, as detailed in Chapter 7.

The image of the scholar as recluse is a romantic myth. This book could not exist were it not for the support and collaboration of many people. First place among these is unquestionably held by my wife, Leslie, who not only typed every word of every draft – and there were many – but also offered helpful criticism regarding sentence structure, choice of vocabulary, and readability. Her dedication to this book has earned her its dedication in return, a tribute far more real than symbolic.

Less direct but no less appreciated have been the support and encouragement given me over the years by Dr. Janet Whatley, who chaired my department for the past few years, and by Dr. Timothy Murad, her successor. In addition to other matters, these two colleagues – scholars in their own right – paid me the highest compliment an author can receive: They read my works. The support of my parents, Willy and Elisabeth Weiger, always there when I needed it, deserves a special note of thanks.

To Elizabeth Maguire, humanities editor of Cambridge University Press, I wish to express an appreciation that goes beyond the normal indebtedness of an author to his editor. The support she gave me from the outset, the faith she maintained in my work, and the goodwill and patience with which she managed the problems that came her way helped to bring this undertaking to fruition. Janis Bolster spent many hours with the manuscript and offered valuable editorial comment for which I shall always be grateful. Martin Dinitz, my production editor, provided direction that turned a manuscript into a book.

I should like to thank the University of Vermont for providing me with a year's sabbatical leave, during which I was able to travel, read, think, write, and above all, rethink and revise. Chapter 3, in particular, was supported by a research grant awarded me by the university's graduate college. My indebtedness must also include the students of my course on Cervantes. Their stimulating questions over the years have provided me with much food for thought. Finally, I wish to thank Liverpool University Press, publishers of the *Bulletin of Hispanic Studies*, for permission to include in Chapter 1 the article which I published in that journal and which served as the nucleus of its namesake here.

Chapter 1

Don Quixote:
the comedy in spite of itself

Cervantes was one of the very few artists the world has known who made absurdity a positive value.
– William Byron, *Cervantes: A Biography*

Midway in the journey between London and Canterbury, Chaucer's host urged the monk to recite his tale, concluding with this epigrammatic counsel: "But be nat wrooth, my lord, though that I pleye, / Ful ofte in game a sooth I have herd seye!"[1] It is unlikely that Cervantes was familiar with Chaucer, but he surely would have agreed with the truism expressed in the prologue to "the Monk's Tale." In point of fact, Chaucer's aphorism, that truth is often spoken in jest, finds its echo in *Don Quixote* in a context of marked pertinence to the subject of this chapter: Surprised that Sancho Panza is not the buffoon that a reading of *Don Quixote*, Part I, might lead some to expect, a character in *Don Quixote*, Part II, observes that "jests turn into truth, and the mockers find themselves mocked (II, 49).[2] The reference to mockers is an allusion to the duke and duchess, who, basing their conception on their reading (or their misreading, as we shall see) of Part I, treat Don Quixote and Sancho as objects of amusement and ridicule.

Before one sets out to comment on Cervantes' works, a perennial question must be addressed, particularly with respect to his masterpiece: Was *Don Quixote* written in earnest or in jest? The question does not, of course, turn its back on the self-evident. *Don Quixote* is undeniably a funny book. At the same time, the abundance of serious themes, many of them commonplace in others' works of unquestionably earnest intent, is similarly beyond dispute. Needless to say, the element of parody underlying the work permits a humorous resolution of many grave matters, but this is not sufficient to let us smile away, as Lord Byron would have it, the ethical, psychological, historical, and aesthetic concerns that so engage modern scholars. If we presume to probe Cervantes' work, we must first know whether he meant us to take him seriously. No doubt many of his truths are said in jest. Whether the jest served the truth or the other way around, or, perhaps, whether the two alternated in these functions, needs to be examined.

Asking how Cervantes' contemporaries and subsequent generations
reacted to his work is one way of addressing the question. P. E. Russell,
in an oft-cited essay, argues persuasively that the readers of Cervantes'
time thought of *Don Quixote* as a funny book. He poses an interesting
question, although his answer to it remains incomplete: "But what of
Cervantes? Did his contemporaries all fail to get his point, or was his
intention what they thought it to be? There is certainly no evidence in
those chapters in Part II where the success of Part I is discussed to suggest
that Cervantes thought his readers had misunderstood him." Russell goes
on to say that Cervantes did "claim that to write humorously requires
great genius."[3] I shall return later to this important observation.

Russell's documentation leaves little room for doubt with respect to
what Cervantes' contemporaries thought of *Don Quixote*. It was a book
of entertainment, a source of laughter, a satirical commentary on those
who wrote and those who took seriously the romances of chivalry – in
a word, it was burlesque. Anthony Close has taken up Russell's line of
investigation to demonstrate that it was a subsequent age – the Romantic
– that was largely responsible for the philosophical and mystical interpretations that underlie most present-day readings of the work.[4] Although no reader fails to see the humor, I think it safe to say that rare
indeed is the analysis today that does not take the meaning of *Don Quixote*
seriously, whether the particular concern be of a literary, linguistic,
philosophical, historical, or psychological nature. (Taking the work seriously is not, of course, equivalent to seeing the protagonist in a heroic
light.)

Nothing of the foregoing review tells us what Cervantes meant to
convey. Russell's question remains only partially answered. What Cervantes' intention was is not necessarily delineated by the reactions of his
contemporaries. Moreover, as I propose to show, Cervantes does provide
evidence to suggest that what his readers thought of the book was at
odds with his own purpose, even as he relished the popular success of
its comicality. I do not pretend to reveal what Cervantes "really" meant,
for this task is beyond my capability, but it is possible to infer Cervantes'
reactions to those who read *Don Quixote* and to deduce therefrom that
his own intention differed from the reception given to his work.

Discussions of Cervantes' literary theories invariably include Don
Quixote's definition of poetry: a maiden who "does not care to be pawed
nor dragged through the streets, nor exhibited at street corners nor in
palace corners"(II, 16).[5] It is customary to relate this passage to similar
panegyrics in *La gitanilla*, *El licenciado Vidriera*, and the *Viaje del Parnaso*,
but I know of no study that has linked the statement with Sansón Carrasco's description of the 1605 *Don Quixote*:

> Children paw it, youngsters read it, grown men understand it and
> oldsters applaud it; and finally, it is so dog-eared and so much read

by all sorts of people. . . . And those who have indulged themselves
most in its reading are the page boys: Some pick it up when others
put it down; some rush at it and others ask for it. [II, 3][6]

Although the purpose of these passages is as different as the dissimilar
contexts in which they are found, the disparity of the circumstances is
reduced somewhat by the prior declaration in each of the two chapters
that the 1605 *Don Quixote* had attained a publication of twelve thousand
and thirty thousand copies, respectively. The connection is tenuous, to
be sure. The two references to publication figures are intended to attest
to the popularity of Cervantes' masterpiece, and to this extent Sansón's
description is germane to the matter of sales figures. The praise of poetry
does not seem to have any bearing on such matters until we recognize
its discriminating function: What the one – poetry – is, the other – *Don
Quixote* – is not.

   E. C. Riley offers a clue: "In its essence [poetry] itself is idealization;
it itself is made allegory, an essentially poetic form foreign to the novel.
Poetry may represent the finest human concepts and aspirations, but it
floats above the everyday world of historical contingency that is the
domain of the novel and, to a certain point, of the drama."[7] Cervantes'
"true history," despite its legitimate claims to poetic truth, has as its
stuff the quotidian world that Riley describes as the novel's domain, well
below the heights at which Lady Poetry soars. What is striking is that
Cervantes' own definition should thus classify, by elimination, his *Don
Quixote*.

   Poetry not only is on a higher plane but is not for the masses. In this
light, Cervantes' frequent sarcastic remarks about the paucity of poets –
three and a half, he says in *Don Quixote*, II, 4 – not only are satirical but
fit well his definition of the art as the property of a select minority. *Don
Quixote*, however, is a work enjoyed by the masses for its humor, a
result achieved by the author's genius: To write humorously and wittily
requires great ingenuity. It is well to note an additional distinction, one
that separates the essence of a work of art from its reception. The praise
of poetry concerns itself with the nature of the art; the praise of *Don
Quixote* limits itself to the reception given the work by the public, irrespective of its essence and intent. It is important to bear in mind,
therefore, that Cervantes' conception of poetry is not circumscribed by
its subject matter. The definition cited earlier has to do with those who
deal with the art, poets and readers, a select minority capable of serving
the "maiden." Cervantes' understanding of this art embraces a subject
matter far less select than Riley's definition allows. In the *Persiles*, Cervantes writes:

History, poetry, and painting resemble each other and seem so
much alike that when you write history you paint and when you

paint you compose. History does not always deal with matters of
the same weight, nor does painting paint only great and magnificent
things, nor does poetry always communicate in the heavens. History allows base actions; painting, grass and broom in its pictures;
and poetry now and then exalts by singing of humble
matters.[III, 14][8]

Poetry, then, is determined not by its content but by something else.
Cervantes did not codify it, but we may infer from his writings that it
is informed by poetic truths no matter how mundane the subject and
that it is appreciated by a comparatively small number of people. Whether
he considered *Don Quixote* to belong in the realm of poetry is a matter
apart from the book's popular reception as entertainment for the masses.
But if he did intend to compose a poetic work of art, Russell's research
has shown that no one else of Cervantes' time shared such a perspective.
It was a funny book and Cervantes clearly appreciated his own talent
for humor. It was, however, only in the 1615 *Don Quixote* that he boasted
of it, and it was not until the *Viaje del Parnaso* (published only a year
earlier) that he prided himself on his talent for calculated absurdity generally, as we shall see. What is more, in the prologue to the *Persiles*,
written only a few days before his death, in 1616, he dealt with the matter
of his humor one more time, as we shall also see. In short, Cervantes
left us a number of remarks on his success as a humorist. What I propose
to show in the pages that follow is that despite the pleasure he found in
his gift for writing wittily and the satisfaction he derived from having
that talent extolled by large numbers of readers, he had aimed elsewhere
and, in my view, depicted his readers as having failed to see beyond the
burlesque.

    In the village priest, Cervantes gave us an avid reader who, like the
majority of his contemporaries, would find *Don Quixote* amusing for its
comic elements.[9] Of course, it is more accurate to personalize the name
by removing the italics: It is the risible antics of his neighbor Don Quixote
that provide the curate with entertainment. The priest who fails to appreciate the abstract qualities of the *Curioso impertinente* – ostensibly on
grounds of lack of verisimilitude and decorum – but enjoys it nonetheless
sees in the quixotic way of life not the source of philosophical inquiry
but an escape from the boredom and drudgery of the everyday Man-
chegan world.

    Close refers to the priest as "jolly Pero Pérez."[10] E. T. Aylward con-
cedes that the priest comes "to be cast in a progressively more comical
light," but argues that both the priest and the barber are introduced in
I, 5, "for the purpose of counterbalancing Don Quijote's foolishness
about the novels of chivalry."[11] It is essential to recall, however, that

both of these characters are introduced in the opening chapter as the protagonist's debating partners in matters such as who was the best of the knights they had read about (not which was the best of the books), hardly an introduction befitting those who supposedly counterbalance Don Quixote's belief in the knights' historicity. Moreover, it is well to note, as Martín de Riquer does, that in the scrutiny of the library "several books are burned without having been examined, which undoubtedly would have been saved if the priest had seen them."[12]

Perhaps the most telling statement about the curate's sensibilities comes in the initial chapter of Part II. After first agreeing not to touch upon matters of knight-errantry so as not to bring about a relapse of the protagonist's madness, the priest changes his mind, encourages Don Quixote (whom he addresses as such, not as Quixada or Quixana) to reveal his plan for knights to aid the king against the Turks, and eggs him on to describe the faces of the heroes of the romances, "gustando de oírle decir tan grandes disparates" ("for he enjoyed hearing him say such gross absurdities").

This is no idle description. It is a key delineation, and I shall return to it frequently in the pages that follow. Riley has discerned that for Cervantes, "*disparate* is no heedless term of abuse, but one of the most meaningful in his critical vocabulary. It frequently occurs in his criticism, and it is the keyword in the condemnation of the romances of chivalry."[13] At the other extreme is the irony in Don Quixote's testament: The curate and his surrogate, Sansón Carrasco, are named executors and are asked to relay Alonso Quixano's apologies to Avellaneda (if they find him) for having provided the latter with the opportunity to write *disparates* (in the spurious *Don Quixote*).

There is more than a little poetic justice in bequeathing to the curate and Sansón the task of looking for yet another Don Quixote, as it were. That other work is filled with "so many and such gross *disparates*"(II, 74). That is also what is wrong with romances of chivalry in general, avers the canon of Toledo, who finds them filled with "so many and such inordinate *disparates*" (I, 47) and "so many and such *disparatados* matters" (I, 49). And this is precisely what the priest enjoys about Don Quixote, "for he liked to hear him say such gross *disparates*." It is this pleasure that, his better judgment to the contrary notwithstanding, attracts the priest to the entertainment provided him by his parishioner. In the examination of Don Quixote's library, the priest spares Antonio de Lofraso's *Los diez libros de Fortuna de amor*, citing its humor and *disparates*: "Such a funny and *disparatado* book as that has not been written and . . . in its way, it is the best and most unique of all of this kind that have been published, and he who hasn't read it can be certain that he has never read anything pleasurable." Cervantes adds that the priest puts it aside with very great pleasure (I, 6). Although the priest admits that the romances are "full of *disparates*" and that "neither such deeds nor such *disparates*" ever took place, this opinion does not prevent him from enjoying them, and he considers them as beneficial as chess, handball, and billiards "in well-ordered republics," (I, 32), thereby setting himself in opposition to what the canon will say in I, 47: "Truly, Sir Curate, as far as I'm concerned I find that these that they call books of chivalry are harmful to the republic." We need to take with a grain of salt, therefore, the priest's response to the canon: "He told him that, because he was of the same opinion and abhorred books of chivalry, he had burned all of Don Quixote's, which was a lot" (I, 47). We know, of course, that the number fell far short of "all."

The stretching of the truth tells us more than the incidental fact that the sycophantic priest echoes the opinion of his ecclesiastical superior. Added to Cervantes' own suggestion that the remaining books might have been spared had the priest seen them, the latter's critical posture here cannot be taken at face value. It is worth noting that the curate has, in fact, little to say about the romances of chivalry in this lengthy dialogue. Even his agreement with the canon is only related by the narrator, in contrast with the extensive harangue of the canon's and, curiously, as distinguished from the priest's own lengthy discourse on *disparates*: not those of the romances but those of the national *comedia*. Moreover, it is the canon's depiction of ignorant people, those who "only attend to the pleasure of hearing *disparates*" (I, 48), that we should recall when, in Part II, the priest is described as one who enjoys hearing Don Quixote say "such gross *disparates*."

It is time to define *disparate* in the context of its application in *Don Quixote*. Sebastián de Covarrubias, in his dictionary of 1611, defines it as a "senseless thing, which was not done or said in the proper way, and with a certain aim."[14] The "senseless thing," though not said or done in the way that it perhaps ought to be, may nonetheless be done with a certain purpose in mind. In other words, the matter may be senseless but its utterance or commission may be apropos. Covarrubias himself directs us to the connotation I have suggested,[15] inasmuch as the definition of *disparate* is preceded by the words "the same as *dislate*." The entry for *dislate* not only brings us full circle but provides us with an anecdotal defintion:

> *Disparate*, which was said [i.e., derived] from *dispar* because of not having parity or equality with reason. Juan del Encina was, from what I understood, a very learned man who studied and wrote in Salamanca and . . . composed some highly imaginative verses, of considerable artifice, based on *disparates*, and they provided so much

pleasure that all the rest of his works appositely composed were lost and there remained in proverbial form only the *disparates* of Juan del Encina whenever someone says something senseless. Going along the road one day, an old innkeeper woman heard her servants say, "Juan del Encina, my lord," and she went up to him, looking him up and down, and said to him: "Sir, are you the gentleman who made the *dislates?*" and his embarrassment was so great that he replied with some anger, cursing her. To this danger serious men expose themselves when, for diversion, they write some frivolous things, although they be imaginative and very pleasurable.[16]

The moral is clear, but the point of the anecdote to illustrate the meaning of this kind of nonsense should not be lost amid the humor of having a learned man chagrined by his reputation for nonsensical verses. The anecdote illustrates that even *disparates* may be composed by men of letters for a purpose, in this case, diversion. The matter is no less nonsensical therefore; that it was created purposefully nonetheless and that it succeeded in providing imaginative pleasure are the aspects that relate this definition to that in the *disparate* entry. Covarrubias' anecdote illustrates absurdities as apposite to intended amusement.

In Chapter 6 of the *Viaje del Parnaso*, Cervantes asks: "How can an absurdity please, unless it is committed purposefully?" Earlier, in Chapter 4 of the *Parnaso*, he boasts of having opened "a way whereby the Castilian language can present an absurdity purposefully." Of passages like these Riley has observed:

As long as the author knows what he is doing and where he is going, Cervantes concedes him a good deal of liberty. He is even allowed to perpetrate what would be outrages in other circumstances. . . . *Desatino* ["absurdity"], according to Covarrubias . . . , is a *desconcierto* or something done without discourse of reason and consideration. This, it seems, Cervantes allows when it is in fact committed deliberately. . . . The full idea then seems to be that only an artist's rational purpose, realized in a pleasant apposite or humorous manner, can make a discordant absurdity agreeable, and therefore artistically acceptable. . . . This distinction between the calculated and the uncalculated absurdity is one of the most important in Cervantes's literary theory.[17]

This insightful and fundamental clarification, together with Covarrubias' various definitions, enables us not only to appreciate Cervantes' concern for *disparates* made intentionally and, of greater significance, purposefully ("and with a certain aim") but to seek the specific application of this understanding in *Don Quixote* itself.

The canon of Toledo approaches the romances of chivalry primarily from a classical standpoint. His definition is unequivocal: "This kind of writing and composition falls within that of the fables called Milesian, which are nonsensical stories (*cuentos disparatados*) that seek only to delight and not to instruct" (I, 47). He goes still farther: The romances cannot even provide delight, for they are full of so many and such inordinate absurdities (*desaforados disparates*). This judgment is qualified immediately as he clarifies that "the delight conceived in the soul must be of beauty and concordance." (Riley has concluded that *concordancia* "in Cervantes's literary theory means the harmony established in the mind of the reader by a rapport with the work. It is ruptured by the *disparatado* or incongruously absurd."[18])

The canon has been accused of inconsistency here,[19] but his reasoning is in consonance with his approach. The reason the romances fail to delight is not that they contain *disparates* but that the latter are inordinate, *desaforados* (defined by Covarrubias as "counter to reason . . . lacking consideration . . . nonsensical"). The apparent redundancy of the expression *desaforados disparates* is not a tautology but rather defines, in keeping with the foregoing observations, the nature of the *disparates*. It is not the absurdities themselves but their irrational conception or presentation that prevents the books from providing delight. This is an essential point: The canon's criticism, springing from the Horatian *utile dulci* principle, ultimately settles on the pleasure aspect alone. What is wrong, he maintains, is that the *disparates* fail to delight because they are *desaforados* and lack *concordancia*. This qualification explains an otherwise puzzling oxymoron: "The canon was left to marvel [*admirado*] at the concerted absurdities [*concertados disparates*] that Don Quixote had related, at the way in which he had painted the adventure of the Knight of the Lake, at the impression which the considered lies [*pensadas mentiras*] of the books he had read had made upon him" (I, 50). It is well to note, therefore, that the canon may be moved to *admiratio* by Don Quixote's *disparates*, so long as they are *concertados*. (Alban K. Forcione discusses another moment in Don Quixote's debate with the canon and refers to the "calculated absurdity of Don Quixote's response." In a more recent work, he describes this same passage as "one of [Don Quixote's] masterpieces of coherent nonsense."[20]) This same principle informs Don Quixote's assessment of Sancho's irrelevant proverbs as contrasted with his own: "I bring forth proverbs appositely [*a propósito*] . . . and the proverb that is inapposite [*no viene a propósito*] is a *disparate* rather than an aphorism." Sancho, on the other hand, "pulls them in by the hair and thus drags them and not guides them" (II, 67). Cervantes was evidently fond of this description, for he had said the very same thing in II, 43.

In this light one can appreciate more readily the distinction that Cervantes obviously wishes drawn between his *Don Quixote* and the spurious continuation by Avellaneda. What better way than to have readers – albeit fictive ones – of both works make the distinction for us? Accordingly, Don Jerónimo asks Don Juan, as the latter suggests they read another chapter of Avellaneda's work: "For what reason does Your Grace, Don Juan, want us to read these *disparates*? And whoever has read the first part of the history of Don Quixote de la Mancha cannot possibly find pleasure [*gusto*] in reading this second one" (II, 59). The difference is clear: Avellaneda's continuation is composed of *disparates* whereas Cervantes' original provides *gusto* (which is what the curate found listening to Don Quixote's *disparates*). As for the authentic second part by Cervantes himself, the two gentlemen in question (who intrude into it) "were left to marvel [*admirados*] at Don Quixote's *disparates* as well as the elegant manner in which he related them" (II, 59), a reaction not unlike that of the canon of Toledo.

A distinction emerges in the kinds of *disparates*. The word unquestionably has the connotation it is given in modern Spanish, that is, nonsense or absurdity, and when it is used alone in *Don Quixote*, this is the meaning it retains. When it is modified by a pejorative, the inanity of the matter is increased accordingly, but at the same time the way is prepared for the idiosyncratic approval of *disparates* qualified by commendable attributes. Thus *disparates* that are *desaforados* are opposed to those that are *concertados*. Similarly, books that contain *disparates imposibles* (I, 1) and *fabulosos disparates* (I, prologue) are to be eschewed; those that provide *gusto* because no other book is "as funny or as *disparatado*" (I, 6) are to be spared from destruction.

A unique passage in II, 17, explores the matter under consideration. It is unique because it is the only occasion on which Don Quixote discusses the matter of his sanity (excepting deathbed statements in his Alonso Quijano identity and an occasional retort). As Don Quixote is about to confront the lions, Don Diego de Miranda tries to dissuade him from attempting "such a *disparate*." Both this *disparate* and the essence of his peculiar madness generally are defined by Don Quixote's response: that "he knew what he was doing." The *disparate* is a calculated one.

Like so many others faced with trying to understand Don Quixote, Don Diego "took him to be now sane, and now mad, because what he said was *concertado*, elegant, and well said, and what he did, *disparatado*, reckless, and foolish. And he said to himself, 'What greater recklessness and *disparate* than to want to fight lions by force?'" (There is a possible element of irony in the phrase *por fuerza*, which, more often than "by force," connotes unwillingness. Given Don Quixote's insistence that he knew what he was doing, Don Diego's inability to comprehend it as an act of volition underscores his understanding of it as nonsense.) Breaking into his thoughts, Don Quixote asks: "Who doubts, Don Diego de Miranda, that Your Grace considers me as a crazy and senseless man [*un hombre disparatado y loco*]? And it wouldn't be surprising if I were, because my deeds cannot testify to anything else." What is striking is not so much Don Quixote's awareness that others may think him mad as the implicit distinction between an assessment of him as *disparatado y loco* on the one hand and his rationally calculated behavior on the other. It is, as Covarrubias defined, a senseless thing with a certain aim. Don Quixote recognizes the *disparatado* nature of his action – "I knew it to be an exorbitant temerity," – which is to say that however rash it may be, his behavior is contingent upon an understanding (his understanding, to be sure) of its absurdity.[21]

With the possible exception of the windmills episode, no adventure has received wider critical attention than that of the Cave of Montesinos. The first critique is none other than that of Sancho Panza, who finds it to be "una tan disparatada locura" ("such an absurd madness" [II, 23]) and a collection of "disparates imposibles" (II, 24). It is easy to agree with him if we fall into the trap set by Cervantes and debate the adventure's veracity. If, on the other hand, we accept the general critical judgment, namely, that the whole thing is a dream, and accept as well that Cervantes intends it to be a dream, then we must look for verisimilitude as gauged not by true-to-life standards but by *true-to-dream* referents. While the debate between Don Quixote and Sancho must remain without solution and even Cide Hamete Benengeli is reduced to confessing that Don Quixote could not have fabricated in such a short time "tan gran máquina de disparates" ("such a large assemblage of absurdities" [II, 24]), Cervantes has depicted the distortions appropriate to a dream. In a word, the *disparates* are calculated and apposite.

Much of the Montesinos adventure has its roots in the Knight of the Lake story narrated by Don Quixote in Part I, as Helena Percas has shown.[22] Both stem from Don Quixote's imagination and ultimately from his books. The first is told within the rational context of a literary debate (although Don Quixote sees it as a debate on the historicity of the romances) and causes even the canon of Toledo to admire the *concertados disparates*. The second is the narration of a dream (but told as a true occurrence), the incongruities of which appear to Sancho as *disparates imposibles* but which, when seen from the vantage point of the author (that is, the artist intent upon recreating the dream's distortions), may be recognized as purposeful *disparates*.

In contrast to this account of apposite absurdities, Cervantes presents the subsequent episode of Maese Pedro's puppet show. Don Quixote cites the errors of the play and refers to them as "un gran disparate" (II, 26). Defending himself against the exposure of "niñerías" ("childish trifles"), Maese Pedro is forced to admit that such is the nature of the theater currently in vogue (a renewed attack by Cervantes on the *comedia* of Lope de Vega):

> Don't they show around here, almost as a matter of course, a thousand *comedias* full of a thousand inapposites [*impropiedades*] and absurdities [*disparates*], and despite all that, they have a felicitous run and are heard not only with applause but with admiration and everything? Go ahead, boy, and let him talk, for so long as I can fill my bag, go on and show even more inapposites than there are particles in the sun. [II, 26]

We are reminded of Cervantes' pride in having opened the way to presenting nonsense appropriately ("mostrar con propiedad un desatino"). The *comedia* of the day, however, is emphatically described as being successful at the box office for its *impropiedades*. Although this commentary is interesting for its judgment of the *comedia* – and in this respect repeats the priest's criticism of the theater's *disparates* in I, 48 – the implicit contrast with Cervantes' own talent for apposite irrationality is what attracts us here. Percas has discerned the relationship between the Montesinos and Maese Pedro episodes, although she is more concerned with the antiartistic digressions in the latter than with the essence of the puppet show itself:

> The improprieties and interruptions of the interpreter are impertinent because they break the thread of the fiction. They are, accordingly, inadmissible in poetic creation. The improprieties of the author of the Cave of Montesinos . . . are put there on purpose, in order to create certain grotesque and humorous effects, whose aim is to imitate to perfection the incongruities of dreams. And so these improprieties fulfill an artistic role that is necessary for the creation of verisimilitude.[23]

Needless to say, not all the characters in *Don Quixote* share the requisite sensibility to comprehend the artistic purpose that fashions apposite absurdity. Whereas a minority can comprehend the nature of calculated incongruities, the majority can see only the absurdity of the absurdities. Even so will the duke's ecclesiastic warn that it is "disparate leer tales disparates" ("absurd to read such absurdities," [II, 31]), a criticism leveled not at the romances in general but at the 1605 *Don Quixote* in particular. Although the niece and housekeeper are among those who can see only the reprehensible features, the curate appreciates the pleasures that *disparates* afford. Ruth El Saffar has referred to "the curate's bad faith since he obviously loves the chivalric novels he so piously condemns."[24]

I am not convinced that it is a matter of faith, but the contrast between some of the priest's literary criticism and his evident enjoyment is patent.

Even before the scrutiny of Don Quixote's library begins, we get a glimpse of what will be the salient feature of the priest's character throughout the book. The housekeeper brings some holy water and urges him to sprinkle the study so that "of the many enchanters that these books have, there will not be one here who might enchant us in return for the punishment we wish to give them by expelling them from the world" (I, 6). The housekeeper has committed the same error as Don Quixote: She thinks that enchanters exist because the books speak of them! The priest's reaction is exactly what it will be when he is faced with the absurdities of Don Quixote: "The housekeeper's simplicity brought laughter." Still more revelatory is the conclusion of this same sentence: "and he ordered the barber to proceed to give him those books one by one, to see what they dealt with, for it might be that they would find some that did not deserve punishment by fire." It is immediately following upon the laughter occasioned by the housekeeper's simplicity that the priest commences the scrutiny of the books, and with the express purpose of looking for those that might be worth preserving.

One of those spared is Lofraso's *Los diez libros de Fortuna de amor*, mentioned earlier. John J. Allen sees in the words "tan gracioso ni tan disparatado libro como ése no se ha compuesto" ("a book as funny or absurd as that one has not been composed") a case of "devaluation through hyperbolic praise" that "needs the internal contradiction of 'so droll and absurd' to ensure that it is perceived as irony. Even so, Cervantes is careful to have the curate apply it only to a notoriously bad book."[25] It is true that Cervantes ultimately satirized Lofraso's writings in the 1614 *Viaje del Parnaso*. But, as we shall see in Chapter 7, there are reasons to take seriously the praise bestowed on Lofraso's work in this early chapter of the 1605 *Don Quixote* . Moreover, the preservation of Lofraso's book is consistent with the priest's attitude, provided that, as I suggested earlier, one understands the quality of being *disparatado* in this instance to be laudable because it is humorous, in fact, as funny as it is absurd. (Again, this judgment is to be contrasted with the condemnation of *Don Olivante de Laura*, "por disparatado y arrogante" ["because of being absurd and arrogant"].) Rather than seeing here an evaluation of Lofraso's work that is at odds with Cervantes' views elsewhere, we should regard the judgment made in the library as one made by the priest, a reader who seeks laughter and thereby balances *disparates* with the humor a work contains. Aylward points out that the "term 'disparatado'. . . is used by Cervantes in the library scene in both a positive and negative sense, depending upon certain other literary characteristics of the work discussed."[26]

Unlike a serious literary critic but very much like most readers, the priest responds to a book more often than not according to the pleasure it gives. Although he voices the familiar concepts of verisimilitude, decorum, and other aesthetically charged terms, his appraisal of *El curioso impertinente*, for example, is not truly critical. It is simple and twofold. Above all, he liked it. He says so at its conclusion (I, 35) and again upon expressing his desire to read *Rinconete y Cortadillo*, "for the [novella] of *El curioso impertinente* had been so good" (I, 47). His concern is not directed against the probing of a woman's honorability even to the point of having a third party attempt to seduce her. Rather, what he finds objectionable is such behavior between man and wife, which is to say, the violation of the marriage sacrament, not the violation of literary aesthetics. Nevertheless, he finds the tale good.

Such an approach to literature is a consistent one for the curate. Riley has suggested that the priest's apparent ambivalence regarding *Tirante el Blanco* (he praises the work but condemns its author because the many absurdities are not the result of calculated design) has to do with its indecencies: "There is good reason for interpreting the word [*necedades*] in this context in *Don Quixote* as 'obscenities.'"[27] The twofold criterion for judging literary works is simply that of enjoyment and ethics. In short, he is moved not by the pleasure-and-profit principle but primarily by pleasure and secondarily by ethical propriety. That the latter does not outweigh the former is evidenced by his tendency to praise a work and censure only those portions or features that offend his sense of ethics. Even so will he reject his own role as a damsel in distress when it occurs to him that it is indecorous for him to play the part of a female, but he will continue in a male role because it is ethically acceptable as well as fun.

My disagreement with those scholars who see in the priest the representative of Cervantes' critical opinion is limited to a refutation of their position only to the extent that the latter is unqualified. It is undeniable that among the many things the curate has to say about books, one may discern Cervantes' own views. These may be unequivocal praise (the heroic poems by Ercilla, Virués, and Rufo), evident satire (Feliciano de Silva's *Amadís de Grecia*, the *Espejo de caballerías*, *Palmerín de Oliva*), or irony (*Amadís de Gaula* is first condemned as the originator of the genre, as Cervantes believed it to be, but subsequently saved because it is the best of the very species the scrutiny was intended to purge). I believe it unprofitable to debate what the curate does or does not "represent." What must not be lost sight of is the underlying parodic substance of *Don Quixote*.[28] Accordingly, the priest cannot be a consistent and reliable spokesman for the author unless, of course, we mean thereby a representative spokesman for a particular attitude that the author wishes to bring out in a given situation. In short, within the persona created for him by Cervantes, the priest's posture remains in consonance with his own sensibilities. Even Sancho recognizes that the priest might like to participate in the enactment of pastoral literature, for "he is merry and fond of having fun" (II, 67).

A nagging fact persists: Despite the parody and alongside the irony, despite the burlesque and alongside the satire, *Don Quixote* is replete with serious questions, expounded at length and revelatory of the author's erudition. Parody, though often humorous, is not necessarily funny, and its intent, even when risible, is often wont to be in earnest. Russell's question still pursues us: Did Cervantes intend his work to be no more than the humorous tale his contemporaries evidently took it to be?

Russell's answer, though incomplete, points in the right direction. Cervantes does indeed make the significant claim that "to say amusing things and write wittily is [a talent] of great geniuses." What makes the claim significant is its placement. We find no analogous declaration in Part I. We do find it, and similar statements, in Part II, significantly with reference to the 1605 *Don Quixote*. What is surprising, not to say ironic, is that it is Don Quixote himself who makes the statement. If nothing else, Cervantes places the declaration's importance in relief by putting it in the mouth of the one individual who, more than anyone, wants *Don Quixote*, Part I, to be worthy of high praise. Cervantes unquestionably wishes to relate the talent – his talent – for writing humorously and wittily to the 1605 *Don Quixote*. The irony is that Don Quixote is the one person we would expect *not* to praise the comical aspect of his biography.

The context for this statement is Don Quixote's concern for the nature of the book we know as Part I, the existence of which has just been made known to him. Since it deals with a knight-errant, he convinces himself, it will necessarily be "grandiloquent, elevated, illustrious, magnificent, and truthful" (II, 3). But Sansón's characterization of the work is somewhat different. After describing its popularity in the nonpoetic terms quoted earlier in this chapter, he concludes: "Finally, the aforesaid story is the most pleasurable and least harmful [*perjudicial*] entertainment seen up to now." It is following this statement that Don Quixote, thankful that the work is honest and truthful, declares that it requires great genius to write with humor and wit. Sansón's words recall the curate's definition of pastoral novels, that is, specifically not works of chivalry and therefore harmless: "books of entertainment free of harm [*sin perjuicio*] to others."[29] What is more, in the paragraphs immediately following Sansón's words, the discussion turns to the reception given great works after they are published, at which time envious rivals seek and find faults "por gusto y por particular entretenimiento" ("for pleasure and [their] particular entertainment"). Worried that the book written about him may not have pleased many people, Don Quixote is comforted by Sansón: "Rather, it's the other way around, for just as *stultorum infinitus est numerus,* so the number of those who have enjoyed the said story is infinite" (II, 3).

With the Latin phrase, Sansón and, by extension, Cervantes (inasmuch as he allows the judgment to stand with no comment by Don Quixote) makes the unequivocal connection between *Don Quixote,* Part I, and the readers who have enjoyed it, namely, the infinite number of fools who have "gustado de la tal historia" ("enjoyed the said story"). Even so does the priest find entertainment, "gustando de oírle decir tan grandes disparates" ("enjoying hearing him say such gross absurdities"). Those who find the book amusing are, by Cervantes' own definition, the *vulgo,* the ignorant masses.[30] Works that are "books of entertainment," books that lesser minds judge for their own "pleasure and particular entertainment" are books that are handled by the masses, most of all by page boys in palace corners, for which places poetic works are not destined – in this category falls the 1605 *Don Quixote de la Mancha.*[31]

The foregoing review enables us at last to answer Russell's question. Let me restate it: "Did [Cervantes'] contemporaries all fail to get his point, or was his intention what they thought it to be? There is certainly no evidence in those chapters in Part II where the success of Part I is discussed to suggest that his readers had misunderstood him." I submit that there is evidence to suggest just that conclusion. Cervantes' description of the success of Part I is based on two points: its humor and its popular – in all senses of the word – reception. Its enthusiasts are unmistakably described as dolts. Since publication it has suffered at the hands of envious readers who, for their own particular pleasure and entertainment and without having produced anything of their own (II, 3), have sought out its faults (Cervantes' notorious lapses) and thereby have missed its merits.

Having said this, it is necessary to ask why, if his readers have in fact failed to get his point, Cervantes so clearly emphasizes the book's humor and success in Part II. Although in Part I he occasionally mentions Sancho's humorous effect (in contrast to his more habitual practice of depicting it),[32] it is in Part II that he begins to stress the peasant's indispensability to the work.[33] Sansón reports that "there are those who prize hearing you [Sancho] talk more than the star [*más pintado*] of the whole thing" (II, 3). The priest describes the combination of the two as "this assemblage of *disparates* of such a knight and such a squire, for it seems that they forged them both in the same mold and the madnesses of the master without the inanities of the servant don't amount to a trifle" (II, 2). Don Quixote's defeat deprives the world of the "funniest madman in it"; the viceroy receives unhappily the news of that defeat, "because in Don Quixote's retirement one lost the pleasure that all those who might be apprised of his madnesses could have"; and "with his [mental] health, we lose not only his witticisms but those of his squire Sancho Panza, for any one of them could cheer up melancholy itself" (II, 65). Moreover, what allegedly distinguishes Avellaneda's Sancho from the authentic Sancho and irritates the latter (and, presumably, enables Cervantes to chalk up another point in his own favor, given his opinion of writing wittily) is Avellaneda's failure to have his Sancho live up to the humorous reputation attained in the 1605 *Quixote*:

> "And that Don Quixote," said ours, "did he bring along with him a squire named Sancho Panza?"
>
> "Yes, he did," answered Don Alvaro, "and although he had a reputation for being very funny, I never heard him say a joke that was at all funny."
>
> "That I can believe very well," Sancho now said, "because saying funny things is not for everyone . . . ; for I am the real Sancho Panza and I have more witticisms than the sky rains . . . ; I make everyone who listens to me laugh. [II, 72]

Cervantes describes his readers as fools and depicts the success of his work in bestseller terms: It is "pawed" by all sorts of people. The words he uses are those applied in a pejorative context to describe what poetry is not. He is concerned that more attention is paid to his errors than to the book's merits. All this adds up to unmistakable evidence that the reception given his book, despite its popularity, did not include an understanding of what his intentions were. On the other hand, just as unmistakable is his pride in his achievement, that is, a funny book. This, he points out on numerous occasions, is an uncommon talent. While he quibbles with details in his anger over Avellaneda's book (Don Quixote will now go to Barcelona, not Zaragoza), he is able to have Avellaneda's character confirm that it is precisely in the matter of humor (Sancho's witticisms) that his own work stands out. These matters have to do with the reception of his work, with its success as a comic work, and it is on this aspect of his achievement that he bases its appeal to the masses. But we must remember that this is how he depicts – correctly, to be sure – his readers: as seekers and applauders of humor. His intention is not addressed in these comments.

I think we may ascribe Cervantes' apologies for Sancho's eloquence and wisdom to the same concern. Scholars generally deal with the intrusions of the fictive translator in II, 5, by analyzing the different levels of author. In the light of the argument pursued here, one may suppose that Cervantes, not wishing to persist in the depiction of a fixed character but, desirous instead of presenting an evolution in Sancho's comportment, nonetheless felt a need to account to those who sought only humor in Sancho's behavior. What more fitting humor than to have the translator ridicule the sobriety of the author's representation of the amusing squire?

The fictive translator serves two purposes. As I have suggested, the very idea of an intrusion by one of the figures ostensibly responsible for our being able to read the book, particularly with the aim of ridiculing the veracity of that book, is a comic element. By making fun of Sancho's rationality, an authorial figure is made to insist on the risibility of the circumstances. I am not convinced that the episode is more than moderately humorous. Of course we smile when Sancho corrects Teresa's language, and perhaps we smile when he describes the chivalric adventures in which he and his master will become involved. But this kind of talk reflects his experience with Don Quixote, whose rhetoric he is clearly imitating here. That in itself may be funny, but the joke is really on the translator, who intrudes and reminds us how unlikely it is for Sancho to talk this way. Not only is such mimicking of his master's manner of speech consistent with Sancho's role, but the very fact that it is an attempt to emulate removes the need for the translator's concern. Sancho himself explains that much of what he says is not of his own invention, "for all that I mean to say are the judgments of the reverend father who preached in this town the past Lent" (II, 5). As we shall see, much of Sancho's wisdom is rationalized as being the result of his good memory of the sayings of others.

There is a second motive for the intrusions of the translator here. Not only did the reader of Cervantes' time expect Sancho to adhere to the paradigm of the jester, because that is what seemed to stand out in the characterization of Part I; Cervantes was concerned as well that the development of Sancho's character might be perceived as a violation of Aristotle's requirement of consistency.[34] By having his own surrogate intervene and make the charge himself, Cervantes is engaging in the kind of justification that, via the report made by Sansón Carrasco, points out the charge that the *Curioso impertinente* is irrelevant but nonetheless good and well-reasoned (I, 3). Cervantes knew his readers.[35]

In II, 19, Sancho makes some observations on how love distorts one's vision, whereupon Don Quixote asks where he has heard of such matters. Sancho replies, "Oh! Well, if you don't understand me . . . it's no wonder that my wise sayings are taken for *disparates*. But it doesn't matter: I understand myself, and I know that I have not said many stupidities in what I've said; except that Your Grace, sir, is always the *friscal* of my sayings, and even my doings." Like Don Quixote, Sancho implies that his *disparates* are not unreasonable and conform to his intent. That rationality, however, must give way to the expectations of the seventeenth-century reader, so that the typical linguistic distortion (*friscal* in lieu of *fiscal*) preserves Sancho as a burlesque character.

In the situation just cited, Cervantes is allowing one of Sancho's own traits – his confounding of the language – to compensate for the apparent wisdom of his remarks. In a subsequent circumstance not unlike the one just described, the irony is sharpened by Sancho's own depreciation of the wisdom of his words while at the same time the characteristic orig- inality of his *disparates* is underscored. Sancho asks the self-proclaimed humanist – the compiler of trivia such as revelation of who was the first in the world to have a cold – who the world's first acrobat was. When the "humanist" confesses ignorance, Sancho points out that it was "Lu- cifer, when they tossed or threw him from heaven and he came tumbling down to the abyss." Don Quixote immediately interjects: "That question and answer aren't your own, Sancho; you've heard someone say them." If the matter ended here, we would have only a further example of the need to temper Sancho's wise remarks with some sort of disparagement and no more than that. It is indeed more than that, however, for Sancho himself comments, "In order to ask stupidities and reply with *disparates*, I have no need to go around looking for help from others" (II, 22). His response at once shows up the inanity of the "humanist" for what it is, reduces to an acceptable level any wisdom in his own remarks, and places in relief his acknowledged talent for *disparates*.

As one might expect, it is when the two leading characters are treated as the protagonists of their book that these matters are brought to a head. I refer, of course, to the lengthy portion of Part II that deals with the stay at the ducal estate in which Cervantes gives himself the opportunity to portray the reception of his literary creations at the hands of readers of Part I. For the purposes of my argument in this chapter, I must risk overstating the obvious by insisting on the fact that this is exactly what the drawn-out episode is: Two readers of the 1605 *Don Quixote* are depicted by Cervantes as he understands them to understand his work. Whatever else we may wish to make of this long affair, it is indisputable that in the duke and duchess Cervantes portrays readers of the 1605 *Don Quixote*.

Not surprisingly, the very first thing brought out is the humor that the ducal pair expect Don Quixote and Sancho to provide. (A bit of irony that, so far as I am aware, has not been commented upon is that the duke and duchess never doubt the reality of the characters about whom they have *read*. It is evident that they treat Don Quixote and Sancho in accordance with what they have read, which tells us a great deal about how they have read the 1605 *Don Quixote*. Their acceptance of that volume as a "true history" alerts us to their uncritical approach to the book.) Their interpretation of the book they have read, rather than their observation of the flesh-and-blood people who wander into their lives, informs their understanding of Don Quixote and Sancho and thereby informs us of their understanding of *Don Quixote*.

It would be a repetitive passage indeed were I to list here the many times that words like "laughter," "die laughing," "burst from laughing," and, above all, *gusto* are used in the chapters dealing with the duke and duchess. It is worth recalling that throughout those chapters relating Don Quixote's encounter with Don Diego de Miranda, the latter is never once moved to laughter, not even on the occasion of Don Quixote's helmet overflowing with cheese curds. The word used most often to describe Don Diego's reactions is *admirado*, and although he is torn between considering Don Quixote mad and judging him sane, not even the latter's *disparates* bring forth laughter. We should also recall that Cervantes makes a specific point of the fact that Don Diego has not read the 1605 *Don Quixote*. The ducal pair, in contrast, have read the earlier volume and are thus prepared to find amusement and laughter in the antics of the two whose "history" they know well.

Now, these two reactions – *admiratio* from Don Diego and laughter from the duke and duchess – are singled out by Cervantes as the two possible responses to Don Quixote: "The affairs of Don Quixote are to be greeted either with *admiratio* or with laughter" (II, 44). Riley sees in this declaration a complicated application of neoclassical literary theory: "The explanation of this not altogether obvious distinction is to be sought, I believe, in the idea that the truly 'admirable' must have verisimilitude. When it does not, El Pinciano says, '*admiratio* for the thing is turned to laughter.' "[36] This is adequate as a general observation but fails to come to grips with the two reactions as they are manifested in Don Diego and the ducal couple. It must be borne in mind that Don Diego, who has not read the 1605 *Don Quixote* (or any romance of chivalry, for that matter), but who is a reader of literature nonetheless, approaches the "real" Don Quixote (which is to say the 1615 *Don Quixote*) free of the responses conditioned by a reading of Part I. He has difficulty making up his mind about his guest's sanity or madness, and the basis of his confusion is precisely that the *disparates* – so often a source of laughter elsewhere – are tempered with rational declamation. Don Diego is the only reader in the entire work not tainted by the readings that, their own better judgment to the contrary notwithstanding, intrigue others we have met. Even the canon gets so carried away by the "one good thing" he finds in the romances that he ends up enumerating a veritable catalogue of good things to be found in them.[37] Don Diego is also attracted to works of entertainment, "provided they are of decent entertainment and that they delight with their language and arouse *admiratio* and wonder with their inventiveness"(II, 16).[38] What is more, Cervantes tells us that had Don Diego read the first part, "the *admiratio* that [Don Quixote's] deeds and words aroused in him would come to an end"(II, 17). Stated another way, his reaction to the protagonist is at odds with the interpretation given by readers of Part I.[39]

Don Diego's library is a small one. He opposes his son's desire to be a poet, and it is to him that Don Quixote's noble definition of poetry is addressed. If poetry is not to be pawed on street corners, neither has it entered the tranquility of Don Diego's library. But it is this man, given to the reading of only those few works that conform to Renaissance precepts, who is roused to *admiratio* by Don Quixote's conduct, so very different from his own. Is not Cervantes suggesting that, quit of the prejudiced perspective of a reading of the 1605 *Don Quixote*, which conditions one to see primarily the burlesque qualities of the protagonist, a reader trained in the recognition of preceptist criteria – *utile dulci, admiratio*, wonder and suspense, decent entertainment – will be led to *admiratio* if he will but invite Don Quixote to cross his doorstep?

The duke and duchess are moved to laughter because they *have* read Part I.[40] The duchess is prepared to defend Sancho's humor even against Don Quixote himself. The latter apologizes for Sancho's garrulous risibility: "No knight-errant ever had a squire more talkative and funny than the one I have." But the duchess replies that she considers Sancho's humor to be a sign of *discreción*, "and since good Sancho is funny and witty, from here on I declare him to be clever." What is more, she insists that Sancho travel next to her, because she "gustaba infinito de oír sus discreciones" ("she enjoyed to the utmost hearing his clever sayings" [II, 30]). The echo of the curate's characterization is unmistakable ("gustando de oírle decir tan grandes disparates"). The point is made again in II, 33: "with the *gusto* she had in hearing him."

We should understand that by *discreciones* the duchess has in mind that which gives rise to comicality. If we apply her own logic, it is when someone is "funny and witty" that *discreción* is displayed, so that the latter is a quality of those who produce humor. We know – and, presumably, the duchess knows – that the basis of humor is the discrepancy between expected, logical relationships and their unexpected and surprising inversion. If that is its basis, its essence is determined by the manner in which that discrepancy is applied or, in Kenneth Burke's felicitous phrase, by "planned incongruity."[41] For her part, the duchess ultimately admits that the irrelevance of Sancho's sayings allows her to find them more pleasurable than those that are germane: "For my part I can say that [Sancho's proverbs] give me more pleasure than others, even if [the others] are more apt and more timely" (II, 34). It goes without saying that the one who plans the incongruities is Cervantes, and it is thus that they are "clever." (It is well to recall that in the prologue to

Part I he talks of *fabulosos disparates*, and in Chapter 1 of that volume he speaks of *disparates imposibles*, as noted earlier, in reference to the romances; in the prologue to Part II he refers to himself as an honorable man who has told the story of these *discretas locuras*, these "clever insanities" or, in a freer but, I think, more appropriate translation, cleverly planned absurdities.) Angel Rosenblat points out that the word *discreción*, as the duchess applies it to Sancho, is undoubtedly ironic and gibing.[42] The ultimate irony lies in the fact that the duchess, as depicted by Cervantes, seeks nothing of greater value and does, as noted, prefer irrelevancies to appropriately suited aphorisms. As Cervantes will say in the *Persiles*, "Por la mucha risa se descubre el poco entendimiento" ("a great deal of laughter reveals a small amount of understanding"[II, 5]). If any doubt about the duchess's meaning still remains, it is dispelled by her reaction to Sancho's defense of the existence of knights-errant: "The duchess was dying of laughter from hearing Sancho speak, and in her opinion she took him to be funnier and crazier than his master; *and there were many at that time who were of the same opinion*" (II, 32; emphasis mine).

Why is it necessary to make the observation that I have emphasized? Even more emphasis needs to be given to the phrase "at that time." Cervantes evidently is making a statement on chronological development – of the character, of the readers, or as I suspect, of both. If Sancho now is funnier than his master, then those who are now of this opinion implicitly perceive Don Quixote as something other than the central source of mirth. Moreover, since these readers of Part I evidently seek humor, with which they associate *discreción*, they now focus on Sancho and relegate Don Quixote to secondary importance. This reconsideration of the protagonist is reflected in the Barataria chapters' concentration on Sancho's governorship, despite a structural evenhandedness by Cide Hamete that seems to balance the number of pages devoted to each character's affairs. Accordingly, it is Sancho who sits next to the duchess, Sancho who is given the spoils of chivalry (the governorship), and Sancho who, so they think, will provide the bulk of the humor that these readers previously associated with the 1605 volume. Don Quixote does not seem quite as funny as their reading had led them to expect.

If this attitude betrays a shift in the perception of Don Quixote, the view of Sancho is consistent with the reception given this character from the beginning. After nearly four centuries of criticism and imitations, R. M. Flores concludes that "most of the allusions and references to Sancho show little or no critical insight." Flores adds: "From the very beginning of the [seventeenth] century Sancho was tacitly accepted and used as a tool or vehicle to provoke laughter [and] the final effect was always comical and, not infrequently, gross and derogatory."[43] Flores' research, too lengthy to reproduce here, refers to *tonterías* (foolishnesses) and *necedades* (inanities) strung together, yet demonstrates "how pertinent and valid the *tonterías*" frequently are. Even the artless story of the goatherd and the goats crossing the river is purposeful: "The story ends, as Sancho had all along planned, with the arrival of the dawn."[44]

If I am concerned about Cervantes' intention, I should perhaps show a similar concern that my own meaning not be mistaken. It would be simple to document the burlesque aspects of Sancho's character. I doubt that any reader needs convincing that Sancho is, more often than not, funny, and it is not my aim to corroborate the self-evident. Neither is it my purpose to demonstrate an absence of comicality, for the latter plainly exists. But the fact that Sancho is the source of laughter (or, for that matter, that Don Quixote's antics, no matter how heroically conceived, also are risible) is distinct from the judgment that *Don Quixote* is meant to be exclusively a funny book. Don Diego de Miranda sees no humor in either of the two principal characters. But he, as Cervantes took pains to emphasize, was not a reader of Part I. Nor were the farmers who are left *admirados* by what they judge to be Sancho's *discreción* and who wonder how *discreto* Don Quixote must be, given this quality in Sancho (II, 61).

Of course, even to say that readers of the book find Sancho funny may appear to labor the obvious. My point is not to say this myself but to observe that Cervantes says it. Is he, then, laboring the obvious? To the extent that he points to his success as a humorist, it is doubtless true that he is anything but reticent. But it is one thing for Cervantes to pride himself on the popular success of the book, a success attained by virtue of the burlesque elements that amuse so many a reader; it is another matter for us to assume thereby that the book was conceived to be no more than that. And, I believe, this difference is brought out in the episodes that unfold at the ducal estate.

To a great extent, Cervantes makes his point by indirection. This is not to say that it is veiled or subtle. I am scarcely the first to perceive that the duke and duchess represent the idle rich and that their amusement is derived not only from the truly ludicrous facets of their guests' behavior but at the expense of the protagonists. Cervantes depicts two avid readers of his work whose entertainment – specifically, whose laughter – is predicated upon making sport of his two major characters. If all this is well known, is it also well understood? It is fine to ascribe it to whatever reasons Cervantes may have had for satirizing the idle aristocracy, but this does not go far enough to explain why such satire is achieved at the expense of his own protagonists.

We ought to distinguish between Don Quixote and Sancho in this sequence of events. Don Quixote begins this adventure with the feeling that "it was the first day that he wholly recognized and believed himself to be a true knight-errant and not a fantastic one, seeing himself treated in the very way that he had read that real knights were treated in past centuries" (II, 31). This statement frequently raises eyebrows because it seems to imply that before this moment – that is, from his first sally through the windmills adventure, the galley slaves, the events at Juan Palomeque's inn, the confrontation with the lions, the intervention in Maese Pedro's theater, and so forth – he has never fully believed in his own persona. But Cervantes' carefully constructed sentence does not say that. What it does say is that it is the first time he believes his treatment to be in accordance with the *books* that he has read.

Immediately following this appreciation of being taken as seriously as he has taken the books he wants to emulate, Don Quixote is faced with the embarrassment of Sancho's behavior with respect to his ass. His anger brings forth a lengthy tirade, the essence of which may be summarized as follows: Just now, when we were about to be accepted by these noble people, must you reveal our humble origin? "Don't you understand . . . that if they see that you are a coarse boor *or a burlesque fool,* they will think that I am some fake or some swindler of a knight? No, no, friend Sancho; flee, flee from these obstacles, for whoever falls into the habit of being garrulous and funny, at the first kick he will fall and *end up as a miserable buffoon*" (II, 31; emphasis mine).

In unequivocal terms, Cervantes portrays the distinct reactions of Don Quixote and the duchess to Sancho's comicality: "Each word that Sancho said pleased the duchess as much as it drove Don Quixote to despair" (II, 39). Although from the outset Don Quixote has played the role of teacher and has had reason to criticize Sancho's conduct and use of language, not until the events at the ducal estate does he show so much embarrassment, chagrin, and – a significant emotion – despair concerning Sancho's behavior. Inasmuch as the entire sequence of events here is predicated on the nobles' reading of Part I (and the improvisation of details related to them of the earlier portions of Part II), I think it not unreasonable to view these chapters as an understanding of that reading, in turn presented as Cervantes wishes to portray that understanding.

A number of scholars have speculated about the identity of the historical personages that may have served Cervantes as models for the duke and duchess. In the absence of any convincing documentation, it would be fruitless to pursue this conjecture. Even the assumption that a specific couple served as inspiration at all remains hypothetical. On the other hand, we do have a duke and duchess; that is, we are given figures representative of a certain class and its attendant power, which to no small extent included the patronage of artists. That our duke and duchess remain anonymous throughout the many chapters in which they figure so prominently may be a precautionary device on Cervantes' part, if indeed he had in mind living people who inspired his fictional creations. In the absence of evidence, then, we can deal only with the textual material Cervantes left for us, and that text gives us two characters whose importance in the book does not give them a name, a point of interest in itself in a work in which the use of names has given rise to countless scholarly investigations. We must reach the only conclusion within our grasp (other than to dismiss any significance altogether), and that is the obvious one: The duke and duchess are representative of their class and thus convey how *Don Quixote* – personified on the fictive level in Part II as Don Quixote and Sancho – entered the houses of that class and provided a reason for laughter. Unless one wishes to argue that the duke and duchess are portrayed sympathetically, unless one is prepared to argue that the duke and duchess treat their guests with goodwill, unless one believes that Cervantes applauds the ducal pair's character – unless one accepts such suppositions, it is necessary to conclude that the duke and duchess belong to the *vulgo* as Cervantes has earlier defined it: "Todo aquel que no sabe, *aunque sea señor y príncipe*, puede y debe entrar en número de vulgo" ("Everyone who is ignorant, *though he be lord and prince*, can and must be counted among the *vulgo*" [II, 16; emphasis mine]).

Of what are the duke and duchess ignorant? I think it plain that to the extent that they are judges of *Don Quixote*, they are ignorant of everything but the burlesque. When Sancho is given the opportunity to exercise gubernatorial power, the farcical context created by the duke and duchess does not preclude his praiseworthy conduct in office. However, the conversion of the quixotic ideal (Dulcinea) by the duke and duchess into something base and ludicrous is no better, and probably worse, than Sancho's "enchantment" of the peasant girl. Their use of a young boy to play the part of Dulcinea shows the same insensitivity to Don Quixote's ideal as that of the authors of *Man of La Mancha* when they thought it amusing to have Dulcinea and the prostitute be one and the same person. If the ducal pair can emulate Sancho in their enchantment of Dulcinea and La Trifaldi, what does this tell us about their comprehension of *Don Quixote*? As the preceding pages have suggested, the duke and duchess demonstrate by their insensitive behavior toward Don Quixote and Sancho what their reading of the 1605 *Don Quixote* has led them to seek.

The ducal couple represents a pair of readers created by Cervantes, but another reader was to be thrown in his face and, to use a popular expression that may apply literally, with a vengeance. It has been suggested that the appearance in 1614 of Avellaneda's false continuation of the *Quixote* provided Cervantes with a number of artistic opportunities to weave more intricacies into the various authorial levels and the fiction-within-fiction distinctions (or indistinctions), as well as the relationship of art to reality generally. The spurious *Don Quixote* also provided Cervantes with the documented reaction of a reader of his own 1605 *Don Quixote*. If we set aside Cervantes' anger – inspired by the deprecatory remarks in Avellaneda's prologue as much as by the feeling of having been unfaithfully plagiarized – we can perceive some of what I have tried to bring to the fore in this chapter. It is customary to see in Avellaneda's book firsthand evidence of a contemporary reader's response to Cervantes' work. Avellaneda did not take into account any serious literary or philosophical endeavors that Cervantes may have had in mind, and thus his work confirms the research of those who, like Russell and Close, have shown that *Don Quixote* was received simply as a funny and entertaining book. But to agree that it was so received is not to say what was or was not in Cervantes' mind when he wrote his book. Let us, therefore, look not for Avellaneda's understanding of Cervantes' book, nor for Cervantes' understanding of Avellaneda's book, but for Cervantes' reaction to Avellaneda's understanding.

We already know two things that are really two sides of the same coin. Cervantes has Avellaneda's Sancho described as not as amusing as the original Sancho. Furthermore, on his deathbed Don Quixote wants to apologize to Avellaneda for having provided him with the material to write so many *disparates*. The word *disparates*, left unqualified, leaves no doubt in our minds: Avellaneda may have tried to be amusing (because, as everyone agrees, that is what he took Cervantes' book to be), but his Sancho is not funny and his *disparates* are simply absurd. What is more, as quoted earlier, Don Jerónimo points out that anyone who has read the Cervantes book cannot possibly find *gusto* in the Avellaneda sequel, which he describes as "these *disparates*." Stated another way, Avellaneda's *disparates* lack apposite humor and fail to reflect purposeful incongruity.

It is in Don Juan's reply that Cervantes lets loose his most telling charge. Despite all that which Don Jerónimo has just said, it would still be a good idea, he adds, to read the Avellaneda work, "for there is no book so bad that it does not have some good thing" (a favorite maxim of Cervantes'). In other words, Avellaneda's failure to be funny and his inability to provide *gusto* are not, in and of themselves, sufficient to brand the work a bad book. But then Don Juan continues: "What in this one *displeases me most* is that he portrays Don Quixote as already out of love with Dulcinea del Toboso" (II, 59; emphasis mine). Herein lies, I am convinced, the key to the question we have been probing. Leaving aside the matter of humor, Cervantes says, it could still be a good book were it not for the fact that *the essence of Don Quixote has been misunderstood.*

Avellaneda has distorted the quixotic ideal beyond anything the duke and duchess have attempted. It is grotesque to debase Dulcinea, but to represent Don Quixote as not enamored of her reveals a failure to comprehend the nature of Don Quixote the personage, of *Don Quixote* the book, and of that unique kind of madness we call quixotic. Even if one accepts the notion that Cervantes wrote his book only to ridicule the romances of chivalry,[45] it is necessary to recognize, to understand, that the knight – seriously or in jest – is inextricably bound to his ladylove. Not only did the romances require this commitment, but it would be de rigeur for a consciously conceived parody. If many a truth has been spoken in jest, this is a truth that, in the context of an understanding of *Don Quixote* as a parodic imitation of the romances, does not and cannot lose its veracity by virtue of its presentation in jest. In a word, the reader (Avellaneda) of *Don Quixote* has misunderstood Cervantes' intention.

Don Quixote is then placed in the unique position of leafing through Avellaneda's book. We may infer that this is a representation of the initial thumbing through the volume that so startled and angered Cervantes himself. Of course, that moment is depicted here as Cervantes cares to have us envision it. Don Quixote's cursory inspection of the volume reveals three faults: the deprecatory prologue, the use of Aragonese rather than Castilian, and the failure to get Teresa Panza's name right. (Scholars have been intrigued by the last two points for a number of reasons not germane to the question before us here.) What it all boils down to is a personal reaction of anger to the personally insulting remarks in the prologue along with a simple and direct accusation that Avellaneda has his facts all wrong.

The appearance of the Avellaneda book has provided Cervantes with the opportunity to demonstrate how his own book could be and was misunderstood. He takes pride in his own talent for writing wittily and recognizes immediately what others have repeated ever since, namely, that he succeeds in the humorous aspects whereas Avellaneda is unable to rise above farce. Nevertheless, the matter of humor is set aside as an insufficient criterion for judging the book's worth. It is, rather, in the essence of the quixotic ideal – quixotic madness, if you will – and in the fundamentals (language and "historical" accuracy) that the original has been misrepresented. As if to ward off charges that his displeasure is the result of another's using his creations, Cervantes has Don Quixote say (the pun is lost in translation): "Retráteme el que quisiere . . . pero no me maltrate" ("Let anyone who wishes portray me . . . but let him not mistreat me"[II, 59]).

Unlike Cervantes' own *Quixote*, which was "pawed" by people of all sorts, Avellaneda's book is described as passing "from hand to hand but not stopping at any because everyone gives it the foot"(II, 70). It is not unlikely that, in addition to characterizing the reception of Avellaneda's work, this remark was as well a comparatively polite response to an obscene assessment of the 1605 *Don Quixote*, attributed to Lope de Vega: "And as for your nothing of a *Don Quixote*, / it goes from asshole to asshole through the world / hawking spices and bastard-saffron / and it will come to rest on a dung heap."[46] But Cervantes' criticism is aimed not at the *quality* of Avellaneda's book but at its failure to capture the essentials of his own creation. It is clear that in the criticism of Avellaneda's work there is an implicit charge: If you do not take Don Quixote's love for his ideal seriously, even within the context of a parody filled with my evident talent for humor, you have misunderstood my book.

Throughout this chapter I have referred to the question of taking Cervantes in jest or in earnest. By the idea of taking him and his work seriously I have not intended to convey the notion that he be taken literally or that we go to the extremes that fired Unamuno's interpretation of the protagonist as approaching sainthood. To see in Don Quixote a noble soul, spurred by the impossible dream of reestablishing the mythical Golden Age in the face of a hypocritical society, is indeed a valid interpretation. But I do not suggest that this was Cervantes' intention. Nor am I able to deny it. If this appears to be at best circular reasoning or at worst a failure to come to grips with the implications of my own thesis, I must remind the reader that I have not set out, in this chapter, to delineate Cervantes' meaning. Rather, I have tried to address the question whether his masterpiece was intended to be a funny book or whether, in addition to (but not instead of) the burlesque, he intended to convey something that engages the reader's intellect. The preceding pages demonstrate, I believe, that in his portrayal of the readers of his book, Cervantes betrayed a dissatisfaction with their intellectual capacity to see beyond the risible.

What, then, did he intend to do? If one looks at those passages in the book in which the content is indisputably serious, the Cervantine process is patent. For instance, the discourse on the Golden Age is addressed to uncomprehending goatherds; the speech on arms and letters is pronounced amid an audience involved in a drawn-out farce; the definition of poetry is counterbalanced by a challenge to lions; the advice on how to govern oneself and others is presented within the topsy-turvy context of a peasant farcically turned governor. The list is very nearly endless and the conclusion obvious: Serious matters are presented in burlesque garb so that the effect is one of incongruity. It is, of course, a calculated incongruity, and as so many characters are made to remark, one is never quite sure whether the protagonist is mad or sane, which is akin to saying that the reader is never to be quite certain whether the book is to be taken seriously or not.

Nevertheless, all the evidence we have forces us to believe that the foregoing conclusion was not evident to Cervantes' contemporaries. "Lope de Vega belonged to the category of those who found the knight objectionable, dismissing him as an *extravagante* and the book as worthless," writes Russell. Because of the animosity and rivalry between Cervantes and Lope, I shall not pursue here the latter's reaction to *Don Quixote*. Worth repeating, however, because of the ironic reversal implicit in its observation, is Russell's subsequent sentence: "Lope doubtless took this line because he liked the romances of chivalry and perhaps thought . . . that those who laughed at them did so because they missed their real point."[47] If readers laughed at the romances because they missed their real point, is it unreasonable to assume that readers of *Don Quixote* laughed at it for the same reason?

A play by Pedro Calderón de la Barca, though no longer extant, is cited by Russell primarily because of its title, *Los disparates de don Quijote*, from which one may infer that even philosophically oriented artists like the author of *La vida es sueño* saw Cervantes' hero only as a burlesque figure. The play, evidently staged in Madrid in 1637 (Russell cites N. D. Shergold's finding) some two decades after Cervantes' death, would only confirm what I agree is an indisputable fact: the reception of *Don Quixote* as a funny book. But Calderón's interpretation offers us no clue about whether his view was at variance with Cervantes' intentions.[48]

Guillén de Castro (1569–1631), the Valencian dramatist best remembered for his *Las mocedades del Cid*, wrote three plays based on Cervantes' works. Two of them are grounded in the 1605 *Don Quixote*: *Don Quixote de la Mancha* and *El curioso impertinente*; the third is an adaptation of a novella, *La fuerza de la sangre*. The first of these, despite its title, is really a dramatization of the Luscinda–Cardenio–Dorotea–Fernando affair of the original, Don Quixote's role being relegated to that of ludicrous madman whose amusing and at times silly interventions in the principal plot confirm once more a burlesque reading of Cervantes' work or, perhaps, a belief that such an interpretation would be the appropriate one for the theatrical crowds. Russell cites this play in support of his argument, as does Close, who believes the drama to have been written between 1605 and 1615. This chronological detail assumes some importance for us, as I shall explain shortly. First, it is necessary to consider Close's argument.

In Chapter 5 of *Don Quixote*, Part I, the protagonist engages not in the emulation of chivalric heroes, as is his habit in the remainder of the book, but in the impersonation of literary characters. This difference in his behavior will have a bearing on our investigation of the phases of the work's composition, as we shall see in Chapter 7. Here I wish to take up Close's argument that the interpretation of the protagonist in accordance with his conduct in I, 5, supports the conclusion that "Cervantes's contemporaries understood very clearly" the burlesque characterization of Don Quixote. Close reminds us that Avellaneda's spurious continuation, in effect an imitation, represents the hero as Cervantes had portrayed him in I, 5, rather than as he developed him subsequently. Avellaneda's "work might be said to present us with a case of arrested development: Don Quixote's psychology arrested at the point which Cervantes reached in Part I, Chapter 5." Close goes on to observe that "Avellaneda's hero is a much more wooden, much less individual, much less responsive character than Cervantes's. Perhaps because Avellaneda's conception is cruder, it clarifies the root-motive of Don Quixote's behaviour in Cervantes's novel – the urge to play-act chivalresque fiction – by copying it in the oversimplified manner that I have described." Close goes on to suggest that Guillén de Castro's play, in which Don Quixote at one point "resolves to 'be' Leander crossing the Hellespont to visit Hero," is further evidence of this understanding of the hero's original characterization.[49]

I submit that Close's felicitous phrase "arrested development" illustrates my own line of reasoning as well as it does his own. It is correct to conclude that Cervantes' contemporaries received his book as a work of humor. But the fact that imitators selected the characteristics of the hero as he was portrayed in the early pages of the book, characteristics that Close himself agrees are different from the more fully developed psychological features of Don Quixote as revealed in subsequent pages by Cervantes, confirms that there are two models to imitate: One is the simple character who impersonates heroes of books; the other is the more individualized character who emulates heroes of books by living life in accordance with the principles of those books. Moreover, the fact that imitators like Avellaneda and Castro chose to borrow the more primitive characterization, which is to say that they neglected or refused to appropriate the subsequently developed character, tells us a good deal about the difference between the response to the book by Cervantes' contemporaries and what Cervantes put into his book. Free to choose for their own purposes between a crude conception (to use Close's words) and a more complex personality as developed in Cervantes' later pages, they settled on the former, that is, on the Don Quixote that they so "clearly understood."

As regards the dates of composition, staging, and publication of the three plays by Castro, these details take on some importance for the question before us in this chapter. The matter of chronology bears directly on our understanding of Cervantes' response to his readers. The Valencian dramatist was praised on two occasions by Cervantes: once in the *Viaje del Parnaso* (published in 1614 but, except for the epilogue known as the *Adjunta al Parnaso*, completed in 1612), in which Castro was praised in general terms, and again in the 1615 prologue to Cervantes' own dramatic works, in which Castro was lauded for his "suavidad y dulzura" ("smoothness and sweetness"). The words were not chosen idly, as Alberto Porqueras Mayo has shown.[50] Of interest is the fact that the prologue to the 1615 *Don Quixote* contained no reference to Castro, nor was he mentioned anywhere in that volume, despite his having written three plays on topics inspired by Cervantes' works, including the 1605 *Don Quixote*, the popularity of which Cervantes so evidently wished to accentuate in the 1615 volume. One wonders why, for instance, Sansón Carrasco did not report the fact that Don Quixote was as well the subject of a stage play or that *El curioso impertinente*, whose allegedly irrelevant but nonetheless "well-reasoned" plot was discussed, had been dramatized by a leading playwright.

Castro's *Don Quixote de la Mancha* was long thought to have been composed shortly after 1605. Hugo Rennert believed that the dramatist took advantage of *Don Quixote*'s immediate popularity. He offered no documentation, and yet Courtney Bruerton, in an attempt to date Castro's theatrical works according to their versification patterns, simply accepted Rennert's supposition and said, "I agree." More surprising is Bruerton's citation of an entry in the *Encyclopaedia Britannica* to the effect that "by June, 1605, the citizens of Valladolid already regarded Don Quijote and Sancho Panza as proverbial types," a statement that led him to conclude that "1610 would seem to be the latest probable *terminus ad quem*."[51] What seemed to be probable, something in turn based on irrelevant observations and impressionistic conclusions, was thus used to date both Castro plays inspired by the 1605 *Don Quixote*, a determination not questioned until 1980, when I published an article on the matter in *Segismundo*.[52] There is textual evidence to preclude a composition date earlier than 1615, and for reasons detailed in my article, I fix the date in the period 1615–18.

In view of my conclusion that neither of the two plays based on the 1605 *Don Quixote* was composed before the completion of the *Don Quixote* of 1615, there is no mystery with respect to neither's being mentioned in *Don Quixote*, Part II. Accordingly, while Castro's *Don Quixote de la Mancha* obviously reflects a burlesque reading of Cervantes' original, one cannot point to Cervantes' silence as a tacit acceptance of the interpretation. For instance, he might have objected quite strenuously to Castro's *El curioso impertinente*: The first act – dismissed by some critics precisely because it is not faithful to the original[53] – has Lotario betrothed to Camila and thus makes much more readily explainable Anselmo's fear that Camila might again yield to Lotario's advances. Whereas this situation may seem psychologically more acceptable to an audience than Cervantes' version, it is clear that the essence of the Cervantine tale has been radically altered. In short, here is an obvious instance of a portion of *Don Quixote*'s having been misinterpreted, either by design or by failure to comprehend the original. Yet Cervantes bestows high praise on Castro. It seems unlikely that either of the two plays reached Cervantes' attention before July of 1615, the date of the *aprobación* of the volume in which he praised the Valencian.[54]

What may in fact have come to his attention was the third Castro play, *La fuerza de la sangre*, based on Cervantes' novella published in 1613. William Byron notes that in January of 1615, "Guillén de Castro had adapted *The Call of Blood* [*La fuerza de la sangre*] for the Madrid stage."[55] He cites no source, but his information probably goes back to a 1935 document by one San Román, which reveals that *La fuerza de la sangre* "was in existence on January 21, 1615."[56] This date would be too late for the text of *Don Quixote*, Part II (first *aprobación* of February 1615 and *privilegio* of March 1615) but not for the volume of plays (*aprobación* of July of that year). The Castro adaptation of *La fuerza de la sangre*, though clearly inferior to the original, is comparatively faithful to it. It certainly would be reason enough for Cervantes to praise Castro's talent if his pleasure was at least partially based on his satisfaction at having one of his works not only dramatized but produced in the very medium associated with Lope de Vega, that same Lope who, he grudgingly admits in that same prologue, had run off with "the monarchy of the *comedia*." The praise bestowed on Castro in the 1615 prologue to Cervantes' plays (more enthusiastic than the passing reference in the *Viaje del Parnaso*, composed prior to the *aprobación* of the *Novelas*, dated July 1612) can be ascribed to this recent development: a play based on his own work, perhaps the first such occurrence in his experience.

While the foregoing argument supports the observation that Cervantes' *Don Quixote* was received as a source of laughter but forbids the deduction that Cervantes' failure to object was a tacit agreement with such an interpretation of his work, the following one helps to support my contention that Cervantes did believe that his readers had misunderstood him. A few days before his death in April of 1616, Cervantes wrote the prologue to the *Persiles*. Here he brought up the subject of how others viewed him and how he did not share that view. To be sure, some of this explanation was couched in a false modesty typical of prologues. Since the choice of words was his, however, I see no reason not to accept them literally. He related the chance meeting with a student who, upon recognizing him, exclaimed: "Yes, yes; it's the healthy cripple, the famous everything, the merry writer and, finally, the joy of the muses!"

Cervantes replied: "That is an error which many ignorant enthusiasts have made. I, sir, am Cervantes, but not the joy of the muses, nor any of the rest of those trifles that you have said."

The words "merry writer" and "ignorant enthusiasts" merit scrutiny. My translation of *alegre* as "merry" rather than "happy" or "cheerful" is influenced in part by translators' renditions in other passages as well as by analogous contexts elsewhere: When, after the realization that the frightening noises have been caused by fulling mills (I, 20), Sancho proceeds to ridicule his master by imitating Don Quixote's heroic speech of the night before, he engages not in parody but in burlesque. In point of fact, both he and Don Quixote use the verb *burlarse* to describe Sancho's conduct. Don Quixote thereupon calls Sancho *señor alegre*. Clearly, the adjective is meant to describe not happiness but the jocose, burlesque ridicule employed by Sancho in his imitation of a heroic attitude that, it has turned out, was not called for. Now this is, in miniature, the response given to the novel as a whole by Cervantes' contemporaries. Here Cervantes allows the perpetrator of the burlesque imitation to be called *señor alegre*. We know, accordingly, why he rejects the label *escritor alegre* for himself.

We should note here an insightful observation by Howard Mancing, who points out that Sancho's speech just before the comic denouement of this episode is an eloquent, logical petition replete with stylistic devices from classical rhetoric. Mancing observes that it is remarkable that "no critic of the novel has ever commented on this extraordinary passage. Perhaps this inattention is due in part to the fact that *other, more obviously comic scenes in the same chapter have attracted greater attention.*"[57]

Cervantes' use of *alegre* in such contexts is found elsewhere. Tomé Cecial, Sancho's neighbor whom Sansón Carrasco recruits to play his "squire" and to disguise himself with a false nose in the manner of a burlesque, is described as "hombre alegre y de lucios cascos" ("merry and scatterbrained man" [II, 15]). In II, 67, when the suggestion is made that Don Quixote and Sancho turn to the imitation of pastoral literature, the priest is thought to be an excellent possibility for this new role playing, "según es de alegre y amigo de holgarse" ("inasmuch as he is merry and fond of amusing himself"). Less direct but in the same vein, Vivaldo, specifically in order to ease the weariness of travel and so that Don Quixote may "proceed with his *disparates*" (I, 13), humors the latter by pretending not to know what knights-errant are (though he subsequently reveals his intimate knowledge of Don Galaor, brother of Amadís de Gaula). Vivaldo is described as "de alegre condición" ("of a merry disposition"). Now, in these examples of Cervantes' use of *alegre*, translators of *Don Quixote* have been inconsistent. It is clear, however, that they do not see in these contexts a meaning akin to "happy" or "cheerful" but prefer some word or phrase that emphasizes the joker or the jester, which is to say that the word *alegre* evokes a quality associated with those who produce comicality. Tobias Smollett's eighteenth-century translation, for example, renders *señor alegre* as "Mr. Joker"; Samuel Putnam writes "my merry gentleman"; Walter Starkie puts "Master Merryman"; J. M. Cohen renders it "Master Joker." In translating the description of the priest as *alegre*, Smollett calls him a "merry companion"; Putnam labels him "so jolly"; Starkie describes him as "frolicsome"; Cohen characterizes him as "gay and fond of his amusements."[58] I need not produce an exhaustive list to make the point that translators have found that Cervantes' use of *alegre* in these instances reflects a character fond of mirth. It follows, therefore, that when he insists that the designation *escritor alegre* is an erroneous one, Cervantes rejects a label that he himself would use when describing a character disposed to merriment.

Those who have applied this term to him are identified as *aficionados ignorantes* ("ignorant enthusiasts"). We know that in Cervantes' vocabulary, those who are ignorant are the *vulgo*. Here in Cervantes' last written words, ignorant people who have thought him to be *escritor alegre* are identified as his enthusiasts. Conversely, in rejecting the label of merry writer as a "trifle" that is the error of ignorant enthusiasts, Cervantes conveys that to think of his work as the product of an amusing writer is the mistake that has been made by the very people who have enjoyed his writing, people who are ignorant, people who, in a word, have not understood him.[59]

Of all the differences between the two parts of *Don Quixote*, none is more intriguing than the importance that the existence of Part I is allowed to have for Part II. I shall not enter the very interesting discussions that, particularly in the last decades, have attempted to provide a literary analysis of this phenomenon. To keep within the bounds of the present chapter, then, and to bear in mind the matters brought forth in it, I submit that the evidence allows the conclusion that Cervantes' consciousness – "self-consciousness" is perhaps more accurate – of his earlier volume reveals a sensitivity to the reception given to that volume and that this reception of the work as a funny book helped to shape much of the second part.

The 1615 *Don Quixote* insists upon the humor as it presents the "history" as one that leads to *admiratio*. The chapter headings play with the reader. Chapter 9, for instance, is headed "Wherein is told what therein will be seen"; Chapter 31 will "deal with many and grand things"; Chapter 40 is "of things that pertain and touch upon this adventure and this memorable history"; Chapter 54 is "of things dealing with this history and none other" and so forth. Although the headings of the first part occasionally refer to the humorous nature of this or that episode, the playfulness evident in those of the second part is not there.

We have already seen other examples of the insistence upon humor, beginning with Don Quixote's own statement concerning the need for genius in this respect. Don Quixote himself is depicted as laughing twice as frequently in 1615 as in 1605.[60] Perhaps most telling is the response to Avellaneda's book. On the one hand, the superiority of Sancho's humor to that of Avellaneda's Sancho is one of the criteria adduced for the identification of the authentic Cervantine character. On the other hand, Cervantes allows Don Juan to suggest that it would still be worthwhile to read Avellaneda's book, were it not for the inaccuracy of basic facts and the unpardonable misconstruing of Don Quixote's love for Dulcinea. The two points are of course not mutually exclusive, and that they are not, I venture to say, supports and illustrates my contention. Avellaneda's work is unworthy because it fails to understand the essence of the Cervantes original. This essence is distinct from the humorous aspect of the book, as the discussion of the issue brings out. Even though the humorous quality is *not* the essence, that quality is an uncommon one – it requires genius to write wittily – and if that is what the reading public sees in Cervantes' work, he will be proud of it, for it confirms his genius and his ability to win over that *vulgo* which applauded Lope de Vega. (I am cognizant of the fact that the crowds that attended the plays, particularly the rowdy *mosqueteros*, constituted a population distinct from those who were able to read Cervantes' book. It is the concept of the *vulgo* as that majority who, literate or not, lacked the intelligence, wisdom, or learning to appreciate the nature of the parody that links Cervantes' readers with the ignorant spectators who applauded Lope's *comedias*.) Like Lope, he will not hide his contempt for the *vulgo*, although when he specifically identifies the popularity of the 1605 *Don Quixote* with the infinite number of fools, he uses Latin to make the point, perhaps to underline the notion that the *vulgo* that reads his book most likely will not recognize itself. In the prologue to his last work, as we have seen, he will go so far as to say that the enthusiasts who called him a merry writer show ignorance, the key quality that for him signifies *vulgo*.

Not as direct but no less clear a message can be gleaned from *El licenciado Vidriera*. The tale of the "man of glass" is frequently compared to *Don Quixote* because both works depict madmen of sorts. What is germane to the issue before us here is that the central portion of the tale portrays the deranged licentiate spewing forth incisive maxims and sarcastic observations about most facets of society, thus attracting the crowd that follows him from square to square. The learned man is thus pursued by the *vulgo* that is drawn to his pronouncements. These acerbic aphorisms are rarely amusing if we perceive them via the mentality of the times. They may make us smile today, for our reaction is frequently colored by a disapproval of the objects of the licentiate's satire, but the Spaniard of 1613, though he could appreciate the satire and the wit, would not find most of them funny.[61] We may, however, refer to them as *disparates* for two reasons. First, the rapid-fire series of sardonic remarks is let loose in a shotgun manner. One might easily say that the protagonist repeatedly "shoots off his mouth," a slang expression of our own that parallels the basic meaning of *disparar*, "to fire or shoot."

The licentiate's remarks may be said to be *disparates* for a more significant reason. Although the aphorisms frequently hit their mark, they resemble Sancho's proverbs in that they lack cohesion. I should like to borrow Ruth El Saffar's interpretation, according to which the crowd's harrassment has forced the licentiate "to release his own over-all knowledge in bits and pieces which never find their way into a coherent and potentially alternate system." Moreover, the protagonist "fails as an author because he does not communicate by his own words nor does he transform." He is "another in Cervantes's gallery of authors who have failed." Finally, the work "represents the nadir of Cervantes's confidence in both his possibility for success and the possibility that wisdom and intelligence have any meaning in a world governed by ignorance and prejudice." The licentiate's aphorisms become "a machine-gun fire of hateful statements lacking all cohesion and order"[62]

Given El Saffar's interpretation and the points made in this chapter, one can better understand the licentiate's words to the crowd after recovering his sanity: "What you used to ask me in the public squares, ask me now in my home, and you will see that he who, *so they say*, answered you well extemporaneously, will answer you better with deliberation" (*Obras*, p. 888; italics mine). The outcome, as readers recall, is that he is now ignored and leaves to seek success as a soldier. Much has been made of the irony implicit in the attention given his aphorisms during his illness in contrast to the apathy shown him after his recovery. El Saffar's analysis allows us to add an important nuance.

It is true that the sententious remarks are inspired by the particular and dissolve into generalizations, a characteristic of the *comedia* as well.[63] They are pithy statements critical of the society and its mores. They are not without significance and in this respect do not merit the label of *disparates*. We know, however, that for Cervantes *disparates* are absurd by reason not necessarily of their content but rather of their context. The charge leveled at the *comedia* of the day by the canon of Toledo is that they are "conocidos disparates" ("notorious absurdities") that have "neither head nor feet"; that is, they are disjointed. Nonetheless, the canon continues, "the *vulgo* listens to them with pleasure" (I, 48). One

observer has summarized all this as follows: "For the Canon, *comedias*
that are 'disparates' are those that lack 'traza,' meaning 'plan' or 'invention,' and do not coherently develop the 'fábula,' which is the 'plot' or
'action' of the play."[64] Both the canon's definition and his observation
on the *vulgo*'s reaction may be applied to *El licenciado Vidriera*. It goes
without saying that Cervantes has put all these elements together in his
novella intentionally, so that although at the fictive level the overall lack
of cohesion among the several aphorisms betrays a series of *disparates
desconcertados*, at the literary level we may speak once more of a calculated
series, or *disparates concertados*.[65] But at the fictive level it is the incohesive
sequence that attracts the *vulgo*, whereas the remarks delivered with
deliberation lead the audience to disappear. At what I have termed the
literary level – that is, at the level of Cervantes and his creation as opposed
to the fictive results thereof – one perceives why it is necessary to create
absurdities that seem to lack integrity, that reflect an apparently episodic
plot structure, and that point at "another in Cervantes's gallery of authors
who have failed." I submit that there is a correspondence between the
licentiate and Cervantes himself. Having succeeded in attracting the crowds
in public squares where his witticisms could be heard (and where *Don
Quixote* was "pawed"), he nonetheless failed to be appreciated for what
he had meant to convey with deliberation and purpose.[66]

Even as the narrator of *Don Quixote* insists upon the humor – the
reader is told to "expect two bushels of laughter, which is how you will
be affected by finding out how Sancho conducted himself" as governor
(II, 44) – those who experience Sancho's comportment must confess,
along with many a reader, to be *admirado* to see how such an unlettered
man can say so many wise things, "so outside all that those who sent
us [the duke and duchess] and those of us who came here had expected
of your intellect"(II, 49). Although Cide Hamete Benengeli insists on
seeing things to laugh at, he must also record that *admiratio* is the reaction
of those who make their own judgment in the face of the laughter the
readers of Part I (the duke and duchess) led them to expect. The statement
just quoted goes on to declare that "burlas se vuelven en veras y los
burladores se hallan burlados" ("jests turn into truths and the mockers
find themselves mocked"). Indeed, if Chaucer could say that truths are
spoken in jest, Cervantes points out that we may even mistake the one
for the other.

To sum up: In 1605 Cervantes published a parody consciously patterned upon a variety of literary antecedents, among them the romances
of chivalry, the pastoral romances, even epic poetry. The basic assumption of the plot was a humorous one: A fifty-year-old man not only
believed the romances but believed himself capable of being one of their
heroes; his companion would be not only his squire but eventually a

governor. This aspect of the plot overshadowed the mock-serious parody of the literary models and the ethical and aesthetic questions posed but did not prevent the book from being a popular success. Ten years later Cervantes published the sequel, in which he continued his original approach and, because he knew that the public would expect another funny book, not only continued its humor but repeatedly underscored the risible qualities of his work and its characters. In 1615 he said that to write wittily requires genius. In 1605 he had said that the story of Don Quixote was so extraordinary that it was doubtful there could be a genius keen enough to have hit upon the idea (I, 30). When, at times, his more serious intentions seemed to diverge from the expectations of the reader, Cervantes applied immediate corrective measures, such as giving Sancho a malapropism to counterbalance a wise observation, or having his surrogate authors express disbelief, or having Don Quixote or Sancho himself explain a source for Sancho's wisdom, or having the narrator tell the reader that something was a matter for laughter when otherwise there might not have been cause to see humor.

I must confess that, aside from the underlying concept of having an ignorant peasant be a governor at all, I for one find very little to laugh at during the entire sequence of the events surrounding Sancho's governorship. There is, in fact, only one point at which laughter is specifically recorded (the judgment over the tailor's caps in II, 45), although the narrator has assured us two bushels of laughs throughout the governorship. The governorship of Sancho Panza is a satire and a parody, and in this sense it is comic. But it is not composed of funny situations, unless one is predisposed to see it that way. The doctor's refusal to let Sancho touch any food, along with the duke's warning not to eat or sleep, may seem funny, particularly given Sancho's penchant for doing both. However, if we see him as the butt of the joke, the lack of food and sleep loses its humor, especially in light of the responsibilities that he discharges with care and that eventually prove too much for him. But the reader of the 1605 *Don Quixote* expected Sancho to be funny, and so in 1615 Cervantes went along with that expectation. See how funny it is, he seems to have been saying, even as he portrayed pathos, political satire, the cruelty of humor at others' expense, and as he probed the most serious literary questions of his day. Yes, it is a funny book. But it is only the *aficionados ignorantes* who cannot see beyond the tears of their own laughter.

In a recent book, Carroll B. Johnson recounts an experience repeated in several Madrid theaters. A film in which young love was understood by the audiences as what it is also included a sequence in which two people in an old-age home fall in love and carry on a relationship corresponding to that of an adolescent romance: love poems surreptitiously passed from table to table at mealtimes, melodramatic declarations of love, lingering glances after mealtimes, and so on. Johnson observes: "In every theater the audience's reaction to this segment was laughter, from raucous guffaw to nervous titter. [The audience] experienced the idea of older people in love as shocking . . . and retreated into the safety of tradition by turning the two lovers into a pair of clowns."[67]

This response to the portrayal of old people engaged in lovemaking, namely, considering it risible, is indeed a conventional one. Leaving to one side the psychosocial response of security in the face of potentially unorthodox behavior, the guffaw and titter witnessed by Johnson are the reactions of a community accustomed to thinking that such behavior is not the expected norm and is, therefore, a source of humor. It is analogous to the sort of laughter provoked by a dignified individual's slipping on a banana peel. The behavior itself is not funny: An elderly, dignified person falling down or falling in love is not in itself a comic event, unless and until that event is seen in a context in which laughter is the expected result. I daresay that had the audiences in Johnson's anecdote not seen first the segment on young love, had they instead attended a movie solely devoted to the depiction of elderly love, the reaction would have been altogether different. In the same way there is a difference in our response to the dignified individual and the banana peel. In a Charlie Chaplin film we are predisposed to laugh; faced with a grandparent's fall our laughter is far less likely.

My point is an obvious one. The audience observed by Johnson found the depiction of love among the elderly risible because they had arrived at that segment of the film with a set of preconditioned reflexes. Not only has erotic behavior among the aged traditionally been an object of humorous treatment in literature, particularly dramatic literature, but the contrast with the film's first half helped to set up the corresponding contrast between sympathy and ridicule. The same kind of opposition – taking Don Quixote in earnest or in jest – based on the same criterion – prior conditioning – is at work in the reception of the 1615 Don Quixote. I have suggested in this chapter that much of Cervantes' emphasis on humor in the 1615 volume serves a dual purpose: First, his evident talent and the resultant reputation for it made him proud to underscore his genius for writing wittily. Second, his awareness (as a result of the reception given the 1605 Don Quixote) that his public saw primarily, if not exclusively, the humor of his work moved him (in the 1615 Don Quixote) to point to the humor even in situations that more properly should have been identified for their pathos (witness the many laughs promised for the reading of the chapters dealing with Sancho's governorship).

Johnson, writing from a perspective unrelated to mine, makes an observation that complements my arguments in a suggestive way. The episode in question is the nocturnal appearance of Doña Rodríguez in Don Quixote's bedroom (II, 48). We are in the presence of an encounter, in erotic circumstances, between two middle-aged people. Johnson comments:

> On the surface, the sight of these two mid-lifers alone in Don Quixote's room in the middle of the night, each bundled up in several layers of clothing (and in Don Quixote's case in the bed-clothes as well), both so preoccupied that their own sexuality would run away with [them], both adopting exaggerated defensive postures, is ludicrous or embarrassing, analogous to the episode of "love in the old folks' home" in the Spanish film described earlier. This is probably why the human dimension of this episode has received scant critical attention, and this is certainly why Cide Hamete Benengeli makes fun of the two of them. One might inquire here why Cervantes goes out of his way to ascribe the ridicule to Cide Hamete and does not indulge...himself in his capacity as principal narrator... For Cide Hamete what is ludicrous is the couple's elaborate avoidance of sexual intimacy. For most Christian readers... what is either ludicrous or embarrassing is that two senior citizens like Don Quixote and Doña Rodríguez should find themselves in a sexual situation at all.... The Arab narrator observes the scene from another, different perspective and finds it risible. There is a strong suggestion here that Cervantes, a fiftyish Christian like Don Quixote, turns the stated reaction to this scene over to Cide Hamete because *he himself finds it not humorous, but pathetic.*[68]

The implications of the insightful final sentence cannot be overstated. Johnson's suggestion, that in a major episode of the 1615 *Don Quixote* Cervantes saw pathos but allowed his surrogate author to represent it as humor, supports the basis of the thesis put forth in this chapter.

I close this chapter with commentaries from two recent articles that, though written from still other perspectives, make observations that bear upon the thoughts I have expressed. On Sancho's governorship:

> At one level, of course, the episode is an opportunistic use of Sancho by Cervantes to turn the practical joke against the jokers. But in doing so he engages the serious Renaissance theme of the good governor. Without doing violence to Sancho's "character," and yet using our clear sense that he has changed during his association with Quixote, Cervantes is able to draw more serious implications from the episode than his figure would seem to allow. The whole

episode must be understood not as a farcical interlude but rather as a Shakespearian sub-plot in which the major theme is expanded and universalized through repetition in a comic and earthy mode.[69]

And on Don Quixote's circumstance: "That an *hidalgo* should fancy himself to be an heroic *caballero* is of course comical and satirical. But it will make no difference to insist that his book is only a comic epic, or a comic epic in prose, because *his situation is in any case that of the epic hero.*"[70]

The emphasis is mine, for it reinforces a position taken in this chapter. To perceive and appreciate the comicality of *Don Quixote* is fitting. To insist on this feature as its only or primary intention is to miss the substance of the protagonist's circumstance.

Chapter 2
Gilt o'erdusted:
the problem of originality

The two most engaging powers of an author: new things are made familiar, and familiar things are made new.

– Samuel Johnson

If Cervantes had intended to write only a funny book, the question of its originality would be of a different order. The central premise of the plot – that an individual could accept the books of chivalry literally – was already present in the *Entremés de los romances*; and critics are still continuing to find sources for this or that episode, not to mention the many historical figures that are offered as models for major and minor characters. It goes without saying that Cervantes, who prided himself on his inventiveness, would have objected that the essence of originality (had such a word occurred to him) lies elsewhere. The basis of *Don Quixote* – which is not to say its meaning or intention – is parody, which by its nature depends on established and more or less recognizable models.

The question of the multiplicity of authors – indeed of the reader's participation implied by the invitation of the 1605 prologue – has fascinated Cervantists for some time. An exploration of this topic would divert us from our task in this chapter, but it bears remarking that one implication of Cervantes' removing himself as author and yielding to various levels of historians and interpreters is a claim not to have originated *Don Quixote*. In addition to its importance for an understanding of Cervantes' probing of literary aesthetics, the literary joke of assigning the authorship of his masterpiece to someone else betrays that the concept of originality, to the extent that it means origination, is itself a problematic question. But this question is not limited to *Don Quixote*.

"I am the first to have 'novelized' in the Castilian language," asserts Cervantes in the 1613 prologue to his *Novelas ejemplares*. He is of course referring to having written novellas. Does he also wish to imply the novelty of these tales? Although it is true that to be first is at least to some extent tantamount to being novel, the converse does not inevitably follow. Novelty may, for instance, be revealed not only in the first statement of an idea but as well (and often more profoundly) in its restatement. When we admire someone's analysis of a matter by exclaiming, "I've never heard it put quite that way before," we are admittedly implying that we have indeed heard whatever it is before, just *not put quite that way*. If this appears at first to be an artificial dichotomy between chronological priority and intellectual novelty, we shall soon see that it is in fact a rich paradox that reflects the struggle of an artist to resolve the sometimes juxtaposed but often antagonistic urges to be first as well as best, to be original as well as ingenious. Indeed, novelty often is more closely allied to the ingenious use of tradition than to the process of origination: "Literary history understandably dwells on innovation and originality, though the wholly original and traditionless poet – *überlie-ferunglos*, as Goethe once imagined him – would ultimately become a tradition in himself. Novelty emerges . . . through the talented use of sources and conventions."[1]

Cervantes' claim to be the first to compose novellas in the Castilian tongue plunges us into the midst of the problem under consideration in this chapter. J. D. M. Ford's assessment, made well over half a century ago, that it is a "claim that cannot be contested,"[2] retains its validity even when we read Cervantes' statement in the context of his own qualifying remarks:

> I allow myself to understand (and so it is) that I am the first to have "novelized" in the Castilian tongue; for the many novellas that are in print in Spanish are all translated from foreign languages, and these here are my own, not imitated nor stolen: My ingenuity engendered them and my pen gave birth to them, and they are now growing in the arms of the printing press.

Ruth El Saffar reminds us that a number of scholars have taken issue with the supposition that Cervantes' tales owe much to his Italian predecessors: "Hainsworth finds, in fact, very little that resembles the *novella* in Cervantes's short stories. . . . Hainsworth emphasizes, against modern prejudices, the originality in Cervantes's idealistic tales. . . . When we consider the [characteristics of these] tales, we must agree that they are strongly divergent from the clear-cut, almost anecdotal novellas of the Italian tradition."[3]

It may appear only natural that Cervantes' prologue should display his own critical understanding of the contribution made in his tales, an understanding that goes beyond the notion of being first and embraces the very stuff of the Spanish *novela*. Accordingly, his insistence on being first assumes more than a claim of chronological priority. It is the *novelty of the character* of his tales that Cervantes wishes to bring forth, by which he means to distinguish them from *other* novellas, in fact, from the "many novellas that are in print in Spanish." The matter of others' works as

translations diminishes in importance as we read Cervantes' more em-
phatic insistence upon the *Novelas ejemplares* as his own, "not imitated
nor stolen" but engendered by his ingenuity and given birth by his pen.
Similarly, the prologue to *Don Quixote*, Part I, insists on the protagonist's
thoughts as "never imagined by anyone else." The more we read Cervantes' words, the more we are struck by his desire to underscore the
ingenuity displayed in his novellas and by his pride in their having been
created by him.[4] Moreover, we should recall Don Quixote's response
to translations: After making exceptions for translations of works originally in "the queens of languages, Greek and Latin," he then suggests
that translating is like copying and requires neither ingenuity nor eloquence. In typical Cervantine fashion, he next hastens to present the
other side of the coin: that translation is nonetheless a worthy occupation,
particularly in comparison with lesser matters with which people could
occupy their time. But then the extremes meet as he mentions two Italian
works whose Spanish translations are so well done that they "felicitously
put in doubt which is the translation and which the original" (II, 62).
What emerges here is consistent with Cervantes' views on the concepts
we are exploring in this chapter, namely, that originality in its chronological sense may be subordinated to its own restatement.

How may we accommodate this greater emphasis on artistic novelty
to his earlier statement that he is the first to have written novellas in
Spanish? Cervantes not infrequently concerns himself with the question
of being first. Moreover, as is the case with so many other aspects of
Cervantes' art, the concept of anteriority is examined from a multiplicity
of vantage points. As is also the case so often in the works of Cervantes,
numerous matters are presented with an appreciation for irony. The
phrasing of the sentence we have been considering, therefore, needs to
be studied with some care. What I have rendered as "I allow myself to
understand (and so it is) that I am the first to have 'novelized'," reads in
the original as follows: *Me doy a entender (y es así) que yo soy el primero
que he novelado.* The clause *me doy a entender*, literally, "I give myself to
understand," appears to present no ambiguities. Yet one major dictionary
does register an intriguing definition for part of the expression (*darse a*)
and goes on to suggest a discordant, exaggerated, and perhaps unreasonable connotation for what is being "given to understand."[5] Whether
Cervantes consciously avails himself of the ambiguities contained in the
expression *darse a entender*, or whether he simply applies the equivoque
intuitively, is difficult to discern. In either event, we may readily document that this expression is repeatedly used in a great variety of contexts,
most of which are replete with ambiguity, at variance with a more literal
reading of the passage in question. For the moment, I simply present

the hypothesis that Cervantes is employing a construction with inherently discordant and ambiguous connotations when he asserts that he allows himself to understand that he is the first to have novelized in Spanish.

In the prologue to the *Novelas ejemplares*, Cervantes not only proclaims his understanding of being first but adds parenthetically that it is so. A quick reading suggests no more than iteration for the sake of emphasis. Yet the assertion of truth here is directed at us from two sources: what Cervantes has given or allowed himself to understand, as well as what *it is*. Stated another way, Cervantes' claim is presented as being based on what he perceives or allows himself to perceive (a subjective apprehending of the truth) and, in addition, based on what is so (an assertion of absolute truth). To wander into a discussion of relative truth versus absolute truth, of appearance and reality, of perspectivism in Cervantes' works, would not be without profit. Such an excursion, however, would no doubt restate what so many of the best studies have already explored. But we should recognize the relationship between these themes and the sentence we are examining. To be specific, the parenthetical "and so it is" is not merely a commonplace to reinforce the preceding "understanding" that he is the first. The two expressions reflect a manner of approaching reality familiar to readers of Cervantes: what one believes or takes to be the truth ("I allow myself to understand") and what is the truth ("and so it is").

So frequent is this type of iteration in Cervantes' writings that it is easy to dismiss it as merely an idiosyncrasy of his prose. What makes it significant, however, is that the mutual reinforcement of such iterative assertions reflects subjective belief even as it invokes some sort of disinterested or absolute confirmation of that perception. In the most famous adventure in all of Spanish literature – Don Quixote tilting at the windmills – the protagonist explains the transformation of the "giants" into windmills as enchantment by declaring, "I think, and so it is true" (I, 8). Not only does Don Quixote express his belief, but he at once confirms that his understanding is also the truth. Not dissimilar is the subsequent declaration in the same chapter that the Benedictine monks "must be, and are, undoubtedly, some enchanters." What must be (individual perspective) and what undoubtedly is (absolute truth) are once more distinguished by their very power of mutual reinforcement. The construction employed by Don Quixote is not a rarity in Cervantes' works, nor is it confined to those who see illusions. An antithetical version of Don Quixote, a charlatan who consciously tries to deceive others by making *them* attempt to see illusions (Chanfalla, in *El retablo de las maravillas*), similarly declares to his companion that those who are approaching "must be, as they are undoubtedly, the governor and the aldermen." This statement of fact, rather than being a possible illustration of the phrase in a situation *not* charged with multiple interpretations, is presented at the beginning of a work whose central and ironic theme will be the necessity for all concerned – particularly the governor – to question their very identities.

It would be no difficult task to adduce a veritable catalogue of similar constructions in Cervantes' writings.[6] What is to the point here is that the expressions of the sort we find in his statement that he is the first to have "novelized" in Spanish are readily related to Cervantes' acknowledged concern with the nature of truth. Although it is frequently stated that he paints truth as a relative concept, it is more accurate to say that he understands truth as an absolute concept that we may *claim* to possess but that, because of our human limitations, we are unable to grasp in its totality. Thus what we perceive to be true may indeed be true (the two parts of the constructions we have been considering), yet it may be only a portion of the absolute truth. Inasmuch as Cervantes understands this paradox, his statement about chronological priority needs to be examined in this light.

If, then, the phrase *darse a entender* has the unreasonable, exaggerated, and discordant connotations recorded by María Moliner, and if the bipartite construction reveals a subjective perception as well as a perhaps ironic summoning of what is beyond our grasp (the absolute truth), how are we to deal with Cervantes' claim that he is the first to have written novellas? It is worth recalling that in another prologue (to his *Ocho comedias y ocho entremeses*, 1615), published only two years after the *Novelas ejemplares*, Cervantes claims that it was he who dared to reduce from five to three the number of acts into which plays now (1615) are conventionally divided. Moreover, he asserts in the very same sentence that he was the first to represent the hidden thoughts and imaginings of the soul by displaying "moral figures" in the theater, a matter I shall return to shortly.

It is surely not happenstance that it is in this same prologue that Cervantes, in a mixture of disappointment and respect, credits Lope de Vega with having run off with the monarchy of the Spanish *comedia*. One naturally wonders why Cervantes, while admitting Lope's supremacy in the theater, should care to claim precedence in the matter of the number of acts. The question seems to become academic when we recall that Lope himself did not take credit for this purely structural innovation, a fact of which Cervantes could scarcely have been unaware, for in the well-known *Arte nuevo de hacer comedias en este tiempo*, Lope affirmed that "Captain Virués, a worthy wit, divided [the *comedia*] into three acts, which before had gone on all fours, as on baby's feet, for [*comedias*] were then infants."[7] Although it is not my purpose here to establish who did originate the three-act formula, a brief look at how this innovation was perceived will help us to place Cervantes' understanding of it in a clearer light.

Cristóbal de Virués, a Valencian contemporary of Cervantes' (who, like Cervantes, had been wounded at the battle of Lepanto in 1571), did indeed claim to have been the first to have written a Spanish play in three acts, as he affirms in the prologue to his drama *La gran Semíramis*.[8] J. P. W. Crawford observed that it is "true that Avendaño's *Comedia Florisea*, in three acts, was printed in 1551, but the Spanish plays with which Virués was acquainted were written in four or rarely five acts, and he had good reasons to believe himself the inventor of a new form."[9] Nonetheless, aside from the comment of Lope de Vega himself, we possess no contemporary corroboration of Virués' claim. In fact, the diarist Diego de Vich (1584–1657) attributed the three-act format to yet another Valencian, Andrés Rey de Artieda.[10] How does all this relate to Cervantes' assertion?

It is difficult to take Cervantes seriously, given the date of the prologue to his theatrical works. Not only had Lope de Vega declared that it was Virués who first fixed the three-act formula, but he had done so in a work published as long before as 1609, the date of the publication of the earliest known edition of the *Arte nuevo*. Subsequent editions (or reprintings with slight variations) during Cervantes' lifetime appeared in 1611, 1612, and 1613. It is highly unlikely that Cervantes remained ignorant of Lope's poem, including the reference to Virués and the origin of the tripartite format. Moreover, any suggestion that Cervantes might have wished to take credit from Virués is negated by the nature as well as the chronological span of the laudatory references to the Valencian made in three of Cervantes' works: In *La Galatea* (published in 1585), Cervantes not only praised Virués' knowledge, valor, ingenuity, and virtue but went so far as to promise to spread far and wide the fruit of his ingenuity, so that it might be known, admired and esteemed. In *Don Quixote* (1605), Cervantes had the curate spare Virués' epic poem *El Monserrate* for reasons not unlike those for which he subsequently praised his own novellas: It, and works by Ercilla and Rufo, "are the best that have been written in the Castilian language and may well compete with the most famous of Italy; keep them as the richest jewels of poetry that Spain has to show" (I, 6). Finally, in the *Viaje del Parnaso*, published only one year before the prologue to the plays (though written by 1612), Cervantes once more paid tribute to Virués as one of a famous group of Valencian poets. In short, no motive for eclipsing Virués' claims to fame can be inferred from Cervantes' references to Virués, which span some three decades.

It is, of course, possible to assume that some of Cervantes' earliest plays – works that most scholars agree existed but that have since been lost – may have been composed in three acts and that, chronological accuracy aside (for he need not have been aware of the dates of Virués' or Avendaño's works), Cervantes may honestly have believed himself to have anticipated what later became the conventional number of acts for a *comedia*. He did not, in point of fact, say that he was the first but only that he had dared to take the step, a claim that in any event brings to the fore how unusual – one might say, how original – it was at the time. If he did believe he had anticipated most if not all of his contemporaries in the matter, there is no reference to a title that might help substantiate the claim. (We should note in passing that in the very collection the 1615 prologue heads, the figure of "Curiosity" in *El rufián dichoso* asks the figure "Comedia" why, among other changes from older customs, the latter has "reduced to three" the number of acts she at one time comprised. The reply is that times change things, an explanation that is further used to justify the violation of the unity of place, the explanation being labeled an "excuse for such a *disparate*.")

Perhaps greater significance may be attached to Cervantes' more substantive claim that he was the first to present "moral figures" in the theater. Once more, however, we find that Cervantes was by no means the first, although some commentators have perceived a distinction between the traditional allegorical figures (Faith, Hope, Charity, Death, Fame, Fortune, and the like) and Cervantes' representation of Necessity, Hunger, Curiosity, and similar figures.

Riley points out that Cervantes

> ... does not say that he was the first to bring allegorical figures onto the stage, but that he was the first to represent imaginings and secret thoughts by bringing allegorical figures on the stage. There is a difference. An allegorical figure is usually the personification of a mental concept, to be sure; but Cervantes is not referring to animated ideas.... He is surely talking about giving external dramatic form to what is going on in the mind of a character.[11]

We should bear in mind, however, that it was with tongue in cheek that Cervantes praised Cide Hamete Benengeli for a similar accomplishment: "He depicts the thoughts, discovers the imaginings, answers the unspoken, clarifies doubts, resolves objections and finally, reveals the atoms of the most captious desire" (II, 40).

If it is, then, in a more modern kind of allegorical figure that Cervantes finds his own originality, the claim about such an innovation reflects an intriguing juxtaposition of inventiveness and restatement. Once more it becomes clear that although it is a claim to chronological priority, Cervantes' assertion carries meaning principally in its suggestion of novelty

as a creation whose "originality" lies more in the ingenuity of its presentation than in its absolute newness.

In Chapter 22 of the second part of *Don Quixote*, an individual who
describes himself as a humanist is introduced to guide the protagonist to
the famous Cave of Montesinos. For reasons that are never made clear,
this person is presented as the cousin of the licentiate whom Don Quixote
met earlier. In short, Cervantes creates a new character who remains
anonymous and who is referred to alternately as the guide or the cousin,
the latter being the more frequently used appellative. The Spanish word
for cousin – *primo* – of course can mean "first" as well and is used in
this sense on several occasions in *Don Quixote*. If this connection seems
either too obvious or too far-fetched, its relationship to the character
becomes patent when we are informed that the sort of book this "humanist" is most inclined to compose is exemplified by his *Supplement to
Virgilio Polidoro*, which, as he himself describes it, "deals with the invention of things. . . . Virgilio forgot to tell us who was the first in the
world to have a cold, and the first to take the cure for syphilis." Sancho
Panza, it will be recalled, is quick to meet the pseudoscholar on his own
terms: "Tell me, sir . . . , could you tell me, for surely you must know,
since you know it all, who was the first to scratch his head, for I am
convinced it must have been our father Adam?" The cousin agrees, giving
as his reason the self-evident observation that Adam was the first man
in the world. Sancho prods further: "Who was the first acrobat in the
world?" In the face of the cousin's inability to respond without further
research, Sancho answers that it was Lucifer, prompting Don Quixote
to observe that "there are some people who wear themselves out learning
and discovering things that, once learned and discovered, don't matter
one bit for our comprehension or retention."

Most scholars rightly consider Don Quixote's comment a sardonic
interpretation of the decadence inherent in the compilation of data for
its own sake, an accumulation that then is allowed to pass for erudition.
But the aspect that gives rise to the lengthiest reaction is the book of
"firsts" that the cousin is composing. In short, one of Cervantes' specific
targets for ridicule is the undue attention that learned pedant and witty
peasant alike may pay to the question, who did what first? Is there a
relationship between the banter in *Don Quixote* and the claims to being
first that Cervantes makes in the prologues cited?

E. R. Curtius lists four typical categories for introductory passages:
(1) the topos "I bring things never said before"; (2) a dedication; (3) the
topos "the possession of knowledge makes it a duty to impart it"; and
(4) the topos "idleness is to be shunned."[12] Commenting on these topoi,

Alberto Porqueras Mayo concludes that only the first enjoyed any vogue in the Spanish Golden Age.[13] In other words, the declaration of originality is in keeping with a tradition, specifically one of which Cervantes and his contemporaries were fond. The deeper significance of originality is accordingly subordinated to the convention of finding things that the author may include in his prologue as "firsts." That the accumulation of "firsts" is satirically presented in the pseudoscholarship of the humanist cousin tells us a good deal about Cervantes' contention in the prologue to his own *comedias* that it was he who dared to reduce the number of acts of a *comedia* to the number long since in vogue at the time of the prologue's publication. Taken at face value, Cervantes' claim may be ascribed to the convention of the prologue, as categorized by Curtius and specified by Porqueras. Given our understanding of Cervantes' art generally (with respect to his reshaping of earlier genres and modes), we may easily see in the utilization of the topos an ironic inversion of its traditional intent.

If we sense bitterness in the prologue to the *comedias*, the focal point of Cervantes' claim to precedence becomes picayune. If he really meant to make a case for having been the first to determine the number of acts or the first to present allegorical figures, precisely at a time when he had more reason to emphasize (as he did) his own successes, particularly *Don Quixote*, Part I, and the *Novelas ejemplares* (as well as his evident hopes for *Don Quixote*, Part II, and the *Persiles*), the contention becomes truly contentious.[14] The more we attempt to understand it, the more it pales in comparison with the greater triumphs of both Lope and Cervantes. Bearing in mind what we have come to understand about Cervantes' perception of being first, it is in the very triviality of the number of acts that Cervantes leads us to consider the importance of something other than being first.

The final sentence of *Don Quixote*, Part II, boasts of another first: "I shall be satisfied and proud at having been the first to have enjoyed fully the fruits of his writings." Whatever other irony we may perceive in the fact that this sentence is attributed to Cide Hamete Benengeli, we are presented with a claim that is at once not verifiable yet irrefutable. On the one hand, how can we substantiate that no previous writer has ever fully enjoyed the fruit of his writings, inasmuch as this must remain a subjective judgment? Yet on the other hand, Cervantes' declaration that he has indeed lived to enjoy fully the fruit of his literary labors is, as he says, a statement of pride and satisfaction, quite at variance with the apparent bitterness expressed in the prologue to the plays. The assertion assumes an altogether different significance, of course, when we place it in the context of the matters discussed in my Chapter 1. If Cervantes believed, as I do, that his work was not understood, the sentence at the conclusion of the 1615 *Don Quixote* must also be seen as another declaration of a "first" that is not to be taken at face value.

It should be recalled in passing that in Spanish, more so than in English, to be first is not always limited to chronological priority but may in fact be synonymous with "foremost." Our own use of the Italian *prima donna* exemplifies this connotation, as does our word "prime." That it held ironic possibilities for Cervantes is reflected in the best-known pun of this sort, namely, the dubbing of Don Quixote's nag Rocinante, "a name that, in his opinion, was high-sounding, sonorous and significant of what it had been when it was a nag, before what it was now, first and foremost [*antes y primero*] of all the nags in the world" (I, 1). On a different level is the satirical treatment given to the concept of being first as equivalent to being foremost in Don Quixote's evaluation of the poetry of young Don Lorenzo de Miranda. The very concept of being first is reduced to social terms, devoid of aesthetic significance:

> Your Grace should strive to carry off the second prize, for the first is always awarded as a favor to someone of high rank, the second goes to the one who merits first place, and thus the third is in reality second, while the first, by this reckoning, would be third. . . . But for all of that, the first prize carries with it a great distinction. [II, 18].

The final sentence, which appears to add the ultimate ambiguity, is in the original charged with sarcasm to reinforce the preceding proposition, for it reads: "Gran personaje es el nombre de 'primero'" ("The name 'first' is a great personage").

Once again, but with a different purpose in mind, we need to enter Don Quixote's library (I, 6). Not surprisingly, the inquisition commences with what Cervantes understood to be the prototype of such literature, the *Amadís de Gaula*. The curate avers that

> " . . . this book was the first one of chivalry printed in Spain, and all the rest have their beginnings and origin in this one; and so, it seems to me that, in view of its role as dogmatic founder of such an evil sect, we should without any excuse whatsoever condemn it to the fire."
>
> "No, sir," said the barber, "for I have also heard that it is the best of all the books of this genre that have been composed; and so, in view of its being unique in its art, it ought to be pardoned."
>
> "That's true," said the curate, "and for that reason we shall allow it to live for the time being."

In this parody of the Inquisition, with its aim of ridding the world of the "false" books of chivalry, the founder of this literary "sect" is initially condemned solely because he is the originator. That is, the salient feature of the *Amadís* as perceived by the curate is that this book was the first. For this reason alone the curate deems it proper, "without any excuse whatsoever," to condemn *Amadís de Gaula* to the flames. Yet after the brief evaluation by the barber, the curate not merely modifies his views but proclaims in parallel terms that it is for the very reason that the book is "unique in its art" that it ought to be spared! What exculpates the *Amadís*, which had initially been unpardonably condemned for being first, is the qualification that it is the best. In addition to the evident irony in having those who supposedly seek to condemn books of chivalry agree to preserve the genre's prototype because it is judged to be good, we should note a distinction that is more readily attributed to Cervantes himself than to his parodic characters: To be the first and to be the best are so different that the distinction may literally be a matter of life and death.

It is fruitful to link the topic under discussion here to that well-known theme which pervades Cervantes' writings: *Cada uno es hijo de sus obras*, ("Each one is the child of his own works"). This aphorism, as readers of Cervantes are well aware, is best understood when it is placed in contradistinction to the notion that one's worth is determined by one's ancestors. In other words, the viewpoint expressed in this maxim embraces more than a statement of individual worth, for it includes as well an implicit contrast between those who originate and those who perceive the origination in and of itself as cause for renown. There is an assumption implied in the *cada uno es hijo de sus obras* theme that distinguishes those who do things first from those who do things well (and, perhaps, from those who simply do them). Don Quixote presents the problem in his definition of the two kinds of lineage by means of the metaphor of the pyramid as he explains that

> ... there are in this world two kinds of ancestral lines. In the one case, there are those who trace their descent from princes and monarchs whom time has little by little reduced until they come to end in a point like a pyramid upside down; and in the other case, there are those who spring from the lower classes and who go upward, one step after another, until they come to be great lords; the difference being that the former were what they no longer are, while the latter are what they formerly were not. [I, 21]

Those without value are the ones who *merely* descend from the originators of great lineages or who have not accomplished anything that might have enabled them to rise in stature. Where the two converge is the point at which members of either group have done something sufficiently worthy (*obras*). In contrast, those who are only the children of these worthy individuals are, unlike the latter, not the children of their own works, and hence less worthy. Conversely, those who form the "lower classes," from among whom may spring others who do make something of themselves, are, unlike the latter, not the children of their own works either. In a word, *obras* determine the worth of the individual, whether or not he or she is the first.

That the foregoing argument is related to the evaluation made of the *Amadís* by the barber and the curate becomes clear when the next volume in Don Quixote's library is subjected to scrutiny: the *Sergas de Esplandián* or *Exploits of Esplandián*, described by the barber as the "legitimate son of Amadís de Gaula." The curate's response is unhesitating: "The merits of the father are not going to be of avail to the son."[15] This condemnation of the *Esplandián* because its only claim to fame appears to be its derivation from the original (and better) *Amadís* places the *hijo de sus obras* theme more in an ethical than a societal context. Although the examples most often given deal with sociological status (as in the pyramid metaphor), other illustrations of the theme (such as the literary comparison between original and sequel) reveal a more global appreciation of its significance.[16] The child (*Esplandián*) is being condemned not because it is not the father (*Amadís*) but because it is judged as having nothing *other* to say for itself than that it is the father's child. *Amadís*, as we have seen, is spared because of its being judged best, *after* having been condemned as being first. Accordingly, the *hijo de sus obras* theme reflects a manner of judging not only social status, moral worth, and esteem of people; it reveals to us as well a perspective from which Cervantes probes the value of creatures and creations generally.

The curate's change of mind as the result of his concurrence that the *Amadís* is not merely first but unique in its art helps us to understand the response to the literature of chivalry voiced in I, 47, by the canon, who readily boasts of being well versed in the genre: "I know more about books of chivalry than about the *Súmulas de Villalpando*." Not only does he claim familiarity with such books, but he admits to having had a "certain temptation to compose a book of chivalry . . . and, to confess the truth, I have more than a hundred pages written already" (I, 48). The canon's having written the beginning of a book of chivalry not only complements Don Quixote's desire to pick up his pen and conclude one (I, 1) but actually takes the canon a step further than Don Quixote, for the canon has indeed begun to write his book. On the other hand, the canon's inability to finish writing such a book is matched by his earlier confession that he has not managed to finish reading one, for "although I have read . . . the beginning of most of those in print, I have never succeeded in bringing myself to read any of them from beginning to end, because it seems to me that, more or less they are all the same thing" (I. 47). As Bruce W. Wardropper puts it, the "sameness of their subject matter has prevented his being able to finish reading even one."[17] As in the scrutiny of Don Quixote's library, therefore, the obstacle to considering the books worthy is their lack of uniqueness – in a word, their lack of originality.

After the curate recounts to the canon the scrutiny and burning of Don Quixote's books, the canon expresses his amusement,[18] adding that, despite all the bad things he has said about such books, he has found in them *one good thing*. As Wardropper observes:

This compromising with his academic principles is his undoing. As he makes his point – namely that the novel offers a wide field for an intelligent author – a flood of other *good things* sweeps into his mind. . . . It is easy to see from a comparison of his two speeches that what the canon knows to be good literature is very different from the writing he feels to be good.[19]

Commenting on this discourse, Riley has written that the canon "follows up his adverse criticism of the novels of chivalry . . . with a sort of blueprint for the ideal romance. . . . This well-known passage is central to Cervantes's theory of the novel."[20] Riley goes on to make the following balanced assessment:

What we have here is not so much a theory of The Novel as a theory of a certain type of novel. . . . It is certainly not the sum of [Cervantes'] theory and still less a description of his own achievements. It accounts well enough for the *Persiles*, but only very partially for the *Quixote*, and not at all for such things as the psychological exploration of characters in *novelas* like the *Curioso impertinente* and the *Celoso extremeño*, or the comic "realism" of *novelas* in the low style like *Rinconete y Cortadillo* and the *Coloquio de los perros*. It does nothing to explain the complex creative processes of *Don Quixote*. This is not to say that Cervantes excludes such accomplishments from his ideal romance, for he expressly allows the writer room to include many varieties of fiction. . . . Apart from its significance as a point of departure, the chief importance of the passage lies in the attempt to raise the novel to the level of the most esteemed form of poetry.[21]

Regarding our concern for Cervantes' attitude toward his art as an exercise in originality, the varied yet complementary observations offered by Wardropper and Riley prove illuminating. Wardropper cautions against equating the canon's stance with that of Cervantes himself. The canon's apparent vacillation – what Wardropper felicitously terms his "fine inconsistency" – does, of course, reflect Cervantes' dual concern: an appreciation of received tradition in juxtaposition with a yearning for originality. On a level quite removed from the canon's ambivalence about what he "knows to be good literature" and "the writing he feels to be good," Cervantes finds himself confronted with the comprehension of classical and neoclassical precepts, on the one hand, and, on the other, his own ambition (repeatedly expressed in many of his works) to be recognized for his inventiveness. (On yet another level is the question of catering to the *vulgo*, a matter touched on in my Chapter 1 and one that, ironically, is as much in conflict with originality as it is with classical tradition by virtue of its attendant need for self-imitation – that very "sameness" which the canon deplores in the books of chivalry.)[22] The one good thing that the canon finds worthy in the books – the wide field for displaying one's intellect – which, to the extent that his debate relies on academic principles, is (in Wardropper's words) his undoing, follows immediately upon the curate's account of the book burning.[23]

The wide field for displaying one's intellectual capabilities is, accordingly, the very first good thing that leaps to the canon's mind when he is prompted to react to the otherwise risible burning of the books. From a somewhat different perspective, as we have noted, Riley similarly observes that he "expressly allows the writer room to include many varieties of fiction." I would approach with more caution Riley's conclusion that the "emphasis on variety, underlining the importance of the action, reflects the priority given to plot over character by Aristotle."[24] We need to recall Wardropper's wisdom in warning us not to equate the canon's views with those of Cervantes. Cervantes' writings generally reveal that insight into his own characters and their functioning as individuals overshadows his concern for plot development.[25] It is, as I see it, in variety and the room it affords to the writer's intellect that much of Cervantes' concern for originality finds its significance. Similarly, Riley's indisputable conclusion that "the chief importance of the passage lies in the attempt to raise the novel to the level of the most esteemed form of poetry" should be viewed in a complementary fashion. Although Cervantes has the canon make an unequivocal declaration – it is the *epic* that may be composed in prose as well as in verse – the ultimate importance lies, in my view, less with the epic per se and more with the fact that the epic represents "the level of the most esteemed form of poetry." The chief importance of the passage lies in the revelation of Cervantes' lifelong quest for a literary work aesthetically worthy of the highest esteem, whatever the mode or genre.[26]

It is clear that despite many references to being first, Cervantes' deeper concern is for novelty in an artistic fashion, rather than priority on a chronological scale. More specifically, Cervantes does not prize novelty for its own sake. As in his satirical treatment of the immateriality of learning who was first, he deals in a parallel way with those who seek to learn trivia simply because the data appear new.

El retablo de las maravillas provides several examples, beginning with an ironic description by the charlatan Chanfalla of the nonexistent marvels as "the never-seen-nor-heard things." In this account Chanfalla evidently plays on the "I-bring-things-never-said-before" topos while having in mind things that will in fact never be seen or heard;[27] in addition, the description follows immediately (in the same sentence) upon the definition of illegitimacy and impure (i.e., Jewish or Moorish) blood as "these two well-worn infirmities." In turn, the credulous mayor seizes upon the newness of the marvels (rather than upon their wondrousness) as the salient feature: "Now I notice that every day new things are seen in the world." Only a few moments later in this work, Cervantes makes use of a multiple play on the value of newness as the governor lays claim to being a dramatic poet whose nearly two dozen plays are "all new." This phrase alludes at once to the many such poets that exist (all claiming to be famous yet copying from one another), to the commercial (rather than artistic) demand for new titles, and to the *comedia nueva* in general. Once again, the only characteristic that the insignificant governor calls attention to is the plays' newness. (That Cervantes himself, in the dedication to the Count of Lemos that precedes the very collection in which this play is found, should seize upon the newness of his own plays as their one worthy feature, while putting this same claim in the governor's mouth, confirms once again his use of introductory passages to present the topos of novelty with tongue in cheek.) Yet another manifestation in the same play of the ludicrous contexts in which the quality of newness may be found is the response of Juana Castrada when asked by her father why, since she was earlier frightened by mice, she now asks to be shown bears and lions: "Everything new is pleasing, father."

On a farcical level as well is the situation of the deceived husband in *La cueva de Salamanca* who is led to believe that those who were involved in the hanky-panky are demons conjured up by the roguish student. Pancracio voices his desire to see what "will be the newest and rarest thing ever seen in the world." When, contrary to his belief (apparently based on the same "wisdom" that informs Sancho regarding enchanted people [*Don Quixote*, I, 49]) that devils do not eat, these "devils" insist that they are of the variety that do eat, Pancracio asks them to stay, "for I want to see what I have never seen." A more direct mockery of novelty is Don Quixote's response to the story that Sancho relates in the darkness during the adventure of the fulling mills (I, 20). It is an old and well-worn tale; yet Don Quixote calls it "one of the newest tales, story or history, that anyone could think up in the world." The irony is heightened by the juxtaposition of "newest" with *consejas*, "folk tales." Consequently, it is not only farce but a continuation of this ironic motif that we find in Sancho's explanation of the noises accompanying the movement of his bowels: "It must be something new; for adventures and misadventures never begin for something insignificant." And certainly nothing is more revelatory of the pejorative possibility of newness than Cervantes' repeated references to Avellaneda as the new historian, the modern author of his, Avellaneda's, new history.

The examples just adduced are for the most part humorous. If one reads them exclusively in this way, the erroneous interpretation of Cervantes as an author primarily of comedy forbids the appreciation of the truth of the jest. The matter of Sancho's bowels, for instance, is undeniably low comedy. But to fail to see the cynical purpose behind the linking of bowel movements to "something new," in turn related to so many sardonic depictions of novelty, is to miss the ethical purpose and significance of which these witty elements are the substance.

As in many languages, the word "new" is in Spanish readily defined as "recent." That is to say, something may be described as new without any attendant connotation of absolute newness or uniqueness; the word indicates simply that whatever is being described is qualified as being so recently. As an example, Cardenio (I, 27) describes the man who agreed to deliver a letter from Luscinda as "the new messenger," the idea plainly being that making deliveries is not the man's custom. What it assuredly does *not* convey is the suggestion of originality (that is, that such a kind of messenger is a new phenomenon). For this reason, I do not concur with Joaquín Casalduero's reading of Cervantes' description of Leonora and Loaysa (*El celoso extremeño*): They are "the new adulterers" but not, as Casalduero would have it, new in kind.[28]

Many more examples from Cervantes' writings could be adduced to confirm what the discussion presented here makes clear. Being new, like being first, is not in itself a seriously extolled attribute. In this matter Cervantes approximates his English contemporary Shakespeare, who observed:

> One touch of nature makes the whole world kin:
> That all with one consent praise new-born gauds
> Though they are made and molded of things past,
> And give to dust that is a little gilt
> More laud than gilt o'erdusted.[29]

This is, of course, another way of describing the principle I mentioned at the outset: Novelty may consist of the restatement of an idea. It is, in fact, with respect to a topos as often identified with Shakespeare as with Cervantes, the "all-the-world-is-a-stage" metaphor, that Cervantes gives us an insight into his appreciation of the restatement of received tradition.

Don Quixote describes the comedy we call life, "where some play the parts of emperors, others those of pontiffs – in short, all the characters that a drama may have – but when it is all over, that is to say, when life is done, death takes from each the garb that differentiates him, and all at last are equal in the grave." To this Sancho responds, "It is a fine comparison... though not so new [for] I have heard of it many times before. It reminds me of that other one, about the game of chess. So long as the game lasts, each piece has its special qualities, but when it is over they are all mixed and jumbled together and put into a bag, which is to the chess pieces what the grave is to life." Don Quixote observes, "Every day, Sancho..., you are becoming less stupid and more clever" (II, 12).

Curtius traces the "all-the-world-is-a-stage" topos back to Plato; when he moves forward to Cervantes and Sancho's reply that it is a fine comparison but not so new that he has not heard it many times before, Curtius concludes: "Thus does Cervantes make fun of a literary cliché. Witty – indirect – mockery of a fashionable ornament: That is the first form in which the theatrical metaphor meets us in the Spain of the seventeenth century."[30] I cannot accept Curtius' interpretation of the treatment by Cervantes as mockery. My earlier examples give some indication of how Cervantes does mock notions. Sancho's reaction to the topos here simply, in all senses of the word, confirms how widely disseminated and well understood the metaphor has become. Cervantes' version is a wider-reaching one than that of Shakespeare, for whereas the latter limits his analogy to the *chronological* development of the parts we play, the Spanish writer emphasizes the *variety* of roles played by men and women during the comedy of life. That distinction in itself should reveal Cervantes' sensitivity to the richness of the image. Moreover, Sancho's instant linking of the stage metaphor to the chess analogy is hardly mockery but yet another reflection of the concerns of this chapter: On the one hand, the concept need not be new in order to be a "fine comparison"; on the other hand, the metaphor lends itself readily to restatement. It is here that Cervantes and Shakespeare converge: "Newborn gauds... are made and molded of things past."

The insistence on a wise observation's lack of originality serves another purpose in accordance with the subject of Chapter 1. The fact that Sancho is maturing runs counter to an expectation of him as a static source of laughter. The emphasis on the observation as a time-honored metaphor helps to explain why it is plausible to have Sancho give voice to it. By the time he is governor, the denial of originality has become a frequent recourse. Sancho's resolution of the money concealed in the borrower's cane is first explained sardonically: "Those who govern, even if they are fools, are perhaps guided by God in their judgments"; the sentence then goes on to state that "further, he [Sancho] had heard another case like that one related by the priest of his hometown" (II, 45), thus attributing the felicitous judgment more to Sancho's memory than to his intellect. The subsequent resolution of the riddle of the man and the bridge is similarly rationalized: "I in this case have not spoken on my own, but rather there came to my memory a precept, from among many others that my master Don Quixote gave me" (II, 51). The disclaimers of originality have served to retain the image of a Sancho in keeping with humbler expectations.

"Originality would seem to depend, after the accumulation of experiences, upon the aptness with which they are recombined," writes Harry Levin.[31] The concept of a new combination as a kind of originality – what Shakespeare viewed as a remolding – is found as well in Frederick R. Karl's description of Fielding's "reshaping of narrative, character, plot, theme, and language." Karl similarly describes the work of Laurence Sterne, who, "like Joyce after him established a unity or order upon disparate materials that was not anything substantially new but that *appears* new because every synthesis creates different shapes."[32] This critical appraisal may be applied even to the *Beowulf* poet: "All the events he relates, including, of course, the basic story of Grendel and his dam, are based on traditional materials. The poet's originality lay in his combination of these elements to create a new work of art."[33]

It is in this sort of artistic refashioning that Cervantes finds significance, and so we can understand in a clearer light his variegated references (in turn a reflection of his kaleidoscopic perspectives and resultant perceptions) to the concept of newness. The examples presented here thus far illustrate novelty in a pejorative context, ranging from satire and farce to dismissal of originality in concepts that are otherwise praised for their universal – hence not "new" – validity; in addition, Cervantes reveals his continuing concern for the concept of originality as a problem in aesthetic awareness. Here again we find the vantage points to be multifarious.

In the early pages of this chapter I temporarily set aside the importance Cervantes attaches to artistic originality that is specifically Spanish. His insistence on being the first to have composed novellas in Castilian belongs in a context that once again is somewhat distinct from chronological precedence, though not entirely unrelated to the concept of priority. Stated another way, the two notions – being first and being first in Spanish – are mutually reinforcing ideas in Cervantes' mind, and so the one gives value to the other. Accordingly, Cervantes' praise of the epics by Ercilla, Virués, and Rufo ("the best that have been written in the Castilian tongue and may well compete with the most famous of Italy; keep them as the richest jewels of poetry that Spain has to show") is not to be dismissed as a mere bibliographical reference or to be interpreted as an apology for the best that Spain has managed to produce. Cervantes' respect for the classics as well as for the masterpieces of Italy is liberally sprinkled throughout his works. Consequently, his praise of works (his own as well as others') should be read in a context of pride, although not vainglorious chauvinism. He understands the artist's pride at seeing a creation that has taken into consideration the best (be it of antiquity or of Italy) and that has refashioned such paradigmatic (hence no longer dogmatic) precedents.

Cervantes' assertion that, aside from his own, "the many novellas that are in print in Spanish are all translated from foreign languages" seems to echo a complaint by no less a poet than Garcilaso de la Vega, who, writing in 1533 of Boscán's translation into Spanish of Castiglione's *Il Cortegiano*, said: "I hold to be very great the benefit which is done to the Castilian language by translating into it things which are worth reading; for I know not why it has always been our misfortune that hardly anyone has written in our language anything except that which could very well be dispensed with."[34] Russell points out that Garcilaso's "judgment, of course, is absurdly harsh. Garcilaso rejects, by implication, a timeless work like the [*Celestina*]. . . . But his comment tells us how Spanish writing in the period we have been discussing seemed to one who had thoroughly imbibed the ideas and tastes of Italian humanism."[35] It goes without saying that Cervantes was writing his own thoughts well over half a century later. We should not lose sight, however, of the previously quoted passage from *Don Quixote* concerning the two translations from Italian that "felicitously put in doubt which is the translation and which the original." It is the ingenuity required for restatement that Cervantes prizes, whether the reshaping is in a temporal, cultural, generic, or linguistic context.

This consideration permits us to appreciate, for example, what moves Cervantes to call a fictive version of himself that "modern Spaniard and new author of new and exquisite books," as he does in the *Persiles* (IV, 2). As usual, there is irony in this self-description, for the title of the work discussed in this passage is first called *Flor de aforismos peregrinos*, and it is subsequently suggested that it could well have been titled *Historia peregrina sacada de diversos autores*. Both titles bear the word "peregrine," with its connotation of "strange," which is to say, novel. The concept of originality flies in the face of the very basis of a collection of aphorisms, which normally reflect traditional wisdom; yet the manner of gathering the aphorisms is indeed "peregrine," for it is done by happenstance, as the author meets people who might contribute to the anthology. This brand of novelty also gives rise to the second title and evidently places in an incongruous context the very next sentence, which is the description of the "author" just cited. (We should recall that the humanist "cousin" in *Don Quixote* had described his imitation of Ovid – significantly subtitled *Spanish Ovid* – as being "of new and rare invention.")

As we strive to keep up with Cervantes' presentation of what is new, he seems eager to let us know that it is scarcely new, while he simultaneously leads us to see the entire representation as something quite original after all. Consequently, if the author of the aphorisms is not original, much less the "author" in the first place, in the long run the latter turns out to be Cervantes: the author in the final analysis. And it is in this kind of restatement that Cervantes perceives originality or, to use a word he much prefers, *invención*. Accordingly, it is "not surprising that Cervantes should carry out his attack on the old conventions not by *avoiding* them, but by recalling as many of them as possible in his 'new' work."[36]

C. S. Lewis has observed of medieval authors that "far from feigning originality, as a modern plagiarist would, they are apt to conceal it. They sometimes profess to be deriving something from their *auctour* at the very moment when they are departing from him."[37] This observation may not, of course, be applied to Cervantes without some obvious qualifications. In point of fact, we have already seen several examples of the converse: Cervantes frequently feigns originality at the very moment when it appears most evident that he is anything but original or, at any rate, when no one would take him seriously. Nonetheless, the process described by Lewis is analogous to that which we have been observing in the present chapter. Cervantes feigns originality while poking fun at it; he flaunts novelty while flouting it; he denigrates renditions not in the original tongue while applauding selected translations. Moreover, Lewis's words are almost identical to those of Ramón Menéndez Pidal: "Cervantes, precisely at those moments when he follows the *Entremés de los romances* most closely, appears more original than ever."[38]

The art of Cervantes is not confined to origination. Of course, it goes without saying that although he did begin with "gilt o'erdusted," what he gave to dust was more than "a little gilt." Stated another way, we may better appreciate Cervantes' art and his approach to artistic creativity if we bear in mind that he did not so much create a tradition as create within a tradition. Lest this appear no more than sophistry, I hasten to add that this assessment by no means relegates Cervantes to the status of follower: He did create; he did bring about new artistic approaches to the apprehending of reality; indeed, he created memorable characters.

But we are not diminishing him or his work when in the face of words like "create," "new," and "memorable" we affirm that these things are not synonymous with initiating. None other than Cervantes himself has made the distinction for us. Let us not forget his own artifice of claiming *not* to have originated his own masterpiece.

Restatement through ingenuity assumes primary importance. If it seems necessary to labor the qualities of newness or of being first – in a word, originality – such claims are often made not only because of the irony and the satire inherent in their witty presentation but also because, unlike the medieval audiences, the Renaissance public expected novelty to be the claim of the author. Like the historian who explains his raison d'être as exploring the past in order to understand the future (when his real motive is his intellectual curiosity), because he has come to know that this is what people expect him to say, Cervantes speaks – particularly in introductory passages – of being first or of presenting unheard-of matters because he understands the convention. Yet even here, Cervantes takes precisely the topos that is ready-made for the author's expression of originality and refashions it so that it at once parodies the very quality it supposedly flaunts and demonstrates the ingenuity that he really treasures.

Whereas national pride is of no little importance in declarations like those cited earlier, the deeper significance lies in the appreciation of an art: the art of the artist in question, hence the art of that artist's culture, and, consequently, an art attributable to that artist's time and nation, in this case, the Spain of Cervantes. This art takes the best of what has gone before and of what has been created elsewhere, and re-creates to the point at which even a translation (which is otherwise relegated to the mechanics of transcribing) may "felicitously put in doubt which is the translation and which is the original."

We should read with care the analysis of the *Novelas ejemplares* made by Peter N. Dunn. It is an illuminating and succinct study, devoid of impressionistic readings. Dunn calls our attention to the reports of the official censors, noting their appreciation of Cervantes' inventiveness. Indeed, Cervantes himself prided himself on this quality. But, as we shall explore in Chapter 4, the term *invención* is taken from rhetoric. Rather than defining what in modern terms we understand by inventiveness, the term alludes to the process of *finding* the appropriate elements to put together the plot of a literary work. We should recall, for instance, Don Diego de Miranda's remark about his perusal of the books in his library. None of these books, it bears noting, was of an imaginative sort: They were either devotional or historical. It is the latter that he leafed through more often, provided that they gave delight with their language and aroused wonder with their *invención* (II, 16). Needless to say, today we would not praise books of history for their inventiveness, although we would praise the discerning selection of material by their authors. It is this aspect, rather than originality, that Cervantes prefers to stress. Moreover, it is not wholly accurate to say that Cervantes proclaims his novels to be "original."[39] Cervantes does not use the word "original." What he does say is that his novels are not imitated or stolen. It may be legitimate to call the absence of plagiarism originality, but we should not mistake it for an artistic claim. As Vicente Llorens has remarked, we should exercise caution with respect to "the debatable Romantic concept of originality."[40] That this is not merely a semantic issue but a reflection of a received tradition is revealed in observations like the following:

> Originality is a word that makes most modern critics and teachers of medieval poetry slightly uneasy; we have good reason. Nineteenth- and early twentieth-century critics ... so insisted upon "originality" as a criterion of literary value, so often preferred the "personal" to the traditional, and therefore so often undervalued the artistic uses of conventions and traditions, that we who study and teach this literature are still forced to spend a good deal of our time demonstrating to our students – and to our colleagues – that medieval literature can be, and usually is, valuable precisely because of its traditional nature, its very lack of "originality" in the modern sense of that word.[41]

The apparent limitation of this comment to the medieval period should not allow us to miss the relevant point, an understanding of originality that persisted in the Renaissance.[42] Clearly, Cervantes understood the concept discussed here, namely, "the artistic uses of conventions and traditions." If we, then, from our own vantage point, wish to label this artistry originality, well and good. My intent is not to deny Cervantes' originality (as we understand this term) but to explore his attitude toward its ramifications as a concept.

An attempted justification of Cervantes' claim to being first is not supported by Dunn's dismissal of interpolated tales in the *Guzmán de Alfarache* on grounds that they served to create a contrast within a work different from themselves, whereas Cervantes clearly intended his novellas to make up a collection. The function, as well as the name *novela* that Cervantes gives to *El curioso impertinente*, forbids such a criterion for definition. Moreover, it seems *post hoc ergo propter hoc* reasoning to dismiss Timoneda's tales because *they* are scarcely original.[43] The other works dismissed by Dunn are rightfully discarded, provided we are really speaking not of who was first but of whose artistry is the more ingenious. The word "original" is indeed replete with ambiguity. Despite these details, I find myself ultimately in perfect agreement with Dunn when he concludes that with respect to all those tales that antedated Cervantes, the latter's only interest could have lain in surpassing them. This accurate perception has moved us away from the question who was the first and back to the more significant matter of aesthetic ingenuity and Cervantes' attitude toward it.

Two examples of purposeful restatement will illustrate the possibilities for the process envisaged by Cervantes. My aim here is not to present my interpretation of these passages but to display them as models for the way in which Cervantes could take an existing work of art and reshape it to accommodate it to the new circumstances.

In Chapter 2 of Part I, Don Quixote arrives at the first inn (which he, of course, takes to be a castle), and addressing the prostitutes (who, he believes, are ladies of the castle), he paraphrases a well-known ballad. The original reads:

> Nunca fuera caballero
> de damas tan bien servido
> como fuera Lanzarote
> cuando de Bretaña vino:
> que dueñas curaban dél,
> doncellas del su rocino.[44]
> [Never was there a knight
> so well attended by ladies
> as was Lancelot
> when he came from Britain:
> for duennas cared for him,
> maidens for his horse.]

The first four lines are later recited (I, 13) exactly as quoted here in an attempt to explain the tradition of knights-errant, from King Arthur's time to "our Christian ballad." But, in I, 2, that tradition is carried one step further as Don Quixote reworks it to suit his own circumstances:

> Nunca fuera caballero
> de damas tan bien servido
> como fuera don Quijote
> cuando de su aldea vino:
> doncellas curaban dél,
> princesas del su rocino.

The verse portion leaves off at this point, as Don Quixote goes on to tell the prostitutes his horse's name, now that he has revealed his own, something he had preferred to postpone until his deeds revealed it to them. However, "the press of accommodating this old ballad of Lancelot to the present purpose" causes him to do so now.

Some interesting changes are to be observed. Not only has the name of the hero been made to fit our protagonist, as was to be expected; not only has "Britain" become "village," as might also be expected; but duennas are no longer present, a detail consistent with their treatment elsewhere, their place being taken by "doncellas" ("maidens") as the "doncellas" of the original are raised to "princesas" ("princesses"). Just so will "esa bellaca jodía" ("that rascal of a Jewess") become "la doncella Herodías" ("the maiden Herodias") in *El retablo de las maravillas*, under different circumstances, to be sure, but in accordance with the same accommodating procedure. Perhaps most interesting for our purposes here is that Cervantes has his protagonist articulate that process: He feels, says Don Quixote, a need to accommodate an old ballad to his present circumstances.

The same ballad undergoes further refashioning in Chapter 31 of Part II. This time it is Sancho who invokes the old lines, citing his master as his immediate source, in keeping with what we have come to recognize as a consistent pattern. Sancho wants his ass cared for and asks a duenna to see to it, basing his reasoning on a new distortion of the old ballad, a variation in accord with his particular circumstance. Sancho recites three lines:

> cuando de Bretaña vino,
> que damas curaban dél,
> y dueñas del su rocino.
> [when he came from Britain,
> for ladies cared for him,
> and duennas for his horse.]

There is no question that we have here both parody and farce. The farce lies in the very nature of the facts (that it is an ass that is to be cared for, that a lady-in-waiting should wait upon the ass, that a Sancho Panza should be in a position to make the demand, that Sancho should see the relationship between these circumstances and those of Lancelot). The parody lies in the perfect accommodation of the old ballad's functional purpose, the restatement remaining faithful to the paradigm of the original.[45] I shall return later in this chapter to the question of parody as it relates to farce and imitation. For the present, let us note that in addition to the comical effect, the restatement of the traditional ballad in the two instances cited reveals, particularly when we bear in mind Don Quixote's recitation of the ballad in its original form in I, 13, a purposive distortion quite apposite to the manner in which the characters perceive their reality. Cervantes wishes to portray not that reality but their perception of it.[46]

Cervantes does not let the matter rest here. It turns out that a maiden does in fact attend to Don Quixote. But instead of providing him with a finger bowl for his hands after dinner, the *doncella barbera*, or "damsel barber," washes his beard. The farcical element is evident. Were it not related to the essence of the ballad that has been with us since early in Part I, we could dismiss the scene here as no more than farce. By having a damsel minister to Don Quixote, in implicit accordance with his own modification of the ballad, Cervantes subsumes the immediate farce in the ongoing parody.

Sancho is impressed by the novelty of the treatment given his master. He declares that this is why it is good to live a long time: "to see a great deal; although they also say that he who lives a long life must go through a lot of trouble, even though going through one of these washings is pleasure rather than travail" (II, 32). Once more we note familiar themes. Sancho's articulation of an adage must degenerate into burlesque, and his desire to see a novelty for its own sake rather than for its merit reminds us of similar statements by the mayor and Juana Castrada (*El retablo de las maravillas*) and Pancracio (*La cueva de Salamanca*). But if Sancho expects to be washed by a maiden (like his master) or even by a lady (as his version of the ballad suggests), the result is mortifying, for it is not a *doncella barbera* but a *pícaro barbero* who, along with other rascals, has treated Sancho's beard with dirty cloths, murky soap, cold water, and dirty hands. The farce is even more evident in this treatment than in that dealt to Don Quixote, to be sure. Nonetheless, our awareness of the distortions these ludicrous ministrations convey, with respect to the recurrent ballad and its modifications, permits us to see a larger design.

A similar process, but of a different order, may be discerned in a sequence that has its climax in the Cave of Montesinos (II, 23). Don Quixote finds himself unable to pay the required sum of money that presumably would enable him to alleviate Dulcinea's distress. He immediately promises "not to eat bread off a tablecloth . . . until vengeance had been had." This apparently ludicrous promise is readily placed in context when we recall that the words are a portion of a famous vow, having its origins in the ballads of the Cid:

> Rey que no face justicia
> no debiera de reinar,
> ni cabalgar en caballo,
> ni con la reina holgar,
> ni comer pan a manteles,
> ni menos armas armar.[47]
> [A king who does not do justice
> ought not to reign,

> nor ride around on horseback,
> nor go to bed with the queen,
> nor eat bread off tablecloths,
> much less wear arms.]

These lines were well known to Cervantes' readers, partly because of the popularity of the ballad; partly because Guillén de Castro's famous play *Las mocedades del Cid* presented yet another variation of Jimena's bold complaint; and partly because Don Quixote's own inspiration is a ballad about the Marqués de Mantua, another widely known poem. Don Quixote knows these sources well, as his earlier paraphrase in I, 10, reveals: "I swear . . . to lead the life led by the great Marqués de Mantua . . . which was not to eat bread off tablecloths, nor to go to bed with his wife, and other things." In the Montesinos episode, however, Don Quixote mentions only the portion about not eating bread from a tablecloth, appending the phrase "con las otras zarandajas que allí añadió" ("with the other trifles that he added there"). Now, it goes without saying that to swear not to sleep with one's wife is hardly a trifle, particularly in comparison with not using tablecloths. If Don Quixote could remember that portion in I, 10, his dismissal of it along with the other "trifles" in II, 23, suggests a purposeful omission on Cervantes' part. Inasmuch as the immediate cause of the vow is the failure to attain his ladylove – that is, his impotence with respect to disenchanting her and restoring her to her pristine beauty – the vow of sexual abstinence until vengeance (i.e., disenchantment) is realized becomes an implicit ingredient of the otherwise incongruous oath uttered in the Cave of Montesinos. The reshaping of models thus becomes an underlying and pervasive aspect of Cervantes' approach to his material. What frequently seems only funny at first ultimately reveals an artistically conceived, which is to say, original, use of incongruity.

On a level somewhat removed from the concerns of this chapter, the concept of imitation is related to the question of the imitation of nature by art (and the potentially converse interpretation of this axiom). It is this aspect that has interested most of the scholars who have occupied themselves with the problem, along with the related question of verisimilitude. These are facets that are not the central concern of my explorations here. Riley observes: "Some of the dangers of the theory of imitation were at any rate mitigated by the complementary notion that art perfected nature. This, it is true, gave rise to further difficulties, but it did mean that art was not just 'copying.' It serves also as a reminder that imitation did not imply what we now understand by 'realism.'"[48] Subsequently, in another reference to the discussion with the canon of

Toledo, Riley reinforces my previously stated suggestion that in the long run the chief value of that passage lies less in the attempt to define a specific genre than in the unrestraining potential of variety:

> The same liberty is available to the novelist. The variegated items enumerated by the Canon as his recipe for the ideal romance reflect something of the idea. Cervantes's claim that he has the "ability, sufficiency, and wit" to deal with the whole universe is also a probable reminiscence of the vast range permitted to the poet. But merely finding something to say was the least of his problems. It was shaping what nature offered into a work of art which was unified and credible in conformity with required standards that was difficult.[49]

To omit the final sentence of Riley's paragraph would be to cite him out of context. Although I agree with the rest of that paragraph, the last sentence – which is irrefutable in the abstract – does not, in my opinion, fully reflect the attitude of Cervantes. I use the word "attitude" as distinct from "comprehension," for although Cervantes unquestionably understands what Riley accurately describes, it is the response that interests me. "Conformity with required standards" becomes in Cervantes' hands a principle that with great dexterity – to the point where he may even proclaim its clumsiness – is stood on its head.

In the prologue to *Don Quixote*, Part I, Cervantes approaches the "idle reader" directly with this proposition. If the protagonist is described as the stepson rather than the son of the author (because, of course, Don Quixote will be the son of his own works), the book, as distinct from the hero, is presented in the opening lines as the child of Cervantes' intellect. And the bargain that is struck between the author's "sterile and poorly cultivated *ingenio*" and the idle but "very dear reader" is that, concurrent with the use of banal commonplaces, Cervantes will not "go along with the current of custom." The reader is presented with a *double* inversion of the conventionalism: The traditional claim to novelty is first converted to an apology for a dry and shriveled work and subsequently presented as defying custom! Since nature ordains that each thing engender its likeness, posits Cervantes, "What could the sterile and poorly cultivated *ingenio* of mine engender but the story of a dried up, shriveled, capricious child, full of thoughts so disparate and never before imagined by anyone else?" We are once more presented with the paradox of the introductory topos: The child shall be like the father (in violation of the *hijo de sus obras* maxim) to the extent that it is dry and shriveled. Yet in the same breath we are told that it is unique (today we would say original); full of thoughts never before conceived.

Similar declarations are made in the equivalent to a prologue by Chanfalla in *El retablo de las maravillas*, as we have noted. The two statements share a parodic treatment of the novelty topos, although they are far removed from one another in nearly every other aspect. In the prologue to his novel, Cervantes operates on three levels as he deals with the subject of originality: In the first place, the very introduction of the matter is in conformity with convention; secondly, he parodies the concept by suggesting that the originality of his work lies specifically in its desiccated and emaciated nature; finally, his claim to originality is ultimately based on the desire (articulated by the "friend") to undo the harm of the books of chivalry, which is to say that his "never before imagined by anyone else" thoughts are *derived* from these other books. (C. B. Johnson has shown that even the phrase just quoted is not original with Cervantes. Taken from Huarte de San Juan, it typifies Don Quixote's madness.)[50] The prologue flirts with the concept of originality:

> And now [continues Cervantes' imaginary friend] we come to the list of authors cited, such as other works contain but in which your own is lacking. . . . You have little need to refer to them, and so it does not matter; and some may be so simple-minded as to believe that you have drawn upon them all in your simple unpretentious little story. . . . This is especially true in view of the fact that your book stands in no need of all these things whose absence you lament; for the entire work is an attack upon the books of chivalry of which Aristotle never dreamed . . . and of which Cicero had no knowledge. . . . All that you have to do is to make proper use of imitation in what you write, and the more perfect the imitation the better will your writing be. . . . Let it be your aim that . . . the simple not be bored, but may the clever admire your originality.[51]

Not originality itself, of course, but the attitudes of writers toward it are satirized in this prologue. This is how we must read the mock-ignorant declaration that there are no marginal notes in the book because "I do not even know which authors I am following in it." In fact, in an anticipation of the pseudoauthor device, Cervantes disclaims most of the prologue by suggesting that it does not originate with him at all: "Listening in profound silence to what my friend had to say, I was so impressed by his reasoning that, with no thought of questioning them, I decided to make use of his arguments in composing this prologue."[52] The prologue, as is readily discernible, plays with the concept of originality on every conceivable level, even to the point of having the author feign silence and an uncritical attitude concerning the arguments of a fictive interlocutor.

Among these arguments is the conventional response to artistic imitation, and the writings of many theorists will confirm the source of these remarks. Such an excursion would provide the necessary comprehension of the context within which Cervantes thought and wrote, but I venture to suggest that an unequivocal application of the imitation principle, particularly in the context of the prologue under consideration, would be as misleading as an unquestioned acceptance of any of the other points made there by Cervantes. Unless we are to dismiss our appreciation of Cervantes' sensitivity regarding the problem of originality, we cannot accept at face value, much less ascribe to docile acceptance of a Renaissance precept, his "friend's" advice that *all* he needs to do is to take advantage of imitation in what he writes.[53] Either Cervantes will aim to produce worthy artistic imitations of recognized models or he will, as with other elements of his art, invert the very concept in its reelaboration at his hands. We cannot have it both ways.

The suggestion in the prologue that "the more perfect the imitation the better will your writing be" finds its analogue in *Don Quixote*, I, 25. However, we must approach the Sierra Morena episode with caution, for it contains as well the echo of the prologue's description of the "dried up, shriveled, capricious child, full of thoughts so disparate and never before imagined by anyone else." The modern reader may be perplexed by the suggestion of the perfect imitation that Cervantes' "friend" advises him to produce. Placed within the serious tradition of the preceptists, the matter is so easily clarified that my raising it at all seems unwarranted. Again, Riley provides the most concise explanation:

> Here, and even more when the Canon speaks of "verisimilitude and . . . imitation, in which is found the perfection of what is written," we are reminded of El Pinciano, who says: "the poet who looks to imitation and verisimilitude best attains poetic perfection." El Pinciano describes imitation as the "form" of poetry, and for Cervantes verisimilitude and formal aesthetic qualities meet and mingle inextricably in imitation, for imitation of the impossible is an aesthetic *disparate*.[54]

However, I submit that we will fall into the very trap that Cervantes has, with no little relish, laid for us if we take the advice of the fictional friend at face value, particularly within the satirical context of the entire prologue. Accordingly, I suggest that Cervantes is consistent in his sardonic approach when he advises himself to compose a perfect imitation. He not only mocks the dry erudition of works that incessantly cite other writers but also plays with *us* in having his friend advise the use of an alphabetical catalogue of *authors* with which to give an *impromptu authority* to the book. (Consider the "professional humanist" in II, 22, who has authorized his findings with more than two dozen authors.)

Marthe Robert has noted that *Don Quixote* and Kafka's *Castle* are "works of such unfettered genius that the usual concept of imitation is inadequate." Quixotism, according to Robert,

> . . . instead of accepting imitation *along with* its ideological support . . . , dissociates them in such a way that it can imitate obsolete forms *in order to* weigh them against the fragile, questionable claims of the new forms it is in the process of creating. This perfectly controlled simulation, which provokes the most bitter academic arguments, allows the quixotic author to write *as if* he shares the ideas of the imitator (to some extent he does share them and the simulation is only partial). He is then free to parade openly all the affirmation of authority and implicit values that imitation carries in its wake.[55]

If we approach the Sierra Morena episode with the foregoing observations in mind, the satirical nature of the imitation of knightly penance does, as I have suggested, find its echo in the prologue. As Don Quixote prepares to imitate Amadís or Orlando, he tells us that his will be "such a rare, such a felicitous, and such an unseen imitation."[56] Evidently this will be one of those "never before imagined by anyone else" thoughts that the prologue warns us about, as well as one of the "never seen deeds" that the narrator will recount. Riley summarizes:

> The artistic nature of his attempted imitation is but one facet of his penance in the Sierra Morena; I do not want to exaggerate it. This episode in chapter 24, however, holds a unique place among the endeavors of Don Quixote, and occupies a sort of dead-centre in the action of Part I. . . . The imitation of Amadis lacks any rational purpose other than imitation for its own sake, it is inappropriate to the needs of the imitator and could only be comically superficial. This happens to be a misuse, of which Cervantes is critical elsewhere, of an accepted principle of art.[57]

I suggest that it is a confusion of levels to attribute to Don Quixote the serious articulation of the imitation precept, then to call his application of it devoid of rational purpose, and finally to criticize Cervantes for having misused an accepted artistic principle. Riley is of course correct in his observation that Don Quixote first voices the literary precept and then parodies its realization. This is, after all, the pattern of many of the protagonist's misadventures, particularly in Part I. But precisely because it does conform to the behavior of Don Quixote, it seems to me that an irrational response, most especially in the confusion of literary precepts with real-life situations, needs to be perceived as consistent with Cervantes' art.

J. B. Avalle-Arce approaches the episode from a slightly different perspective. Don Quixote's behavior, he believes, must be seen "not only as emulation of conduct but as well, and this is the key, as an *artistic* imitation." Avalle repeatedly stresses Don Quixote's lack of motivation, citing the protagonist's own admission that he has no cause for complaint against Dulcinea, as Amadís had against Oriana. Don Quixote's penance, accordingly, becomes a "pure act of will" by which he "confuses, no doubt on purpose, artistic imitation . . . with emulation of conduct."[58]

What is missing from these analyses is Cervantes' treatment of parody. Although it is well known that the models for the penance and even the madness are to be found in the romances of chivalry (notably but not exclusively those of Amadís and Orlando alluded to by Don Quixote), the protagonist's imitation here is informed only nominally by these romances. The latter provide the formula, but what animates Don Quixote's behavior here is his observation of Cardenio's conduct as the result of the latter's lovesickness. Even the letter to Dulcinea is immediately inspired by the discovery of Cardenio's letter and verses. In point of fact, it is the reading of these verses that sets off the sequence culminating in the apparently unmotivated behavior of Chapters 25 and 26. The intention to do penance, to perform acts of madness, to enact things never seen before, finds its stimulus in the madness of Cardenio. It is after Don Quixote beholds Cardenio's antics that he decides to do likewise, ostensibly because the heroes of the romances did so. It is for the Sancho Panzas of this world to witness and recount to the conventional curates and barbers that Don Quixote does what he thinks literary tradition expects of him.

Once alone – figuratively freed from the conventions that an audience imposes – Don Quixote reconsiders and subsequently reworks the entire proposition. It is, accordingly, of no little significance that the very person who articulates the imitation principle is the one who takes it upon himself to vary the imitation to the point of refashioning it altogether. Nothing could be more symbolic of the parodic originality illustrative of the reshaping principle than Don Quixote's solution to the lack of a rosary: Naked from the waist down, he tears a strip from the tail of his shirt, makes eleven knots in it and recites a million Hail Marys.[59] Consequently, the Sierra Morena episode, like the prologue, not only is the parody it so evidently is but constitutes as well an exploration of the concept of imitation. The comic elements do not preclude such an exploration. Don Quixote's imitation is so "rare" that by definition it ceases to be imitation and becomes an original manifestation. We should not allow ourselves to be led astray from this central significance of Don Quixote's behavior in the Sierra Morena by observations that underscore its irrational or apparently purposeless nature. It is the curate, we need

to remember, who voices the opinion that Don Quixote's conduct constitutes "useless penance" (I, 26), "vain penance" (I, 27). As Marthe
Robert observes, "Don Quixote's genius, in fact, is to discover what
everyone has known all along but no one has the inclination, courage or
folly to pursue in a new way."[60]

One of those things that we have known all along is the real identity
of Dulcinea. It is in the Sierra Morena that Don Quixote first reveals it.
Of course, we know that her name is really Aldonza Lorenzo; it is Sancho
who learns this fact only now. But the significant revelation lies in Don
Quixote's explication. To bridge the gap between the farcical level of
confusing the lady and the wench and his own level of perception, he
tells the racy anecdote of the widow who preferred the uncouth and
ignorant but youthful fellow to the learned but elderly philosophers
because the lad, *for her needs*, knew as much philosophy as Aristotle. In
a corresponding manner, continues Don Quixote, Dulcinea is equivalent
to the highest princess. What is more, "I paint her in my imagination as
I desire her" (I, 25).

We shall hear variations on this conception of Dulcinea on other occasions (notably in II, 32). It is here, however, in the Sierra Morena, as
Don Quixote is about to impose upon himself the apparently senseless
penance, that he articulates the essence of Dulcinea and, by extension,
the essence of what motivates his every action. Whether it be madness
or folly, heroism or asceticism, imitation or invention, the confusion
between life and art is, as Avalle-Arce's insight implies, less involuntary
than one might suppose.

As I shall discuss in Chapter 4, Don Quixote's way of looking at the
world revolves around the search for metaphor. Animated by the chivalric romances, he does not simply see his environment in chivalric
terms but seeks those elements that, in objects and beings otherwise
unlike, may be interpreted in chivalric terms, thereby making these objects metaphorically alike. For instance, an inn and a castle are dissimilar
objects. Yet their function and even some of their structural components
have enough in common so that a metaphoric relationship can be established. Don Quixote, guided by his romances, spots that relationship
and realizes the metaphor: For his chivalric purposes the inn *is* a castle.
His understanding of the racy anecdote is based not on its erotic content
(which he glosses over because it runs counter to his perceived vital
interests) but on his recognition of its metaphoric process. Accordingly,
just as the widow could recognize the features that a young fellow had
in common with the antonomastic philosopher (pleasurable stimulation),
so Don Quixote sees in Aldonza the requisite characteristics of the peer-
less lady of his imagination. There, in his imagination, in accordance

with his needs (informed by his books) he "paints" her, which is to say that he poeticizes her through metaphor.

It is in the Sierra Morena episode that a central part of Sancho's nature is developed: Out of his earthy background come the endless proverbs that parallel his master's allusions to the romances of chivalry. The immediate pertinence of these proverbial truths is of secondary importance to the fact that they represent Sancho's own variety of artistic imitation. If Don Quixote cites texts that are beyond Sancho's reach, Sancho will bring forth quotable material from his own cultural store. In the same way, Don Quixote, availing himself of the formulas of his romances, creates the reality of Dulcinea by imitating poets (whose ladies, he reminds us, do not always exist historically), and so produces an essence that transcends physical attributes. That in his penance he inverts Orlando's defiling of the trees, by inscribing poetry on them instead, shows how imitation, refashioning, and originality are interwoven and, indeed, interdependent. The significance of Don Quixote's penance lies not in its immediate acts but in its reliance upon the romances for its pretext and precedent, upon the the irrational behavior of Cardenio for its stimulus, and upon the articulated recognition of Dulcinea as a concept rather than as a woman for its substance.

From Don Quixote's point of view, the penance has served a purpose. When Sancho reports the fabricated details of his supposed visit to Dulcinea, he claims to have informed her that Don Quixote was "doing penance, naked from the waist up" (I, 31). Now, the reader will recall that Don Quixote was naked from the waist *down*. We may account for Sancho's error in a number of ways (his memory fails him; amid the confusion of lies he confuses details of truth; he reports a more decorous version in consonance with what he would have reported to a lady), but what is remarkable is that Don Quixote allows this error to stand unchallenged. He does correct Sancho's reporting him to have been cursing his fortune, and therein lies the key: In keeping with the Aristotelian principle of poetic truth (articulated in I, 25), the representation of Don Quixote as cursing his fate is not in accord with his image as blessing his fortune for permitting him to adore Dulcinea. Similarly, the image of nudity from the waist down depicts a sexual crudity not in accord with the image he means to convey to Dulcinea. Sancho's emendation, which Don Quixote believes to have been communicated to Dulcinea, represents his madness in symbolic fashion devoid of base connotations. Don Quixote, therefore, believes his antics to have achieved the desired effect.

The reappearance of Andrés in this same chapter (I, 31) underscores the point: The reader remembers the grievous outcome of this adventure, whereas Don Quixote recalls his perception of its success. The contrast, made embarrassingly clear to Don Quixote at this juncture, corresponds to the opposition between what to the reader appears to be senseless behavior in the Sierra Morena "imitation" and what from Don Quixote's perspective achieves its purpose, namely, the communication to his lady of his mad passion for her.

I began this chapter with allusions to imitation and parody, two terms that have been repeated in the discussion of the Sierra Morena episode. A source of confusion, I suspect, is the belief that parody is necessarily funny. To be sure, parody does, more often than not, involve humor, although it is not always clear whether the humor was the intent or the corollary. The *Princeton Encyclopedia of Poetry and Poetics* offers some help: "One fundamental distinction can be made between comic parody, which is close to burlesque, and literary or critical parody, which follows more closely a given author's style or a particular work of art." Critical parody is then defined as "the exaggerated imitation of a work of art . . . based on distortion, bringing into bolder relief the salient features of a writer's style or habit of mind." Finally, and highly significantly, parody "usually makes its point by employing a serious style to express an incongruous subject, thus disturbing the balance of form and matter."[61]
    A similar distinction is made in a study by Margaret Rose specifically devoted to parody, with added interest for us here because of the work chosen to exemplify some of the points made. Among several other referents, parody may be defined by "its usage as comedy in literary texts or in speeches as a rhetorical device ('specific parody') [or by] the structure of texts in which parody is not just a specific technique but the mode of the work itself ('general parody' as in Cervantes' *Don Quixote*)." Rose also makes the point that "the attribution of the comic effect to parody has misled many literary historians into seeing the parodist as merely a mocker of other texts." Furthermore: "A history of parody will show . . . that parody has served to bring the concept of imitation itself into question, and that while imitation may be used as a technique in the parody it is the use of incongruity which distinguishes the parody from other forms of quotation and literary imitation, and shows its function to be more than imitation alone." Finally: "In works such as *Don Quixote*, in which parody has had the [alleged] function of both destroying a specific target and refunctioning that target for a new audience (or for a similar audience whose expectations for the old text are to be revised) parody has been described as the transformation of one genre into another."[62]
    It may seem that we are once again exploring issues raised in Chapter 1, and to a certain extent this is so. The result of the parody in *Don*

Quixote indisputably includes laughter, which is to say not that laughter was not intended but rather that it was not necessarily Cervantes' central aim in the composition of the work. Putting to one side the burlesque facets is not, I must insist, tantamount to seeing a heroic, noble figure in, say, the Sierra Morena, where in fact we are presented with a pathetic attempt to imitate the behavior of madmen and fictitious knights. But there is an important distinction between the ludicrous fictive results and the serious literary procedure, the latter analogous to the "critical parody" of the Princeton definition and in keeping with the "general parody" set forth by Rose. As a matter of fact, it has even been suggested that "Don Quixote's attitudes and actions – e.g., his penance, his ordeals, his readiness for martyrdom – can be interpreted as a sustained parody of the actions and attitudes celebrated in literary saints' lives."[63]

A recent article by Lowry Nelson is even more to the point, and once more the matters explored in our first two chapters come together here:

> Our appreciation of *Don Quixote* would be disastrously diminished if we had to view the novel as farce or burlesque or through the crudities of near-contemporary translations, imitations, and adaptations. . . . We need not be caught in the . . . limitations of the unrigorously used terms "burlesque," "farce," and "parody."
>
> In ordinary language we often use "parody" as an all-purpose word to mean burlesque, travesty, take-off, farce; and usually we think of it as describing something enjoyable and risible, but somewhat trivial and perhaps disrespectful and malicious. Yet I would strongly urge that "parody" be used as a neutral, non-derogatory term of literary criticism, divested of any presumptive triviality.[64]

There is a brief passage in *Don Quixote*, Part II, that illustrates the procedure. Every editor has had to deal with its anomalies, though there is little agreement among them. I refer to the paragraph that opens Chapter 53 of Part II and announces the end of Sancho Panza's governorship:

> Pensar que en esta vida las cosas della han de durar siempre en un estado, es pensar en lo escusado; antes parece que ella anda todo en redondo, digo, a la redonda: la primavera sigue al verano, el verano al estío, el estío al otoño, y el otoño al invierno, y el invierno a la primavera, y así torna a andarse el tiempo con esta rueda continua; sola la vida humana corre a su fin ligera más que el tiempo. . . . Esto dice Cide Hamete, filósofo mahomético; porque esto de entender la ligereza e inestabilidad de la vida presente, y de la duración de la eterna que se espera, muchos sin lumbre de fe, sino con la luz natural, lo han entendido; pero aquí nuestro autor lo dice por la

presteza con que se acabó, se consumió, se deshizo, se fue como en sombra y humo el gobierno de Sancho.

[To think that in this life matters pertaining to it should last always in the same state is fruitless; it seems rather that it goes the other way around, I mean, in a circular way: spring follows summer, summer high summer, high summer autumn, and autumn winter, and winter spring, and in this way time keeps on going like a continuous wheel; only human life speeds to its end faster than time itself. . . . This is what Cide Hamete, the Mohammedan philosopher says; because this matter of understanding the flightiness and instability of our present life, and the permanence of the awaited eternal life, has been understood by many without the light of faith but with nature's light; but here our author says it because of the rapidity with which Sancho's government was ended, consumed, undone and disappeared in shadow and smoke.]

Two things undoubtedly strike the reader immediately: the number and the sequence of seasons. The phrase "high summer" is my own interpretation of estío, for in modern Spanish the words verano and estío both mean "summer" (the latter somewhat more poetic). According to a tradition that goes back to the Middle Ages in Spain, the year was indeed calculated in five, not four, seasons.[65] Most translators get around the problem by avoiding it and registering only one word – summer – and not making any reference to a fifth season. Even some specialists have overlooked the matter. Henryk Ziomek, for instance, has studied the use of numbers in Don Quixote and has reported that "in the ancient world, the number 'four' represented the cycle of the seasons of the year (as Cervantes expresses it, II, 53)."[66] L. A. Murillo's excellent study The Golden Dial, the subtitle of which is Temporal Configuration in "Don Quijote," reflects the author's concern with the seasons, and though there is a brief analysis of the philosophical significance of the passage in question and of its relationship to Sancho's experience, as well as the cited clarification of the number of seasons, the inverted order receives no attention, and the translation offered (Thomas Shelton's) gives the normal one. Augustín Redondo's study of the governorship episode as an application of the "world-upside-down" topos makes no mention of the passage at all, nor does a study by J. M. Sobré on the "hero upside down," despite a passing reference to Cide Hamete as "the anti-poet, the opposite of a Virgil; he is the poet upside-down."[67]

One who does see and even translate the five seasons is John J. Allen (who renders estío as "harvest season"). He notes perceptively that "the seriousness of the analogy (death : governorship) and the level of style contrast with the mock-epic invocation of Sancho's first arrival at Barataria." However, he does not take the matter further, nor does he deal with the inverted order.[68] Casalduero sees what he calls an "evident irony" in Cervantes' pointing out that this beginning (of the chapter) refers to the end of Sancho's governorship and to the rapidity with which it was concluded.[69] Riquer reports the suggestion of a colleague: that *estío* is equivalent to *sama'un* (a period of forty days beginning in late June), a designation used in North Africa; this explanation would account for Cervantes' familiarity with the term and for its attribution to the Moorish pseudoauthor.[70] Rudolph Schevill suggests that the inverted order was written intentionally so as to make the pronouncement risible by revealing that the Mohammedan philosopher says things backwards.[71] The risibility, though intended, is, I think, incidental.

Aside from the interesting, though surely coincidental, irony of having the beginning of the end related precisely in Chapter 53, that is, one chapter beyond the number of chapters that make up the first *Quixote*, there is no little irony in attributing the universal truth to the Moor invented by Cervantes, together with the insistence on the universality as transcending the Catholic faith. But beyond the irony – or, more accurately, underlying it – is the purposive distortion characteristic of Cervantes' parodic pattern.[72]

He begins by invoking the most noticeable natural evidence of the sequence of events: the seasonal progression that moves at once ever forward and ever in a circular configuration. Had the sentence suggested that, say, spring followed autumn, the nonsensical sequence would have degenerated the declaration to the level of farce. The sequence in the text, however, is neither nonsensical nor farcical but is the normal sequence – only presented in reverse. Redondo's reading of the entire governorship as animated by the world-upside-down topos finds further corroboration in the passage under consideration here, a passage summarizing the end of that topsy-turvy world as it *re-turns* the sequence. Seen in this light, the invocation that begins the governorship in Chapter 45 is not only in mock-epic contrast with the seriousness of the passage that announces the end in Chapter 53, as Allen has suggested; the earlier invocation is as well a parallel on the parodic level. If the sequence of seasons typifies the repetitive and circular shape of worldly events, the daily voyage of the sun around the earth (as it is perceived even in post-Copernican society) epitomizes the same principle:

¡Oh perpetuo descubridor de las antípodas, hacha del mundo, ojo del cielo, meneo dulce de las cantimploras, Timbrio aquí, Febo allí, tirador acá, médico acullá, padre de la Poesía, inventor de la música, tú que siempre sales, y, aunque lo parece, nunca te pones!
[Oh perpetual discoverer of the Antipodes, torch of the world, eye

of the heavens, sweet stirrer of water-cooling jugs, here Thymbrius,
there Phoebus, now archer, now physician, father of poetry, inventor of music, you who always rise and, though you seem to,
never set!]

It is tempting to dismiss this as farce or, at best, mock-classical invocation. What suggests the farcical is the inclusion of the *cantimploras*,
jugs that were filled with water surrounded by ice or snow for cooling
and that, because of the movement of the sun, were themselves moved
to keep the water cool. But this is not nonsense. The movement of the
jugs corresponding to the movement of the sun is literally a down-to-
earth counterpart of the lofty epithets of epic incantations. If it is not in
keeping with epic poetry, it is clearly in accord with the proverbial
perspective personified by Sancho Panza. We smile as we note the incongruity of the pedestrian among the elevated – and then realize that
this is precisely the circumstance that the invocation introduces: a peasant
among the governing class.[73] The calculated incongruity, patterned after
the epic paradigm, parodies heroic literature, restates it to accommodate
the new circumstances (as Don Quixote had fashioned a rosary), and,
along with providing the humorous aspect, leads to an appreciation of
the parodic intent of the work as a whole.

That the sun rises perpetually and never sets though it seems to is not
only a statement of the circular nature of temporal events but another
of those truisms typical of *Don Quixote*, "where commonplaces are set
up and reduced to rubble, though sometimes sympathetically."[74] This
point, so evident in the invocation of Chapter 45, has been overlooked
in the "beginning of the end" statement of Chapter 53 amid the appreciation of the more serious tone or the efforts of various editors to
"correct" Cervantes' inversion of the chronological order. It is necessary
to recognize the basic similarity of the two pronouncements. In both,
time marches on and runs in cycles; in neither is there any originality in
the fundamental substance. The jugs of the first statement find their
corresponding incongruity in the inverted order and, perhaps, in the
unorthodox number of seasons. Just as the interpolation of the jugs
betrays the parodic (but not farcical) intent because the original paradigm
is perfectly imitated, so the inverted (but not chaotic) sequence of seasons
reveals the fundamental mark of parody.

Don Quixote leaves us with the notion that intention is at least as much
to be valued as accomplishment: Let it be said, he muses in the Sierra
Morena, that if he did not achieve great things, he died in their undertaking (I, 26). Not unlike this affirmation is the declaration made after
the ride on the wooden horse Clavileño: "The illustrious knight Don

Quixote de la Mancha concluded and ended the adventure of the Countess Trifaldi . . . just by undertaking it" (II, 41). Evidently we are again in the world of parody, and there is no point in elaborating here on what is self-evident. On the other hand, the emphasis on intention as compared to substance finds its analogue in Cervantes' primary concern for the manner in which art is presented.

Jacques Maritain has described that phase in which human creativity "passes from the *object* depicted to the *mode* with which the artist performs his work."[75] The episode of Don Quixote in the Sierra Morena serves as a convenient illustration of this point of view, for certainly the "objects" are scarcely original and yet I have been able to speak of originality because of what Maritain terms the "mode" with which the author goes about his art. A. F. G. Bell has observed that it is Cervantes' "chief originality that his marvelous imagination is brought to bear on the common things and ordinary events of everyday, illumining them with extraordinary power. It would almost seem that the characters and events must be ordinary. . . . Thus . . . the hero, transformed from the perfect Amadis to the lowly and very human Knight of La Mancha, becomes a natural and very living figure."[76] Seen in this light, much of Cervantes' originality consists of yet another sort of inversion or restatement, a process that could well be described as a transposing downward. What Bell perceived has itself been restated in somewhat more recent terminology by Herman Wouk, who observes that Cervantes "moved the art [of narrative] away from high life and the beautiful people to all life and to all people. [Cervantes] looked to ordinary life rather than to high life for his substance."[77] By the phrase "transposing downward" I by no means intend to convey a pejorative view. On the contrary, to deal at length with a protagonist endowed neither with superior characteristics nor with base and purely risible attributes was a challenge of formidable proportions. And there seems no doubt that Cervantes perceived it as a challenge.

Competition played more than a small part in the development of Cervantes' art. In addition to the immediate challenge presented by contemporary rivals, Cervantes sensed as well a need to compete with other literary landmarks of different times and places. In the prologue to the *Novelas ejemplares* he looked forward to the completion of his *Persiles*, "a book that dares to compete with Heliodorus," a reference to the latter's *Ethiopic History*. The competitive urge must be kept in mind whenever we consider the matter of imitation, for it allows us to see the latter concept in yet another light. As Casalduero has observed, Cervantes "does not try to imitate the ancients; what he wants is to enter into competition with them."[78]

Although Casalduero places this observation in a baroque context, it seems to me more applicable to Cervantes as an artist of the Renaissance. The author of *Don Quixote* and the *Persiles* reflects the

> ... tremendous outpouring of the creative spirit in the Renaissance, a spirit found in every aspect of its life: the rise of national patriotism, the thrust toward power of the upper middle class, the expansion of the geographical world through voyages of discovery. This same spirit is found in all the arts at this time: painting, sculpture, architecture, music, and literature. *All were determined to produce new and more ambitious masterpieces.* And this is particularly true of the two great national states, Spain and England. In neither of these countries were writers overwhelmed by the achievements of Italy. Ariosto may be magnificent, but Spenser hopes to *outdo* him – and, of course, ends by *doing something quite different.* Italian comedy may be highly amusing, but Lope de Vega will show them *something new* with the love-making of his witty society ladies.[79]

We may quarrel with such a limited description of this one aspect of Lope's theater, but the underlying significance of the observation remains valid. Similarly, no matter how we approach the bulk of Cervantes' works – as serious attempts to emulate, as comic parodies, as modern novel or modern epic – they almost invariably appeal because they are a new elaboration and therein find their originality.

It is in this spirit of competitive emulation with its resultant restatement that we ought to read Cervantes' otherwise ambiguous claim in the dedication to *Don Quixote*, Part II, in which he predicts that his nearly finished *Persiles* will be "either the worst or the best [book] that has been composed in our language." We note once more the emphasis on the work as one composed in Spanish, yet this book "dares to compete with Heliodorus." Cervantes' comment that it may possibly be either the worst or the best underscores his urge to be competitive. It is true that he appears to correct himself by adding immediately that he regrets having said the worst, "because in the opinion of my friends, it will reach the utmost goodness possible." Were this apparent second thought a true correction there would have been no need for him to permit the passage to remain intact. The feigned regrets, prompted by anonymous and probably fictitious friends (a favorite artifice in Cervantes' preliminary pages), are a likely response to Avellaneda, who, in his own prologue to the spurious *Don Quixote*, had accused Cervantes of lacking friends. Cervantes' reply in the dedication of his own Part II not only suggests that he has friends but conveys that they have resolved whatever doubts he himself has had, for they have expressed positive judgments about the work in progress. This perspective should be added to the unqualified declaration of Avalle-Arce, who writes of Cervantes' "attitude of courageous self-confidence [that led him to declare] that the

Persiles will be the best book of entertainment written in Spanish, and this in the dedication to no less than the second part of the *Quixote*."[80]

A similar aspiration is expressed in the prologue to the *Comedias y entremeses* published in the same year: Cervantes declares that he would like his plays to be "the best in the world or, at least, reasonable."[81] Finally, it is in a similar context that we may view the 1592 contract for Cervantes' plays with its stipulation that they "turn out to be among the best ever represented in Spain." I speculated earlier that in addition to any personal difficulties (which might, in fact, have been alleviated had the works been produced), Cervantes' motive for not following through with the delivery of his plays in 1592 might reflect his intuitive recognition that they would not be well received – quite the opposite of the self-confidence that does indeed emerge in the satire of the 1615 prologue to the theatrical works. My previously expressed conjecture, that this prologue not only reflects Cervantes' belated self-confidence but intimates that originality in the Lopean *comedia* is made up of trivia, can now be viewed from an additional perspective: Cervantes' art is a "reasonable" one, a *rational* creation superior to the extravagances of the theater then in vogue. His work just might, he would like to think, be more than that: It may be the best in the world. The bravado of the 1615 prologue is made all the more prominent by the parallelism of the respective sentences and by another restatement, which today we might term "one-upmanship": What in 1592 was required to be the best in Spain is in 1615 described as possibly the best in the world.

We have come a long way. In contrast to the mock-serious denigration of being first and of presenting something new, we now discern in Cervantes' writings a desire to compete and to emerge as the best. To a large extent, the determination of qualifications such as "good" or "best" (and "reasonable" as we have defined this term) rests upon the way in which the art is presented. Inasmuch as we have come to relate Cervantes' perception of originality to a reelaboration or restatement, this concentration upon manner is hardly surprising. An otherwise gratuitous remark in the *Persiles* is accordingly placed within an easily appreciated context: Mauricio and Ladislao might not have gone on listening to Periandro's long narrative, which they judged somewhat lengthy and not altogether pertinent; however, they remained "waiting to hear the end of his story, at least for the gracefulness and good style with which Periandro related it" (II, 11). In other words, the manner complements the matter, the one making the other worthwhile. The manner alone, however, is not sufficient to compensate for the absence of underlying truths:

> for not in elegance
> and manner of speech lies the foundation

and the principal substance
of truthful narration,
which in pure truth has its sustentation.[82]

If the matter is based on universal truths, then the very novelty of the story may be matched by the manner in which it is related. Such is the reaction of Fernando to the captive's tale: "To be sure, captain, the manner in which you have told this strange event is such that it equals the novelty and strangeness of the case itself" (*Don Quixote*, I, 42). Not unlike this response is the licentiate's comment on the otherwise unbelievable *Coloquio de los perros*: "Although this colloquy may be fictitious and may never have occurred, it seems to me so well composed. . . . I appreciate the artifice of the *Coloquio* and its inventiveness, and that is sufficient. Now let's go to . . . refresh the eyes of our bodies, for I have already refreshed those of my intellect." This, as readers of Cervantes are well aware, is an echo of the judgment made of the *Curioso impertinente* by the curate, who has difficulty accepting the verisimilitude of the tale, but "as far as the manner of telling it is concerned, it does not displease me" (*Don Quixote*, I, 35).

Availing himself of the epic, the ballad, the romance, the pastoral, the allegorical fable, the colloquy, and the Italian novella, Cervantes emerges with a restatement whose manner enhances either the otherwise prosaic or the "legitimate marvelous."[83] Such originality is acceptable even to that grand inquisitor of the library, the curate, who finds that this manner does not displease him. Precisely because it is true that Cervantes always retains respect for the principle of plausibility – Forcione calls verisimilitude Cervantes' major aesthetic preoccupation[84] – the oft-quoted criticism of the *Curioso impertinente* causes the originality of the manner to stand out. (The more familiar criticism, the tale's alleged irrelevance, is first reported in the 1615 *Don Quixote* by Sansón Carrasco.) The curate's concern in 1605 is for the apparent lack of verisimilitude in the tale. We must not lose sight of the fact that Cervantes himself is allowing this criticism of his "major aesthetic preoccupation" to be brought to the fore. To some extent the purpose of this introduction of the matter is to prepare the way for the literary discussion to follow. At the same time, however, Cervantes is allowing his inquisitor to expose his tale's most vulnerable element, its plausibility, while allowing its most creative – original, if you will – attribute to override preceptist considerations. In its manner the tale is novel. Cervantes is indeed the first to have "novelized" in Castilian.

The lines from Samuel Johnson that serve as epigraph for this chapter find a counterpart in Ximénez Patón, a friend of Lope de Vega's: "In order for the things one says to possess *gracia* [charm], novel things should be said like ordinary ones and ordinary ones like novel." I take the translation from Alan S. Trueblood, who makes the following comment: "Ximénez Patón may be recalling Socrates in the *Phaedrus*. . . . If so, he has passed over Socrates' irony in evaluating favorably as *gracia* what Socrates ridicules as sophistry."[85] It is well to accept Trueblood's reading of Ximénez Patón as ignorance of Socrates' (or Plato's) meaning, for both the Greek and the Spaniard help us to see the contrast with Cervantes, in turn illuminated by the Johnson quotation. Socrates derides the intent to "*disguise* the new in old fashions and the old in new fashions."[86] The emphasis is my own, since the criticism deals with appearances. Just so does Ximénez Patón advise the presentation of the one as the other. Johnson, on the other hand, commends an author for the artistic recreation: What might seem startling is presented so that we may appreciate it in intelligible circumstances, and what has been prosaic is presented anew in a manner worthy of *admiratio*. Therein lies the originality of Cervantes.

Chapter 3

The reality of illusion

*My purpose is to tell of bodies which have been transformed
into shapes of a different kind.*

– Ovid, *Metamorphoses*

"Dogs," writes E. C. Riley, "do not hold conversations in Spanish."[1]
If we, the readers of *El coloquio de los perros* (*The Dogs' Colloquy*), do not
believe that dogs converse, the same skepticism is displayed by the first
(fictional) reader of this tale, the licentiate Peralta. Perhaps more intriguing is the fact that its first (fictional) listener, the dog Cipión, shares
the doubt, despite his own speaking role in the story. The parallels do
not end there: All three levels – the real reader, the fictional reader, and
the fictional listener-participant – agree, explicitly or implicitly, that their
incredulity will not interfere with the reading or recitation of the work.
Disbelief is suspended, not merely as a literary convention but in the
face of rational processes that inform us to the contrary.

Peralta does not care to debate the veracity of the dogs' colloquy and
is content with having appreciated its artifice and creativity. We, the real
readers of fiction, share that perspective inasmuch as none of us stops to
insist upon the implausibility of the dogs' speech. We are likely to agree
with Peralta's metaphor: The reading of the colloquy has refreshed the
ojos del entendimiento, perhaps best rendered in English as "the mind's
eye." (In *La Galatea*, Cervantes speaks of the *ojos de la imaginación*, the
eyes of the imagination.)[2] There is in this phrase a perspective so elemental
that one tends to overlook it in the course of literary analyses that seem
more rewarding. The illusion that is fiction, mere words impressed upon
paper, creates a visual image in the mind's eye despite the evidence
transmitted to the brain via the eyes of the body: still words on paper.
Peralta's locution not only is a description of the process of reading
literature but defines the basis of illusion generally. The mind as well as
the body has a sense of vision, and what informs the one may supersede
what informs the other. Generally speaking, we tend to think that we
credit what the physical senses convey: Seeing is believing. But just as
we "see" the "reality" of literature while physically seeing only words,
so we are likely to see objects and events whose physical realities are at
variance with the information provided by the intellect: Believing is
seeing.

To clarify my meaning, I quote from a recent essay that at once shares my viewpoint and diverges from it: "Writers write. That is, they communicate through words without speaking. They address in the mind's eye and the mind's ear absent readers [and construct] a context that readers would naturally see if they were to experience the discourse as a live interchange."[3] The words used here could be my own – "a context that readers would naturally see" – if the conclusion were different. What readers naturally *see* is dependent not upon a hypothetical experience of a "live interchange" of the discourse but upon an actual experience of the transmitted context. When I say "actual" I do not mean vicarious. The latter has to do with the plot: The reader experiences vicariously *that which occurs* in fiction. But what the reader *sees* – in the mind's eye, to be sure – is in fact seen in the sense that that image, conjured by mere words on paper, is transmitted as surely as though it were being perceived visually. When that reader par excellence, Don Quixote, "*saw* Reinaldos de Montalbán leave his castle and rob those he came upon" (I, 1; emphasis mine), the point is made so casually that few readers stop to notice the significance of the verb.[4]

The detail in the opening chapter of the 1605 *Don Quixote*, the "seeing" of fictive characters, is elaborated in the corresponding chapter of the 1615 volume. Anxious to counter the charge that his storybook heroes are figments of people's dreams, Don Quixote replies that the truth of their existence

> . . . is so certain that I am prepared to say that with my own eyes
> I saw Amadís de Gaula, who was a man of tall build, fair com-
> plexion, well-kempt though black beard, half mild and half severe
> in countenance, succinct in words, slow to anger and quick to calm
> that anger; and in the way in which I have delineated Amadís I
> could, in my opinion, paint and describe all the many knights-
> errant that populate the histories of the world, for by the appre-
> hension that I have of the fact that they were as their histories relate,
> and by the deeds that they performed and condition they had, and,
> by virtue of good philosophy, their features, their complexion and
> stature, can be deduced.

Cervantes associates a precise mental image of a literary character with the reading process on a number of occasions.[5] Moreover, Don Quixote, egged on by the curate, does indeed go on to describe in detail several more heroes of the romances. The passage excerpted here, therefore, not merely is evidence of a madman's obsession with the reality of his il-lusions but is in keeping with Cervantes' representation of the act of reading and its consequences. One need not be mad in order to see, in the mind's eye, the vitality of fictive creations. On the contrary, the only way to apprehend literary art is to convert its symbols into images as real as those apprehended by the sense of sight. The other part of the process – not apprehending but conveying literary images – is animated by the same insistence on having the reader or listener "see" what the words project. The procedure is epitomized in the *Persiles* (III, 17), as the narrator intrudes to ask of the reader:

> Do you see her crying, do you see her sighing, do you see her beside herself, do you see her brandish the murderous sword, do you see her kiss the bloody shirt? . . . Well, just wait until the morning and you will see things that will give you something to talk about for a thousand centuries, if you should live so long.

An interesting variation is found earlier in the *Persiles* (III, 1). Following an encomium of Lisbon typical of Renaissance descriptions of such cities, the speaker is asked not to say any more: "Leave something for our eyes, Antonio, for praises should not tell it all: Something should be left for the vision." It is theoretically possible, therefore, to compose a description so graphic that there is nothing left to see that has not already been seen with the mind's eye.

When Don Quixote relates his tale of the Knight of the Lake, he is convinced that his listeners will *see* what he is narrating:

> Is there a greater joy than to *see*, *so to speak*, here now revealed in front of us a large lake of pitch, boiling and bubbling, and swimming about in it many serpents, snakes and lizards? . . . And could there be anything better to *see*, after having *seen* this, than to *see* coming out of the door of the castle a goodly number of maidens, whose festive and showy costumes, were I to set forth and describe them as the histories tell us, would be a never-ending tale? . . . What must it be to *see*, then, what they *tell* us? . . . What, to *see* him having water poured? . . . What, to *see* him served by all the maidens? . . . And, believe me, your grace, and as I've told you before, *read* these books and you will *see*. [I, 50; emphases mine][6]

As I shall point out later in this chapter, Don Quixote is quick to note the clues that people look for when they accept or reject his perceptions. Sancho's insistence on the names of the "phantoms" who tossed him in the blanket results in Don Quixote's exhaustive string of names in the very next adventure (sheep perceived as soldiers). I do not mean to imply that Don Quixote is a charlatan; rather, in his need to convey the illusions he perceives, he betrays the urgency to have those illusions confirmed for himself, thereby confirming his chivalric world. The passage just quoted is an attempt to persuade the canon to see in the romances what he, Don Quixote, sees. The emphasis on seeing in this passage suggests

THE REALITY OF ILLUSION

that he understands his interlocutor well. Don Quixote was most likely not in hearing distance when the canon expounded on the *disparates* of the romances, but it is interesting to note that the canon's way of perceiving literature is for the soul to conceive the delight "of beauty and harmony that it *sees* or contemplates in the things that [the sense of] sight or *the imagination* place in front of it" (I, 47; emphasis mine). Small wonder, then, that the canon's reaction to Don Quixote's recitation is *admiratio*. He is amazed by the *concertados disparates* and by the way in which Don Quixote has "painted" the adventure. Of course, he is also amazed by the knight's madness. But surely one reason for his wonderment is the essence of his own definition of the reading process that Don Quixote's narration has just put into practice. As we shall soon have occasion to note, this same process underlies Don Quixote's attempts to convey his illusions in a number of situations as he strives to communicate the images that his mind's eye apprehends.

Now, the word just used echoes that of Don Quixote: "for by the apprehension that I have of the fact." The original reads, "por la aprehensión que tengo de que." Cohen does not translate the key word but renders it "for my absolute faith in the details." Putnam similarly writes, "for I feel sure that they were." A most interesting interpretation is given by Smollett in his translation of 1755: "for, according to the ideas formed by reading these histories." These translations reflect an important connotation revealed in the eighteenth-century *Diccionario de Autoridades*, which defines *aprehensión* as follows:

> Although in its literal and straightforward sense one understands by this word the act of apprehending or retaining a certain thing by grabbing and taking hold of it, in its common and usual sense this word is restricted to the explanation of the vehement and tenacious imagination with which the mind conceives, thinks of, and ponders a certain thing that ordinarily startles and disorients it.

For *aprehender*, the same dictionary gives:

"To take and hold on to things, retain them and bring them to oneself; what is properly understood by which the mind conceives, imagines, and retains with vehemence."[7] It is the vehemence and tenacity described in these definitions that fire Don Quixote's understanding of his readings, and one can see that quite apart from the particular madness in his case, there is in the word chosen for him by Cervantes, *aprehensión*, an accepted understanding of how the mind, particularly in matters that may startle and disorient, grasps and retains the image it forms of its environment.

Exegesis would lead us to metaphysical and philosophical exploration, a topic of no small interest and one that is the concern of many scholarly studies. It is rather on a more elemental – fundamental, if you will –

plane that I wish to concentrate in the pages that follow. Although the metaphysical implications are in the long run the matters of consequence, the basis for the latter is to be found in the consideration of the illusion–reality problem on the physical level. Inasmuch as illusion – that is, the phenomenon of illusion irrespective of the veracity of its cause – is real, Cervantes' treatment of the phenomenon merits exploration.

The best point of departure may well be the point of greatest familiarity: Don Quixote transforms windmills into giants. (It is of importance to bear in mind that from his perspective the transformation occurs the other way around: An enchanter has converted the giants into windmills, a declaration that not only intimates a changed visual perception but significantly concedes Don Quixote's own perception of the objects *as windmills*, following his physical experience with them.) What to us appears to be the transformation of windmills into giants has a rational basis. It is the result of pure ratiocination bereft of experiential disillusionment. If we are to believe the chronicler of his affairs, the protagonist's prior experiences would not have included an interest in windmills. (We recall his selling tillable land in order to buy romances of chivalry.) But windmills no doubt were commonplace for a man of Sancho Panza's background (hence his insistence on their reality as windmills is not so much the voice of common sense as that of experience in agrarian matters). Don Quixote's apprehension of the world through the book-lined walls of his study has "programmed" him to see giants where others may see windmills. E. H. Gombrich concludes that "perception itself is the product of habituation, although at 'bottom' it is automatic and 'programmed' to seek out certain natural features of the visual field."[8]

At times the illusion is other than visual. Though Don Quixote "sees" giants where others see windmills because that is what his readings have prepared him to encounter, it is not his perception but his behavior toward the goatherds in I, 11, that is in accord with a literary preconditioning. The well-known discourse on the utopian or Golden Age that Don Quixote pronounces before the group of illiterate and uncomprehending rustics is a good example of the purposive incongruity discussed in Chapter 1, but this becomes clear only when we see it as part of the programmed response we are exploring here.

The unquestionably humorous picture of our gentleman addressing ignorant goatherds on matters of mythology and philosophy must be tempered with our knowledge that Don Quixote's library, which directs his apprehension of and approach to the world, has led him to believe, by way of his readings of pastoral literature, that to philosophize with shepherds and their like is the *expected* thing to do. If this is madness, then it is the familiar folly of accepting what he has read as historical truth and of living that fiction as though it were fact. Given this basic flaw as the point of departure for Don Quixote's conception and perception of his environment, it is consistent for him to address goatherds in consonance with what he had read about pastoral behavior. To view this episode as a humorous caricature of a mad knight waxing philosophical in the wilderness before a group of dumbfounded peasants is to miss the consistency with which Cervantes has depicted the protagonist's *logical* behavior, given Don Quixote's dependence on what he has read of the world. What is at issue here is not a failure to see the goatherds for what they are. Rather, Don Quixote responds to them in keeping with what they are according to his previous experiences, which is to say, in books. The illusion here is not optical. Don Quixote sees the goatherds as goatherds but envisages an encounter with the literary rustics of his library.

The philosopher José Ortega y Gasset asks: "These giants may not be giants, but – what about the others? I mean giants generally? Where has man taken giants from in the first place? Because *in reality* there have never been any nor are there any. Whenever it may have been, the occasion on which man for the first time thought up giants is not essentially different from this Cervantine scene."[9] Ortega's well-known statement represents the quixotic transformation of windmills to giants as a distortion of physical reality, but one that corresponds to a creative process responsible for the ideation of mankind's myths. The quixotic imagination is therefore analogous to the poetic process, the perception of reality in metaphorical terms.

But it is not only the process of poeticization that characterizes Don Quixote's perception of giants where others see windmills. On a much simpler level is the plain substitution of one object for another. As Marthe Robert has put it: "In the case of the windmills, he seems to be the victim of an optical illusion."[10] At first glance this would appear to be the prosaic antithesis of the process I have been describing. Yet the two points of view are not mutually exclusive. The preconditioning of his many years as a bibliophile may easily be seen as allowing just such an illusion to come to the fore. The very idea of the windmill–giant confusion not exclusively as the product of a fertile imagination but as a physical phenomenon, an *optical illusion*, is an insightful observation.

Cervantes understood the nature of optical illusions. I do not mean to imply that he had scientific knowledge; it is nonetheless clear from his works that he had enough of an appreciation of the phenomenon to use it as a plot device on numerous occasions. I should clarify at the outset that I am using the term "optical illusion" in its broadest sense and not solely in its dramatic application to mirages. When people look ahead on a long stretch of railroad track and see two parallel rails converge, they experience a classic example of an optical illusion. This kind of "seeing things" is corrected by the spectators because they know – which is to say that they bring to bear their knowledge of how railways are constructed – that parallel rails do *not* converge. A variation is the situation in which shadows on a road are mistaken for patches of ice, or, conversely, patches of ice are ignored because they are seen as only shadows. The driver who "sees" patches of ice when there are only shadows brings to bear a set of expectations that precondition a perception of a physical phenomenon that a passenger unaccustomed to driving in northern climates may not see or comprehend. The passenger may even draw conclusions about the driver's imagination or driving skills. The passenger may, in fact, find it easy to believe that the operator is a "crazy driver."

At least some of this sort of predisposition to illusion is at work in the windmill episode. It is possible to propose its explanation by turning to the denouement of the adventure of the fulling mills. Don Quixote's response to Sancho's mockery of his master's inability to recognize these other mills for what they are could readily be applied to the windmills: "Am I obliged, being, as I am, a knight, to recognize and distinguish sounds and know which ones come from fulling mills and which ones don't? What's more, it could be, as indeed it is, that I have never seen them in my whole life, whereas you, base peasant that you are, must have seen them, since you were born and brought up among them" (I, 20). The rationalization that Cervantes puts in Don Quixote's mouth supports the contention that in addition to – but not, of course, instead of – the philosophical representation of the appearance–reality theme inherent in such transformations, Don Quixote's predisposition quite naturally leads him to suffer not only delusion but illusion. The delusion spawns the illusion: Believing is seeing. As Gombrich puts it: "Expectation created illusion."[11]

There is an important corollary to Robert's observation that in the windmill episode Don Quixote appears to be the victim of an optical illusion: We are dealing with a *physical* process. To say that the protagonist has been "programmed" or psychologically conditioned by his voracious reading only partially explains why he should mistake one thing for another. The July heat and the heavy armor (pointedly emphasized in Chapter 2) are two additional factors that support the likelihood of an optical illusion. Cervantes adds another element: distance.

Readers tend to overlook the evident fact that the windmills are – in fact, must be – espied from afar. The narrative plunges us so rapidly into the action that we are likely to envision the episode as beginning at a point at which Don Quixote is already quite close to the objects. Yet Cervantes lays down some clues that demand a sighting from a distance great enough to permit the discernment of a large number of structures. Although the narrator and the protagonist disagree on the nature of the objects, they are surprisingly in accord about their number. According to the narrator, "descubrieron treinta o cuarenta molinos de viento" ("they discovered thirty or forty windmills"); according to Don Quixote, "se descubren treinta, o pocos más desaforados gigantes" ("thirty, or a few more, inordinate giants reveal themselves")(I, 8). We should not lose sight of Cervantes' play on the word *descubrir*, a play lost in translation: The narrator tells us what the characters discovered, but the protagonist, using the same verb, gives us its reflexive form (equivalent to the passive voice), the author hinting thereby that it was the objects that were revealing themselves to be what Don Quixote was inclined to think they were.

The ability to perceive more than thirty of the objects requires a substantial distance between object and observer, given the size of a typical windmill. That narrator and observer coincide in the number reinforces this point. It is this apprehension from afar, a perception made credible by the combination of preconditioning, atmospheric conditions, inordinately heavy dress, and the distortion that distance in itself permits, that the protagonist carries with him even as he nears the objects: "But he went along so set in his belief that they were giants that he neither heard the shouts of his squire Sancho *nor did he notice, although he was already quite near,* what they were" (I, 8; emphasis mine). In other words, the illusion created from afar was not shattered by nearness because Don Quixote, intent upon the attack, was not paying any further attention to what his eyes might have revealed upon closer inspection. From a metaphysical standpoint, the fact that he was no longer seeing the objects may simply reinforce the well-known interpretations of this adventure as well as of the protagonist. For the purposes of the analysis presented here, however, the fact that Don Quixote was no longer taking notice of the windmills, together with other observations made earlier, enables us to appreciate Cervantes' familiarity with the physical aspects of the illusion, namely, atmospheric conditions and distance. (In *La Galatea*, one character says to another: "Perhaps you looked at her from afar, and the distance of the place . . . made her seem something other than what she ought to be" [Book II].) It bears noting that it is Cervantes himself who makes the point for us as he concedes that Don Quixote does not notice although he is already quite near. The potential distinction in perception between what is seen from afar and what may be noticed when one is quite near is thereby overtly set forth. Yet Don Quixote makes no notice.

The optical illusion initiated from afar is maintained at close range because the observer, so set upon that initial interpretation nurtured by his preconditioned expectation, no longer relies upon his sense of sight as he approaches. From a psychological point of view, this mind-set is consistent with Don Quixote's apprehension of phenomena that attend his chivalresque understanding of objects and events. The blindness is purposefully rationalized by Cervantes as he explains that even though Don Quixote is now quite near he no longer is paying attention to visual clues. If it appears that I am making too much of the point, one must ask why Cervantes sees fit to make it at all. The need to explain the continuing illusion by justifying its persistence despite the proximity of object and observer is a need created by the narrator. What I have referred to as blindness in fact mimics the temporary blindness one experiences after looking at a bright object. Even though the eyes are subsequently closed or averted, the image just seen persists. Cervantes' specific reference to Don Quixote's no longer noticing what is now in front of him (windmills) supports the mind's-eye image of what his long-range perception had impressed upon him (giants). The intellectually stimulated illusion has spawned a mind's-eye image, blinding him to a corrected perception until the physical shock "opens his eyes," so to speak, but without a rejection of that earlier perception, for it is of metamorphosis, not correction, that he subsequently speaks. His explanation, based on his readings, is not that windmills have been changed into giants but that an enchanter has transformed the giants so that they are now windmills. That is, he as well as Sancho now sees them as windmills. In short, from a distance Don Quixote saw giants; close up he at first maintained that illusion inasmuch as he did not rely upon his eyes; and only after the physical disaster does he see the objects as windmills.

Only slightly less familiar than this episode is that of the blanket tossing. On this occasion Don Quixote sees exactly what everyone else sees. It is his interpretation of the perpetrators that insinuates the illusion. Don Quixote fails to come to his squire's aid because the phantoms not only tossed Sancho but immobilized Don Quixote (or so the latter claims). If in the windmill adventure it is possible to perceive Don Quixote as the victim of an optical illusion, the blanket-tossing rationalization depicts him in the role of illusionist.[12] What is of interest to us here is his attempt to make Sancho believe the metamorphosis. Of course, as readers of the book are reminded on numerous occasions, Sancho never fully accepts his master's point of view. But the reason for Sancho's conviction that his tormentors were flesh-and-blood human beings is not only the obvious physical discomfort inflicted upon him by the "phantoms." Sancho insists:

I am convinced that those who had fun with me were neither phantoms nor enchanted men, as your grace says, but men of flesh and blood like us; and all of them, as I heard them call each other by name while they were tossing me, had their own names: for one was called Pedro Martínez, and the other Tenorio Hernández, and

I heard that the innkeeper was called "Lefty" Juan Palomeque. So, sir, your not being able to jump over the yard wall or get off your horse was due to something other than enchantments. [I, 18; emphasis mine]

Don Quixote realizes that he has failed to convince Sancho of the enchanted nature of the affair. In other words, he has failed to convey the illusion. He has not failed, however, to grasp the reason for Sancho's resistance to the illusion: The conventional wisdom regarding the significance of a man's name as an indication of his manhood (existence) has been accepted by Sancho as evidence of his tormentors' physical reality. This clue to the workings of Sancho's mind does not escape the alert Don Quixote.

Anxious to reestablish his influence on Sancho, Don Quixote asks him to be patient, "for the day will come when you will *see by the sight of your eyes* what an honorable thing it is to be in this profession" (I, 18; emphasis mine). The redundancy cries out for our attention. Despite the talk about intangibles like honor and glory, it is a *visual* confirmation that Don Quixote wishes to impose. His opportunity comes almost immediately as a huge cloud of dust (the well-known adventure of the flocks of sheep) inspires him to announce that the awaited day is already here.

To some extent it would be possible to argue that Don Quixote's perception of the sheep as armies is simply a variation of the windmill illusion; that is to say, for reasons already explored, Don Quixote is the victim of an optical illusion. But Don Quixote is still smarting from his failure to convince Sancho of his illusions. His eagerness to convey his own illusions to Sancho is in keeping with his anxiousness to have those illusions shared by his disciple and companion. More specifically, he needs to convince Sancho of the reality of the illusion. Michael Bell has taken this argument a step farther by suggesting that it is the reader who is obliged to see the illusion: "Even while passionately moved to participate, [Don Quixote] *sees* it, and therefore requires us to see it, as literally a passing spectacle."[13]

Mindful of the relationship between the reality of a man and his name, Don Quixote proceeds to pour forth a veritable who's who of legendary warriors, even to the point of recounting some of their lineages and describing their coats of arms. Sancho is at first easily led on and even suggests joining in the battle, a prospect that causes him to ask where to leave his ass. Don Quixote begins an answer but is reminded of the overriding aspect of sharing the illusion. Interrupting his own response to Sancho he urges: "But pay attention to me and *look*, for I want to give you an account of the most important knights that are in these

armies. And so you may *see and note* them better, let's go over to that
hill there" (I, 18; emphasis mine).

The narrator gives us the precise circumstances of the illusion as he
describes how Don Quixote and Sancho settled themselves on a rise
"from which the two flocks that for Don Quixote had become armies
would have been readily seen, if the clouds of dust raised by the animals
had not confused and blinded their vision; nonetheless, seeing in his
imagination what he did not really see nor was there to see, Don Quixote
raised his voice."

What is so often called Don Quixote's idealism is revealed here in its
true character by the narrator's words. It is idealism not in the sense of
being guided by ideals in contradistinction to practical matters but rather
in the metaphysical sense of apprehending reality on a plane that transcends physical phenomèna. This distinction explains Don Quixote's
interruption of his own parenthetical remarks to Sancho concerning the
ass and Rocinante. Even though this parenthesis in the description of the
imagined armies seemingly reflects Sancho's potential acceptance of the
illusion, Don Quixote rejects the prosaic concerns voiced by his squire.
Yet Don Quixote's re-creation of his illusion for Sancho's benefit is
almost entirely dependent on particulars: the innumerable string of names,
family backgrounds, lovers' quarrels, clothing, colors, geographical details, and historicolegendary allusions.

The metaphysical significance of the quixotic illusion is dependent
upon the physical realization of that illusion: "Seeing in his imagination
what he did not really see nor was there to see, he raised his voice." The
ideation of the illusion, spawned perhaps by an optical illusion in turn
responding to an urgent need to compensate for his earlier failure to
convey the illusion of phantoms, is followed by the raising of his voice:
"That knight you *see* over there... But turn your *eyes* in this other
direction and you will *see*... "(emphasis mine). In a final outburst enumerating still more military squadrons, Don Quixote's store of names is
at last exhausted as he describes troops "whose faces I recognize *and see,*
although their names I don't remember" (emphasis mine).

The path along which Don Quixote travels is as follows: (1) an assurance that Sancho will recognize the value of knight-errantry by means
of what he will see; (2) an insistence that if Sancho will look and listen,
he will see the account given by Don Quixote; (3) a prolonged enumeration of names coupled with a renewed assurance that Sancho will
see what Don Quixote is describing; (4) a desperate insistence that he,
Don Quixote, does see what he is describing. The alternation of assurance
and insistence leads to a curious order: Those whose names he cannot
recall have faces that he recognizes and sees. Would one not expect that
he should *first see and then recognize?*[14]

The inversion suggests two things: First, his insistence that he sees the faces reflects an urgent attempt to underscore the recognition with the underlying need of the illusion, namely, his conviction that *he* does see them. More significantly, the quixotic illusion springs from cognition to actualization: The protagonist must first make the connection with his predisposition to find what his books have preconditioned him to seek. When he "recognizes" giants in La Mancha, then he "sees" them. It is not the other way around. Accordingly, what occurs in the sheep episode is not a glimpse of sheep that he converts to soldiers. What the narrator tells us is that Don Quixote sees a large and dense *cloud of dust*. Moreover, Don Quixote himself says it is a dust cloud and tells Sancho so. Since, however, the quixotic illusion functions on a believing-is-seeing principle, the dust cloud contains what Don Quixote's conviction leads him to see. Finally, his efforts to share the illusion are informed by what Sancho has suggested would be indicative of reality, that is, names.

Don Quixote resorts to his usual explanation moments after the ig-nominious encounter. He does not deny Sancho's perception of the arm-ies as sheep but argues in typical fashion that the envious enchanter has transformed the squadrons of soldiers into droves of sheep. But then follows a curious statement: "So that you may disillusion yourself and see that what I'm telling you is true, get on your ass and follow [the sheep] and you will see how, as they move off a bit into the distance, they will reassume their original shape and, no longer sheep, be [once more] real and true men, as I first described them to you" (I, 18).[15] Don Quixote immediately retracts the suggestion that Sancho follow the sheep, in view of his need for ministration; the vomiting that follows is sufficient to drive the question of illusion from our minds. Nonetheless, the process described by the protagonist merits our attention. Although the *inter-pretation* made by Don Quixote is in keeping with the confusion of reality we have come to expect, the *rationalization* of the confusion betrays a familiarity with optical as well as fictional illusions. (I am not suggesting that the protagonist is aware of optical – that is, purely physical – illusions as playing a role in his apprehension of phenomena. The narrator, on the other hand, does describe a process that we may readily relate to that involved in visual illusions, a process the protagonist is inadvertently describing despite his own more fanciful interpretation. At a later stage, however, he will actually describe the process of optical illusion, not metamorphosis, though still informed by his fantasy: "I do not mean that [enchantments] change things from one entity to another really, but rather that it seems that way" [II, 29]. The same point is made in the *Persiles* [I, 18]: Potions may cause us to see one thing for another, but "there are no people who change their original nature into another.")

In Don Quixote's mind, presumably, the transformation of objects in relation to their distance conforms to their relative distance from him. Accordingly, the metamorphosis is, to his way of thinking, determined by the enchanter's desire to distort reality primarily for him. Such an interpretation is in keeping not only with the protagonist's eccentricity but also with his egocentricity. That is why the description of the process is in fact the reverse of what we would normally expect: In proportion to the distance from the protagonist, we are told, the likelihood increases that "they will reassume their *original* shape," namely, the shape of soldiers and not sheep. If this is well-understood quixotic originality (with respect to ontological perspectives), what has gone unobserved (so far as I am aware) is how the process described by Don Quixote adheres to the simple physical distortion produced by an optical illusion: The distance between the observer and the object may directly affect the perception of that object. It is when they move off into the distance, Don Quixote declares, that the sheep appear as men.[16] He does not deny that seen up close their appearance is that of sheep, for such is the nature of an optical illusion.

It bears remarking that Aristotle, with the intention of proving that sight can occur only through a medium (such as air), illustrates the point by noting that an object placed too close to the eye cannot be seen.[17] Proximity may thus distort as well as distance. That Don Quixote interprets the metamorphosis as the workings of an enchanter needs no further comment; that he recognizes the transformation as having occurred is a concession to the deceptive nature of physical phenomena. This admission, however, does not mean that his own perception has altered as a result. Just as the traveler recognizes that the parallel lanes in the distance only seem to converge but the illusion persists nevertheless, so Don Quixote, informed by his literature, persists in seeing the illusion while "correcting" the optical manifestation in accordance with his "knowledge."

This process, so very ordinary when one pauses to consider it, underlies the perception of the barber's basin as Mambrino's helmet. Cervantes leads the reader to understand rather clearly that it is not quixotic madness alone that allows a perception of the basin as headgear. First, the circumstances themselves invite such a perception, for "it began to rain a bit. . . . Not far off Don Quixote spotted a man on horseback who wore on his head a thing that shone as if it were of gold" (I, 21). We note here that some distance is once more important enough to mention, although not so much as to invite a potential distortion of the magnitude of a sheep–soldier confusion. Moreover, these opening sentences in themselves suggest how easily we, the readers, could be led to identify what so far is only an unqualified "thing that shines" as a gleaming sort of headgear. What is more, the narrator goes to great lengths to explain the prosaic circumstances: "The fact of the matter [regarding] the helmet, the horse, and the knight that Don Quixote saw was this: ... the barber carried a brass shaving basin with him and as luck would have it ... it began to rain, and so that his hat, which must have been new, would not become stained, he put the basin on top of his head, and since it was clean, it gleamed from half a league away." Once again the distance is a matter to be noted. Furthermore, the narrator has taken pains to provide us with the facts requisite to a plausible association: The gleaming object is headgear, and its glitter suggests a sort of helmet.

Of course, the particulars are once more in keeping with the protagonist's preconditioned penchant for seeing matters of chivalry at every turn. What must not be overlooked, however, is that, especially in this episode, the narrator spells out the circumstantial conditions that reasonably could lead to Don Quixote's perception. To some extent, in fact, this perception is more reasonable than the observation made by Sancho, whose interpretation follows a trajectory from apparent neutrality ("a thing that shines") through chivalric acceptance (not as a helmet but as the spoils of battle, a basin worth eight *reales*) to compromise (*baciyelmo*). Don Quixote extends the interpretation of the object to embrace the perceptions of others to whom it will seem to be something else.[18] But their perceptions will not affect the illusion that he alone sees, an illusion informed by his visual apprehension of the object as headgear and sustained by the preconditioning of the romances. Once again, it bears remarking that Don Quixote agrees that it looks like a basin but insists that his familiarity with the object – he almost articulates here the influence of predisposition – permits his interpretation:

> Do you know what I think, Sancho? That this famous part of this enchanted helmet, by some strange accident must have come into the hands of someone incapable of recognizing or valuing it and, without knowing what he was doing, seeing it to be of the purest gold, he must have melted the other half in order to take advantage of the value and from the other half he made this piece, which *looks like a barber's basin*, as you say. But, be that as it may, for I, who know it, am not affected by its transmutation.[Emphasis mine]

It would be pointless to attempt to draw consistent parallels between Don Quixote's illusions on the metaphysical and physical levels. No such relationship exists on any continuous basis. The foregoing discussion has been intended to show that a general comprehension of how simple optical illusions function does inform the comparatively more dramatic illusions that typify Don Quixote's distortion of the physical phenomena he encounters. Of course, it is not Don Quixote but Cervantes who reveals an understanding of visual illusion. Accordingly, Don Quixote is not the only character affected by such deceptions of the eye. Sancho, too, has analogous experiences.

We are given a graphic example in the incident in Barcelona harbor. In an episode that has its counterpart in the blanket-tossing affair, Sancho is tossed about by the crew of the galley "so rapidly that poor Sancho lost the sight of his eyes and without any doubt thought that the very devils were carrying him" (II, 63). Don Quixote on this occasion is not moved to fanciful interpretation but, like our hypothetical traveler, sees an optical illusion that his knowledge corrects but does not prohibit: He perceives Sancho's being tossed about as "Sancho's flight without wings." But if Don Quixote is able to compensate for the visual illusion in this instance, Sancho is convinced that "these indeed are really enchanted things and not those that my master says." The connection with the blanket-tossing is not limited to the mere fact of Sancho's being tossed about. It will be recalled that Sancho, on that earlier occasion, insisted on the flesh-and-blood nature of his tormentors not only because of what he felt but because they called each other by name. This symbolic act of mundane reality was sufficient to dispel for him his master's interpretation of the event as enchantment. In the episode of the tossing by the crew in Barcelona harbor, however, the narrator points out that despite the horrendous noise with which the crew raised and lowered the sail, the crew members themselves remained "silent, as if they had neither voice nor breath." This, then, is what predisposes Sancho to accept the goings-on as enchantment, a veritable optical illusion, for the movement of the many oars looks to Sancho like the simultaneous motion of so many reddish feet.

This episode is introduced with the pointed declaration by the narrator that Sancho has never in his life seen galleys before (II, 62), a comment that helps to make the illusion a plausible one. If in the Mambrino episode it is deemed important to make the helmet a reasonable sort of illusion, then here as well we are inclined to sympathize with the image of a waterborne centipede in the mind of one who has never before seen the sea (II, 61), much less such galleys. We thus have further evidence of Cervantes' comprehension of the role played by prior disposition in the formation of optical illusions. This is why, on its most elemental level, the windmill–giant perception is not the depiction of a realistic–idealistic dichotomy and may be considered perspectivistic only if we consider the predisposition of the perspective.

The moments discussed in the preceding pages reflect a progression that I am scarcely the first to notice, namely, Sancho Panza's gradual approach toward quixotic perspectives. Stated in terms appropriate to the concerns dealt with in this chapter, the instances selected here reveal a Sancho who is ever more inclined to accept illusion. Concurrently, these same moments reveal a Don Quixote whose perspective allows an increasing appreciation for the effects of illusion.

Don Quixote's rationalization of the enchanter's transformation of the giants into windmills is blunt: "I think, and so it is true." A similar order informs his perception of the sheep as armies: "I recognize and see." The latter instance, however, already suggests a different perception dependent upon one's distance (although Don Quixote's interpretation of that distance is related to the distance he believes to exist between him and his inimical enchanter). In the basin–helmet controversy, Don Quixote continues to hold on to the illusion but ultimately allows the possibility that to Sancho the object may appear to be a barber's basin and, more significantly, that to someone else it may appear to be something altogether different. By the time we reach the Barcelona harbor, Don Quixote's perception of Sancho's wingless flight is in keeping with the kind of optical illusion most of us experience, that is, tempered by our knowledge of what is in fact occurring despite the visual evidence to the contrary.

In these same instances, Sancho begins with a bald refusal to accept the illusion. Not only does he not see giants; the peasant lectures the gentleman on the nature of windmills, explaining away the illusion with concrete facts: "Look, your grace . . . , for those things that appear over there are not giants but windmills, and what on them seem arms are the blades which, tossed by the wind, make the millstone move" (I, 8). Like Don Quixote in Barcelona harbor, Sancho recognizes the illusion and corrects it.

When we get to the sheep episode, Sancho is disposed to share the illusion but cannot yet bring himself to accept it and ends up by rejecting it outright: "I hear nothing but a lot of bleating of sheep and lambs" (I, 18). We might conclude the same thing about the Mambrino episode were it not for a curious construction chosen by Cervantes for Sancho's apparent neutrality. When Sancho is confronted with his master's insistence that he see a "knight coming toward us, on a brown spotted horse, wearing a golden helmet on his head," his response is that he sees only "a man on an ass, brown like mine, wearing on his head something that gleams" (I, 21). What is significant for us here is that Sancho introduces this observation with the construction, "Lo que yo veo y columbro." The first part is clear ("What I see") and the second produces a typically Cervantine effect, for *columbrar* means to glimpse or make out. More intriguing is the definition in Covarrubias' dictionary of 1611: *Columbrar* not only is imprecise in its degree of perception but is specifically related to seeing at a distance. Covarrubias defines it thus: "To descry something from afar that can barely be distinguished and recognized for what it is."[19]

If Don Quixote first recognizes and then sees, Sancho Panza sees and barely recognizes. The apparent neutrality in his observation of neither barber nor knight, neither basin nor helmet (although he does see an ass where his master sees a horse), is tempered by his use of *columbro*, an imprecision with telling effect. By the time we reach the Barcelona harbor incident, Sancho is described as having "lost the sight of his eyes . . . and *without any doubt* [he] thought that the very devils were carrying him." Now it is Sancho who is firmly convinced that "these indeed are really enchanted things and not those that my master says" (II, 63).

From the Mambrino episode (I, 21) to the Barcelona harbor incident (II, 63) represents an enormous leap. It is well to consider briefly what may be regarded as a midpoint in this progression, namely, the adventure of the wooden horse Clavileño. It will be recalled that Sancho claims to have raised his blindfold slightly and caught a glimpse of the earth, which seemed to him to be "no larger than a grain of mustard seed, and the men who were walking on it not much bigger than hazelnuts, so that you can see how high we must have been flying then" (II, 41).

Whether Sancho really believes he saw what he describes or whether he invents it is a matter that Cervantes takes pleasure in leaving in perpetual doubt. My task here would be made easier, of course, if we knew for certain whether what Sancho reports is his interpretation of something he actually perceived or what he consciously imagines he would have seen. Since we must be content with the ambiguity left us by Cervantes, I shall assume the distinction to be irrelevant to the matter of concern here, inasmuch as we do know that he did not view the earth from on high. It follows, therefore, that whether he did peek (thereby perceiving as "earth" and "men" a grain of seed and some kernels) or whether he made it all up (thereby revealing his ignorance of proportion, as the duchess is quick to point out), his predisposition to accept the illusory distortions that great distance creates is patent. Had he claimed to have seen men in their normal size or had he reported seeing seeds and nuts – the former a blatant fabrication, the latter a reversion to his insistence on windmills and sheep – it would be, in all senses, a different story.

The ensuing discussion becomes a parodic debate on optics:

> "Friend Sancho," said the duchess, "watch what you're saying, for apparently you did not see the earth but only men walking on it. It is clear that if the earth appeared to you as a grain of mustard seed and each man like a hazelnut, one man alone would have covered the entire earth."
>
> "That's true," replied Sancho, "but despite all that, I spotted it from one side and saw all of it."

"Look, Sancho," said the duchess. "From one side you can't see all of what you look at."

"I don't know anything about looks," answered Sancho. "All I know is that your ladyship ought to understand that, since we were flying by means of enchantment, it was by enchantment that I could see the whole earth and all the men no matter which way I looked at them. And if I am not believed in this, your grace will probably not believe either how, uncovering myself up to my eyebrows, I saw that I was so close to the sky that between it and me there wasn't the length of a palm and a half. . . . And it happened that we passed by the part where the seven goats are." [II, 41]

By this time it is clear that Sancho has yielded to the temptation to invent and enlarge his tale.[20] As was the case with Don Quixote in the sheep adventure, the doubts of his interlocutor provoke increased efforts to substantiate the illusion. If Don Quixote saw soldiers conjured from sheep, Sancho sees goats conjured from stars. (As most editors point out, the goats are the Pleiades.) But once again it is parody, not farce, that I wish to stress here. The discussion centers around the perception of objects from afar, and that discussion is a parody of a debate on such matters. Nearly lost in the translation is the emphasis and play on the word *mirada* (a glance, a look, as well as a *manner of looking* at things). The connection is more evident in the original because in Cervantes' time the *vos* (used with the second person plural form of the verb, though applicable to a single individual) yielded the form *mirad*. In the two admonitions to Sancho just quoted, it is this form, *mirad*, that sets up Sancho's reply to the duchess, which I have rendered, "I don't know anything about looks." (The original reads: "Yo no sé esas miradas.") The parodic element is accordingly contained in the mock-serious treatment of Sancho's perspective. Although the duchess is obviously leading him on (ultimately leading the discussion to a farcical level), the issue is joined not over whether Sancho sneaked a look but over what he saw and how he perceived what he spotted.

The duchess suggests that Sancho's sightings are out of proportion. Sancho could not have seen the entire earth, she says, but he did see, she allows, the men walking on it. Of course, she points out, were the earth to appear as small as a grain of mustard then men could not be as large as hazelnuts. Moreover, one does not see the totality of anything by looking at it only from one side. Such a discussion with Sancho could not have occurred in Part I.[21] Aside from the parody (and the continuing farce at the ducal estate generally), the discussion has as its premise Sancho's capacity for illusion. Part way between the prosaic insistence on windmills, sheep, and a barber's basin, on the one hand, and a conviction that the events in Barcelona harbor "indeed are really enchanted things," on the other, Sancho's distortions of what he sees or thinks he sees or would have seen from Clavileño reveal the effects of his quixotic education. An incipient though still imperfect ability to apprehend reality by yielding to the imaginative interpretations afforded by the deceptions he has learned to associate with distance, the curvature of the earth, the effects of squinting and the like – such is the revelation of the Clavileño episode regarding Sancho's manner of perception at this stage. If rational observers can see bears and goats as they perceive the heavens from earth, why may not Sancho be disposed to see earth as a mustard seed and men the size of hazelnuts as he supposedly spots, or imagines that he spots, earth from the heavens?

Franklin O. Brantley has traced the recurring theme of the flight to the heavens from Plato and Cicero through Boethius, Boccaccio, and Chaucer to Cervantes. Among the characteristics common to such flights are that "the Earth is so petty that it appears a mere dot in the Universe" and that "humanity viewed from above appears to be a chaotic chorus ... while all the rest of the Universe is marked by perfect harmony." Brantley remarks that it is "not surprising that Cervantes should have been acquainted with this tradition... What is surprising is that Sancho himself should know something about these episodes, or rather, that Cervantes should expect the reader to accept such knowledge on the part of Sancho." The subsequent explanation offered, namely that "these ascents from literature had probably become part of the folklore by that day and so were the property of the illiterate as well as the literate," misses the point.[22] The episode is a climactic one in Sancho's development, as Brantley's study convincingly shows. From this standpoint, the experience on Clavileño is one of *disillusionment*.[23]

On the other hand, the episode is pivotal in another sense: It reveals at last Sancho's capacity for *illusion*. (I am evidently differentiating between optical illusions and the type of deception practiced by Sancho in his "enchantment" of Dulcinea.)

I do not think it necessary to argue for Sancho's familiarity with the literary tradition. If it is Cervantes' purpose to show an attitudinal change in Sancho, then it is consistent with other such reactions to phenomena to depict a response in consonance with the individual's predisposition. It should not be forgotten that just before the encounter with the duke and duchess, Sancho had decided to give up the quest (II, 29). Sancho's predisposition to be figuratively disillusioned about the value of a governorship has conditioned him to see the pettiness of worldly power. The earth accordingly appears to him as it has to others of literary tradition – and to many twentieth-century voyagers with no such traditions – as a small place indeed, no larger than a grain of mustard seed.

The lack of correct proportion implicit in the comparison of the "men" with hazelnuts may, on a simple level, answer Brantley's question concerning Sancho's acquaintance with a literary tradition. The purposeful distortion most likely is Cervantes' way of making such a familiarity acceptable, corresponding as it does to Sancho's frequent distortion of the names of literary personages. (Sancho's malapropisms often serve to make plausible his discussion of serious topics, as we saw in Chapter 1.) More significant than Sancho's way of handling a cultural tradition, I would suggest, is Cervantes' treatment of a topos: Cervantes reshapes the traditional theme. In the present instance we may go so far as to say that it is a literal reshaping, for the proportionate size of men and the earth has been inverted.[24] It goes without saying that this distortion produces a comic effect. It needs to be said, however, that Sancho's growing ethical awareness is revealed in his perception of the insignificance of a world ruled by men "too big for their breeches." If the topos has as one of its characteristics "humanity [as] a chaotic chorus," then Sancho's perception of such chaos among those who would presume to govern the earth is not unlike Don Quixote's earlier perception of unwieldy giants.

The Spanish phrase *el engaño a los ojos*, "visual deception," is frequently used to describe the baroque representation of the appearance-and-reality confusion. This *engaño a los ojos*, observes Américo Castro, has an artistic slant as well as an ethical one.[25] Applied to the Clavileño episode, the concept makes it possible to think of Sancho's perception of the world and its distorted men-giants as the ethical aspect of Cervantes' artistic representation of that statement. But there is a third dimension, underlying the other two – the substance, as it were – and it is the element I have been emphasizing in this chapter. The physical *engaño a los ojos*, the reality of illusion, is what allows Cervantes to lead us to the artistic *engaño* and its ethical interpretation by Sancho. If Sancho did indeed peek and thereby did glimpse something, that thing, that physical reality, most likely was a grain of mustard seed and a fallen hazelnut, as his initial perception suggested to his mind. The more intriguing ethical, social, and psychological interpretations that emerge therefrom depend upon that visual perception.

In short, the metaphysical significance attached to an episode like that of Clavileño ultimately rests on the physical apprehension of reality. (Perhaps it would be more accurate to say that it rests *first* on the physical apprehension.) Stated quite simply, in the present instance any comical, ethical, social, or psychological aspects of Sancho's description have their basis in *what he did in fact see*. The illusion is not a grain of mustard seed or a hazelnut; these are the reality from which subsequent illusions – Sancho's own as well as those of his interlocutors – are derived.

It may be objected that my assumption that Sancho did peek and did see something is not supported by the text. It is, of course, true that the text does not say that he did. Neither does it say that he did not. The familiar corrective explanation of the narrator is not found here. But in the final analysis, whether he in fact saw anything is not the determinant point. The essential question is what he saw in his mind's eye. I think a case can be made to support the suggestion that he did peek. Not only does he make a point of wanting to peek and, despite his master's admonition against it, insisting that he did so, but his own self-description as a *curioso*, together with his skeptical nature (we recall, for instance, the Micomicona illusion, nearly shattered by the revelation of his spying on the couple as they embraced; his perception of the resemblance of the duke's majordomo to the "Countess" Trifaldi; etc.) suggests that rather than obey his master, Sancho did sneak a quick glimpse. The more rapid the glance, the more likely the vision of a grain of mustard seed and a hazelnut. But even if he did not actually look at the ground, his predisposition to see the earth from on high as most of us would expect to see its details in reduced form would be enough to substantiate the point I wish to bring out. What is seen, with the physical eye or the eye of the mind, is the basis for the consequent illusion and, in this case, subsequent fabrication.[26]

Sancho's account of his ascent to the heavens is eventually relegated to the same realm as that of Don Quixote's descent to the Cave of Montesinos. Such "visions" and the observer's attendant attempt to share the reality of the corresponding illusion conform to a conception that transcends *Don Quixote*. In the *Persiles* (III, 16) we come across the following declaration:

> Matter and matters occur in the world that, prior to their occurrence, even if the imagination could cause them to occur as they do, it would not succeed in plotting. Accordingly, because they happen so rarely, many are taken to be apocryphal and are not considered to be as real as they in fact are. So it becomes necessary to support them with oaths or at least the credibility of the person who related them, although I say that it would be better not to tell them, as those old Castilian lines advise.[27]

Taken as a strictly literary commentary, the passage is calculated to arouse the reader's sense of *admiratio* for what follows. Interpreted in a more global way, the statement is an aphoristic observation not unlike our "truth is stranger than fiction," together with an earthy admonition concerning the reception likely to be given to such accounts by unimaginative listeners. It is not necessary to stress how this declaration by Cervantes in his last work may be applied to numerous situations in several of his works and, of course, to the Montesinos and Clavileño episodes in particular. It is, in short, a statement on the reality of illusion.

In addition to having transcendent significance and introductory purpose for Chapter 16 of Book III of the *Persiles*, the passage cited follows the episode of the flying woman in the two preceding chapters. Succinctly put, the incident is that of a woman whose fall from a tower, slackened by the billowing of her dress, appears to the observers as human flight. The optical illusion is corrected immediately. And yet Cervantes persists in making references to the incident as it was illusorily perceived: as that of a flying woman. This emphasis on the illusion cries out for the reader's attention.

Cervantes at once explains the nature of the illusion and hastens to reassure his readers that "the thing is possible without being a miracle" (III, 14),[28] but we are alerted to his preoccupation with the visual illusion and, significantly, his preparation of the setting as conducive to such illusion:

> The hour was noon, the sun's rays struck the earth from directly overhead, the heat was setting in and the shade of a high tower of the house invited them to spend the siesta there, for that period of the day threatened to be extremely hot. [After Bartolomé prepared lunch], they satisfied the hunger that was beginning to bother them. But scarcely had they raised their hands to lift it to their mouths when Bartolomé, raising his eyes, said in a loud voice: "Everybody out of the way, for someone is flying down from the sky and it won't be good for any of you to get caught underneath."
>
> They all raised their eyes and saw a figure coming down in the air and before they could make out what it was, it was already on the ground almost next to Periandro's feet. [There follows a sentence explaining what had in fact occurred.] The event left her overwhelmed and frightened, as it did all those who had seen her fly. [III, 14][29]

It is well to take a careful look at the construction of this passage. Although the use of the preterite tense in the original conveys the information that they did satisfy their hunger, the context unequivocally clarifies that the woman's flight occurred before such satisfaction could be realized. I make this point because the hunger they were suffering evidently ties in with their general state of mind, a state emphatically affected by the heat of the midday sun. Moreover, Cervantes frequently uses the verb I have rendered as "bother" – *fatigar* – in contexts of hunger, thirst, and the heat of the sun's rays.[30] That the characters in the *Persiles* are in these ways "bothered" provides the requisite predisposition for an optical illusion. That such is Cervantes' purpose is evidenced by his insistence, specifically following the rational explanation of the fall, on referring to the incident as something that overwhelmed and frightened "all those who had seen her fly." Moreover, immediately thereafter Cervantes calls the individual in question "the flying woman." Finally, on summing up the recent events – just before the passage on *admiratio* cited earlier – Cervantes once more refers to the miraculous flight of the woman.

Although Cervantes hastens to steer us away from a supernatural interpretation, his characterization of the fall as a miraculous flight is especially remarkable not only because the nature of the "flight" has long before – in fact, almost simultaneously with the incident itself – been clarified; it is noteworthy as well because of the contrasting description given to the similar fall of Periandro. The latter had rushed to the top of the tower to fight the man who caused the woman's fall. In the ensuing struggle, both men fell to the ground, Periandro's opponent being killed by the knife that passed through his chest and Periandro himself taking the same fall, but "since he did not have flaring clothes [as did the woman] to support him the impact had its effect and left him almost lifeless" (III, 14).

There is a great to-do made of the possibility of Periandro's fall being fatal, but, of course, he recovers. Given the nature of their respective falls, then, one would expect a reaction of wonder at Periandro's survival rather than at the woman's flight. Yet it is the latter that calls forth Cervantes' assessment that it is "more to be wondered at than believed." Whereas Periandro's hurtling from the tower is plainly called a fall, the woman's fall is repeatedly referred to as a flight. (Only very much later, in one of the several concise summaries of earlier episodes, is a reference made to "how Periandro's fall was held to be a miracle" [IV, 8], a recollection at odds with the narration of that event.) It is evident that what distinguishes the two falls, at least during the narration of their occurrence, is not the nature of the falls themselves so much as the visual perception they induce. Periandro's fall, the result of an act of heroism, is filled with pathos. The woman's fall, as a result of the optical illusion of flight caused by the billowing of her clothes, arouses awe and *admiratio*, to the point at which Cervantes twice feels the need to dispel any supernatural interpretation. Leaving to one side the concern for ecclesiastical censorship and literary decorum, what emerges is the continuing vision of the woman's fall as the optical illusion it was initially and momentarily. The heat of the noontime sun, the travelers' hunger, the visual difficulties posed by sun and shade, and, finally, the appearance of the woman's clothes, which served her as parachute, all combine to depict with no little accuracy the conditions that may lead to an optical illusion.

In contrast to the farcical world of *El retablo de las maravillas*, where there is mischievous deception, or to that of *Don Quixote*, where there is an existential need for illusion, the perception here in the *Persiles* is shared by everyone. To a large extent this difference is in accord with the varieties of genre involved, as well as with the intrinsic purposes of the respective works. For the concerns of the present chapter, however, the episode of the flying woman is significant beyond its own immediate function in the plot of *Persiles y Sigismunda*. The point, made repeatedly by Cervantes, that *all* the observers shared the same illusion is, as well as an expression of his concern for plausibility, a plain statement regarding the nature of visual perception. If a leap from a cliff onto a frozen sea (*Persiles*, II, 20) requires at least a tacit desire for some broken bones in order to assure a modicum of verisimilitude, the vision of a human fall slackened by billowing clothes resembling wings is possible without supernatural interpretations. But just as our hypothetical travelers of some pages back realize that the parallel rails will not converge and nonetheless continue to perceive them as convergent, so the characters in the *Persiles*, aware of the nature of the woman's fall, retain the image of a flying woman. (It is well to recall the earlier remark about the image that persists once we have seen a brightly lit object.) Cervantes has described the conditions and the responses of observers of an optical illusion.

There remains a further stage of visual illusion, one in which the illusory features dominate the optical perception. In the instances selected thus far, there has been no doubt that *something* is being perceived. The common elements have been the physical reality of the objects in question and the diverse interpretations that may be made of their perception. Even in the instance from the *Persiles*, in which the perception by the characters is uniform, Cervantes permits us to see not only the difference between the omniscient narrator's clarification (fall, not miracle) and the temporary illusion of a flying woman, on the one hand, but also the difference between that momentary illusion (temporary belief in the miraculous) and the prolonged illusion of a falling woman whose billowing clothes make her appear to be flying (a natural trompe l'oeil). In other words, what I have termed "illusion" in the instances examined up to now has been, in each case, the undisputed sighting of something that *appears* to be something else.

In Cervantes' play *Los baños de Argel*, we come upon an optical illusion of a different order: a mirage. There is no better way to describe it than to let Cervantes' own character, a guard of the Christian captives in Algiers, tell it as he relates it to the Christians:

This morning as the sun rose its rays left an impression on the clouds of such a formation that, although they were false, I believe them. They showed an armada, powered by sails and oars, rapidly moving along the calm sea to dock in Algiers. The eyes that see all this make out the prows, sterns, and oars of the false galleys so clearly that there are those who declare and those who swear that they saw the boatswain giving orders and the oarsmen obeying all at the same time. There are even some who say they saw your dead prophet on a flag on the topsail of one of the vessels. . . . By means of these formations that the sun with its rays has printed on the clouds, it has in a thousand ways produced fear in us. . . . There are more than twenty wounded and more than thirty dead. But now the sun has broken up the armada and you can go back to your games. [*Obras*, p. 310]

This passage has a number of significant elements. In the first place, the optical illusion narrated here completes the series ranging from the shared perception of an object that conveys diverse signals (basin–helmet), through diverse perceptions of an object (sheep–soldiers), to perceptions of objects that only appear to be what they in fact are (hazelnuts–men), and finally to the mirage, perception of what is not in fact there. Secondly, the very use of the mirage confirms Cervantes' appreciation of the phenomenon for literary purposes. Moreover, although the speaker is narrating a past event, he uses the present tense to express his belief, specifically in conjunction with his assertion that what was perceived was false: "Although they were false, I believe them." It may be argued that the present tense of the verb (*creo*) is required by the *romance* versification (assonance in *e-o*), or that the tense is in reality the historical present so frequently found in narrative literature. Both of these are valid observations. There appears to be another facet, however, particularly when we bear in mind a favorite type of construction in Cervantes' works, namely, the bipartite declaration of absolute truth and individual perspective, which we discussed in Chapter 2. In the statement under discussion here, the absolute assertion declares the vision to have been a falsehood while the individual perspective betrays belief.

The paradoxical statement thus reflects the paradox we have noted in optical illusions, a paradox reinforced by the disparity of the tenses. Although the observer is intellectually aware of the falsity of the visions, his belief that he saw them transcends the historicity of the incident. Although he knows that the galleys were false, the mirage nonetheless did occur – the reality of the illusion – and so he continues to believe (present tense) that he did see them. The ambiguous construction, like so many others in Cervantes' writings, is in keeping with his representation of reality not as a dichotomy between the poetic-universal and the historical-particular but as coterminous perceptions. Paul Ricoeur cites Roman Jakobson to the effect that

... what happens in poetry is not the suppression of the referential function but its profound alteration by the workings of the ambiguity of the message itself. "The supremacy of poetic function over referential function," [Jakobson] says, "does not obliterate the reference but makes it ambiguous. The double-sense message finds correspondence in a split addresser, in a split addressee, and what is more, in a split reference, as is cogently exposed in the preambles to fairy tales of various people, for instance, in the usual exhortation of the Majorca story tellers: *Aixo era y no era* (it was [so] and it was not)."[31]

This same function is found in the guard's description of the images produced by the mirage: "Although they were false, I believe them" – *aixo era y no era.*

Cervantes, anxious to avoid any suggestion of the supernatural, explains the phenomenon as the qadi attempts to rationalize what has occurred by recounting similar experiences: "Frightful squadrons formed of fantastic shadows have often been seen in the air, which meet with all the artifice and skill of real ones charging each other in the middle of a battlefield; clouds have rained blood and mail, and bits of scimitars and shields" (*Obras*, p. 312). The king refers to Christian miracles that do, he allows, occur at times. The present situation, however, he finds unique because without any mystery at all the sun's rays, on meeting the clouds, formed such an enormous armada. Nonetheless, he is reminded, this little trick (*burleta*) has cost him the lives of more than thirty Christian captives.

Although the philosophical and cultural implications are not without interest, this episode, when seen in the context of the present chapter, completes the sequence of illusions examined here. More so than any of the illusions studied previously, this most plausible of all – a true mirage – causes the most serious harm: twenty wounded and thirty dead. Cervantes, who was neither philosopher nor scientist, drew upon the knowledge of his time: "Meteorological writings formalized [the] constant opposition between sun and cloud; and poets, stimulated by personal observation as well as by the technical exposition of the process, often based their images on it."[32] Moreover, "many writers reported the occurrence of other strange and wonderful apparitions in the heavens. Fulke recounted the appearance of castles, cities, battles, monsters, and assorted religious symbols. Shakespeare's Antony recalls having seen in the sky

A tower'd citadel, a pendent rock,
A forked mountain, or blue promontory
With trees upon't, that nod unto the world.

Antony suggests that these apparitions are various cloud forms, and perhaps today these phenomena would be called mirages."[33]

To the extent that they concerned themselves with the difficulty in distinguishing appearance and reality, Cervantes and his age were not unique. How that particular age, that particular culture, and that particular artist perceived and responded to the perennial paradox is the subject of numerous studies, major and minor. It is, of course, at this ontological level that the reading and study of Cervantes' works is, intellectually, most rewarding. In the foregoing pages I have not attempted to come to grips with the metaphysical significance of the episodes scrutinized. Rather, my intention has been to seek the physical underpinnings, as it were, of the artist's philosophical response to the deceptive nature of appearances. A close reading of Cervantes' works does not allow us to say, with Prospero, that therein lies "the baseless fabric of this vision."[34] The illusion, more often than not, was based on reality.

Chapter 4
The illusion of reality

Seeing is believing.
    – Plautus

Following the scrutiny and burning of the books, Don Quixote's library is walled up. He subsequently attempts to locate the room, searching for the door with his hands while "rolling his eyes round and round over everything" (I, 7). The sense of touch and an exhaustive use of the sense of sight do not reveal his library, the disappearance of which, he is now told by his niece, was effected by an enchanter. This is the first occurrence in the book ascribed to an enchanter. (Enchanters are mentioned earlier, but this is the first occasion of an enchanter allegedly participating in the action.) Mark Van Doren went so far as to suggest that Don Quixote gets from his niece the idea of enchantment as a useful dodge for rationalizing disasters.[1] We may raise our eyebrows: The notion of enchanters clearly originated in the romances Don Quixote has read. It is true, however, that this introduction of enchanters' doings into his own life is spawned not by his imagination but by the plotting of the niece and the other supposedly rational souls involved in the deception. It is precisely one chapter later that the first optical illusion, animated by his readings and rationalized by the accommodation of the niece's explanation, takes shape: the adventure of the windmills.

The windmills episode marks the beginning of the action of the second sally. The first, accordingly, takes place before the workings of an enchanter supposedly bring about a rearrangement of his physical surroundings. Before this experience, Don Quixote's apprehension of reality does not include optical illusions. That first sally limits such matters to a chivalresque *interpretation* of what he sees, without the distorting effect on his visual perception that we come to know in subsequent sallies. Here I mean to differentiate a purely imaginative interpretation from an optically distorted perception. Chapter 3 dealt with the latter. The description of the first inn, however, belongs in a category of illusion apart from those based on optical apprehension. The description of the first inn and how Don Quixote takes it to be a castle is a process related to, but distinct from, those employed in the situations explored heretofore:

> At dusk, his horse and he were tired and dying of hunger; and . . .
> looking all around to see if he could spot some castle or some
> shepherds' hut . . . he saw, not far from the road along which he
> was going, an inn, which was as if he saw a star that was heading
> him not merely to the gates but to the palace of his salvation. [I, 2][2]

Several requisites for an optical illusion are present: hunger, fatigue,
poor illumination. Yet the first description of his perception is purely
metaphorical: It "was *as if* he saw a star," and the "palace of his salvation"
is not very different from the label any hungry and weary traveler might
apply to such an establishment at the end of a long day's journey. Of
course, the perception is soon carried further, but it bears remarking that
the very first encounter with a physical object in the character's career
as Don Quixote is initially reported in metaphorical terms that, by definition, remove the object from its ordinary referents. Before we may
proceed to outright fantasy, the narrator leads us by the hand, so to
speak, and allows us to follow a plausible association. For a fatigued
traveler as nightfall approaches, an inn that he does see may readily be
envisioned as if he saw a star guiding him to a palace.

The narrator next takes us a step farther:

> And since all our adventurer thought, saw, or imagined seemed to
> him to be made and to occur in the way that he had read, as soon
> as he saw the inn it appeared to him that it was a castle with its
> four turrets and pinnacles of shining silver, not without its draw-
> bridge and deep moat, together with all those attendant things with
> which such castles are depicted.[3]

Clearly, there is no optical distortion at work here. The narrator himself
stops to explain that everything is conditioned by Don Quixote's readings. The details "seen" by Don Quixote are seen only in the mind's
eye and correspond not to physical objects imperfectly perceived but to
the fictive circumstances he has read about. Even the verb used – *se
pintan*, literally "are painted" or, as I have put it, "are depicted" – describes castles not as they are but as they are portrayed, that is, with
reference not to what Don Quixote sees but to what he has read about.
The details of the castle are the product of the same process that enables
him to see, and later to describe, the heroes of his books. This process
is distinct from that which sees windmills as giants, sheep as armies, a
basin worn on the head as a helmet, and so forth. To be sure, these
situations, discussed in the previous chapter, assume the characteristics
of chivalric literature on the same basis as does the inn's conversion to
a castle. That is why, for instance, the barber's basin is perceived as
Mambrino's helmet and not, say, as a bishop's miter. But the fact that
it is perceived as headgear does have, as we have seen, a basis in observable

reality. Moreover, changed circumstances reveal objects in a new light – windmills perceived as giants are subsequently seen as windmills; clouds of dust perceived as armies are then recognized as sheep – and once again, although the particular manifestation is informed by the romances, the optical illusion that permits the interpretation is capable of being analyzed as such. But there is no illusion of an optical nature in the perception of the first inn as a castle.

The perception of turrets, pinnacles, moat, and drawbridge is presented not as an optical phenomenon but as a mental process whereby physical reality is not actually seen; rather, it is replaced in the mind's eye by what the protagonist has hoped or expected to see. Don Quixote sees the structure not as it is, nor as castles are constructed, but as they are "painted." We are reminded of the fictive friend of the prologue who advises the author to paint his intention ("pintando ... vuestra intención"). The prologue of course presents the perspective of the author, whereas the passage in I, 2, depicts the viewpoint of the character. But the two passages share the linking of purpose and painting. If this association seems less clear in Don Quixote's case than in Cervantes', it bears noting that the protagonist perceives the building as a castle not because he recognizes features of castles but because he envisions such features as they are painted. In a word, he sees in his mind's eye what he saw when he read his books.

Don Quixote's way of looking at the world involves the search for metaphor. When, for instance, he sees the virtues of maidens in prostitutes, the features of castles in inns, or for that matter, the beauty of Dulcinea in Aldonza, he is engaging in the classic exercise of metaphoric perception: the recognition of like or analogous elements in objects or beings otherwise unlike. The referent, of course, is the literature he has read.[4] We have here an interesting variation on the Horatian *ut pictura poesis* formula. The comparison of poetry and painting in relation to the activity of the author requires no comment. But the suggestion that the character's use of metaphor to seek chivalric qualities in mundane things and people is related to the painting process is a unique representation of his poeticization of the prosaic. To be sure, in the passage under discussion Don Quixote is not said to be painting; rather, he seeks elements of castles as they were painted in the romances. But in later moments he paints Maritornes in his imagination (I, 16), paints Dulcinea in his imagination (I, 25), refers to the sheep in the form in which "I first painted them for you" (I, 18), and claims to be able to paint all the knights-errant he has read about (II, 1). Even the canon is said to be amazed at the way Don Quixote "painted" the adventure of the Knight of the Lake (I, 50).

Angel Sánchez Rivero has made the insightful observation that on approaching the first inn, Don Quixote, hoping to find *either* a castle *or* a shepherds' hut, expresses the polarity of heroic dream and animal necessity, a dichotomy that will later be resolved by the introduction of Sancho Panza.[5] Accordingly, the absence of a Sancho precludes the intercourse, emotional as well as verbal, that underlies attempts to share illusions.[6] The conversion of inn to castle is therefore an internalized illusion, wholly imaginative, and so devoid of a physical basis. In this early phase of the novel, we may speak not of optical but only of mental illusions. As the work evolves into subsequent phases, the illusions are presented still as illusions, but with a plausibility grounded in optical distortions and animated by the protagonist's belief in living the life of his romances.

Cervantes plays with the problem of illusion in *El retablo de las maravillas* (*The Showcase of Wonders*). This one-act farce describes the irrationality of the "pure blood" delusion and is filled with apparent illusions. Yet it is, in point of fact, totally devoid of any illusion, physical or otherwise. The "illusions" presented by the charlatan are *not seen by anyone*, although the other characters' code of social ethics – the butt of Cervantes' satire – forces them to insist that they do see the illusions. We may say that the people of this play, by virtue of the ethos of their time and society, have been preconditioned to see the illusions. Though of course they do not see them (for there is nothing to see), much of the humor of the work derives from two particulars. First, the faith that the perquisites of legitimate birth and membership in the *cristiano viejo* or "Old Christian" class will enable them to see the wonders produces comic responses as the characters try to deal with their awareness that they do not, in fact, see anything. Secondly, the several characters, fearing that their inability to see the *maravillas* will be noticed by their neighbors, physically act out the illusions that they supposedly are witnessing. Thus one tries to avoid a pack of mice, another tries to get out of Samson's way, others attempt to flee a bull, and one goes through the motions of dancing with Salome. In this play we have the other side of the coin: In a work whose principal purpose is to show the illusory nature of certain beliefs that underlie the social structure, the very illusions qua illusions are nonexistent. As Calderón would say a few decades later, life is a dream and the dreams are naught but dream. (Cervantes himself had said in Book VI of the *Galatea*: "Es nuestra vida un sueño, un pasatiempo, un vano encanto" ["Our life is a dream, a pastime, a vain enchantment"].)

Another nonillusory situation will help us to see the significance of a circumstance studied in the previous chapter: the description of the warriors Don Quixote believed he saw (the flocks of sheep). I suggested that the sequence (*conozco y veo*) was the reverse of a normal, physical perception, for it would be expected that one sees first and recognizes subsequently. But as I argued in detail, the essence of quixotic illusion is that believing is seeing. We may place this perception in relief by contrasting the sheep episode in *Don Quixote* with a passage at the beginning of Book IV of *La Galatea*.

In an episode resembling that of the Dorotea–Fernando affair of *Don Quixote*, Rosaura tries to persuade Grisaldo to keep his promise to marry her, despite his father's arrangement of a marriage to another woman. Threatening suicide, Rosaura attempts to convince Grisaldo of her determination: "Y porque claro *conozcas y veas* que la que perdió por ti su honestidad, y puso en detrimento su honra, tendrá en poco perder la vida" ("And so that you may clearly *recognize and see* that she who lost her purity for you, and put her honor in danger, will think little of losing her life" [emphasis mine]).

Not only are we not dealing with illusions here, neither is it a matter of physical sighting. In the circumstances just described, Rosaura is asking for mental recognition first, whereupon intellectual and hence moral vision will, she hopes, follow. The situation here seems normal to us: It is not out of sequence. It is to be expected that one must first recognize the significance of the circumstances before it is possible to see the consequences. But it is this sequence – mental recognition prior to physical sighting – that Cervantes depicts in the perception of the clouds of dust raised by the sheep in *Don Quixote*. The contrast with the situation in *La Galatea* enables us to appreciate the depiction of the illusory process in the sheep–armies perception.

As if to underline the point, the episode in *La Galatea* goes on to provide us with the other side of the coin. Among others present, Teolinda recognized her twin sister, Leonarda, and revealed her presence, so that Leonarda *saw* Teolinda *and then recognized* her ("Y como . . . viese a Teolinda, luego la conoció" [Book IV]). Unlike the mental recognition of a moral problem and, unlike the quixotic illusion, the recognition of one's sister is depicted as we would expect: First the person is seen and then she is recognized. This sequence is restated not long afterward as "they *saw* some shepherds coming from afar, who were *then recognized*" ("vieron venir de lejos algunos pastores que luego fueron conocidos" [Book IV]). An earlier passage illustrates the matter in a similar fashion: "As soon as Elicio *saw* them, he *recognized* that it was Daranio . . . and that the rest were all neighbors" ("Luego que Elicio los vio, conoció ser Daranio . . . y los demás ser todos circunvecinos" [Book II]). On the same page we read: "And as soon as Lenio *saw and recognized* them" ("Y así como Lenio los vio y conoció").

I have begun this chapter with some examples that, by way of contrast, place in relief the propositions set forth in Chapter 3. What follows is not intended to contrast with but rather to complement what I have termed the reality of illusion. By examining some passages from *La Galatea*, we may appreciate the converse: the illusion of reality. If this seems less startling, it is by no means less interesting. We are dealing with the substance of the writer's art: the conjuring of images transmitted from the artist's imagination to that of the reader.

The many surrogate authors created by Cervantes, of whom Cide Hamete Benengeli is the best known, share an attribute that might well be described as that of the conjurer.[7] Unlike the deus ex machina, Cervantes' stand-ins are conspicuous as they point out, guide toward, comment on, and even criticize the action that they present or describe. Although these figures sometimes direct their charges against Cervantes' own lapses, we have seen that such criticism is frequently brought to the fore in order to defend his purpose, ward off charges that he is ignorant of literary precepts, and, most important, underscore his intention to present the matter in question irrespective of the apparent violation of decorum. The matter of *disparates*, discussed so extensively in Chapter 1, is only one example of how something apparently in violation of aesthetic exigencies may have meaningful, artistic purpose, as a result of which such presentation stands justified. The direct challenge of the translator regarding the implausibility of Sancho's manner of speaking to his wife in II, 5, is another instance.

The experimental urge is evident in all the major works. It lies at the heart of the declaration in the prologue to *Don Quixote*, Part I: "I do not care to go along with the current of custom." It is reflected in his conviction that the epic may be written in prose, that is, in a form other than the conventional one. It reveals itself in his belief that by writing plays in three acts long before Lope he was daring, and in his assertion that the *Persiles* dares to outdo Heliodorus.

Even when he appears to apologize, Cervantes adverts to his daring. In Chapter 44 of the 1615 *Don Quixote*, Cide Hamete refers to the interpolated tales of the first part. Such stories are "more serious and more entertaining," an implication that they provide both profit and pleasure. But in this second part he will not again "dare to reach out to other digressions," in turn an implication that what he did in 1605 was daring. (It bears noting parenthetically that one of the reasons given for not continuing with such tales is that readers might skip them or read them cursorily, thereby missing their craftsmanship and elegance. Not only do readers often so react even today, but in Cervantes' words we may see yet another allusion to the failure of his readers to understand the 1605 *Don Quixote* as he intended.) To some extent the issue discussed here deals with the interpretation of literary theory: unity contrasted with variety. For our purpose here, however, we observe one more instance in which Cervantes points to a work in which he has been daring.

In the dedication of his first major work, *La Galatea*, Cervantes speaks of his daring. In point of fact, the work is framed by suggestions that publication itself is daring, a topic I shall explore from a different perspective in Chapter 6. Toward the end of *La Galatea*, we are told that because of the poor reception given to good works in Spain, distinguished poets "communicate their lofty and exotic concepts only with their intellects, without daring to publish them for the world." And in the final sentence of the book, Cervantes promises a sequel that, if the first part is well received, "will have the daring to come out shortly" (Book VI). More directly significant for our purpose here is *La Galatea*'s prologue. Cervantes alludes to those who, fearful of bad reputations, "do not dare to publish." He, in contrast, has "given indications of being daring in the publication of this book." It is true that in this prologue Cervantes expresses reservations about his book's shortcomings, but we must remember that expressions of humility were part of the topos of affected modesty found in prologues generally. What bears noting is that the profession of humility is countered immediately with the assertion of daring. By seeing the contrast not as modesty (real or feigned) in opposition to braggadocio but as an uneasiness in conjunction with daring, we can sense the feeling of experimentation that Cervantes' attitude conveys. To accept the author's reservations as expressed in the prologue as earnest misgivings about the value of his work would be equivalent to taking literally his protestations of a sterile *ingenio* in the prologue to *Don Quixote*, Part I.

We ought to understand that when Cervantes speaks of his daring, as he does often in his works, he means to convey the excitement of publishing his attempts at subjecting conventions to untried referents and new dimensions. A brilliant essay by Mary Gaylord Randel has already explored one important aspect: Asking readers not to circumscribe their perspective by seeking only "Cervantes, the apprentice novelist," Randel convincingly demonstrates how *La Galatea* reveals "the ultimate impotence of words" and aims at a "testing of the limits of language and poetry."[8] This approach helps us to see a new purpose in the curate's description of *La Galatea* as proposing something but concluding nothing (*Quixote*, I, 6): Cervantes is letting us know that this was the point and that his perennial promises to bring out a sequel (again putting a convention to his own use) were never meant to be fulfilled![9]

Alongside the claim that his talent for verse is inferior (now given new meaning, thanks to Randel), Cervantes' remarks about his *Galatea* allude to another familiar attribute: *invención*. We have considered this word to a limited extent in our exploration of his attitude on originality, and many critics have explicated its use in a number of ways. Here I should like to examine it once more, but from a different angle. Let us look at the context in which it appears when he writes of *La Galatea*.

In the scrutiny of Don Quixote's library, the book is described as having "some good *invención*; it proposes something, and doesn't conclude anything: it is necessary to await the promised second part; perhaps with amendment it will gain the clemency that now is denied it." It is tempting to accept the curate as Cervantes' spokesman here, particularly in view of his declaration that he has been a great friend of Cervantes for many years. But we must recall our discussion in Chapter 1. Though an avid reader, the priest is scarcely one to echo the literary sensibilities of Cervantes. If he finds the *Curioso impertinente* good, he nonetheless criticizes the very kind of daring we are discussing here, namely, the departure from conventional conduct. What the priest is expressing here is precisely what could be expected of someone who represents norms, standard behavior, adherence to precepts, and, as his conversation with the canon reveals, a desire not to rock the boat. Accordingly, he assumes that the sequel will reveal *amendment*!

Although it is dangerous to see the curate as Cervantes' spokesman, we may nevertheless see in the word *invención* a favorite quality that Cervantes frequently attributes to his works. But what does it mean here? Putnam, for instance, translates the line in question as "good plot." On the other hand, Cohen renders it "clever ideas." Though less accurate technically, Cohen's insightful version reflects the germ of Cervantes' meaning.

In the prologue to *La Galatea*, Cervantes asks the reader to overlook any objections that might be made "en la invención y en la disposición." Now, these two words, *invención* and *disposición*, are not idly chosen. We find them over and over again in treatises on rhetoric and dialectic. Classical thinking divided rhetoric into five faculties: "invention (the logical argument), disposition (the arrangement of the parts), style, memory, and delivery." By the Renaissance, there had been

> ... established a link between rhetoric and poetic that was to persist through the Renaissance and beyond. ... At the same time, as the Ciceronian parts of "invention, disposition, and elocution" had been extended to all forms of composition, a common ground was seen for poetic and rhetoric. ... *Elocutio* provided a basis for joining poetic and rhetoric on the level of language; the relationship was extended, through *inventio* and *dispositio*, to the whole of the two arts.[10]

In Spain we discover Francisco Sánchez (1523-1601), known as *El Brocense* (and praised by Cervantes in *La Galatea* and the *Viaje del Parnaso*), defining our key words as follows: "*Invención*... finds the arguments to explain the topic under consideration," and "*disposición* is the appropriate placement of what has been found."[11] Another contemporary (and friend of Lope de Vega), Ximénez Patón, declared that rhetoric had borrowed *invención* and *disposición* from dialectic.[12]

It is true that "invention," when applied to literature, was associated with plot. But it was not synonymous with making up a story. As El Brocense's definition makes clear, invention had to do with the discovery of appropriate elements of the topic. Stated in a literary context, as Robortello interpreted Aristotle's *Poetics*: "In so far as a poet uses a true plot, he does not invent, and hence his work resembles the activity of a historian; his truly poetic activity... bears upon elements other than the plot."[13] It follows, then, that when Cervantes expresses his satisfaction with the *buena invención* of *La Galatea*, what he claims is not that he has created a good plot, as Putnam would have it, but that he has given evidence of "clever ideas," to use Cohen's words, or, more to the point, good ideas appropriate to that plot. It is the appropriateness (which, in Cervantes' writings, is better interpreted as purposiveness) of the elements selected (or "discovered," to use the term of the rhetoricians) that amounts to what the literary preceptists designate proper imitation.

The problematic concepts of invention and imitation are frequent concerns of literary criticism, as we saw in Chapter 2. The prologue to *La Galatea*, however, alludes to a second element: disposition. As the word suggests, and as all rhetorical definitions agree, this aspect has to do with the placement or arrangement of the matters that invention has "discovered." Again, we should qualify the arrangement by seeking its appropriateness. And, of course, what is appropriate for Cervantes is what is apposite to his purpose.

His purpose in *La Galatea*, he tells us in its prologue, is to please. Once more we recognize a term from literary precepts: To please, to give pleasure, is one-half of the Horatian maxim of pleasure and profit, and we find it in the very sentence in which the rhetorical terms *invención* and *disposición* are used. Failings found in these two aspects, says Cervantes, should be excused by the reader's *discreción* and by the author's desire to please. Should he not succeed, Cervantes promises future works of greater pleasure and artifice. Although he does make mention of profit in this prologue, the reference is to the utility of the study of poetry, not to the fruits of the reading of his book. The stated purpose of *La Galatea* is to provide entertainment. Years later, in the scrutiny of Don Quixote's library, the priest will declare that pastoral novels, among which is *La Galatea*, are simply books of entertainment.[14]

So the invention, which is to say the selection of the topics to be

considered, and the disposition, by which is meant the arrangement of
the constituent parts, serve a clearly stated purpose: to please, to provide
entertainment. Much has been said, in this book as well as in numerous
other studies, about the invention of Cervantes' plots. Here we shall
concern ourselves with the disposition or arrangement that he hopes will
please.

In the fourth book of *La Galatea*, there occurs a debate between Lenio
and Tirsi, the former arguing that love's effects are harmful, and the
latter taking the opposing position. We shall have occasion to deal with
Lenio's views in our discussion of the faculties of the soul in Chapter 5.
Here I shall discuss not the merits of Lenio's posture but its function as
an analogue of the matters just introduced.

Seen in the context of pastoral literature, the debate is properly read
as part of conventional *cuestión de amor* dialectic.[15] I should like to suggest
a new and, no doubt, controversial perspective: I propose that we view
Lenio, our disenamored poet, as a spokesman for Cervantes. My proposition is controversial not only because the equation of a character and
the author is always a precarious inference (and I have argued against
such identifications in the cases of the curate and the canon) but because
we know that Lauso, another character in *La Galatea*, bears Cervantes'
own pseudonym.[16] I must emphasize that I am not suggesting Lenio as
Cervantes' alter ego. I simply posit that in Lenio's world view, as voiced
in the novel, we may recognize the perspective of his creator.

To some extent it is possible to defend my thesis by means of the
conventional debate itself. Not only does Cervantes frequently accuse
love of upsetting the proper balance of the soul's faculties, but his works
generally portray victims of love's power in accordance with the de-
nunciations made by Lenio in his diatribe. Even Don Quixote's madness
has been attributed to his having "love – often simply sex – on the
brain."[17] The argument seems to become moot when we recall that Lenio
ultimately yields to love's might. But I suggest that love's triumph, or,
from a different perspective, Lenio's defeat, serves to underscore my
proposition. Let us begin at the beginning.

The disenamored shepherd is almost as much a contradiction in terms
for pastoral literature as the disenamored knight is for the literature of
chivalry. If in the end Lenio succumbs to love, his introduction as es-
chewing it suggests an individual at odds with the conventions of his
circumstances. One of these conventions, of course, is that the shepherds
who populate these books are poets. That he fails in his purpose may
make him the first of those in "Cervantes's gallery of authors who have
failed."[18] But it is not necessary to pursue the theme of love, no matter
how central it is to the plot. Let us, as a first step, simply acknowledge

that in this matter Lenio stands apart from convention, and ultimately is defeated by it.

The debate is initiated by Lenio's reaction to a poem by another shepherd. Now this poem is *not* about love. What prompts Lenio to praise it is that it is unlike the poems that he hears "at every step." The latter not only deal with love, as we might expect in the world of the pastoral; more significantly for us, such poems are "so badly arranged and intricate" ("tan mal dispuestos e intricados"). What is more, some are so difficult to grasp that even their authors could not understand them. We may attribute some of this objection to Cervantes' lifelong espousal of clarity in poetry, but it is important to see here a key word. What I have rendered as "arranged" is in the original *dispuestos*, the past participle of the verb *disponer*, which of course also gives us *disposición*. What Lenio objects to, then, in addition to the content, is the disposition of the conventional poems that he hears wherever he goes. In short, he deplores both their *invención* and their *disposición*.

Lenio introduces his response with the supposition that his audience must think him "daring" in view of his "little *ingenio* and less experience." Finding confidence, however, in the belief that some innate *ingenio* along with a bit of experience often will "discover new paths . . . , I should like to dare today to display in public the reasons that have moved me to oppose love." Do we hear in this preamble some of the phrases associated with the traditional affected modesty of prologues? Perhaps. I suggest that what has a familiar ring is the Cervantine phrasing I have commented on before. Not only does Lenio advert to daring and confidence (specifically with reference to publication in its most literal sense), as Cervantes does in the prologue to *La Galatea* itself; the allusion to the "little *ingenio*" finds its echo in the prologue to the 1605 *Don Quixote*, in which Cervantes apologizes to the reader for his "sterile and badly cultivated *ingenio*." And surely the reference to new paths presages Cervantes' claim, in the *Viaje del Parnaso*, to have opened the way with his novellas.

Tradition, partly in the guise of his opponent's "age, experience and customary studies," and no less in the expectation and desire of the other shepherds that the "disenamored opinion of Lenio not prevail,"[19] is Lenio's true adversary in the polemic. It bears noting that some of the audience, particularly some *caballeros*, that is, specifically *not* shepherds of the tradition, think that Lenio's presentation seems to reveal "a richer vein than a pastoral *ingenio*."[20]

This last point, the essence of which is repeated following Tirsi's rebuttal (and with reference to both debaters), is a familiar recourse. Even in a genre whose most conspicuous artifice is that of the literate shepherd, Cervantes feels the need to defer to the exigencies of verisimilitude. If the reader has difficulty accepting Sancho Panza's wisdom, either a surrogate author will voice that disbelief or the peasant's good sense will be attributed to the teachings of others. Here, in *La Galatea*, the logical argumentation of shepherds is similarly rationalized:

> If you knew . . . how the renowned Tirsi's upbringing was not among trees and forest groves . . . but in royal courts and well-known schools, you would not wonder at what he has said but at what he has failed to say. And although the disenamored Lenio, because of his humility, has confessed that the rusticity of his life can promise few tokens of *ingenio*, nonetheless I assure you that he spent his best years not keeping sheep in the hills, but on the banks of the clear Tormes, in worthy studies and clever conversations.

We should not let the concern for plausibility divert our attention from the characterization of Lenio. Unlike Tirsi, the representation of the accepted tradition, whose recitation serves simply to "confirm once more the reputation as clever that everyone thought him to enjoy," Lenio is presented yet again as the one who has prefaced his oration with pro-testations of humility and few guarantees of *ingenio*. He does not, I must repeat, represent an incarnation of Cervantes (the allusion to the river Tormes, which is to say, the University of Salamanca, is not an auto-biographical element, inasmuch as Cervantes had no university education that we know of). But he is, as I have suggested, an analogue of Cer-vantes, and so we should read these words not in a literal but in an analogical sense. The poet who opposes the accepted tradition and its disposition, and claims modestly not to provide much evidence of *ingenio*, nonetheless has spent his best years not idling among the flowers but in worthwhile preparation for the time when he "dares . . . to display in public" – that is, publish – his own efforts. Of course, as we know, he eventually succumbs to the pastoral fashion, but even then it is important to note his wording. Leaving to one side the expected confession of love's power (which we may interpret as the power of tradition), Lenio's sub-mission is yet another reiteration of the daring he shows in competing with the renowned Tirsi.[21] In short, the issue is not limited to the content of the debate but embraces as well the daring required to oppose the convention that Tirsi represents. That Lenio ultimately fails is a de-nouement familiar to readers of Cervantes. More specifically, such fail-ures typically embody conversion to an arena or perspective other than that originally espoused by the upstart. In some works this takes the form of a return to sanity; in others it is a return to society or a social milieu more acceptable to the individual's coterie; rarely, it manifests itself in the character's death. Here, in *La Galatea*, it is Lenio's fate to join his fellow shepherds in the pangs of love.

It bears remarking that at least four Cervantine characters are described as having "strange" motivations. Don Quixote, of course, "hit upon the strangest thought ever hit upon by a madman" (I, 1); Anselmo (*El curioso impertinente*) describes his own malady as "a desire so strange and out of ordinary usage" (I, 33); Tomás Rodaja (*El licenciado Vidriera*) suffers "the strangest madness of all the madnesses theretofore seen" (*Obras*, p. 880); the fourth is Lenio, whose aversion to love is described as "this strange condition that he had" (*Galatea*, Book I). Needless to say, the common element – what makes them strange – is their unconventionality. And it is this quality that they share with their creator: "I do not care to go along with the current of custom."

Nothing of all this needs to be viewed as any sort of heroic idealism. I do think it warranted to conclude, however, that whether he is writing of his own efforts to be daring or depicting the aberrant behavior of some of his characters, Cervantes evinces a penchant for experimentation, availing himself pragmatically of the conventions at his disposal. In Chapter 2 we saw that his originality reveals itself not in opposition to but within a tradition. It is in the reshaping of what is already at hand that he excels. Just so will Don Quixote make use of the materials in his library, accommodating their conventions to his own needs. Anselmo's impertinent curiosity is the logical extension – "insane" or "strange" as it may be in relation to accepted behavior – of love's concomitant, jealousy, and of the literal implications of the honor code. Tomás Rodaja's antisocial personality leads, again logically, to an existence removed from the flesh-and-blood society he so acerbically probes.[22] Finally (though really first chronologically), Lenio takes on its own terms the convention of the world into which he wanders by participating in a typical debate on the central question of that world, but stands it on its head by denying the validity of its premise and disposition. It is when the abstract realm of logic yields to empirical probing that the experiment leads to his capitulation. We understand, then, the curate's expectation that the sequel to *La Galatea* may be its amendment.

As we saw in Chapter 3, Cervantes recognizes that the reading of literature is contingent upon visual images formed in the mind of the reader. Accordingly, the disposition of the elements that conjure up those images bears upon his approach to the presentation of literature. Although terms like "disposition" and "invention" are proper to rhetoric and dialectic, we have seen that Cervantes has borrowed them for the prologue to his first published book, a work of imaginative literature. Though there is no way to document the connection, I believe that he saw a correspondence between the arrangement of the material and Aristotle's concern for visualization:

Watch these points, then, and also the perceptions that necessarily attend on the poetic art. We have spoken about them in our published discourses; anyhow, in constructing one's plots and working them out in language one should put them directly before one's eyes as much as possible. That way, seeing most vividly, as if he were actually getting close to the events as they happen, the poet can devise the appropriate "business" and discrepancies are least likely to escape his notice.[23]

Gerald F. Else, whose translation I have used here, comments that Aristotle "must refer to perceptions of a different order from the visual quality of a mask or a costume: some kind of visual effect *inherent* in the nature of poetry."[24] Leon Golden translates the final sentence as follows: "For by visualizing the events as distinctly as he can, just as if he were present at their actual occurrence, he will discover what is fitting for his purpose, and there will be the least chance of incongruities escaping his notice."[25] Although the text clearly states that the poet should visualize his plot as if he were seeing the events himself, an interesting variation occurs in Valentín García Yebra's commentary to his trilingual edition: The poet should put himself in the place *of the spectator.*[26]

To disregard this Aristotelian prescription because it refers to drama, particularly to tragedy, would not be germane, inasmuch as dicta from the *Poetics* served as bases for literary theory generally throughout the sixteenth and seventeenth centuries (witness the concerns for imitation, verisimilitude, etc., in other discussions). As a matter of fact, an analogy with theater was very likely an influential factor in Cervantes' understanding of his art. In whatever Renaissance translation the *Poetics* came to Cervantes, I suggest that its perspective, together with his own frequently expressed lifelong attraction to the theater, contributed to the way in which he envisaged his relationship with his readers. Our discussion in Chapter 3 showed us two aspects of this concern: his understanding of the reading process as a kind of seeing, and his interest in the variegated optical illusions that the writer can plausibly create. A third manifestation of a theatrically oriented approach to his fiction is the conjuring function of so many of his surrogate authors, whom we may frequently picture as pointing or pointing out (witness Maese Pedro's presentation of his puppet show). A related artifice is the not inconsiderable number of authorial voices that ask us or the fictional characters to look, to see, to listen.

Underlying these matters – the substance, as it were – is Cervantes' concern for the reader's visualization of the plot. If he did not quite think that this quality was inherent in the nature of the medium, to paraphrase Else's interpretation of Aristotle, he no doubt understood that the arrangement of his words would shape the visual image conveyed to the reader.

In accordance with the *in medias res* convention, the opening lines of *La Galatea* plunge the reader into the midst of the shepherd Elicio's verse recitation. The narrator follows immediately with a geographical location, the banks of the Tajo, following which he provides some particulars of Elicio's love for Galatea. It is important to note that the narrator's very first words enable the reader to picture Elicio in a physical setting.

This preamble leads to the unfolding of the plot: "And so, one day . . . , finding himself in the midst of a delightful meadow, enticed by the solitude and by the murmur of a delightful brooklet that ran along the plain, taking a polished rebec out of his purse . . . " (Book I).[27] Before the shepherd starts to sing, then, the reader has a complete mental picture of the physical circumstances in which Elicio "finds himself one day." (The fact that the description is of a typical *locus amoenus* is but another instance of Cervantes' handling of a conventionalism.) Some seven stanzas into his recitation, Elicio breaks off because "there sounded to his right-hand side the cries of Erastro, who with his flock of goats was coming along toward the place where [Elicio] was."[28] Why, one might ask, would a reader be concerned to know whether the sounds were coming from the left-hand or the right-hand side? The answer must surely lie in Cervantes' desire to implant in the reader's mind a picture as graphic as that provided by stage directions.

A paragraph later Erastro is still described as "coming" (*venía*), accompanied now by his mastiffs, who, being individually called by their names, "were coming along toward him." What a few moments earlier had been only Erastro's cries are now, with greater proximity, identified as the calling of the dogs' names. It is following this sequence that the preterite tense is finally used to denote that Erastro has reached Elicio: "In this manner Erastro arrived [*llegó*] where he was pleasantly received by Elicio." The reader, guided by visual and acoustic clues, has been able to visualize the action of the scene from Elicio's presence in the meadow to the sounds from his right, the approach of Erastro with his goats, and finally the arrival of the dogs, whose names can now be identified. (The dogs, we are told, guard Erastro's sheep, so that the latter, not clearly discernible from afar, subsequently are identified as another constituent of the group that has arrived. If in our study of illusions we appreciated Cervantes' handling of objects perceived from a distance, here we may admire his treatment of the matter with respect to the reader, who is dealt with in accordance with Aristotle's prescription.)

Following a verse dialogue sung by both shepherds, the narrator tells us:

Erastro was already preparing to proceed with his song when they heard a not small clamor and noise along a dense hillock that was at their backs; and both of them getting up on their feet to see what it was, they saw that from the forest a shepherd came running out with the greatest of speed, with a bare knife in his hand and the color of his face gone from him; and that behind him there came another fleet shepherd who in a few strides overtook the first one, and grabbing him by the collar of his jacket, he raised his arm as high in the air as he could and ensconced a sharp, unsheathed dagger that he carried twice into his body. . . . And this was done with such speed that Elicio and Erastro had no time to impede him, for they arrived just as the wounded shepherd was already breathing his last.[29]

John T. Cull believes that this passage suggests how deceptive appearances are when things are seen from a distance. He makes some perceptive remarks:

The abrupt change of focus of the action is announced with a noise. The difference between near and far is stylistically suggested by the use of the diminutive (hillock) and the litotes (not small) to indicate the diminution of what is distant, and the retardation of the narrative rhythm, focusing on concrete details (sharp, unsheathed dagger) to evoke immediate distance. Nevertheless, the use of the euphemism "ensconced" plants a doubt about the true nature of the action, although it may be a faithful representation, given the perspective of the observers.[30]

In view of our examination of Cervantes' method of portraying the illusions created by the deceptiveness of appearances, I submit that here is no such situation. The procedure used in this scene does depict masterfully, as Cull details, the perspectives required for the representation of the near and the far. But I would prefer to label the use of "ensconced" (*escondió* in the original) not euphemism but metaphor. Furthermore, I prefer to accept the implications of Cull's own concession: It *is* a faithful representation of what the observers saw, and hence of what Cervantes wants the reader to see. The distance from which Elicio and Erastro and the reader see the action makes it improper for the narrator to tell us that the dagger entered the body. What the narrator narrates is what the reader is expected to *see*, and since the reader's perspective here is that of Elicio and Erastro, the only thing that can be seen (not inferred) is the disappearance of the weapon into the body or, as our narrator would have it, its ensconcement. The scene in question should as well be compared to the one previously examined. The rapidity of the movement here, in contrast with the studied approach in the earlier passage, reveals Cervantes' control of our visualization of the action.

In the foregoing discussion it has been possible to use the analogy of a theatrical presentation to correspond to Cervantes' art of conveying to the reader a scenic image of the events, physical setting, and relative distances involved in a static focal point. What follows can best be compared to a modern film. Although the analogy of a revolving stage might seem less of an anachronism, I am describing not a physical reenactment – a "real" play with scenery, actors, voices, and sound effects – but the mental transmission, via words on paper, of images from author to reader.

The reader of *La Galatea* sees "the three shepherds [Elicio, Erastro, and Lisandro] with their gentle flock of sheep coming down along a ravine, [and] as they went up a slope they heard the sound of a mellow flute, which was then recognized by Elicio and Erastro as being Galatea playing it. And it was not long before some sheep were to be seen along the peak of a hill and then, behind them, Galatea." We note once more the verisimilitude implicit in hearing the sound of the instrument before it is close enough to permit recognition of the person playing it. And although it does not take long, some amount of time is required before the sheep are seen, and still a bit longer before Galatea herself comes into view. Of course, this is the sort of scene we are now familiar with, and in fact, such scenes will be so frequent that there is no need to make further reference to them. The scene here continues as Galatea, seeing her flock joining that of the shepherds, "called her gentle yearling, which the rest of the sheep followed, and set her on a path in a different direction from that which the shepherds were taking." Elicio laments Galatea's failure to reciprocate his love, whereupon Erastro, "seeing that Galatea was moving on and leaving them," says to her: "Where are you going or from whom are you fleeing, beautiful Galatea? If it is from us, who adore you, that you are moving away . . . "[31]

Our field of view has remained constant: We have seen the shepherds coming down, have heard the flute, have seen Galatea's sheep and Galatea herself approach, and finally, thanks to the words of the narrator and Erastro, have visualized Galatea's continuous moving off into the distance. It is as Erastro's words come to an end that our perspective begins to change: "Are you laughing at what I am saying, Galatea? Well, I am crying at what you are doing." The narrator continues:

Galatea was unable to answer Erastro, because she was guiding her flock toward the brook of the Palms, and lowering her head from afar as a sign of farewell, she left [the shepherds] and, when she was alone, while she was nearing the place where she thought her friend Florisa would be . . . she sang. . . . Galatea's concluding the song and her reaching where Florisa was occurred simultaneously.

[While they occupied themselves picking flowers] they saw a shepherdess suddenly coming down along the brook . . . and they saw that she was little by little coming toward where they were; and although they were quite close, she was coming along so absorbed in and transported by her thoughts that she never saw them until they cared to show themselves.[32]

In a sort of mental motion picture, our minds have shifted the field of vision in accordance with the narration. Having visualized the setting from the perspective of the shepherds, we are now guided to a new vantage point as we envision the scene from the perspective of Galatea. Along with her, we leave the shepherds behind, join her friend, and visualize the ensuing events (the arrival of the new shepherdess) within the framework of this new field of vision. The change from one setting to another is scarcely a novelty; what merits our appreciation is the transition. Very much in the manner of a modern movie camera, Cervantes has allowed our minds to see the scene shift from one vantage point to another and, concurrently, to shift the focal point of our interest.

Movement may be multidirectional. Silerio's tale in Book II of *La Galatea* is, like so many of the pastoral novel's narrations, related during the wanderings of the interlocutors. (We quickly become accustomed to reading that a song or tale reaches its conclusion concurrently with the end of a journey or that a story is halted because the shepherds have reached their destination.) The story in question begins with Silerio's promise to inform the shepherds of his misfortunes as best he can "along the way." The shepherds consider this a good idea, and so, "putting him in the middle, with leisurely strides they resumed the path to the village, whereupon [Silerio] began the tale of his miseries." Throughout the narration, therefore, we sense a movement in the direction of the village. Sometime later, Silerio stops:

Silerio would have gone ahead with his tale, had he not been interrupted by the sound of many flutes and well-tuned pipes heard at their backs, and, turning their heads, they saw coming toward them up to a dozen graceful shepherds arranged in double file, and in the middle there came a comely shepherd. . . . He carried a staff in one hand, and with a solemn pace he moved along little by little, and the rest of the shepherds [accompanying him were] walking with the same measured pace and all of them playing their instruments. . . . As soon as Elicio saw them, he knew the shepherd in the middle to be Daranio, and the rest to be neighbors who wanted to be at the wedding [and] were heading for the village in the same

manner.... And at this point the happy crowd of shepherds arrived
... and renewing the music and renewing the gladness, they once
more resumed their original path, and now that they were reaching
the village together, there reached their ears the sound of the
disenamored Lenio's flute.... And as soon as Lenio saw and recognized them, without interrupting his mellow song, he came
toward them singing.[33]

Shortly thereafter: "Lenio would have replied, were it not for the fact
that they saw the beautiful Galatea and the clever shepherdesses Florisa
and Teolinda coming toward where they were.... They [the three she-
pherdesses] arrived and were happily greeted by the shepherds." There
follows a song by Erastro; then "Erastro finished his song and the path
leading to the village came to an end," whereupon Book II itself ends.[34]
Let us examine the foregoing sequence with some care.

The reader is first presented with the measured strides of the shepherds
on their way to the village, Silerio in their center narrating his tale. It is
from behind them that they hear the sound of musical instruments, and
as they literally turn their heads to see the second group of shepherds
approaching double file, the reader's vision turns figuratively in a corresponding direction. We may appreciate a certain symmetry: In the
group nearby, Silerio occupies the center position as his listeners – including us – focus attention (the shepherds' ears and our mind's eye) on
him and his tale. The approaching group has placed Daranio in a corresponding position, because of the central function of his role as bride-
groom. As the two groups merge (and we note once more that the sound
from the distance, complete with "stage directions" for our visualization,
precedes the recognition of those coming from afar), the narration of
past events during the journey to the wedding is subsumed by the immediate object of the journey: Daranio's wedding. As the groups move
on together, a new sound is heard, closer to the village: Lenio's flute.
The reader's inner eye is now drawn in that direction, as the narrator
tells us that Lenio first sees, then recognizes, the groups on whom we
have been focusing, whereupon he comes toward that focal point, bringing together the two directions of movement. Yet another movement
from afar brings toward us the three shepherdesses; their actual arrival
follows, and, Erastro's subsequent song having reached its end, the journey to the village is brought to its conclusion, as is Book II.

Although we have here no left or right indications, we do have one
clear reference to "backstage" ("at their backs"). The references to measured and solemn paces, the landmark of the town toward which the
motion is directed, the relative positions from which sounds emanate –
all permit the reader to visualize, in the manner of a spectator, the move-

ments and the physical relationships among the characters. It is another example of Cervantes' concern for the spatial disposition of the images received by the reader.

The treatment of sounds here is more than an ancillary facet of the disposition. Cervantes understands that sounds as well as sights convey to the mind the information necessary to picture objects and events. Consider the following from Book IV of *La Galatea*:

> When [Galatea and Florisa] were ready to turn around and leave [Teolinda], they saw four men on horseback and a few on foot crossing a gorge that was a bit away from the path where they were, and whom they immediately recognized as hunters by their dress and the hawks and dogs they brought along. And watching them attentively to see whether they knew them, they saw two shepherdesses . . . coming out from some dense shrubs that were near the gorge. They had their faces covered with their white kerchiefs, and, one of them raising her voice, she asked the hunters to stop, which they did, and both of [the shepherdesses] going up to one of [the hunters], who in his appearance and bearing seemed to be their leader, they took hold of the reins of his horse and spent a bit of time talking with him, without [our] three shepherdesses being able to hear a word of what they were saying, because of the distance from the place, which prevented it. They saw only that in the short time that they spoke with him the gentleman dismounted, and having – insofar as could be judged – ordered his companions to turn back . . . , he took the two shepherdesses by the hand and little by little began to accompany them right into a dense wood that was there, all of which, seen by . . . Galatea, Florisa, and Teolinda, determined them to see, if they could, who the disguised shepherdesses and the gentleman taking them were.[35]

In addition to a number of now-familiar aspects of Cervantes' treatment of such descriptions, we note here a fidelity to detail that lets us, along with the three shepherdesses, observe and share in the conclusions reached. (We need to bear in mind that we are not permitted any insight beyond what is observable by the three women.) We know on what basis they judged the men to be hunters; we know that it is necessary to concentrate on the latter's features so that recognition can occur; we know the physical surroundings as well as if we ourselves had undertaken a panoramic exploration; we even accept the shepherdesses' reasoning about why one of the hunters seems to be the superior of the rest, an inference borne out by the subsequent deduction that he has instructed the others to depart. What is striking in this passage is the acoustic verisimilitude.

The detail provided at the beginning regarding the gorge's being "a bit away" from where the three women are leads to the necessity of their being unable to distinguish the words exchanged by the hunters and the newly arrived shepherdesses. The fact that one of the latter has to raise her voice to ask the hunters to stop accounts for our shepherdesses' (and our) being able to understand that request. Otherwise, it is made emphatically clear that the distance prevents them (and us) from making out a single word of what the others say. We may infer what is transpiring, but the narrator is very explicit: Our deduction is limited to what can reasonably be judged from such a distance.

In the paragraph just concluded I have spoken of necessity and requirement. It bears remarking that the demands made by distance are created for this scene by Cervantes, a good example of *invención*. It would have been possible to have the narrator tell us what transpires between the hunters and the girls who hail them. (In the long run, we do learn this, but only after Galatea and her friends get close enough to overhear.) The passage we have just read and examined is, with respect to the exigencies of the plot, superfluous. But insofar as invention means the finding of the appropriate elements, and disposition refers to their apposite arrangement, the passage substantiates the connection between these matters and the requirements of verisimilitude, in addition to satisfying the Aristotelian prescription for visualization. Beyond the simple invention of a plot, Cervantes seeks to expand the dimensions imposed by the printed page by experimenting with perspectives that allow the reader's mind to function as it would if it shared the fictive circumambience.

If *La Galatea* does not offer conclusions, the curate is nonetheless correct in his observation that it proposes something. It is a proposition, an experiment. Like other Cervantine "inventions," its point of departure is an established convention. I have not set out to provide its explication. Rather, I have chosen one aspect of Cervantes' "daring" experimentation. His concern is reflected in the title of this chapter: the illusion of reality.

In his first major work, Cervantes, among many other things, experiments with the manner of conveying not merely the story line and the psychology of his characters but the graphic images required for a proper visualization of the plot. Since the reader is not provided with actual pictures or sounds, it is a challenge to the artist as writer to enable his reader to see, and frequently to hear, the physical environment in which the plot takes place.

That such concerns would always remain with Cervantes may be seen by taking as an instance a sentence depicting Don Quixote's confrontation with the Benedictine friars: "He placed himself in the middle of the road along which the friars were coming and, *when they came close enough so that it seemed to him that they could hear what he said*, he said in a loud voice..." (I, 8). The inclusion of the portion that I have italicized is not, it might be argued, essential to the plot. It is, however, essential to Cervantes' craft. The preoccupation with the reader's visualization of the spatial relationships that correspond to the verisimilar exigencies of the circumstances is one of the ingredients of the substance of Cervantes.

In an effort to demonstrate Cervantes' more masterful manipulation of point of view in 1615, Allen has compared a scene from Camacho's wedding from the *Don Quixote* of that year with the description of Daranio's wedding in *La Galatea*. In the latter, the account

> ... proceeds through a straightforward omniscient description of the decorations and the music, the lament of the rejected Mireno, the large number of guests and the sumptuous feast, and the fine wedding attire of the bride and groom. The third-person objective account is varied only by the interjection of [a dialogue, the reading of some verses, and the praise of Galatea's beauty].[36]

Given the selection, Allen's remarks cannot be faulted. That the passage is not representative of many other descriptions in *La Galatea* is patent to the readers of this chapter. What Allen goes on to say of *Don Quixote*, however, is of great interest:

> In contrast to the parallel presentation of the wedding in *La Galatea*, Cervantes makes us see it through the eyes of his characters, deepening our involvement with and understanding of *them* at the same time that he advances his narrative. *Events* become *experiences*, and therein lies the modernity of the passage. . . . Both at the same party, Sancho counts wineskins and Don Quixote memorizes verses, and their eyes are ours. This is the world of the modern novel.[37]

The emphasis on the words "events" and "experiences" was placed there by Allen; I have added the italics to the word "them," for herein lies the difference, or the modernity, to use Allen's term. We have seen through the eyes of characters before, not only in *La Galatea* but in works antedating Cervantes. What finally occurs in *Don Quixote*, as Allen rightly makes clear, is that the visualization is not circumscribed solely by the physical limitations that we have discussed heretofore. Rather, the image conveyed to the reader is defined by the psychology of the fictive viewer. It bears remarking that the description from the 1615 *Don Quixote*, in which each character sees those objects and actions that are consistent with his psychology, is distinct from what is typical of the 1605 volume, in which they focus on the same things but see them differently (helmet–

basin, armies–sheep, etc.). What is more, the several surrogate authors, like the Cervantine characters that they must ultimately be recognized as being, similarly present the "true history" through the eyes of the observer. It is when the translator, for instance, refuses to recount the author's description of Don Diego de Miranda's house, or refuses to believe the speeches attributed to Sancho, that this treatment reaches beyond the baroque and well into the future of imaginative literature. Even so do we today question the points of view of the historians themselves. The fruits of Cervantes' daring to experiment with the disposition of his fictional world have ripened to provide the basis for – the substance of – the epistemological inquiries of what once was perceived primarily as a funny book.

Chapter 5

The faculties of the soul

> *The prophet David... tells us... three things that certain*
> *learned philosophers tell us are in the soul and are properties*
> *of it, and they are these: intellect, will, and memory.*
>   – Juan Ruiz, Libro de buen amor

Intellectum tibi dabo, et instruam te in via hac, qua gradieris: firmabo super te oculos meos. So reads the eighth verse of the Thirty-first Psalm (Vulgate), in which Juan Ruiz, archpriest of Hita, claims to discern the three faculties of the soul enumerated in the epigraph to this chapter.[1] We may accuse him of reading too much into the words of King David – "I will instruct thee and teach thee in the way thou shalt go. I will guide thee with mine eye" (Psalm 32 of the King James version) – but he does go on to make the point that will provide the substance of this chapter: "And when the soul with good intellect and goodwill and with good memory chooses and loves good love, which is the love of God, and places it in the cella of memory so that it may remember it, [it] leads the body to do good deeds, through which man attains salvation."[2]

    Commenting on this passage, Otis H. Green observes that *intellectum* here serves "as one of the three faculties of the soul, the *entendimiento* or reasoning power; the other faculties being the *memoria*, i.e., the faculty that integrates the personality, and the *voluntad* (will), the appetitive faculty that reaches out and embraces the good which the reason has made apprehensible."[3] Although Cervantes was not familiar with Juan Ruiz, he not only inherited the understanding of the metaphorical representation of the soul as comprising three faculties, as defined and qualified by the archpriest, but as we shall see, he made use of the triad in contexts not unrelated to that of the fourteenth-century work. It is significant that in the latter, all of this righteous talk about the soul's faculties serves to introduce not a treatise on the love of God (although that is what the words deal with) but an *ars amandi*. This ambivalence is important for us here because it illustrates the potential ambiguity of the faculties, for their inherent ambivalence allows both a virtuous and a self-serving interpretation. For instance, Green cites a fifteenth-century work to the effect that "*voluntad*, the most active of the three faculties, could also be translated *desire* and frequently meant *love*...: '*Voluntas voluntad* is the desire for that which we have not obtained. And *voluntad* is delight (good or bad) in what we have obtained."[4] Whether this faculty is perceived as desire or whether it adheres to the definition given previously – "the appetitive faculty that reaches out and embraces the good which the reason has made apprehensible" – becomes a concern for moralists as well as a source of literary conflict and may determine the difference between serious intent and burlesque farce, as we shall see.

If the reference to the Bible as a source for the triad seems contrived in the passage from the *Libro de buen amor*, the reference to "doctores philósophos" or "learned philosophers" suggests an allusion to Aristotle, known antonomastically as "the Philosopher." Although Aristotle was not the formulator of the triad, he did play an important role in leading the way. Moreover, Cervantes was most probably under the impression that the metaphor of the soul as composed of the three faculties of intellect, memory, and will did originate with Aristotle: Cervantes' immediate source was El Pinciano, who, in turn, thought Aristotle to have stated the equation. In his *Philosophía antigua poética*, published in 1596, El Pinciano (the name by which the Aristotelian theorist Alonso López Pinciano was known) wrote that the faculties "are three: intellect, memory and will . . . according to the Philosopher in his *Ethics*."[5] El Pinciano's work had a profound influence upon Cervantes, as revealed in a number of ways that are significant for literary theory.[6] To my knowledge, no study has explored the importance of the three faculties in Cervantes' works or offered more than a passing reference to the commonplace of the triad.[7]

Although it is true that Aristotle dealt at length with what he termed faculties or potentialities of the soul, particularly in the *Nicomachean Ethics* and *De Anima*, the triad specified by El Pinciano never appeared as a discrete configuration of Aristotle's depiction of the human soul. There was, however, one point at which he did come tantalizingly close to the three faculties that will engage our interest in this chapter: In the *Ethics* he said that "there are three elements in the soul which control action and the attainment of truth: namely, Sensation, Intellect, and Desire." Sensation was immediately set aside, because it "never originates action, as is shown by the fact that animals have sensation but are not capable of action."[8] H. Rackham clarifies that Aristotle meant "rational action, conduct. The movements of animals, Aristotle appears to think, are mere reactions to the stimuli of sensation."[9] With respect to the other two, Aristotle wrote:

> Pursuit and avoidance in the sphere of Desire correspond to affirmation and denial in the sphere of the Intellect. Hence inasmuch as moral virtue is a disposition of the mind in regard to choice, and choice is deliberate desire, it follows that, if the choice is to be good,

both the principle must be true and the desire right, and that desire must pursue the same things as principle affirms.[10]

The ethical concern for the nature of desire, so carefully delineated here by Aristotle, presaged what would later become a preoccupation of moralists (as well as subject matter for burlesque), namely a differentiation between moral will – which is really what is defined here – and self-serving, often lustful, appetitive desire. This point was explicated elsewhere in the *Ethics* when Aristotle discussed the portion of the soul that is "the seat of the appetites and of desire in general [and] does in a sense participate in [the rational] principle, as being amenable and obedient to it."[11] Desire is, accordingly, subordinate to reason or intellect, a matter that will later be a point of controversy.

It may be helpful to think of this kind of soul – the material soul, as Aristotle referred to it – as a concept somewhat akin to the mind, though the two terms are not equivalent. Unlike Plato, who divided the soul into parts or properties, Aristotle analyzed its functions:

Aristotle fell back upon the notion of "faculties" or capacities: each sense organ has a specific capacity to elicit its proper object from a near chaos of physical impingements, and by extension the material soul, as a sort of organ, is endowed with faculties that allow it to perform its inductive functions properly. These faculties – common sense, imagination, reason, and memory in the medieval scheme (although Aristotle himself lodged all memorative functions in the faculty of the imagination) – work together.[12]

Although it was Aristotle's perspective that led to the understanding of the faculties, Plato had earlier suggested an analogy that would eventually reappear in Christian terms. Plato described a tripartite soul – intellect, emotion, desire – based on human behavior: We "learn with one part of ourselves, feel anger with another, and with yet a third desire the pleasures of nutrition and generation and their kind."[13] This division, in turn, corresponds to the "three kinds of people, the [rational], the irascible or spirited, and the [appetitive]. All men have appetites, some have both appetites and irascibility and a few have these two faculties plus reason. It is their reason which keeps the other faculties under control."[14] This attempt to relate the soul's properties to man's nature by finding corresponding divisions would emerge anew in Saint Augustine's formulation of the soul's faculties as corresponding to man's creation in the image of the Trinity.

It is not necessary to be a philosopher or a theologian in order to understand that human beings have an ability to reason and a capability for volition. The faculties of intellect and will are readily observable in human behavior, particularly as distinctive characteristics of the species. Memory, on the other hand, is not as directly observable, and one tends to see its workings rather than to see it working. Whether it was on a par with the other faculties in the medieval scheme is, some say, an arguable point.[15]

Plotinus saw in the memory the potential for discriminating between the moral and appetitive levels of volition: "Only by memory does the embodied soul possess an image of itself. It is through desire for the lower that the soul enters into the body, and it is by desire for the higher that the soul can recall memory of its activity in the intellectual sphere and aspire eventually to forget all the lower... in contemplation of the divine."[16] This concern would also emerge once more in the Christian era, in a way best expressed by Bonaventure:

> The cause is that our soul, distracted by the tasks and cares of daily life, does not penetrate into its own secret place with the aid of the memory; that blinded by the vain images of worldly things, it does not reflect on its own essence with the aid of the intellect; and that, seduced by the attractions of concupiscence, it does not return to the true self with the desire [i.e., the will] to enjoy the inner peace and gladness of the spirit.[17]

Bonaventure's pessimism regarding human failure to measure up to the possibilities inherent in the soul's faculties is, as one might expect, the very stuff of many a literary work. In fact, we find a paraphrase in *La Galatea*: "If the soul finds itself tied up in the subtle net of love... the *memoria* serves only as treasurer and keeper of the object the eyes beheld, and the *entendimiento* [occupies itself] in scrutinizing and getting to know the worth of the one it loves well, and the *voluntad* [serves to] allow that *memoria* and *entendimiento* do not occupy themselves with anything else" (Book II).

The triad, though immediately traceable to El Pinciano's attribution to Aristotle, has its most explicit roots in Saint Augustine's attempt to find analogies in the human circumstance corresponding to man's creation in the image of a triune God: "Since these three, the memory, the understanding, and the will, are, therefore, not three lives but one life, not three minds but one mind, it follows that they are certainly not three substances, but one substance... Therefore, these three are one in that they are one life, one mind, and one essence."[18] (Because in Spanish the word *entendimiento* is normally used in this context and may be rendered as "understanding" or "intellect," and because the English word "will" so often creates awkward sentences when used as a noun, I shall prefer the three Spanish words – *memoria*, *entendimiento*, and *voluntad* – in this chapter.)

By Cervantes' time it was possible to assume a familiarity with the metaphor of the soul as three faculties, even in popular genres like the farcical one-act play known as the *entremés*. In the anonymous (though sometimes attributed to Cervantes) *Los habladores*, we hear that "quien tiene alma tiene potencias. Tres son las potencias del alma: memoria, voluntad y entendimiento" ("whoever has a soul has faculties. The faculties of the soul are three: *memoria*, *voluntad* and *entendimiento*").[19] Moreover, to judge by the kinds of people who utter such phrases in *La guarda cuidadosa*, Cervantes considered the identification of the three elements as faculties of the soul to be a commonplace. The assistant sexton in this play has written a *cédula de matrimonio* publicly attesting to his love for Cristina, presenting as witnesses his heart and soul, that is, "mi corazón, mi entendimiento, mi voluntad y mi memoria." The conversation proceeds to discuss the importance of *voluntad*, whereupon the soldier interjects: "If *voluntades* are taken into account, it's been thirty-nine days since . . . I gave mine to Cristina, together with all the attachments to my three faculties."[20] Given this dialogue between a "miserable sexton" (p. 129) and a "tattered lay soldier" (p. 145), as well as the popular nature of the genre in which it is heard, we may safely conclude that Cervantes expected the topos to be readily recognized and understood.

It is, of course, on such ready comprehension that the pertinence of any topos relies. That the metaphor under discussion was familiar to Cervantes' contemporaries at all social and intellectual levels is the point of Eugenio Asensio's note to the opening passage of *El retablo de las maravillas*: "This mannered way of speaking seemed less so to the people of the time who, since catechism, knew the three faculties of the soul" (p. 169n).[21] The passage in question is Chirinos' promise to bear in mind Chanfalla's advice concerning their hoaxes: "For I have as much *memoria* as *entendimiento*, to which is joined a *voluntad* to succeed in pleasing you that exceeds the rest of the faculties" (p. 169).[22]

The references to the faculties of the soul in the two *entremeses* just cited are similar in character, assume an audience familiar with the allusion, seem to express no more than the extent to which a given character dedicates herself or himself to a particular purpose, and share a farcical context. A close reading, however, reveals one distinction. Whereas in *La guarda cuidadosa* the three faculties are joined together, the assertion by Chirinos allows *voluntad* to exceed the other faculties. The meaning here is evident: *Voluntad* is simply a desire to please her companion and it is not matched by her other faculties. This connotation of *voluntad* is in keeping with the burlesque context. It is significant, however, that one faculty may predominate. Moreover, the utilization of the metaphor in such contexts is testimony to the inversion of the values inherent in memory, intellect, and will. If this is evident in such a farcical context, the allusion to the faculties in more serious circumstances is, though sometimes less obvious, correspondingly more significant. Bearing in mind, then, that Cervantes could assume a familiarity with the topos and that an imbalance among the three faculties was not inconceivable, we may shed new light on some episodes in Cervantes' writings.

The foregoing pages have attempted to give a brief history of the metaphorical depiction of the human soul in terms of its functions, these being the three faculties or *potentiae* by which individuals strive or ought to strive to realize their potentialities. If Cervantes thought the concept originated with Aristotle because El Pinciano had so declared, this is not to suggest that Cervantes first heard of it through El Pinciano's work of 1596, although the attribution of the metaphor to the Greek philosopher undoubtedly provided an added measure of authority. The notion that the human soul comprised memory, will, and intellect was a commonplace of the age, which is to say not only that it was commonly known and figuratively accepted but that, like so many clichés and aphorisms, the equation could readily convey to nearly everyone of the time a kind of shorthand representation of an otherwise complex ontological question. It is, I suspect, the very commonness of the topos that has led scholars to dismiss it as no more than an allusion worthy of an occasional footnote. As I intend to show in this chapter, the triad underlies much of Cervantes' portrayal of the human struggle for self-realization.

At least one author of the period devoted an entire, though brief, work to the subject: Fray Damián de Vegas, in his *Colloquy between a Soul and Its Three Faculties*, published in 1590. Because its content not only relates to but clarifies a number of matters to be addressed in this chapter (and because it is a relatively unknown work), I translate at some length.

The soul, unhappy at the poor service rendered it by its constituent faculties, rebukes the latter, beginning with *entendimiento*:

> You see my flesh go unrestrained
> After the bestial appetite,
> You see of cursed love replete
> *Voluntad* go bolting forth,
> And you [*entendimiento*], who are sufficient
> To reduce them to the bounds
> Of reason, pursuing vice
> You throw yourself along with them?[23]

The soul's body, spurred by an unrestrained *voluntad* equivalent to an animal desire and therefore animated by an accursed love, leads to vice because *entendimiento*, the faculty that is capable of leading its sister fac-

ulties to reason, has itself behaved licentiously. The soul goes on to chide
entendimiento:

> They [your sister faculties] cannot well follow you
> If you don't go and guide them,
> For they have no other light
> Than that which you will give them,
> So that they must go where you go
> To delectation or to the cross.[24]

Again, then, the emphasis is placed upon *entendimiento*'s leading role in
the functions of the three faculties. This is, in fact, *memoria*'s excuse:

> For everything that he [*entendimiento*] understood
> That gave him pleasure, although it be
> Something vain, crude and ugly,
> He has it remembered by me;
> So subject [is he] to novelties
> That, despite me and to my woe
> Garret and storehouse he has made of me
> Of all his vanities.[25]

The abuse of *memoria* – clearly not the "good memory" of Juan Ruiz's
introduction – is accordingly pictured as the result of *entendimiento*'s delight in worldly vanities. (It is interesting to note in passing the context
in which we find novelties [*novedades*], a reflection of the concept as we
explored it in Chapter 2: The purpose of the memorative faculty is to
record the good, and its abuse may consist of an appetite for what is not
memorable, i.e., novelty.) *Memoria* asks of the soul:

> Is there anything more inhumane
> Than that you should like and permit
> That within me there should always be written
> The faults of our sister?[26]

As for *voluntad*, this faculty asks:

> Tell me, how often did we follow
> The body in its crudities,
> And how often to a thousand evils
> Did we go along after appetite?[27]

Finally, acknowledging that it must be used for good if it is to get along
with *entendimiento*, *voluntad* declares:

> I know well when I follow the good
> And also when the bad I follow;

> But in order to succeed with you [*entendimiento*]
> I have to be taken toward the good.[28]

The colloquy makes a number of important points for us. The very
composition of the argument – the soul in conversation with its three
faculties – reflects the Aristotelian view of the faculties as functions, in
contrast to the Platonic conception of them as parts. More directly, this
is a reflection of Saint Thomas Aquinas' belief "that there is a real distinction between the soul and its faculties, and between the faculties
themselves." Furthermore: "In the powers or faculties there is a certain
hierarchy."[29] Will Durant records that the "Franciscans, who sought God
by Augustine's mystic road of love, were shocked by Thomas' 'intel-
lectualism,' his exaltation of intellect above will, of understanding above
love." More specifically:

> Will or appetition is the faculty by which the soul or vital force
> moves toward that which the intellect conceives as good. Thomas,
> following Aristotle, defines the good as "that which is desirable."
> Beauty is a form of the good; it is that which pleases when seen.
> Why does it please? Through the proportion and harmony of parts
> in an organized whole. Intellect is subject to will in so far as desire
> can determine the direction of thought; but will is subject to the
> intellect in so far as our desires are determined by the way we
> conceive things . . . ; "the good as understood moves the will."
> Freedom lies not really in the will, which "is necessarily moved"
> by the understanding of the matter presented by the intellect, but
> in the judgment (*arbitrium*); therefore freedom varies directly with
> knowledge, reason, wisdom, with the capacity of the intellect to
> present a true picture of the situation to the will; only the wise are
> truly free. Intelligence is not only the best and highest, it is also
> the most powerful, of the faculties of the soul. . . . "The proper
> operation of man is to understand."[30]

With this background in mind, it is possible to discern in a number
of Cervantes' works plots whose substructures, as they might be termed,
present an imbalance of the soul's faculties. Sometimes this disequili-
brium is caused by immaturity; at other times an inordinate emphasis
on one faculty is the cause of the imbalance; on still other occasions the
discordance is, as Bonaventure had feared, the result of a moral inversion
of the faculties' proper function as potentialities of the soul (that is, the
result of behavior that is animated instead by the desires of the flesh, as
outlined in Damián de Vegas' colloquy).

La fuerza de la sangre, like so many of Cervantes' works, can be summarized briefly and explicated endlessly. The tale concerns the nocturnal

rape of Leocadia by Rodolfo, the consequent birth of the child Luisico, and the subsequent marriage of the principals. Critical reaction has generally concerned itself with structure and imagery, on the one hand, and, on the other, with the perceived presence or absence of psychological verisimilitude. To oversimplify somewhat, the tale's detractors find difficulty in accepting true love as a basis for Leocadia's desire to marry her rapist; the defenders see the honor code or the neoplatonic understanding of beauty and harmony as bases for comprehending what to the modern reader seems contrived and implausible.[31]

It is not necessary to resort to philosophical schools of thought, much less to psychological analyses, if we understand the relatively simple equivalence of the soul and its three constituent faculties. At Rodolfo's first sight of Leocadia's face, her beauty "began to impress itself in his *memoria* in such a way that it carried his *voluntad* away with it" (*Obras*, p. 890). The third element of the triad is singled out for its absence precisely at the moment of rape: "Blind to the light of *entendimiento*, he stole Leocadia's best jewel in the dark" (p. 891).[32] The initial episode – Rodolfo's rape of Leocadia – is depicted as having taken place in darkness, a fact remarked upon by nearly all of the tale's commentators. That darkness is symbolic of ignorance and sin needs no elaboration here. Let us note, however, that it is specifically the light of *entendimiento* that is missing. (It is interesting to note as well the image of *entendimiento* as a quality that sheds light – an enlightening or illuminating power – just as in Damián de Vegas' colloquy the soul describes the other faculties as dependent upon *entendimiento*'s light.) In *La fuerza de la sangre*, we have not only the inversion of values about which Bonaventure cautioned; we have as well an imbalance of the faculties of the soul: *Entendimiento* is lacking.

The story, particularly this early portion, is replete with references to *voluntad* and its carnal concomitant, *deseo*. Much is made of Rodolfo's excessive freedom and its attendant abuse of *voluntad*. Both principals initially commit the error of consigning the event to oblivion. (We recall Bonaventure's admonition that "our soul, distracted by the tasks and cares of daily life, does not penetrate into its own secret place with the aid of the memory.") Rodolfo's eagerness to forget is ascribed to his youth, which, in an indictment characteristic of Cervantes, forgets the object of desire as soon as the appetite has been sated. Leocadia wishes to banish the experience from memory because of the dishonor it will bring to her family. She soon changes her mind, persuaded by her father's conviction that "true dishonor . . . is in sin and true honor in virtue" (p. 893). In contrast to Leocadia's acceptance of these "prudent reasons" (as the narrator labels them), Rodolfo goes off to Italy "with as little *memoria* of what had happened to him with Leocadia as if it had never happened" (p. 894).

The resolution of the plot is precipitated by Luisico's accident, his recognition by Rodolfo's father (because of the resemblance to Rodolfo), and Leocadia's recognition of the house and "in it the recollection of some *memorias* that I shall never be able to forget as long as I live" (p. 895). But before a harmonious outcome can be brought about, a deception invented by Rodolfo's mother is played out. Rodolfo is shown the portrait of an ugly woman who, so his mother gives him to understand, has been selected by his parents to be his wife. Rodolfo counters:

> There are those who seek nobility; others, discernment; others, money; and others, beauty, and I am of the latter; because nobility, thanks to Heaven and my ancestors and my parents, was left to me by them by inheritance; as for discernment, so long as a woman is not stupid, foolish, or silly, it's enough that she doesn't stand out as shrewd or take advantage of silliness; as for wealth, that of my parents also makes me unafraid of becoming poor; beauty is what I seek, loveliness is what I want. [P. 897]

Margarita Levisi observes: "Psychologically the test reveals in Rodolfo the same passion for beauty that he had applied earlier to evil."[33] El Saffar similarly concludes that "Rodolfo's acceptance of Leocadia as his wife is viewed with benevolence and is taken as sacramental, despite the fact that it was motivated by desires originating out of his lust and love for beauty."[34] We are reminded of Casalduero's warning not to read the lines just quoted from the tale as part of a nineteenth-century dialogue nor to see therein any psychological reality in a modern sense.[35] But it is not necessary to see the story in allegorical terms, as Casalduero would have it.[36]

The tale's final paragraph legitimizes the relationship in divine (sacramental) and human (societal honor) terms. In ethical terms – that is to say, in terms of the ethos implicit in the topos of the faculties of the soul – the moral goodness that Rodolfo has at last attained is revealed in unequivocal, if less evident, fashion: With respect to *memoria*, I have already noted Leocadia's ineradicable memory of the rape; in addition, the image of Rodolfo in his son's face is, as the title of the story suggests, a forceful reminder of the act whose consequences are the subject of the tale. Not only the child's grandfather sees the likeness: In the concluding paragraph, we are told that Rodolfo sees himself in the mirror of his son's face. With respect to *voluntad*, Cervantes takes pains to emphasize that this element alone assures the wedding, "for because it had taken place at a time when marriage was effected with only the *voluntad* of the partners (without the just and holy proceedings and precautions that are used today), there was no difficulty to prevent the wedding" (p. 899). I must disagree with those who see the words just quoted as a device for protecting the author from the Inquisition. The plot of this story does not demand a hurried wedding (as does, for instance, the precipitous marriage of Constanza and the moribund count [*Persiles*, III, 9], which, with no such apology, takes place within two hours of its conception). Cervantes' explanation in *La fuerza de la sangre* calls attention to *voluntad* as the principal factor in the union of the couple, a point consistent with the development of the characters and of the plot as a whole. Moreover, as one glances at the many examples of related cases compiled by Américo Castro (who cites the situation here as an "astute" protection against potential criticism),[37] it becomes evident that Cervantes had recourse to a variety of circumstances in accordance with the plots that he himself created. That in this instance he chose to direct our attention to a time when *voluntad* alone was sufficient for matrimony serves to underscore the importance of *voluntad* to the work under discussion here. The lack of reciprocal *voluntad* at the outset, when only a self-serving carnal desire was at work, is now supplanted with the mutual *voluntad* of the two souls.

We are still left with the third member of the triad, *entendimiento*. There are only two concrete references to this faculty in the tale. The first, cited earlier, is an explicit declaration of its absence: Rodolfo is, at the time of the rape, "blind to the light of *entendimiento*." Highly significant is the fact that, lacking *entendimiento*, Rodolfo remains speechless throughout the rape. Inasmuch as speech, that is, rational discourse, is a manifestation of the intellect, Rodolfo's silence conveys more than the rapist's desire to conceal his identity. In contrast to this dumb behavior at the beginning, he is eloquent at the end, as he responds to his mother's deception with respect to marrying an ugly woman:

> Since the state of matrimony is a knot that nothing but death unties, it is well that its cords be equal and made of the same thread: Virtue, nobility, discernment, and [worldly] goods of fortune can well cheer the *entendimiento* of the man who was fortunate enough to have them in his wife; but that her ugliness should cheer her husband's eyes seems impossible to me. [P. 897]

It is evident that this portion of his statement opposes those traits which gladden the intellect to those which please the senses, particularly vision.[38] A closer reading reveals something else. Five qualities are listed, four that affect *entendimiento* and one that affects the eyes: for the former, virtue, nobility, discernment, and wealth; for the latter, the absence of ugliness, which is to say, beauty. Let us now repeat a later portion of

Rodolfo's statement, which I cited earlier: "There are those who seek nobility; others discernment; others money; and others, beauty." It will be recalled that he then goes on to say that nobility is already his, that discernment is readily come by provided the woman is not stupid or a fool, and that wealth is also his by inheritance, so that beauty is therefore the quality he seeks. Comparing this part of his discourse with the portion just quoted, we notice a striking parallelism: The qualities presented in both parts are identical and are presented in the same order. However, what was given as the initial item in the passage on qualities in general is not found in the list of his particular wants: Virtue is one of the properties that gladden the *entendimiento* of the husband, yet in the list of what he has or may easily come by (nobility, discernment, wealth), virtue is not mentioned.

In point of fact, Rodolfo mentions the qualities not two but three times, each time in the same order. If we compare the specific enumerations, we find the following:

FIRST REFERENCE	SECOND REFERENCE	THIRD REFERENCE
virtue		
nobility	noble	nobility
discernment	discerning	discernment
goods	wealthy	money
		beauty

This comparison confirms that Cervantes was not randomly tossing off a number of attributes but that he had in mind, as shown by the items within the box, a specific order and, as shown by the attributes outside the rules, a desire to place in relief the imbalance as well as the potential balance of these qualities. The properties within the rules may be considered tantamount to a sine qua non; the two outside the rules reveal in a graphic manner a commonplace of neoplatonic thought: Virtue is in the abstract what beauty signifies visibly. As El Saffar has succinctly put it, the denouement of *La fuerza de la sangre* offers "Cervantes's most extreme affirmation of faith in the harmony which beauty and virtue can produce."[39] Leocadia's beauty, accordingly, transcends the physical and symbolizes the virtue that gladdens *entendimiento*. The trio of the soul's faculties has been perfected, and therein lies the significance of Rodolfo's otherwise trite entreaty: "No . . . , it is not good for you to struggle to separate yourself from the arms of the man who holds you in his soul" (p. 898).

Readers, particularly modern readers, have difficulty not only with Leocadia's acceptance of her rapist as her husband. There is also a disinclination to see in Rodolfo any change for the better. A recent analysis by R. P. Calcraft will aid us here:

> [Rodolfo] first looks carefully at the portrait [of the ugly woman, in the test devised by his mother] and then offers his mother *reasoned argument* as to why he would be unhappy with such a woman. . . . It is not by chance that Rodolfo speaks now for the first time in the *novela*. . . . Aware of his privileges and responsibilities, the request that he makes for a marriage partner with whom he may be happy is a perfectly *reasonable* one, and it is no surprise that his mother is delighted with his response. . . . The intensity of the young man's response to Leocadia's beauty is as great as it had been once before, but on this occasion it fills him with reverence rather than lust, the enchanted eyes occasioning the immediate involvement of the soul. . . . In . . . [the] clear parallels to the first encounter we are made aware of a crucial difference in attitude on the part of Rodolfo, the presence and domination of "alma" [soul] over everything else.[40]

The two references to *entendimiento* in *La fuerza de la sangre* occur at key moments at the beginning and end of the tale. Another set of references to *entendimiento* frames the *Coloquio de los perros*. In the tale that introduces it, *El casamiento engañoso*, the supposed chronicler of the *Coloquio* confesses that it was "el gusto, que me tenía echados grillos al entendimiento" ("pleasure, which had my *entendimiento* in shackles" [*Obras*, p. 992]). He subsequently avers that by all rights he should have died upon discovering his wife's deceit, "if I had had *entendimiento* to know how to sense and ponder such a misfortune" (p. 995). The fictional reader of the *Coloquio*, the licentiate Peralta, comments after reading the tale: "Let's go to the Espolón and refresh the eyes of our bodies, for I've already refreshed those of the *entendimiento*" (p. 1026). There is no compelling reason to link the statements, particularly since the contexts are dissimilar. Nonetheless, the fact that the remarks frame the dogs' colloquy does suggest a relevance between them, especially given Cervantes' announced claim that the *Novelas ejemplares* should enable the reader to "get some profitable example" out of them (pp. 769–70). It is appropriate to see a misguided Campuzano, devoid of *entendimiento* in the introductory tale, and an appreciative Peralta, his *entendimiento* nourished by the lessons of the *Coloquio*, as purposive markers surrounding the reading of the novella Cervantes chose to place last among his dozen tales.[41]

All this might be of no more than incidental interest were the story it frames not one whose underlying supposition is the eventual transformation of dog into man, that is, of irrational beast into human endowed with *entendimiento*. The fictive basis for this transition is the witch's revelation that the dogs have descended from a human mother and the prediction that they will, one day, regain human shape. The interpretation of this central point of the tale is not as simple as some would have it. The complexity is brought out in the following passage, as Cipión says:

> For look, Berganza, it would be the most utter nonsense to believe that Camacha could change men into beasts. . . . And if we seem now to have some understanding and power of reason, since we are speaking when we are in fact dogs, or have the form of dogs, we have already said that this is a marvelous and unprecedented thing. . . . Think on what vain and absurd premises Camacha based her argument about our transformation back to human form . . . unless her words are to be taken in a sense I've heard called allegorical, which means that the sense isn't as it sounds, but something else which, although different, may resemble it. So to say [the verses recited by the witch] in the sense I have mentioned, seems to me to mean that we shall recover our form when we see that those who yesterday were at the summit of fortune's wheel are today trampled down and cast at the feet of misfortune and held in low esteem by those who valued them most; and likewise, when we see that others who a couple of hours ago had no place in this world but as a cipher to increase the number of its inhabitants are now so lifted up by prosperity that we can no longer see them. . . . And if recovering our form consisted in this, we have already seen it happen and it happens all the time, from which I gather that it is not in the allegorical but in the literal sense that Camacha's verses are to be taken. However, the answer to our problem does not lie here either, for we have often seen what they say and we are still dogs as much as ever we were.

Berganza responds:

> I declare you are right, brother [Cipión], and that you are cleverer than I thought, and from what you have said I truly think and believe that all that we have experienced up to now and are experiencing is a dream, and that we are dogs. But don't let us for that reason fail to enjoy this blessing of speech which we have and the great honour of possessing the gift of speaking like humans for as long as we can.[42]

We are alerted, gratuitously it might appear, to the fact that the colloquy is allegorical, by which is meant "that the sense isn't as it sounds, but something else which, although different, may resemble it." This is not necessarily allegory as we would define it today but rather an Aristotelian invitation to perceive the tale in a metaphorical sense. On the other hand, the verses, which at first seem wholly symbolic of the millenium, are explained as referring to the daily vicissitudes of life, an everyday consequence of the rotations of fortune's wheel. In this sense, we are told, the day of the animals' conversion to humans is already here and no allegorical reading is required. However, says Cipión, "we are still dogs as much as ever we were." In short, of the two interpretations proposed, allegorical or literal, neither leads to a comprehension of the premise of the tale.

The moral is contained in the final sentence of the passage just quoted.[43] The significance, in contrast, is to be found in the preceding sentence. Riley sees in it "an alarming Lewis Carroll-like suggestion that the *dogs* are dreaming the whole thing."[44] A closer parallel is again found in Calderón's *La vida es sueño*: Not only is life merely a dream, but the dreams themselves are naught but dream. One must continually bear in mind that the colloquy itself is a two-tiered dream. Although Campuzano insists on its veracity in terms that recall Don Quixote's defense of the Montesinos experience as a real occurrence, what he allegedly overheard (and claims to have "seen" in the sense explored in Chapter 3) is evidently a dream. Moreover, in the form that it reaches us, the colloquy is read (whether by Peralta or by us) in a time sequence that parallels precisely the sleep of its fictive author: "The finishing of the *Coloquio* by the licentiate and the awakening of the ensign occurred simultaneously" (p. 1026). Since Campuzano dreamed the original, the dream process is re-created for us as we are forced to picture him asleep whenever we care to read the colloquy. If, then, the protagonists of the dream believe themselves to be dreaming as well, the question to be asked is what animates that dream.

The history of the interpretation of dreams goes back at least as far as the Old Testament (Joseph and the Pharaoh). One need not look to Freud or Jung, for it is evident that writers like Cervantes, Calderón, and Quevedo – to restrict ourselves to one time and place – understood the dream as an artistic vehicle for probing human fears and aspirations. In the two-level story under consideration, the fictive author of the colloquy dreams that colloquy as the result of his having permitted desire (i.e., the base side of *voluntad*) to fetter his *entendimiento*. It is in his syphilitic state that he dreams the entire canine dialogue, including the central episode of the witch Cañizares, who describes herself as wickedly inclined because "el deleite me tiene echados grillos a la voluntad" (delectation has my *voluntad* in shackles" [p. 1017]), a statement that parallels Campuzano's description of "el gusto, que me tenía echados grillos al entendimiento" ("pleasure, which had my *entendimiento* in shackles").

El Saffar has perceived that the central episode of the witch "duplicates

the method of presentation of the story in which it is contained" and
that the witch's words "capture the essence of Berganza's own struggle."[45] The witch's reference to her *voluntad* as having been shackled by
sensual desire also links her circumstance to that of Campuzano, thereby
allowing us to see the interrelationship of not two but three levels: the
witch Cañizares, the dog Berganza, and the ensign Campuzano. (The
partial but not imperceptible phonic resemblance of the three names
should not pass unobserved.) With each of these Cervantes associates
one faculty: It is *voluntad* in the case of the witch and *entendimiento* in that
of Campuzano, as we have noted; *memoria* is the faculty for which dogs
are praised, as Cipión himself points out.[46] Of course, it is not as simple
as that, for the faculties need to be concerted toward a morally commendable aim. It is this potential perfection of the soul that animates the
tale.

Some clarification is in order before we move on. By "perfection" I
mean, of course, the fulfillment of the soul's properties and not necessarily a state of flawlessness. By identifying the potential perfection of
the soul's faculties as that which animates the story, I am not interpreting
its plot but, in keeping with my purpose in this book, attempting to
seek its substance. It is possible to interpret the colloquy and the tale that
frames it in a number of ways, as has indeed been done by a large number
of notable critics. What it "means" is the object of such scholarly interpretation; what animates it is the fact that it is all a dream. When we
recall the comments made about the Cave of Montesinos episode, it
brings to mind that the distortions evident in that dream adventure were
purposefully contrived *disparates*, which is to say, artfully conceived in-
congruencies. (In the *Persiles*, I, 5, Cervantes once more depicts a dream
followed by what the dreamer thinks is a waking state, in which wolves
speak to him in Spanish.) Now, it is all well and good to see our tale
here as a kind of picaresque novel, as social criticism, as an exercise in
authorial distance and control, as an allegory with roots in Aesop and
Apuleius – all legitimate perspectives. However, the fact that it is a dream
that brings forth the plot of the colloquy requires of the reader at least
a minimal (but certainly a constant) awareness of what dreams are: They
are free of the exigencies of coherent logic and they represent a world-
as-it-might-be, were that logic not operative. Inasmuch as the feature of
Campuzano's dream that most obviously defies the world-as-it-is is the
speech of the dogs, it is on the significance of this aspect, the very title
of the tale, that we ought to focus.

As a matter of fact, the protagonists of the colloquy can barely keep
from harping on this point. This constant emphasis brings to our attention that the animals' ability to speak is not an arbitrary literary artifice
that asks the reader to suspend disbelief. On the contrary, the reader is

repeatedly reminded that even the protagonists find it difficult to accept that they, dogs, are thinking and speaking. El Saffar points out that Berganza's narrative is as much concerned with examining his newly found gift of speech as with recounting the tale it is his purpose to tell.[47] What Berganza repeatedly wonders at and, consequently, what Campuzano at bottom dreams about is the potentiality of change, particularly as it is linked to *entendimiento*'s proper function. Because it is a dream, the reader must not fall into the trap of taking literally the circumstance of a talking dog. Rather, the dream reveals the animal nature – bestiality, if you will – of man. Campuzano's flaw is his failure to permit his *entendimiento* to direct his will, the latter emerging as desire rather than as the morally superior *voluntad*. It is this concern that informs his dream: Is his animal self really endowed with *entendimiento*, and sufficiently so to enable this faculty to predominate over those less surprisingly associated with animal behavior?

The tale within the dream – a veritable exemplary tale – of the witch's failure to control her *voluntad* in a morally commendable fashion is indicative of what occurs when *entendimiento* is not permitted to inform *voluntad* and concurrently infringes upon the proper function of the third faculty, *memoria*, rendering it impotent:

> The habit of vice becomes second nature [and] carries with it a chill which freezes the soul and benumbs it even in its faith, so that it forgets itself and doesn't even remember the terror with which God threatens it or the glory which He invites it to share. And in fact, since it is a sin of the flesh and of sensual pleasure, it must of necessity deaden all the senses . . . without allowing them to fulfill their functions as they should.[48]

The charge that the failure to remember both the terror and the glory of God is a failure of the faculties to perform their functions reflects the *tan largo me lo fiáis* of the Don Juan complex: overconfidence in divine mercy irrespective of the proper behavior of the soul's faculties. The philosophy expounded in the witch's words finds its explanation in the following passage:

> The understanding then had to sift the evidence of the senses already organised by the common sense, to examine the exuberant creations of the fancy, to summon up the right material from the memory, and on its own account to lay up the greatest possible store of knowledge and wisdom. It was for the will to make the just decision on the evidence presented to it by the understanding. For man's will, like God's and unlike that of natural agents, is free. . . . It was against the will rather than the understanding that morality habit-

ually set the appetite or the passions. . . . They were not always in opposition; yet, their objects differing basically, at times they must be.[49]

All three levels of our story are thus entwined by the potentiality inherent in *entendimiento*. To say that the commonplace of the three faculties of the soul informs this tale is an exercise in understatement, for I think it plain that without a thorough understanding and a clear application of all the matters brought out in the early pages of this chapter, Cervantes could not have written these two connected tales as they now stand. The metaphor of the soul as three faculties is not incidental but fundamental, and no matter how we may wish to interpret the tale, the workings of the soul's faculties underlie the ethical significance.

By way of a postscript to my approach to the *Coloquio*, it is well to focus on Cervantes' understanding of dreams, inasmuch as the foregoing analysis relies on a reading of this tale as the record of a dream. If Joseph's interpretations of the Pharaoh's dreams constitute our earliest biblical example of the belief that dreams may be subjected to analysis, a more likely though not necessarily direct influence upon Cervantes – to the extent that it clarifies his view on dreams – is found in Plato:

> [I mean those desires] that are awakened in sleep when the rest of the soul, the rational, gentle and dominant part, slumbers, but the beastly and savage part . . . endeavors to sally forth and satisfy its own instincts. You are aware that in such case there is nothing it will not venture to undertake as being released from all sense of shame and all reason. . . . It is ready for any foul deed of blood; it abstains from no food, and, in a word, falls short of no extreme of folly and shamelessness. . . .
>
> But when, I suppose, a man's condition is healthy and sober, and he goes to sleep after arousing his rational part and entertaining it with fair words and thoughts, and attaining to clear self-consciousness, while he has neither starved nor indulged to repletion his appetitive part, so that it may . . . examine and reach out toward and apprehend some of the things unknown to it, past, present, or future, and when he has in like manner tamed his passionate part, and . . . has thus quieted the two elements in his soul and quickened the third, in which reason resides, and so goes to his rest, you are aware that in such case he is most likely to apprehend truth, and the visions of his dreams are least likely to be lawless.[50]

The particular application of many of the points made here to the matters raised in my discussion of the *Coloquio* is patent. Further, the

passage from the *Republic* is clearly evident in a more general treatment
of dreams in the *Persiles*:

> If I were not instructed in the Catholic truth and recalled what God
> says in Leviticus ("Ye shall not be augurers nor shall ye give cre-
> dence to dreams") because the understanding of them is not given
> to all, I would dare to judge the dream that got me so upset and
> that, as I see it, did not come to me by way of some of the usual
> causes of dreams that, when they are not divine revelations or
> illusions of the devil, stem from the many foods that send vapors
> up to the brain, with which they upset the common sense, or else
> from that which man deals with by day. [I, 18]

There are a number of important points for us here. In accordance with
an issue alluded to in earlier chapters and dealt with by, among others,
Castro, Riley, Forcione, and Avalle-Arce, the passage just quoted takes
pains to avoid unchristian and implausible postures. In line with Plato's
observations, Cervantes goes to the prosaic extreme of suggesting that
some dreams may be caused by indigestion. But in the last words cited,
he seems to be paraphrasing another *Republic*, that of Cicero, who in the
Somnium Scipionis observes that "our dreams are commonly begotten by
our recent waking thoughts."[51] If this is not startling information, it
nevertheless is an important point, for it brings to the fore how Cervantes
viewed the dream in an artistic context.

   Don Quixote dreams of Dulcinea in the Cave of Montesinos not as
he envisioned her ideally but as he has seen her really (in Sancho's "enchanted" version, of course). We noted in Chapter 3 that much of Cervantes' treatment of the appearance–reality motif has its basis in the reality
that underlies illusion. While the illusions themselves provide an artistic
representation of psychological, sociological, and ethical perceptions,
their substance more often than not is prosaic and concrete. This same
principle is at work in Cervantes' understanding of dreams. To be sure,
the idea is not original with him, as we have just noted. It may be argued
as well that in order to understand that daytime experiences may inform
dreams one need not consult Plato or Cicero. What I wish to underscore
is that in the *Persiles* Cervantes thought it worthwhile to state the point.
(He had made the point earlier in the *Viaje del Parnaso*, Chapter 6, in
which he listed three causes of dreams, one of which was "las cosas de
que el hombre trata más de ordinario" ["the things with which man
deals most ordinarily"].) If the influence of everyday events (or foods,
for that matter) on dreams is evident to us in our quotidian affairs, we
are perhaps likely to put this knowledge to one side while engaged with
a work of art. It is the essence of Cervantes' art to take the ordinary, the
prosaic, the unspectacular, even the dull and boring, and with this as his

substance, to construct a kaleidoscopic representation of the human condition. The frequent insistence on our *not* interpreting this or that event as miraculous does, of course, have a basis in the works of the literary theorists who taught Cervantes the importance of verisimilitude. At the same time, such repeated insistence serves a concomitant purpose: not that of avoiding the supernatural but that of emphasizing the potential significance of the ordinary.

Cervantes leaves room for divine revelation and infernal illusion. Beyond that, however, dreams in an artistic context must function as they do in the course of natural events. They are informed by real occurrences, real fears, real aspirations, and real imaginings. (We are reminded of Cervantes' claim to being the first to have brought the soul's hidden thoughts and moral figures to the stage. His representation of similar phenomena in dreams is, I think, another manifestation of the same procedure.) Campuzano's dream in his syphilitic state reflects at once his own animal behavior and the struggle to redirect his *entendimiento* together with the fear that upon awakening, that *entendimiento* may no longer be his. The passage quoted from the *Persiles* helps us to see the plausibility of having a dream, however incongruent its content, explain in artistic terms the sorry encounter that forms the plot of the frame story, *El casamiento engañoso*.

The episode of the witch Cañizares also finds its counterpart in the *Persiles*. Readers of Cervantes' last published tale will have no difficulty seeing the parallel in the Rosamunda episode of his last work. Cervantes is unequivocal in his characterization of the woman whom he repeatedly describes as "la torpe Rosamunda" or "la mujer torpe." Although this word's primary meaning today is "clumsy" or "awkward," it also may mean "lascivious," and indeed, Cervantes at one point calls her exactly that: "la lasciva Rosamunda." (The word is related to our "turpitude.")[52] What links all of this to the Cañizares episode (insofar as the condition of the two women's souls is at issue) is Rosamunda's own description of her character in terms that recall the witch's narrative:

> Ever since I first had use of reason I failed to make use of it because I was always wicked. Along with my tender years and my great beauty, my inordinate freedom and my abundant wealth, I was overpowered by vices in such a way that they were and are in me inseparable contingents. You already know . . . that I have desired men's *voluntades*; but time, that robber and thief of women's human beauty, sneaked in for mine so unexpectedly that I found myself ugly sooner than disillusioned. But since vices have their seat in the soul (which does not grow old), they will not leave me and

since I don't offer any resistance but rather let myself go along with
the current of my pleasures [*gustos*]... [I, 20][53]

The immediate context is that of Rosamunda's immodest advances to
Antonio, but the reader of Cervantes readily recognizes Rosamunda and
Cañizares as kindred spirits. This episode in the *Persiles* is not a central
one, although it, along with other secondary plots, serves to place in
relief the moral quest of the protagonists. Given the focus of this chapter,
we can see that Rosamunda personifies Cervantes' continuing concern
for the consequences of an imbalance of the soul's faculties. Had we
begun with this point it would have been a strained allusion, to be sure,
but our familiarity with the topic and the manifest correspondence to
the witch's narrative permit us to see in Rosamunda's words a familiar
pattern.

The rational faculty, which is to say, *entendimiento*, has not been permitted to direct the will, which, allowed to be moved instead by the
force of sensual pleasure, manifests itself as self-gratifying desire. Rosamunda shares with Cañizares the base pleasure of temporal delectation.
Perhaps even more interesting is the comparison that may be drawn
between Rosamunda and Rodolfo of *La fuerza de la sangre*. The latter is
first introduced as a young man of twenty-two whose misconduct is
animated by his "wealth, illustrious blood, twisted inclination, inordinate
freedom and the loose company" he keeps (*Obras*, p. 890).[54] El Saffar
sees in this description a type that "emerges in Cervantes's idealistic
stories as a familiar category to be used symbolically to introduce not
the failures of a particular social class but an abstract force very much
related to the creative process. In *La fuerza de la sangre* Rodolfo epitomizes
all the tendencies outlined in other characters of this type."[55] The example
of Rosamunda shows that these traits may be evinced as well in women.
Rosamunda attributes her wickedness to the overpowering influence of
immaturity, youthful beauty, inordinate freedom – in both works the
original reads *libertad demasiada* – and great wealth, virtually a repetition
of the list detailed for Rodolfo. The difference in the two situations
reinforces the principle at work. Rodolfo matures (a process symbolized
by his voyage to Italy, a frequent theme in Cervantes, who believed
travel to have educational value) and seeks beauty (symbolic of virtue,
as we have noted) and embraces reciprocal *voluntad*, thereby gladdening
entendimiento. Rosamunda, in contrast, refuses to make use of her *entendimiento* and, dazzled by her temporal assets as she seeks not reciprocity
but dominance of men's wills, sees her own beauty turn to ugliness
(symbolic of the vices that have assumed control of her soul).

The relationship between the character type discerned by El Saffar and
the matter under consideration in this chapter is the repeated antithesis

set forth by Cervantes between sensual pleasure and *entendimiento*. We have observed in a number of cases how this latter faculty has been constrained or misguided by the dominance of or insufficient restraint upon *voluntad*, the latter emerging thereby in its hedonistic actualization as pleasure or desire (*deleite* or *gusto*). The opposition thus depicted should not be misinterpreted as a reprobation of sensual delight. Rather, Cervantes here once more follows Thomas Aquinas: "The evil in the sexual act is neither the desire nor the pleasure, but the submergence of the rational faculty which accompanies them. . . . In its Thomist form the [medieval] theory acquits the carnal desire and the carnal pleasure, and finds the evil in the *ligamentum rationis*, the suspension of intellectual activity."[56] It is this principle in contexts other than carnal gratification that motivates Cervantes' description of a lover's *voluntad* as guided not by the intellect but by the irrational power of love, for his desire is not under his control, nor is he himself, but rather it is love that directs his will ("el amor que manda su voluntad" [*Persiles*, II, 14]). In similar fashion does a subsequent passage of the *Persiles* observe that "when amorous passion occupies a soul there is no reasoning with which it can be correct nor reason that it does not trample" (II, 18). Still later in the *Persiles* (III, 5), it is reiterated that "the powerful forces of love tend to upset the most informed minds."

The effects of love may harm not just the intellect but all three faculties (which is to say, the soul), as Lauso makes clear in *La Galatea*. Having turned his back on love and believing himself to have triumphed over it, he declares that "although I slip from its grasp so ill treated, my *voluntad* corrupted, my *entendimiento* upset, and my *memoria* decayed, it still seems to me that I can win the battle" (Book V). Neither love nor love's might is being excoriated in these otherwise trite passages. It is the moral and intellectual upheaval caused by the subversion of the faculties upon which Cervantes repeatedly lays stress.

Domination by love is not something to be blamed on one's fate. The following passage from the eclogue represented in *La Galatea* illustrates (in addition to the ethical polemic of the age regarding the relative influence of destiny or the stars and man's free will) how unrestrained *voluntad* is at least as responsible for events as fate, and probably more forcefully so, since it "permits everything":

> My harsh, bitter fate,
> my inexorable star,
> my *voluntad*, which permits everything,
> have me condemned,
> ungrateful and lovely Belisa,
> to serve and love you forever. [Book III]

Although it is true that the tradition of courtly love ascribed love to fate, and it is this convention that informs Cervantes' references here to fate and the inexorability of one's "star," it is the force of *voluntad* in this passage that stands out.[57]

Nonetheless, love need not be ipso facto the cause of a distraught mind. In the exemplary situation of Persiles and Sigismunda (or Periandro and Auristela, as they are known throughout most of the work), it is the faculties of the soul that make the difference, for "not all loves are precipitous or daring, nor has every lover set the sights of his pleasure on the enjoyment of his loved one, unless it be with the faculties [*potencias*] of his soul" (IV, 11).[58] It is indeed the soul's faculties that animate the relationship of this couple, a matter initially brought up in a paradox described by Periandro, who says that it seems that neither he nor Auristela has "any being at all or freedom to use our free will [*albedrío*]." Only after fulfilling the vow to complete the pilgrimage to Rome "will we be in a position to dispose of our heretofore invalid *voluntades*" (I, 16). This same paradox – a free will but one subject to divine disposition – is repeated later in the book as Periandro says of Auristela that she "is so free and so much mistress of her *voluntad* that she will not surrender it to any prince on earth, because she says that she has surrendered it to the one who is [prince] of Heaven" (III, 13).

It is for this reason, as well as because of her love for Periandro, that Auristela has not responded to Arnaldo's well-intentioned love for her. If we state the situation in terms corresponding to the faculties of the soul, Arnaldo's love has not been allowed to enter Auristela's *memoria*, a problem that Arnaldo attributes to the effect of the misfortunes that have befallen her:

> The misfortunes that you have gone through, beautiful Auristela, must have taken away from your *memoria* those which you had an obligation to remember, among which I wish I myself had been erased from it, for with just the supposition that at some time I had been in it, I would live content, since there can be no forgetting of those of whom there has been no recollection. The present forgetting falls upon the memory of past remembrance. . . . I see as well that misfortunes have the power to erase from *memoria* some obligations that seem powerful. . . . I in the meantime will bear upon the shoulders of my patience my hopes, which are supported by the protection of your good *entendimiento*.

To this Auristela replies: "I have no *voluntad* other than that of my brother Periandro" (I, 17).

Later, Auristela tells Periandro not to let others' beauty take away or erase from his *memoria* what he owes to her, for in her beauty he may "satisfy the desire and fill the void of your *voluntad*, if you observe that, joining the beauty of my body, such as it is, to that of my soul, you will find a composite of beauty that will bring you satisfaction" (II, 2). The response is found in Periandro's words of a few chapters further on:

> The knot with which our *voluntades* are tied no one but death can untie. [Don't believe] that I forget the mines of your virtues and your incomparable beauty, [a beauty] of the body as well as of the soul. This [soul] of mine, which is animated by yours, I offer you once more [with the same] obligation with which I agreed to serve you from the moment when my faculties [*potencias*] were stamped with the awareness of your virtues.

Therefore he asks her to eschew jealousy, which moves *voluntad* to slacken or faint, urging her instead to acknowledge her obligation to her good *entendimiento* by viewing him with a *voluntad* less ready to see careless conduct in his every move (II, 7). She subsequently tells him:

> Only one *voluntad*, oh Persiles, have I had in all my life and that one I gave to you some two years ago, not forced but of my own free will [*libre albedrío*], and it is as whole and firm now as it was the first day I made you master of it and . . . , if it is possible to enlarge, has enlarged and grown among the many travails we have gone through. . . . Up to now my soul suffered by itself alone but from now on I will suffer in it and in yours, although I have said it badly in dividing these two souls, for they are only one. [IV, 1]

We are dealing here with the substance of a work of Cervantes. The interpretations of the *Persiles* offered by scholars are not at odds with the findings presented here, but I venture to say that a comprehension of how pervasively the thread of the metaphorical triad runs through the work will enhance our appreciation of the building blocks, so to speak, with which Cervantes fashioned the opus that subsequently and consequently leads to our appreciation on other and different levels. As the preceding pages illustrate, the *Persiles* in particular lends itself to a clarification of the faculties as Cervantes understood them.

One of the topics alluded to is the neoplatonic equivalence of beauty and virtue, a metaphorical equation we have noted in other works as well. It is from the *Persiles* that the definition can be extrapolated. I have already cited Auristela's reference to the complementarity of beauty of the body and beauty of the soul; a number of related comments complete the definition. When Auristela's illness turns her beauty to ugliness, Periandro remains steadfast, for she "did not thereby seem less beautiful to him because he did not look at her in the bed in which she was lying but in the soul, where he had her portrayed" (IV, 9). Not unlike this reaction is that of the man who loved not the beautiful woman his family had chosen for him but "Leoncia, who is the ugly one . . . , for to the eyes of my soul, because of the virtues that I perceive in the [soul] of my Leoncia, she is the most beautiful woman in the world" (II, 11). To the neoplatonic commonplace that beauty and virtue are mutually reinforcing and metaphorically equivalent because they produce a harmonic whole, Cervantes adds the nuance that the one implies the other. That beauty betokens virtue is scarcely original; that virtue not only implies beauty but is thus perceived in the mind's eye in the face of physical evidence to the contrary is Cervantes' contribution to this topos. (I do not mean to suggest that the perception of virtue as beauty originated with Cervantes. The concept is unmistakably present in Dante, for instance. But its explanation as a phenomenon transcending the physical even to the point of transforming the latter is, in my view, a step or two beyond that well-known metaphor. Not only is the matter taken up elsewhere [La española inglesa] but it underlies Don Quixote's perception of Dulcinea in the nightmare in the Cave of Montesinos, a vision that leads to his description of the cave's grotesqueries as beautiful. Moreover, Don Quixote's insistence, despite his defeat in combat, that Dulcinea remains the most beautiful woman in the world, is in keeping with this understanding.)

We should not miss the qualification that "beauty of the body is *often* a sign of beauty of the soul" (*Persiles*, IV, 4; emphasis mine) or the distinction made in the aphorism that "beauty accompanied by chastity is beauty; that which isn't is no more than good appearance" (IV, 1). Finally, and more directly linked with the soul's faculties, there is Cervantes' comment about the courtesan who falls for Periandro:

> Is there, perchance, in the world an *entendimiento* so keen that, while looking at one of these beauties that I depict, it leaves to one side the beauties of her loveliness and begins to consider those of her humble social conduct? Beauty partly blinds and partly illuminates: It is after the one that blinds that pleasure runs, and after the one that illuminates that the intention to better oneself runs. [IV, 7][59]

The guiding purpose of *entendimiento* recalls matters raised in the early pages of this chapter. We can piece together a more detailed definition of this faculty by extrapolating from the *Persiles* a number of otherwise unrelated statements. For instance, when Auristela is described as so beautiful that she outshines not only all others in the world but even "those that the keenest *entendimiento* can paint in the imagination" (I, 2), we are given to understand that qualities like beauty are received by the imagination through a faculty whose primary property is that of reasoning and understanding. In a different context, Periandro is so upset that "his soul was filled with a thousand imaginings and suspicions as, with the speedy course of his *entendimiento*, he considered what could happen" (I, 2). Again, imaginings are seated in the soul, and it is the *entendimiento* that provides the images by means of its reasoning power. This second example may seem a bit more plausible because we readily understand that it is with the intellect that we weigh consequences by imagining possible outcomes. Nevertheless, it shares with the previous example the capacity of *entendimiento* to compose images.

In point of fact, the *Diccionario de Autoridades*, citing Augustine, gives as its first definition of *entendimiento*, "one of the three faculties of the soul, that . . . understands things it does not see."[60] The wording is somewhat simplistic, to be sure, for we realize that what is meant is the envisioning of matters in the mind's eye. But for our purposes, this eighteenth-century definition helps explain how a dream-fiction may refresh the eyes of one's *entendimiento* (*El coloquio de los perros*); how physical beauty may transcend its own visual reality to disclose virtue or beauty of the soul (*La fuerza de la sangre, Persiles*); how physical ugliness may be perceived as that same virtuous beauty of the soul (*La española inglesa, Persiles*); and how, as we explored in Chapter 3, *entendimiento* informed by *memoria* (conditioned response or programming, as I termed it there) may permit the mind to see something other than the prosaic physical phenomena perceived by the sense of sight. (In *La Galatea*, Cervantes writes that "*memoria* fixed on the object that love put in the soul, represents the living image of the beloved to the intellect" [Book II]).

Entendimiento may be led astray. A lie "creates dissonance in the *entendimiento*" (*Persiles*, III, 10). Accordingly, a soul accepts some thoughts and pursues others, and still others it rejects and forgets; thereby it arrives at a state of calm (*sosiego*), unless it allows itself to be infused with an *error de entendimiento* (*Persiles*, III, 1). The madness of love, it is suggested in *La Galatea*, may bring about such a "blind error of our *entendimiento*" (Book I). Moreover, beauty and wine may distort even "the liveliest *entendimientos*" and, having done so, may erase obligations from *memoria* and in their place put the pleasures of lasciviousness (*Persiles*, II, 15). We have seen a number of such instances in Cervantes' works, and it bears repeating that the evil does not lie in the pleasures but in the disruption of *entendimiento*'s proper function. Such an impropriety causes old King Policarpo (who at the age of seventy has lusted for the seventeen-year-old Auristela) to describe the clock of his *entendimiento* as out of order ("se ha desconcertado el reloj de mi entendimiento" [II, 5]), a metaphor in keeping with this faculty's regulatory function.

Although *entendimiento* is also a factor in *La española inglesa*, it is the impression made upon and retained by *memoria* that underlies the equanimity of the protagonists of this tale.[61] Recaredo is endowed with a good *entendimiento*, as is pointed out more than once, which presumably guides his *voluntad* and impresses upon his *memoria* a love based on irreproachable conduct:

> And this [plan of my parents to have me marry a beautiful Scottish lady] in my view was intended to have the great beauty of this maiden erase from my soul your [beauty], which I have stamped in it. I, Isabela, ever since I first loved you did so with a love other than that whose aim and goal is the fulfillment of sensual appetite: for although your corporal beauty captivated my senses, your infinite virtues captured my soul, so that if I fell in love with you [when you were] beautiful, I adore you [now that you are] ugly. [*Obras*, p. 867][62]

The basis for Recaredo's exemplary attitude is that "the love that he had for her passed from the body to the soul and that if Isabela had lost her beauty, she could not have lost her infinite virtues" (pp. 866–7). Ugliness as well as beauty is metaphorical and directly related to the soul's faculties. Warned that Isabela might be obliged to refrain from bearing him good-will (*buena voluntad*) because of their different nationalities, Recaredo replies: "Let her remember to have some for me, for so long as I am in her *memoria*, I know that the *voluntad* will be good, since in her great worth and *entendimiento* and rare beauty, there is no room for the ugliness of ingratitude" (p. 862). This is precisely what brings about the denouement: Isabela does not go forward with her plan to enter the convent because she recognizes the ransomed captive as her betrothed, despite the written notification of his death: "I have you stamped in my *memoria* and retained in my soul" (p. 871).

To attempt an analysis of the triad as it applies to *Don Quixote* could require a separate volume. Particularly because my primary purpose in this book is not exegesis but the exploration of the substance that may lead us to it, my treatment of the matter in Cervantes' masterpiece must remain synoptic. The reader of *Don Quixote* who has followed my arguments in this chapter will have no difficulty in relating the three faculties of the soul to Don Quixote's essence, even without reference to specific passages in the text. Of these, the epitome is doubtless found in his declaration to Dorotea that he can not marry her (i.e., Micomicona), "so long as I have my *memoria* engaged, my *voluntad* captive, my *entendimiento* lost to [Dulcinea]" (I, 30). I think it safe to conclude that this statement defines the sum and substance of Don Quixote's single-mindedness. If we understand Dulcinea as the embodiment of truth and virtue, the words just quoted are applicable to Don Quixote's psychology at any stage: his belief in her as a knight's lady in accordance with his romances; his belief in her enchantment, which provided him with new purpose in the symbolic restoration of beauty and the reaffirmation of virtue; his declaration at the moment of defeat that she remains the most beautiful woman in the world; finally, amid all the protestations on his deathbed rejecting the delusions of his career, the conspicuous absence of any such abjuration with respect to Dulcinea.

The other side of the coin, so to speak, manifests itself in Sancho's comportment, and with no little irony. To a large extent, Sancho's career is an enactment of the adage that a liar had better have a good memory. The "enchantment" of Dulcinea in Part II is, of course, an outgrowth of a process begun midway in Part I. Having forgotten to take along Don Quixote's letter to Dulcinea, Sancho entrusts to his memory what he thinks to be the gist of its content. The malapropisms that result are familiar to readers of the book, and indeed, we have here a parody (the original letter) turned burlesque (Sancho's version). In the process, Cervantes insists upon the workings of the memorative faculty.

It is Sancho who initiates the sequence by claiming that the loss of the letter does not cause him much concern "because he knew it almost from memory." In response to the barber's request that he recite it, Sancho begins to "scratch his head in order to bring the letter to his memory," eventually coming out with the malapropism of the salutation. Then, twice using the phrase "si mal no me acuerdo" ("if I remember rightly"), he continues with his garbled version, evoking in the barber and the priest their customary reaction: "The two were not a little pleased to see Sancho Panza's *buena memoria* and praised him for it a great deal" (I, 26). What raises the level from farce to irony is that Sancho would perforce be ignorant of the chivalric formulas as well as of the content (directed at the lady Dulcinea but destined for, so Sancho has just learned, Aldonza Lorenzo). Sancho's total ignorance of the literary model for Don Quixote's letter requires his failure to understand its message, with the notable and logical exception of the note about the three ass-colts promised to him. (Once more we note the appositeness of the incongruities that, beyond their comicality, are appropriately Sancho's rendition.) In a word, Sancho's *memoria* serves him not as badly as it might seem, given that his *entendimiento* is incapable of providing necessary comprehension. The irony is that Sancho is unaware that he has not memorized the letter faithfully.

It may be necessary to qualify the statement just made by limiting the unawareness to the point at which the priest and barber hear him recite it several times. Let us examine his recounting of the matter to his master:

"So it would be," replied Sancho, "if I had not taken it into my *memoria* when Your Grace read it to me, so that I told it to a sexton who transcribed it from my *entendimiento*. . . ."

"And do you still have it in your *memoria*, Sancho?" said Don Quixote.

"No, sir," replied Sancho, "for after I gave it [to be transcribed], since I saw that it wasn't going to be of further benefit, I decided to forget it, and if I remember anything, it's that part about *suppressed*, I mean, *sovereign lady*, and the last part: 'Yours until death, the Knight of the Mournful Countenance.'" [I, 30]

The parts that Sancho remembers are the salutation (complete with the correction provided him by the barber) and the signature (containing the sobriquet he himself bestowed earlier upon his master). His claim to have forgotten the rest can be ascribed to two factors: his own assertion that it contained nothing further of benefit (presumably for himself, since the matter of the ass-colts would not be resolved in the love letter) and the realization, now, that he did not memorize it as it was originally written (given his own recognition of the error in the salutation and the amusement of the priest and barber). Not wishing to be challenged, inasmuch as a correct transcription is a necessary part of the fabricated story of his visit to Dulcinea, Sancho, mindful of the dangers of not keeping his lie consistent with the details of the fabrication, prefers to claim that he has now forgotten the text of the letter. Here begins a sequence that will continue throughout the second part of the novel, leading Sancho to invent the enchanted version of Dulcinea in an effort to prevent the real one – that is, Aldonza Lorenzo – from revealing the original lie concerning Sancho's supposed visit.

The irony is compounded by a statement made still earlier. When Don Quixote first hits upon the idea of having Sancho deliver a letter to Dulcinea, he tells Sancho that "everything must depend on your diligence." Sancho echoes: "On my diligence?" (I, 25). Casalduero believes that the thread of the 1615 *Don Quixote* depends on the disenchantment (i.e., begins with Sancho's "enchantment") of Dulcinea, but the spool may have to be wound back to this point in the 1605 volume.[63] By placing the responsibility for communication with Dulcinea on Sancho's diligence, Don Quixote is unwittingly setting in motion the chain of events that begins with Sancho's lie about his delivery of the letter, continues with the "enchantment" and subsequent endeavors to "disenchant" Dulcinea, and culminates in the requirement (plotted by the duke and duchess) that the disenchantment be realized exclusively through Sancho's will. The well-known irony of having Don Quixote reduced to passive spectator in the restoration of his ideal is sharpened when we link it to his own original insistence that all must depend on Sancho's diligence. From Sancho's standpoint, of course, the irony assumes a measure of poetic justice (although he claims not to see the connection).

Sancho's *memoria* is in itself a matter of interest. His use of the previously cited expression *si mal no me acuerdo* (a set phrase in Spanish) is habitual, and the irony lies in his necessary concern for not getting caught in his lie. Although Helena Percas argues that Sancho has an elephantine memory,[64] it is Don Quixote who points out the essential feature, namely, selectivity: "I swear that your memory doesn't fail you when you want to have it" (II, 3). Sancho finds it useful, therefore, when relating once again his fabricated meeting with Dulcinea in terms appropriate to an encounter with Aldonza, to say that as he has described it so it seemed to him, "unless I am short on memory" (II, 8). On approaching El Toboso, Sancho suggests that Dulcinea lives on a dead-end street, "si mal no acuerdo" (II, 9), and Don Quixote, anxious to have Sancho record every gesture, urges him to "have memory" (II, 10). The reverse occurs when it is Sancho's interests that are at issue. When Don Quixote complains of Sancho's loquaciousness, the latter retorts: "If Your Grace had a good memory . . . you ought to remember [that agreement we reached]." To this Don Quixote replies: "I don't remember, Sancho" (II, 20). (It is only a few paragraphs later in this chapter that the narrator tells us that Don Quixote has a great memory.) Sancho's selective memory occasionally takes creative liberties, so that when he is asked how long he has been serving his master (the calculation presumably affecting the salary owed him), he declares: "Si yo mal no me acuerdo . . . debe de haber más de veinte años, tres días más o menos" ("If I remember rightly, it must be more than twenty years, three days more or less" [II, 28]).

Cervantes is consistent in his characterization of Sancho's memory. The recollection of familiar things and the forgetting or garbling of the unfamiliar in the letter to Dulcinea of Part I find their correspondence in the governorship of Part II. Told that a governor needs both letters and arms, Sancho declares that he does not know the alphabet but that it is sufficient for him to have in his memory the Christus (the cross at the head of the alphabet in school primers). The allusion here, of course, is to a self-description we come across frequently in the novel: Sancho is illiterate and therefore, presumably, of pure Christian stock (sufficient, it will be recalled, to make him a count). In this context, the duke's irony is unmistakable: "With such a good memory . . . Sancho will not be able to err in anything" (II, 42).

Sancho "tried to preserve in his memory" the counsels given him by Don Quixote, but "what use are they going to be if I don't remember any?" Nor will he remember them better than "yesteryear's clouds." This forgetfulness is immediately contrasted with Sancho's endless store of proverbs, the facile recollection of which frustrates Don Quixote, who complains: "I am racking my [memory], and I have a good one, and not one [proverb] occurs to me" (II, 43). Needless to say, the *memoria* of each is consistent with his personality.

I have already commented in another context on the appropriateness of ascribing to the recollection of others' ingenuity the wisdom of some of Sancho's judgments during his governorship. The case of the man who carries the gold inside his cane is resolved because Sancho recalls hearing the priest relate a similar case, and "he had such a great memory that, were it not for forgetting all that which he did not want to remember, there would not be such a memory on the whole island" (II, 45). The resolution of the riddle of the man and the bridge (II, 51) is similarly attributed to Sancho's memory, as I detailed in an earlier chapter, and Sancho's advice not to take auguries seriously is once more attributed to his memory of the priest's words: "Y si no me acuerdo mal, he oído decir al cura de nuestro pueblo . . . " ("And if I remember rightly, I have heard the priest of our town say . . . " [II, 73]).

It seems clear that both Don Quixote and Sancho are endowed with good memorative faculties and that their limitations are governed by their respective intellects or *entendimientos* as well as the matters that they believe to be of vital interest to them, which is to say that *voluntad* also plays a role. The account in the foregoing pages is by no means exhaustive, for the three faculties are patent in many an episode. The desire to avoid a catalogue, together with the belief that the point of the discussion has been well illustrated, moves me to bring this chapter to a close. The metaphor of the tripartite soul provides a very large part of the substance of Cervantes' works.

Chapter 6

From happy age of gold to detestable age of iron

Digo que España está en su edad robusta. *[I say that Spain
is in its robust age.]*

– Rey de Artieda, 1581

Stereotypical generalizations are, willy-nilly, part of human nature. It is
natural to wish to reduce to comprehensible simplicity the complex realities of human circumstances. Accordingly, those who speak of Latin
lovers and tempestuous temperaments, sunny Spain and bloody bull
fights, sangrías and siestas, flamenco and fiestas, in the belief that they
epitomize Spanish culture, may be forgiven – perhaps. In contrast, an
unpardonable prejudice persists among scholars, and rare is the Hispanist
who has not been made to sense it. Reduced to practical terms, it is the
matter of considering the study of Spanish easy relative to that of other
languages, and asking what Spanish literature has had to offer other than
Cervantes.[1]

Of the many ironies found in his writings and associated with his life,
none would have surprised Cervantes more than to have found himself,
centuries later, identified as the best of Spain and, as a consequence,
symbolic of the paucity of its men of letters. Like most artists, Cervantes
aspired to excel. It was his fate to have been born at a time when Italian
letters held sway, and even one of his national idols had lamented that
"hardly anyone has written in our language anything except that which
could very well be dispensed with."[2] In Chapter 2, I touched on the
importance of seeing many of Cervantes' claims to originality in a context
of opening the way for the Spanish language. His praise for the epic
poetry of Ercilla, Virués, and Rufo is explicitly grounded in their ability,
Cervantes maintains, to compete in Spanish with the best that Italy has
to offer. The prediction of *Don Quixote*'s success – "There will not be a
nation or a language that has not translated it" (II, 3) – likewise adds to
his personal pride the rare achievement of having other cultures translate
from his original Spanish.

I must caution that in this chapter I am primarily concerned not with
the intrinsic merit of the literary works discussed – those of Cervantes
as well as those of his contemporaries – but rather with Cervantes' per-

ceptions. The irony to which I alluded earlier embraces not only Cervantes' having eclipsed many of those he had intended to laud but also his belief that what today we would call the Golden Age of Spanish letters belonged to the period before the 1605 *Don Quixote* and that the subsequent decades, which we generally consider the apogee of that age, betrayed a degeneration among Spanish poets. As one leafs through the many and scattered pages of Cervantes' works that comment on the poets of his time, there emerges a trajectory from youthful optimism to disappointment in old age. Of course, to a certain extent such a progression is characteristic of many an individual. What bears remarking is that the attitude I am describing is informed not by Cervantes' opinion of his own works but by his opinion of his contemporaries. The references to his having opened the way, to the success of *Don Quixote*, to having been the first to write novellas in Spanish, to having dared to write plays in three acts and bring man's hidden thoughts to the stage – all these claims were made in the last three or four years of his life. As regards his disappointments with respect to his own career, these were related not to any misgivings about the merits of his works but rather to his mistreatment at the hands of Lope, the Argensolas, Avellaneda, and the impresarios who turned down his plays, not to mention the many disappointments and frustrations in the nonliterary side of his life. In short, whatever his dissatisfaction with the reception of his efforts, including the matters discussed in Chapter 1, there is no reason to doubt that he believed his several works to have been good.

An examination of his observations on other poets reveals the trajectory just mentioned. In his late thirties Cervantes published his first major work: the pastoral novel *La Galatea* (1585). The prologue approaches the problem immediately and, in point of fact, comes to grips with an issue that, many believe, did not assume importance until a century later and even then not in Spain. I refer to the so-called quarrel over the ancients and moderns, sometimes called the battle of the books.[3] The age in which he is writing, Cervantes maintains, is a time in which "en general, la poesía anda tan desfavorecida" ("poetry generally is in such disfavor"). Avalle-Arce sees herein the perennial complaint of Spain's poets.[4]

It is important to note two points brought out by Cervantes. The poor reception given to poetry is a part of the ancients–moderns controversy, for "in past times, poetry was, rightly, very much esteemed." The emphasis is placed on the reception of the art. With respect to the poets themselves, however, Cervantes departs from the conventional antagonism between past and present and insists on the fecundity of Spanish poets in all ages, specifically including his own; he mentions "the diversity of keen, subtle and lofty concepts that in the fertility of Spanish *ingenios* the favorable influence of heaven has, to great advantage and in diverse places, produced and does produce hourly in this happy age of ours."

The contrariety set up by Cervantes, then, is between those who respond to poetry and those who create it. The opposition will, in one form or another, remain with him throughout his life, from his frustrations concerning the rejection of his verse and theatrical endeavors to the matters raised in Chapter 1 regarding the reception given to *Don Quixote*. What is essential in this youthful statement is Cervantes' belief in the existence of a great number of Spanish poets at that time. Their purpose, he believes, is akin to what three decades later he will claim to have accomplished himself: "to enrich, the poet taking into consideration his own language and to master the artifice of eloquence that befits it, for loftier and more important endeavors, and to open the way so that, in imitation of him, narrow-minded souls who would have the abundance of the Castilian language cut short by the brevity of ancient language may understand that they have an open, fertile and spacious field."

A number of themes are commingled here. The general context remains the ancients–moderns controversy, but Cervantes does not really take up the argument in antagonistic terms. In contrast to the situation of poetry's reception – it is an art that once was esteemed and has fallen into disfavor – no intrinsic opposition is set up between the poetry of antiquity and that of present-day Spain. The thing for the poet to do is to consider "su propia lengua" ("his own language"), that is, to seek what is appropriate without limitations imposed by another culture and another tongue. (On a number of occasions Cervantes will remind us that the Greeks did not speak Latin because they were Greeks and not Romans and that the latter did not write their masterworks in Greek for the corresponding reason, a statement made as well by Lope de Vega, whose own contribution – and herein lies another of the many ironies – was predicated on an art called new and deemed appropriate *en este tiempo*, in these times, and specifically *en España*, in Spain.)

Two phrases in the prologue to *La Galatea* strike responsive chords in readers of Cervantes: "en la edad dichosa nuestra" ("in this happy age of ours") and "abrir camino" ("to open the way"). The latter, as noted earlier, presages what in the *Viaje del Parnaso* Cervantes will claim to have done for the Castilian language with his *Novelas ejemplares*. In the present context, what stands out is his belief that it is the proper role of Spanish poets in diverse places, which is to say that there exists a profusion of Spanish poets throughout Spain, a point to which I shall return shortly. Equally significant is the phrase "en la edad dichosa nuestra." Three decades later Cervantes speaks of "nuestra edad poco dichosa" ("our unlucky age" [*Viaje del Parnaso*, Chapter 2]). This phrase immediately brings to mind Don Quixote's habitual deploring of the passing

of "la dichosa edad dorada" ("the happy golden age"), as contrasted with
"esta nuestra edad de hierro" ("this iron age of ours" [I, 11]), the latter
depicted at one point as "la depravada edad nuestra" ("the depraved age
of ours" [II, 1]). Granted, the contexts are dissimilar: Don Quixote
compares a mythical age in which the principles of chivalry held sway
with a materialistic present; in *La Galatea*, Cervantes implicitly denies a
contrast in essence by emphasizing the fertility and multiplicity of poets
in existence. Nevertheless, we should not lose sight of the significant
point that links the two kinds of passages: The *Galatea* prologue speaks
of poetic values and narrow-minded souls incapable of realizing the potential for creativity within the framework of a contemporary culture
and its language. The passage is optimistic. Don Quixote's frequent
outbursts likewise speak of a past in poetic terms – be it a utopian, that
is, classical, referent or the values of his romances – in contrast with the
prosaic values encountered in the present reality. The outlook is pessimistic. Implicit in the quixotic vision is the madness of having an old
gentleman embody and seek to restore the poetic values. Implicit in the
Galatea perspective is the faith in a generation of poets worthy of a Spanish
Parnassus. Always mindful of the riskiness of associating Cervantes with
his fictive creature, I nonetheless think it appropriate to see in Don
Quixote some measure of Cervantes' perception of the path followed by
Spanish poetry in the decades since that early optimism.

In the preceding passages I have spoken of poetic values. It bears
keeping in mind that it is in such a general context that words like "poet"
and "poetry" are used by Cervantes. Poetry and those who compose it
are not limited to matters of verse and rhyme, and it is in the larger,
Aristotelian sense of poetic truth that we must understand Cervantes'
references to poetry and poets. To some degree, the definition is in
keeping with the focus of this book, as the *Random House Dictionary of
the English Language* makes clear: "The difference between poetry and
verse is usually the difference between substance and form. Poetry is
lofty thought or impassioned feeling expressed in imaginative words.
. . . Verse is any expression in words which simply conforms to accepted
metrical rules and structure." Of course, this is not to say that distinctions
in genre and mode were not recognized. Not only were Cervantes and
his contemporaries cognizant of such matters, but as is well known, the
differences were hierarchical. Epic or heroic poetry enjoyed supremacy
(as tragedy did in dramatic literature); as I suggested in Chapter 2, however, Cervantes' oft-cited assertion that the epic may be composed in
prose as well as in verse has less to do with generic categories than with
the expression of poetic values generally. Similarly, Cervantes' frequent
references to his own difficulties with versification need not be read as
a confession of failure but can be seen rather as a concession to matters

of form in contradistinction to the more important matter of poetry's substance. It is the latter that Cervantes wishes to extol and to create. If he does not stand out in one form (verse), he may nonetheless succeed in producing poetic art in another, whatever that form may be labeled (prose novel, prose epic, *verdadera historia*).

It is in this broad framework that we ought to see the many observations on poetry and poets, beginning with those in *La Galatea*. The points brought out in the prologue are elaborated in the sixth book of this pastoral novel, particularly in the *Canto de Calíope* or *Song of Calliope*. Although Calliope was, of the nine muses of classical mythology, specifically associated with epic or heroic poetry, Cervantes summons her in the name of poetry generally: "My name is Calliope; it is my duty and nature to favor and aid the divine spirits whose laudable occupation is to devote themselves to the never sufficiently praised discipline [*ciencia*] of poetry." The comments made in the lengthy *Canto* are to be understood, then, in keeping with the broader definition of poetic art just suggested.

The *Canto* is characterized by an emphasis on time and place: the here and now. The ostensible reason for Calliope's appearance is the shepherds' homage to their late comrade Meliso (Diego Hurtado de Mendoza). Before her appearance, therefore, the object of praise was someone no longer living yet known to the other literary shepherds. The arrival of Calliope, who first lists the great poets of the past, thus links the recent past to classical times; next follows the recitation of the *Canto*, which, as Calliope points out in the second strophe, will be limited to poets now living. As regards nationality, Calliope will sing of those "who live in this your Spain and some in the remote Indies subject to it." In contrast to the almost ritual apology for prolixity that precedes or follows (occasionally both) so many of the recitations throughout *La Galatea*, Calliope introduces her *Canto* by promising that, despite its length, she will present it so that they will be "displeased by its brevity." The implication is not only that it will be well told but that – inasmuch as its substance is the enumeration of Spanish poets – it will be only a compendium. The emphasis, accordingly, is on the profusion of those who compose poetry in Spanish.

One of the predominant motifs of the *Canto* is the youth of the Spanish poets. At the same time, their intellectual and artistic maturity is stressed. Cervantes thereby places in relief not only the contemporary character of those whom the muse will immortalize but also an overall sense of optimism with respect to future creativity. Calliope repeatedly refers to her function of eternalizing the poets' fame after their deaths even though they are still alive, which is to say that they have already attained a status worthy of enduring fame, their tender years notwithstanding. The entire poem exudes Cervantes' youthful confidence in the ability of his contemporaries to compete with, equal, and perhaps outshine the poets of Italy and antiquity.

Diego de Sarmiento y Carvajal is "mozo en la edad, anciano en el sentido" ("a youth in age, old man in common sense"); Gutierre Carvajal is a poet of "tierna edad, maduro entendimiento" ("tender age, mature intellect"); Luis de Vargas has a "maduro ingenio en verdes pocos días" ("mature talent in few green days"); Lupercio Leonardo de Argensola is of "edad temprana, pensamientos canos" ("early age, grey-haired thoughts"); to Cristóbal de Virués Calliope says, "se adelanta tu ciencia y tu valor tan a tus años" ("your learning and your valor run ahead of your years"). In another of the many ironies it is Lope de Vega who, at the age of twenty-three, receives the most elaborate encomium of this kind:

> In a genius experience shows
> that in green years and an early age
> learning makes its lodging as well
> as in the mature, ancient and grey-haired age.
> I shall not enter into competition with anyone
> who contradicts a truth so plain,
> the more so if perchance it reaches his ears
> that I say it for you, Lope de Vega.

It is poets like these that make these early years "edad dorada, siglo venturoso" ("golden age, fortunate century"), "la venturosa nuestra edad presente" ("the fortunate present age of ours") in "dichosa España" ("lucky Spain"). There are so many such poets that, walking just a few steps along the banks of the Betis (Guadalquivir) River, Calliope discerns "another thousand Pindus and Parnassus" mountains, and the Tajo epitomizes the abundance of present-day poets in Spain by being graced with "a thousand divine spirits that make our age more fortunate than that of the Greeks and Latins." The reaction to Calliope's acclamation of Spanish poets of the present is found in the words of the "venerable Telesio":

And do not think that the pleasure I have received is small in learning through such a truthful recitation how large the number of divine *ingenios* who live in our Spain today is, because it has always been and is the opinion of foreign nations that there are not many, but rather, few souls in [Spain] who in the discipline of poetry show that they hold it aloft; for it is so much the reverse of what it seems, since each one of those that [Calliope] has named surpasses the keenest foreigner, and they would give clear indications of it if in this our Spain poetry were esteemed as it is in other countries. And so, because of this reason, the distinguished and bright *ingenios* that excel in [Spain], with the little esteem that princes and the *vulgo* show for them, communicate their lofty and exotic concepts only with their intellects, without daring to publish them for the world, and in my view heaven must have arranged it this way, because neither the world nor the ill-considered century of ours deserves to enjoy such tasteful dishes for the soul.[5]

Once more we note the contrast between the reception given to poetry and those who create it. The latter are numerous, as Calliope has detailed, and it is only in the sense that they are not properly appreciated that one may speak of the "ill-considered century of ours," a restatement of matters raised in the prologue. The underlying argument – the substance, as it were – remains the multiplicity of Spanish poets who may compete with and even surpass those of other nations and other times. It is this point that bears stressing, and I shall return to it shortly.

It is of interest to linger a bit and pursue two thoughts raised in the passage just quoted. In an attempt to rationalize the paucity of Spanish poetic productivity relative to that of other nations and times, Cervantes brings up an argument that is not unfamiliar in an altogether different setting. Irrelevant as it may appear at first, I cannot help remarking that a similar case is made in the halls of academe – at least in the United States – when the question of scholarly productivity arises. The well-known yardstick of publication statistics is frequently attacked not only by those who are incapable of producing publishable work but not infrequently by those (or in the name of those) who genuinely love scholarly labors, whose knowledge and perspicacity are admired by their peers, but whose scholarly activity outside the classroom is by and large limited to faculty club or soirée-type discussions. The reasons for these scholars' meager output in published form are varied, often idiosyncratic, and generally immaterial to the circumstances set forth in *La Galatea*. Nevertheless, the phenomenon is analogous. In the attempt to explain how, in the face of so vast an array of poets, "each one" of whom "surpasses the keenest foreigner," such prodigious creativity may go unnoticed, Cervantes submits that the *ingenios* communicate only among themselves. (For the faculty clubs and offices of today we may substitute the literary academies of Cervantes' time or, in the metaphor of pastoral literature, the hills, valleys, meadows, and riverbanks where poetry might be recited and appreciated.) If we extend the analogy a bit further, the point at which it seems to break down illustrates the problem Cervantes wishes to put before us. Those who "appreciate" a professor's publications are, presumably, the institutional administration that supports the activity financially and the readers (students and teachers around the nation and beyond). The corresponding sets in Cervantes' passage are the princes and the *vulgo*. It is because these groups do not value poetic art that those who create it do not "dare" to publish and, consequently, are unable to enhance Spain's fame and prestige. The polarization, therefore, is between a vast number of superb Spanish poets and the patrons – in the two senses that princes and *vulgo* represent – who fail to provide appreciation and support.

To some extent, the specific categories of princes and *vulgo* doubtless are meant to signify the two extremes of society and thus to embrace all of it: Cervantes is to this extent claiming that the Spanish nation does not hold the art of its poets in high esteem. But in light of our knowledge of Cervantes' opinions of princes and the *vulgo*, there is in his statement a hint of what he will later assert unequivocally: "Everyone who is ignorant, though he be lord and prince, can and must be counted among the *vulgo*." The statement in *La Galatea* may thus be seen as an application of a stylistic device delineated by Demetrius: "There are some members [of an oratorical period] which, although not really opposed to one another, are apparently antithetical." Demetrius gives an example from what he terms "the pleasantry of the poet Epicharmus" and observes: "The same thing is said [in both members] and there is no real opposition."[6] If the issue is ignorance of poetic values, the apparent opposition between princes and *vulgo* disappears. As early as the 1580s, then, we discern in Cervantes a posture that sets apart the cognoscenti from the hoi polloi, the latter defined not in social but in intellectual terms.

As regards the poets themselves, however, Cervantes leaves no doubt: His age is more fortunate than those of the Greeks and Romans because of the thousands of poets that grace the Spain of the 1580s. If we recognize easily his use of hyperbole in *La Galatea*, we observe as well its inverse in *Don Quixote* a generation later: Cervantes then can point to only three and a half poets. (In *El licenciado Vidriera* he says that they "no hacen número," usually translated as being "not worth counting" and literally meaning that they do not so much as make a number.) Many critics have commented on this and similarly sardonic assertions, and several – notably Avalle-Arce – have seen the pessimistic statements in *La Galatea* concerning poetry's reception in the larger context of Spain's inferiority complex,[7] but no one has addressed the question raised here: Why does Cervantes exhibit confidence in the multitude of Spanish poets in the 1580s but feel the need to express sarcasm at the height not only of his own fame but of what we now call Spain's Golden Age of literature?

What makes Cervantes' declarations significant is the chronology. Statements about Spain's inferiority, whether in confirmation or refutation, abound, and to this extent Cervantes' comments are simply part

of a conventional concern, even in their extremes of optimism and pessimism, as Otis Green has documented. If we leave to one side the
aspersion cast on those who fail to appreciate poetry – a complaint about
insufficient patronage no less than about ignorance – what is striking is
the change in Cervantes' assessment over the decades after *La Galatea.*
The chapter devoted to this topic by Green is entitled "Spanish Belles-
lettres: From Inferiority to Equality," and the trajectory followed corresponds to the chronological progression suggested by this title. The
quotations offered range from Castillejo's sixteenth-century opinion that
Spaniards "have, until now, been very deficient in all sorts of books for
lack of authors" to Espinel's assessment, published in 1618: "I have lived
in a time when the Spanish Monarchy was so abundantly filled with
gallant spirits in arms and in letters that I do not believe Rome possessed
any greater; and I venture to say that that nation did not have as many,
or of such stature."[8]

If it seems that Cervantes stands alone in his judgment of Spain's
potential grandeur of the 1580s and its subsequent degeneration in the
seventeenth century, it bears pointing out that the belief that the apogee
had been reached in that earlier period was shared by a number of poets
who concerned themselves with drama. The Valencian Micer Andrés
Rey de Artieda, in the prefatory verses to his play *Los amantes* (published
in 1581 and written between 1577 and 1580), asserted:

> I say that Spain is in its robust age
> and if in language and arms it's worthy and is able,
> it seems to me to enjoy what pleases.[9]

Those familiar with the Spanish *comedia* will recognize in Artieda's words
an anticipation of what Lope de Vega would say in 1609 regarding the
criterion of *gusto* in the composition of plays. For our purposes here, it
is noteworthy that the Valencian, a participant in the battle of Lepanto,
believed the Spain of 1580 to have attained puissance in letters as well as
in arms. To go into details here would be to indulge in a study of a
different sort; suffice it to say that Artieda believed that he had contributed
to the development of a dramatic art particularly appropriate to Spanish
custom and taste, as opposed to a straitjacket of preceptist rules (despite
which histories of literature study him in a neoclassical context). Although *Los amantes* is his only extant play and is in four acts, he was
thought by some to have originated the three-act format that became de
rigueur for the Lopean theater of subsequent decades. The point is of
interest because it reflects a perception of Artieda – however inaccurate
historically – as an innovator in matters that later would become symbolic
of the reigning dramatic art.

By 1605, however, Artieda was writing of *poetillas,* or "little poets" just out of swaddling clothes, and of the poet who "in six hours composes a *comedia*"[10] Marcelino Menéndez Pelayo sees in these verses evidence that Artieda, "like Cervantes, was one of the straggling and defeated dramatists and, therefore, one of the malcontents opposed to Lope, to Tárrega and Aguilar, who in his own city of Valencia had supplanted him in the theater."[11] Although Rinaldo Froldi believes the reference to Lope and the Valencians to be in a favorable context, Joaquín de Entrambasaguas notes the displeasure evinced in Artieda's words regarding the rapid climb of Lope and his followers, a reading recalled by Alfredo Hermenegildo, who observes:

> Artieda, with Cervantes, at bottom recognized the genre in which Lope was triumphing . . . The author of *Los amantes* was bothered by the extravagances, anachronisms, and the overt violation of all the old rules, which characterized the new Spanish *comedia*. And he did not comprehend that he, in practice and following a different path, was very close to the dramatic mentality of Lope and the rest of the Valencians.[12]

Another Valencian, and one who also took part in the Lepanto armada, was Cristóbal de Virués. As mentioned in an earlier chapter, he too was singled out as the initiator of the three-act format, partly because of his own claim to that effect and, notably, because Lope de Vega himself attributed the innovation to him in his *Arte nuevo*. But Virués anticipated Lope in a far more transcendental matter, namely, the blending of tragic and comic elements, and on this point Lope credits no one but Nature herself.[13] It was perhaps a result of such disregard for the substance of his contribution to the new art – like Artieda, Virués was consigned to a neoclassical pigeonhole despite his efforts to write something different – that Virués exhibited disappointment in his later years. The man who, in his youth, could write that "this century in which we go about is like those past ones we extol"[14] closed his collection of dramatic and lyric works (published in 1609, the same year as Lope's *Arte nuevo*) with this sonnet:

> I have already fallen from the sublime height
> whither I climbed with sweet delirium
> following the thought and desire
> that were fleeing from the crowd;
>   I was guided in that flight by a heroic light
> with sweet eagerness for noble employment,
> which I now see all changed
> into harsh anxiety of immense grief;
>   Errors, confidences, furies, jealousy,

> ingratitude, envy, perfidy
> have cut the wings of my flights;
>   You, divine pity, you, raise now
> other wings in me with which to the heavens
> I may redirect the flight by a surer way.[15]

One cannot, of course, identify the origin of the qualities that cut the wings of Virués' flights, and it would be folly to identify them with Lope de Vega. The context remains, however, the concluding lines of the volume that contained Virués' five plays, published there for the first time, although Virués, in the prologue, made a point of commenting that they were composed in his youth, which is to say that he was doing this sort of thing long before Lope and his school had reached prominence. By "this sort of thing" I mean not only plays of three acts but also the mixture of the comic and the tragic, the use of the *romance* versification, and other matters that Virués himself considered innovations, as revealed by the individual prologues to several of the plays. The latter, according to Froldi, "are characterized by an intrigue and by characters that will be typical of *comedias*."[16] One can perhaps sense Virués' feelings when, more than two decades after his own works were composed, the elements contained therein were identified as a "new art" of a younger generation. Hermenegildo sees what he calls an "interesting situation" here for Virués, who "found himself shoved aside by the masses. . . . At the same time, and this is the principal characteristic of Virués' vital way, our tragedian yielded to the pressures of the masses . . . and he remained swimming among the waters in a difficult equilibrium that, if it played a role in the formation of the national theater, must have caused him more bitterness than happiness."[17] As for Lope, if he found only the three-act formula with which to credit Virués in 1609, the tribute in *El laurel de Apolo* in 1630, long after Virués had died, appears to be a belated recognition of what Virués never heard in his lifetime:

> Oh unique genius! Rest in peace, you
> to whom the comic muses owed
> the best beginnings they did behold.[18]

Of this tribute William C. Atkinson has written that it "would make of Virués the true founder of the Spanish national drama."[19]

It is not my purpose here to explore the accuracy of the many claims and attributions concerning the formulation of the Spanish *comedia*. What is to the point is that a number of poets whose works appeared in the late 1570s and early 1580s perceived themselves as having divested Spanish dramatic poetry of the shackles of inappropriate precepts while adhering to those classical principles that, they believed, inform art. (If this view appears contradictory, an example is Virués' *Gran Semíramis*: In the prologue he boasts of the novelty of its being the first play in three acts, each of which takes place in a different time and place. However, Virués explains that each act assumes the nature of a separate tragedy and thus preserves the classical unities within the limits of its own dramatic unity.) Nor was it exclusively Valencians who believed themselves to have contributed to the formation of the new theater. The Sevillian Juan de la Cueva (never mentioned by Lope anywhere) maintained in 1606 that it was he who reduced the five-act format to four and that he "introduced other novelties, altering the use of the ancients in accordance with this time and [its] characteristics."[20]

It is against this background that Cervantes' statements about the drama must be seen. Like Virués, Cervantes published his plays years after they, or at least most of them, had been composed. The subtitle of the collection – "nunca representados" ("never performed") – makes two points for us. It is not only a reflection of Cervantes' difficulties with the impresarios who showed no interest in his plays but an indication of his finally having prepared the plays for publication: dramatic literature to be *read* by the literate minority. Even so had Virués addressed the prologue to his works to the "discreto lector," a code phrase in contradistinction to the *vulgo*. I am not suggesting that Cervantes' original intention had been to have his plays published rather than performed. It was the failure to have them accepted for the stage that led to his seeking another audience: readers instead of spectators. The many lengthy stage directions in his *comedias*, so unlike the short and mostly mechanical indications of entrances, exits, and the like, may in fact have been additions to the script when the latter was readied for a reading audience. Wardropper believes that these elaborate stage directions betray Cervantes' desire to control the action rather than yield to the caprices of the professional *metteur en scène*. Doubtless this desire was also a factor, but I do not agree with Wardropper's pejorative tone as he explains that Cervantes addressed "mere readers" when he adopted "incongruently the posture of a narrator, of a novelist."[21] Rather, the stage directions reflect Cervantes' desire to project his dramatizations to that mind's eye of the reader.

With respect to the fact of their publication, I am inclined to accept Casalduero's conclusions, with one qualification. The example of Virués both corrects Casalduero's guess that Cervantes' case is unique and supports the idea of the disappointed playwright:

> Cervantes was hurt by the fact that the theater's doors were closed to him and it appeared to him to be an injustice. Sure of himself, he published his plays. If I am not mistaken, it was an unusual

event at that time. Cervantes published his works not because of having failed but because they refused to perform them. He did not accept the verdict of impresarios and actors. Who knows if they have reached us [in written form] because of not having reached the stage.[22]

The issue of concern remains the chronology. It is in Cervantes' final years that he sends his plays to the printers, and it is then that he makes claims to having "dared" to reduce the number of acts to three, among other matters. In Chapter 2 I discussed the significance that may attach – or that Cervantes might like to attach – to being among the first to write plays in only three acts. As we have seen, others have laid claim to this innovation and still others find it of value to attribute the tripartite formula to this or that poet, an indication of the symbolic importance of this deviation from the established configuration. Cervantes does not say that he was the first. In Chapter 2 we explored his posture regarding "firsts," and so his avoidance of the term here need not surprise us even within the framework of a series of claims concerning his place in the evolution of the Spanish drama. What is placed in relief is the fact that to do such things back in the sixteenth century – say, in the 1580s – was *daring*. First, second, third, or whatever, the kinds of things with which Cervantes and others were experimenting in those pre-Lopean years were unorthodox and bold, corresponding to the efforts revealed in *La Galatea*, as we saw in Chapter 4. But then, Cervantes almost seems to grumble, Lope de Vega, that *monstruo de naturaleza*, entered and ran off with the monarchy of the *comedia*. I read this assertion not so much as a criticism of Lope's art as an expression of bitter resignation at Lope's having absconded with the crown of a creative (and successful) kingdom that Cervantes and others had helped to bring about.

Cervantes marvels at Lope's prodigious productivity, pronounces Lope's plays felicitous and witty, and makes a point of Lope's having seen all his plays performed "or at least having heard that they have been performed" (*Obras*, p. 180). Not only does this situation contrast with Cervantes' failure to get his own plays performed, but it reminds us of the concluding sentence of *Don Quixote*, Part II, published that same year (1615), in which Cervantes (via Cide Hamete) claims to be the first to have wholly enjoyed the fruits of his writings. To the extent that it again deals with "firsts," this sentence is open to interpretation, as I suggested in Chapter 2. On the other hand, if we look at these two passages of 1615 from the perspective of Chapter 1, an interesting reading suggests itself.

The *Don Quixote* assertion, placed in the mock-serious context of Cide Hamete's addressing his pen, is ostensibly based on his having caused people to abhor the "fingidas y disparatadas historias de los libros de caballerías" ("fictitious and absurd stories of the books of chivalry") because of "mi verdadero Don Quijote" ("my real Don Quixote"). The adjective *verdadero* – "real" or "true" – is ambiguous here, for its placement in this sentence suggests an opposition to the fabricated stories of the romances, despite Don Quixote's self-abnegation moments earlier. (He does indeed condemn the romances in his deathbed abjuration, but he simultaneously renounces his identity as Don Quixote, the very *persona* invoked in the sentence under discussion.) The larger context of the paragraph suggests that the opposition is between the true Don Quixote of our narrative and the spurious one of Avellaneda. Now, if we accept his professed intention to destroy the romances, our reading must contrast the latter's "fictitious and *disparatadas* stories" with the self-evident: Don Quixote's adventures also have been a series of *disparates*, but as detailed in Chapter 1, these are absurdities that are calculated and apposite. It is on this contrariety that the parody that is *Don Quixote* rests.

The Moor's statement regarding his having been the first wholly to enjoy the fruits of his writings may be seen as a tongue-in-cheek statement on Cervantes' part. Such a reading not only supports the thesis put forth in Chapter 1 – if the Moor wholly enjoyed the fruits of his writings, the same claim cannot necessarily be made for Cervantes, whose purpose need not coincide with that of Cide Hamete – but also leads us to question the meaning of Cervantes' emphasis on Lope's having wholly ("all his plays") enjoyed the fruits of his writings for the theater. Of course, it bears repeating, the immediate point is the success of Lope contrasted with Cervantes' failure in getting their respective plays staged. However, the framework of the commentary on Lope's success is the development of the Spanish theater. Indeed, although the overall emphasis is on evolution, the language used to describe Lope's role is that of revolution: He ran off with the comic monarchy. (The particular verb used – *alzarse* – though it means "to run off" with something, has as its basic meaning "to rise up." In the *Viaje del Parnaso*, Mercury denies passage to a number of poets because he fears that "se alzasen con Parnaso" ["they might run off with Parnassus"] and found a new empire.)

In the prologue to his plays, Cervantes provides us with a concise history of the Spanish theater's development as he recalls it, including in his summary the names of many poets from his youth as well as more recent practitioners of the "new comedy," all of whom, he says, have contributed to bringing "this great assemblage to the great Lope." Riley finds it surprising that so much emphasis is placed on stagecraft, on sound effects and scenery, when Cervantes evidently considered such matters secondary to the dramatic art itself. He asks, "Is it not curious that Cervantes should linger so long on this aspect of the national *comedia*'s development? Could the old man's accolades have their pinch of irony?"[23]

Although Riley cautiously avoids answering the question by suggesting that at times Cervantes' irony is impenetrable, I propose the following paraphrastic reading from the prologue:

> The history of the theater goes back a long way. Certainly it was already developed in my youth, although the stage settings and mechanical effects were not as elaborate as they are these days. [Here he implies as well that in the sixteenth century poets concentrated on the art of the play, whereas in the seventeenth the newer mechanical devices make up for artistic deficiencies, a complaint also voiced by Lope about those who succeeded him. Scholars who seek to explain Cervantes' exaggeration of Lope de Rueda's simplicities may find an answer in this perspective.] Any strides forward that have been taken since my youth are the achievement of many poets, and I, too, dared to make innovations, such as the now-conventional three-act format and a more modern representation of man's unexpressed thoughts and imaginings. But then a "monster of nature" – by which is meant something counter to the normal order of things – appeared, took over the theatrical domain, subjugated and placed under his jurisdiction ["avasalló y puso debajo de su jurisdicción"] all *farceurs*, and filled the world with *comedias* of his own kind. Back in my day it was daring to be innovative. Today one man rules; he prescribes the formula, elements of which we developed earlier; if they are not done according to his paradigm, my plays are not acceptable to the impresarios and actors who, like Lope, have yielded to what they perceive to be the taste of the *vulgo*. From a generation of a thousand poets attempting bold and artistic dramatic poetry, we have been reduced to an absolute monarchy in which it no longer is worth counting the number of poets, for I can think of no more than three and a half. Indeed, for some time now I have been ridiculing Lope's presumptuous depiction of himself as "único y solo" ["unique and sole"].[24]

If this reading is somewhat oversimplified, it is nonetheless a generally accurate abstract of Cervantes' position. I think that it helps to clear up another doubt raised by Riley, who writes: "Often one reads that the times are disastrous for poetry and, almost at the same time, that the country has never had a greater abundance of poets and that one can scarcely find a poet worthy of the name. Neither the *Parnaso* nor the *Galatea* is free of these common ambiguities."[25] In my view, there is little ambiguity if we keep in mind the focus of the present chapter. Times can indeed be disastrous for poetry even while there exists a wealth of poets. The distinction, as we have seen, is between the reception given to poetry and those who create it. Moreover, Cervantes' opinion of the poets of his youth, colored by the optimism and daring spirit that he rather nostalgically recalls, is opposed by the disappointments of the intervening years, so that he finds it difficult to discern many good poets in the last decade and a half of his life. In the 1615 *Don Quixote*, he charges that "among the unpolished poets of our age it is customary for each one to write as he pleases, and to steal from whomever he wishes, whether or not it is pertinent to their intention, and there is no stupidity that they sing or write which is not attributed to poetic license." As the reader of this book no doubt appreciates, this sentence is charged with meaning for us. The original Spanish bears scrutinizing: "Entre los intonsos poetas de nuestra edad se usa que cada uno escriba como quisiere, y hurte de quien quisiere, venga o no venga a pelo de su intento, y ya no hay necedad que canten o escriban que no se atribuya a licencia poética" (II, 70). I have rendered *intonsos* as "unpolished" despite most translators' preference for the literal "unshorn": Today's poets, Cervantes suggests, are too young to shave, which is to say, they are immature and inexpert,[26] and as a result they are unpolished in their handling of poetic material. Not only are they wont to plagiarize, but their efforts, which are stupidities (*necedades*), are inapposite to their own intentions. We know, of course, how damning an indictment this is, but Cervantes compounds the charge: Not only are the absurdities inapposite; they are not pertinent to the poets' own purpose. (Most translators skip over Cervantes' apparent tautology by translating "no venga a pelo de su intento" as simply "not to the point.") For our purposes in this chapter, the significance of the passage lies in the fact that these charges are directed specifically at the poets *of our age*, that is, of Cervantes' old age.

There is ample documentation, in his own direct statements and in those of many of his characters, to attest to Cervantes' lifelong attraction to the theater. His statements on poets are not to be read as restricted to or even centering on dramatic poets, but I believe that his attitude was animated by his hapless experiences in the theatrical world. Although epic poetry was generally regarded as the highest form of the art, Cervantes did not attempt serious heroic poetry. We do know, of course, that an epic in prose held an attraction for him and that *Persiles y Sigismunda* was the result. We know as well, if indeed not better, that the romances of chivalry whetted his interest sufficiently to enable him to parody them to a degree that scholars only recently have appreciated fully.[27] If he did attempt epic poetry, it was "a mock epic, a classical parody," to use a recent description by Elias L. Rivers, who says of the *Viaje del Parnaso* that

> . . . it is a poem about the status of poetry and poets in the Spain of Cervantes's own time. [I would interject that its focus is the

Spain of Cervantes' last years, though it of course embraces earlier decades as well.] The first-person narrator and protagonist, named Miguel de Cervantes, seems to be nostalgic for an earlier Renaissance humanism; but he is actually aware that, in Spain at least, humanism has broken down and that there are no firm classical standards in literature anymore: "bad" poetry is praised and rewarded financially, while "good" poets starve to death.

Rivers also confronts the question that is central to our chapter here:

His career was interrupted [after *La Galatea* of 1585] for almost ten years; and when he began writing again, he was no longer the same Renaissance man. We don't know exactly what happened to him, spiritually, during these ten years of silence; we do know that, socially, he suffered financial difficulties, that he was excommunicated and sent to prison. There was also the defeat of the Invincible Armada. . . . Should we speak of a *desengaño*, a spiritual crisis in the life of Cervantes? Whatever it was, exactly, it seems to correspond to something akin to what Hyram Haydn has called the "Counter-Renaissance," the skeptical disintegration of that early optimistic synthesis reflected in a classical style of language.[28]

We do know of something that happened to Cervantes in the decade following the publication of *La Galatea*, and it is specifically a matter of his theatrical endeavors. In 1592 Cervantes signed a contract with the impresario Rodrigo Osorio to compose six plays. I have already offered my hypothesis regarding the fate of these plays.[29] My conjecture is strengthened by the declaration of 1614 in the *Adjunta al Parnaso*, in which he speaks precisely of six plays (six *comedias* as well as six *entremeses*) that have not been performed "because the impresarios don't come looking for me nor do I go looking for them." It is in this same passage that Cervantes explains that the impresarios have their "poetas paniaguados," their favorites, and do not care to look for "pan de trastrigo," an idiom meaning "better than the ordinary." Francisco Rodríguez Marín avers that the real reason was not this but Cervantes' confession of a year later (in the prologue to the published plays) regarding an impresario's reported remark denigrating his efforts in verse.[30] The two reasons are not mutually exclusive, and I think it correct to accept them both. Doubtless the deprecatory remark had been made and passed on to Cervantes, who would scarcely include it in a work that purported to separate good poets from bad ones. More relevant to the *Parnaso* is the censure of the impresarios who, content with the box-office success of works by Lope or in the manner of Lope, did not care to accept, much less seek out, works that from Cervantes' standpoint would be better than the ordinary fare. Irrespective of the merits of Cervantes' verse, I think it accurate to say that the statement in the *Parnaso* reflects what Cervantes himself believed. If, as I surmise, the six plays of 1592 are identical to the six of 1614, and in turn are six of the eight published in 1615, we have in these works a continuous thread that represents more than two decades during which Cervantes – whether because of the impresarios' unwillingness to stage his plays or because he refused to accept their terms, financial or artistic – failed to have his plays performed. To conclude that his attitude toward the poets who received the applause of the *vulgo* animated his assessment of poets and poetry in those decades is, I daresay, not unreasonable.

I have remarked several times that the relationship between Cervantes and Lope de Vega abounds with ironies. Among these belongs the irony arising from their respective views on newness as applied to art, specifically dramatic art. I have explored elsewhere Lope's approach to the problem, and I present here only the essence of my arguments.[31] Despite his association with the *comedia nueva* or "new comedy," Lope eschews newness even as he himself contributes innovations in his works. His attitude is not identical with that of Cervantes as described in Chapter 2 (although there are points of contact), for Lope does not play with the concept. Rather, he devotes much energy to presenting his *comedia* as an established art, befitting the Spain of his time. (Even in the *Arte nuevo*, Lope never refers to his art as new – the word in the title modifies an *ars poetica*, not the art itself – and instead insists on his having already succeeded with nearly five hundred plays.) He attacks *gongorismo* as "la nueva poesía" ("the new poetry") and ridicules those who become poets in a day. He is infuriated by the new stage effects, for they detract from the essence of his dramatic art – action in verse – and he mocks his rival (Elena Osorio's lover) as "un extraño pastor de ayer venido" ("a strange shepherd who arrived only yesterday").[32] Whenever he has the opportunity (as in the prologues to his collections of plays or *partes*), Lope brings his reader up to date on how many hundreds of plays he has by now composed, emphasizing thereby not how new but how established and well instituted his art is.

This hasty sketch of Lope's attitude toward newness makes evident the irony to which I have referred. Whatever Lope may have had to say about it, it is with the *comedia nueva* that he was and remains identified, and it is in this light that the disillusionment of poets like Artieda, Virués, Cervantes, and others emerges. I am not suggesting, of course, that Lope was not the leading figure in the codification and popularization of the *comedia*. Although he was not its creator, he undeniably was responsible for its becoming the paradigm of the national theater of Spain. But writers like Cervantes nostalgically recalled not the Lopean formulation and formalization but their own generation's formation of what they had perceived as particularly appropriate for the Spain of their time. It would be irrelevant to argue here the merits of one view or the other, much less of the respective works. Lope's emergence, dominance, and popularity are the issue. Whatever his originality and whatever his debt to his immediate predecessors, in the eyes of Cervantes (among others) Lope was a parvenu – the very quality to which Lope objected in the new wave of *gongorismo*.

It is this perspective, rather than any direct antagonism between the two personalities or their works, that animates Cervantes' disillusionment. When Cervantes composes his own *comedias* with parodies of the Lopean formula (*La entretenida*) or direct challenges to that formula (*Pedro de Urdemalas*), or when he exacts an explanation of the *disparates* of the new theater (*El rufián dichoso*), he betrays not hostility but an "I-could-have-done-it-so-much-better" attitude, a posture not unlike the one he assumes with respect to the romances of chivalry. (Carroll Johnson has made the insightful observation that in the discussion between the curate and the canon in *Don Quixote* regarding the romances and the *comedias*, the same or analogous properties are the object of criticism.)[33] But Cervantes has not had the chance to have his way applauded, for reasons already discussed. If Artieda complains of *poetillas*, Cervantes ridicules *poetillas rateros*, a pun not only on the adjective *ratero* ("thieving" or "sneaky") but, given the context of the sentence from the *Adjunta al Parnaso*, also on *ratón* (mouse), for the reference is to the putrescent blood of the "bad poets" who have been killed in the battle between the good and bad poets, that blood now spawning the aforementioned *poetillas*, who are the size of mice.[34]

It is again – or more accurately, still – the issue we have been exploring in this chapter. From the thousand *ingenios* of the 1580s Spain has degenerated to three and a half poets alongside numerous *poetillas rateros*. Of no little significance is the treatment being given to the earth in the attempt to exterminate the poetasters: with salt, "as if it were the home of traitors." The trajectory from a happy, golden age to a detestable, even depraved, age of iron must be seen against this background of perceived treachery. The hopes Cervantes had for the host of Spanish poets have been dashed. He alone has opened the way, has made sense out of nonsense; and his lament from the *Viaje del Parnaso*, following upon the list of his achievements, is still germane today, though we understand it from the ironic vantage point that the centuries have given us:

> Therefore I am distressed and suffer
> to find myself alone on foot, without a tree's
> caring to grant me any succor.

Chapter 7

Phases of substance

<hr>

Presume not that I am the thing I was.
— Shakespeare, *II Henry IV*

In recent years it has been shown that Cervantes put together the first part of *Don Quixote* in anything but a straightforward manner.[1] To the extent that this finding is already accepted by Cervantists, what follows here is scarcely startling. I shall, however, reveal as inconsistencies a number of matters that, so far as I am aware, have never been thought of as such; and I shall review some others that were identified by scholars before me. Furthermore, these discrepancies (a few of them outright contradictions) not only reflect an earlier draft of *Don Quixote* apart from those proposed by others but also betray an original purpose in which romances of chivalry played a less central role than they do in the longer version that is the finished product. Although scholars have for years pointed to this sentence or that phrase, this paragraph or that passage, as a probable interpolation, I intend to show that embedded in the early chapters of *Don Quixote* is a discrete composition embracing two of the present chapters and parts of two others. If we remove this unit, many of the apparent inconsistencies in what is left take on a more coherent purpose. Geoffrey Stagg has already suggested that the scrutiny of the library could have been a separate composition.[2] I believe this to be so, but I have expanded the hypothesis considerably.

For instance, the books discussed in Chapter 6 during the scrutiny of the library, as well as those cited by the protagonist as he plays various roles in Chapters 5 and 7, are not exclusively of the chivalric world. We know this, yet we have thus far not come to grips with its implications. We are told in Chapter 1 and in a number of later chapters that Dulcinea is the name Don Quixote gave to a real person, Aldonza Lorenzo. Yet in Chapter 5, Don Quixote himself tells us that she is really a reincarnation of a literary character and, as if that were not enough, a character not from a romance of chivalry but from a Moorish novella. Don Quixote's famous "I know who I am" ("yo sé quién soy") is uttered just when he is in the process of claiming to be a variety of personalities, a process uncharacteristic of his conduct during the rest of his career. By labeling these and other textual inconsistencies ironic we may be able to explain them away, but we have not explained them. Nor do we explain them by considering the first eight chapters as an early effort with an integrity of their own. Something is amiss.

Let us begin by considering one of Don Quixote's neighbors: the barber. Among other things, he is fond of romances of chivalry. In fact he is so wrapped up in them that he not only debates about them with the protagonist but, like the priest, argues about the knights as though they were persons, rather than about the merit of the books from which they spring. We are told in the opening chapter of Part I that the protagonist debated with the curate over who was the better knight-errant, Palmerín de Ingalaterra or Amadís de Gaula, "but Maese Nicolás, the barber of the same town, said that none of them could equal the Caballero del Febo [Knight of Phoebus], and that if there was one that could be compared to him it was Don Galaor, brother of Amadís de Gaula." The barber is introduced in Chapter 1 together with the priest, but only the barber is given a name. We must wait until Chapter 5 to learn the priest's name (Pero Pérez), at which time we are introduced once more to Maese Nicolás, "for this was the barber's name." But we already knew his name! Is this Cervantes' carelessness, the narrator's unreliable memory, or a purposive iteration?

More curious is the fact that Maese Nicolás' favorite hero has been identified in Chapter 1 as the Caballero del Febo, protagonist of the *Espejo de príncipes*. Now, although this individual is mentioned by Don Quixote (I, 15, 20) and, in point of fact, there is a poem ascribed to him and dedicated to Don Quixote included among the prefatory verses of *Don Quixote*, the book dealing with his adventures is not among those found, or at any rate mentioned, during the scrutiny of Don Quixote's library. This is in sharp contrast with the treatment given the other two books alluded to in the sentence introducing the barber and the curate in Chapter 1. It was the latter who debated with Don Quixote about the relative merits of Palmerín and Amadís and it is the books relating the adventures of these two knights that not only are found in Don Quixote's library but are spared from destruction. It is true that the barber is the one who urges the priest to preserve the *Amadís*, but this is all part of a series of inconsistencies. Let us examine them.

Given Don Quixote's admiration for Amadís, it is reasonable to assume that in the debates with the curate, it was the latter who favored Palmerín. We are not surprised, therefore, that the priest wishes to condemn the *Amadís* to the flames. His reasoning is that it was the originator of the species. Let us recall, however, that in his arguments with Don Quixote and the barber, the issue was which had been the *best*. Now, during the examination of the library, it is the barber's judgment of *Amadís de Gaula* as the "best of all the books of this kind" that dissuades the priest from going ahead with its destruction, and he is dissuaded for this reason alone. In contrast, in the account in the opening chapter the priest is, at least by implication, reported as favoring Palmerín as the best, and the barber is reported as saying that none of them could equal the Caballero del Febo. Here in Chapter 6, thanks to the barber, it is agreed that the best is *Amadís de Gaula*.

A bit later in the scrutiny, the barber comes across *Palmerín de Inga-laterra*. The priest spares it, as we might expect, given his opinion of it during the aforementioned debates. His specific reasons are three (although he says they are two): He mentions decorum (we recall his later criticism of the *Curioso impertinente*) and his belief that it was written by a Portuguese king, but the very first reason given is that "it is in and of itself very good." Thus both Don Quixote's and the curate's favorites are preserved. The barber's candidate, the *Caballero del Febo*, is not even mentioned. When the curate concludes that the *Amadís* and the *Palmerín* are the only books of chivalry worthy of escaping the flames, the barber brings up one more. It is not the *Caballero del Febo* but *Belianís de Grecia*.

It is tempting to permit the imagination to run free and suggest, for instance, that if the barber enjoyed the *Caballero del Febo* so much, he may have borrowed Don Quixote's copy, something that would explain its absence in the library. But it would be exceeding our license as readers to invent occurrences that are not even hinted at in the text. What we do find in the text before us are a number of inconsistencies, some of them evident contradictions. If in Chapter 1 the curate argues against the *Amadís* being as good as *Palmerín de Ingalaterra*, why in Chapter 6 does he accept the judgment that the *Amadís* is the best of its kind? If in Chapter 1 the barber argues that none can compare with the *Caballero del Febo*, why in Chapter 6 does *he* make the judgment that the *Amadís* is the best of its kind? Moreover, if in Chapter 1 even Don Quixote has reservations about *Belianís de Grecia* because of the implausibility implicit in the inordinate number of wounds the hero gave and received, why in Chapter 6 does the barber select this work to be spared from destruction?

Flores has shown that the "original 'Don Quixote' encompassed only about twelve of the present chapters; and the direct syntactical links that exist between Chapters 3–4 . . . and Chapters 5–6 . . . and the natural flowing of the text from one chapter to the other unequivocally show that this first 'Don Quixote' was written as a continuum without any formal divisions between the various episodes."[3] (This does not mean that it was penned without subsequent interpolations, only that chapter breaks were not part of the original plan.) Accordingly, by ignoring the epigraph of Chapter 6 (which was not part of the original manuscript), not only do we explain the incomplete sentence supposedly ending Chapter 5, but we may also link the matters dealt with in that chapter (or at least in the latter part of it) with the narrative of Chapter 6, the scrutiny of the library. Now the inconsistency noted earlier – the identification of the barber by name as though we had not been told his name in Chapter 1 – may be grouped among the inconsistencies we have noted in Chapter 6. It bears stressing that these matters are inconsistencies *only to the extent that they are compared with Chapter 1.*

My findings point to a separation of Chapters 4–7. More specifically, I submit that in a primitive version there existed as one connected episode the portion that begins in Chapter 4 following Don Quixote's decision to return home and seek out Sancho and ends in the middle of Chapter 7 (with the final reference to the curate and barber until their reappearance in Chapter 26), just before a nearly identical reference to the recruitment of Sancho. In Chapter 4, Don Quixote "determinó volver a su casa y acomodarse de todo, y de un escudero, haciendo cuenta de recebir a un labrador vecino suyo, que era pobre y con hijos, pero muy a propósito para el oficio escuderil de la caballería" ("he determined to return to his home and provide himself with everything, and with a squire, having in mind a neighboring farmer, who was poor and had children, but very appropriate for the squirely position in chivalry").[4] Leaping now to Chapter 7 after the exit of the priest and barber (implied by what follows but never stated, and therefore a brusque transition), we read: "En este tiempo solicitó don Quijote a un labrador vecino suyo, hombre de bien – si es que este título se puede dar al que es pobre – pero de muy poca sal en la mollera" ("At this time Don Quixote enlisted a neighboring farmer, a goodly man – if this title can be given to a poor man – but not very quick on the uptake"). If we excise all of Chapters 5 and 6 and those portions of 4 and 7 that I have indicated, the novel's plot is not adversely affected. To be sure, serious damage is done to our understanding of a number of matters, and this is surely why Cervantes ultimately did put the segment in. It is my contention, however, that the segment was composed separately from and earlier than the remaining portion of what we now know as Chapters 1–8.

For the sake of clarity and concision, I shall refer to the portion I have singled out as phase A, the remaining portion of Chapters 1–8 as phase B, and the text as we now know it as phase C. I believe that phase A was written in the early or mid-1590s and then set aside.[5] Some time later, in the vicinity of 1600, Cervantes penned phase B, which was clearly inspired by phase A (or by a common point of departure) but was written independently of it and without direct reference or access to it. I suspect that, with the germ of phase A still in mind, he thought of a "better idea," which became phase B. Cervantes subsequently retrieved phase A, recognized its potential and interpolated it into phase B, thereby producing phase C. If we view the sentences that frame phase A as links to an originally unbroken phase B, the latter is revealed to have a smooth transition. A large number of textual inconsistencies may now be clarified.

When Cervantes writes in Chapter 2 that there are authors who say Don Quixote's first adventure was that of Puerto Lápice (the encounter with the Biscayan), whereas there are others who say it was that of the windmills, he leaps from Chapter 2 to Chapter 8. That he seems to give the lie to these other "authors" is the source of no little admiration among modern critics for his manipulation of the "true history" theme alongside that of authorial reliability. What the narrator describes immediately is not an adventure at all. What he claims to have found in the annals of La Mancha is that Don Quixote "rode that entire day, and at nightfall, he and his nag were tired and dying of hunger." Without losing our appreciation of the irony, let us neither lose sight of the fact that there is simply no adventure.

What follows at the inn is not properly described as an adventure. It is true that Don Quixote uses the word "adventure" as he awaits the attack upon his arms, but he immediately rejects his own participation because he has not yet been knighted. The episode details Don Quixote's "knighting" and his efforts to keep vigil, but it is not an adventure in the sense of derring-do. It is a preliminary event, and even Don Quixote cannot wait to leave the "castle" and go in search of adventures, a word explicitly used in this context to apply to future events (I, 3). Why does not the narrator, in Chapter 2, mention one of the two adventures following the hero's knighting, adventures that occur earlier than those alluded to, as being among the first? Surely the encounter with Andrés and Juan Haldudo and the confrontation with the merchants may be classified as adventures. What is more, we are told that Don Quixote thinks of them as such, for immediately following the "rescue" of Andrés, Don Quixote spots the merchants from Toledo and imagines this encounter to be *another* adventure (I, 4). But these are events of phase A and not part of the plan for phase B. In the latter phase, the adventures alluded to in Chapter 2 occur following Don Quixote's "knighting" (Chapter 3), his accepting the advice of the "castellan" to seek a squire (early part of Chapter 4), and his doing so (latter part of Chapter 7); and so the first adventures are indeed those of the windmills and the Puerto Lápice, as suggested. It is in the absence of phase A that the first adventures alluded to turn out to be, with no surprise, the first adventures.

Stagg has also noted the discrepancy regarding the adventures. He believes the inconsistency to lie in the fact that Don Quixote is first reported as heading for his village, in accordance with his decision to heed the innkeeper's advice, whereas following the Andrés episode the knight comes to a crossroads and, not certain of the direction to take, leaves it to Rocinante's whim. Since this indecision flies in the face of the earlier resolution, Stagg concludes that the crossroads incident is an interpolation.[6] But in view of my proposition that this is just one more element in phase A, the beginning of which was inserted just after the decision to follow the innkeeper's advice, the crossroads indecision is not a contradictory interpolation but a proper part of phase A, all of which is large-scale interpolation with a unity of its own.

I must disagree with Stagg's conclusion about the reference to the first adventures. Stagg believes that Cervantes interpolated only the one sentence in Chapter 2 that, as we have seen, refers to the "first" adventures but actually names the first adventures of the *second* sally. Cervantes did this, Stagg argues, in order to link the first and second sallies in a belated effort to make a novel out of a story. Once again, the pattern postulated by Stagg – a series of sentences and paragraphs sprinkled throughout in order to bring an early version up to date – is in my view not as convincing as the separate and continuous composition of phase B, in which the links between Chapters 1–3 and part of 4, on the one hand, and part of 7 and 8, on the other, need no further explanation. By removing phase A, we reveal phase B as a discrete composition with an integrity of its own, and some of the troublesome allusions become inconsistencies only if we reinstate phase A. Even the allusion in Chapter 2 to the chronicler of the hero's exploits, frequently cited as a foreshadowing of the direct reference to him in Chapter 8 (though he is not named until Chapter 9), may now be perceived not as a prefiguration but as a part of a continuum.

The depiction of the process that leads Don Quixote to perceive the inn as a castle in this first sally is at variance with the presentation of illusions subsequently used in the novel (as I discussed in the early pages of Chapter 4). A related detail deserves comment here: When Don Quixote challenges Juan Haldudo, the text reads as follows: "'Get on your horse and take your lance' (for he also had a lance leaning against the oak tree where the mare was tied), 'for I will make you aware that what you are doing is cowardly'" (I, 4).

The portion in parentheses represents the intrusion of the narrator. Not only might we wonder why a farmer carries a lance with him, but we ought to notice the effect of the narrator's explanation: Don Quixote's assumption that the farmer is a knight is given a modicum of rational support, at least to the extent that the weapon reinforces the interpretation to which his romances have led him. More than that, however, the emblematic nature of the lance is predicated on recognizing the object for what it is. The narrator confirms that here there is no illusion. Were this episode described in terms we know from subsequent adventures (notably, a basin perceived as a helmet), the narrator most likely would have clarified that what Don Quixote took to be a lance was in reality a staff or some farming tool. The explanation that the farmer really did have a lance is a detail that we do not readily associate with the rest of the novel, and it thus lends further support to the proposition that phase A was composed under different circumstances and with a different approach.

I have already commented on some discrepancies regarding the opinions on books expressed by the barber and curate. Let me restate that these are discrepancies only if we compare Chapters 6 and 1 or, as we may now refer to them, phases A and B. Let us look at phase A more closely. Its centerpiece is the scrutiny of the books. Modern readers who do not avail themselves of the footnotes in scholarly editions frequently infer that Chapter 6 is primarily an examination of books of chivalry. That impression is caused by the fact that we are reading the scrutiny as part of phase C, that is, in the belief that the scrutiny serves principally to illustrate the effect of the romances of chivalry. But it is not a scrutiny of books of chivalry. The inquisition is much broader than that and includes epic poems, pastoral novels, and collections of poems. Among the books is Lofraso's *Los diez libros de Fortuna de amor*, which I commented on in Chapter 1. It will be recalled that the priest spares this volume, partly because its *disparates* are humorous, that is, apropos. An additional reason, however, is that "it is the best and most unique of all the ones of this kind that have been published in the world." This comment reminds us of the barber's words that lead to the preservation of the *Amadís*: "It is the best of all the books of this kind that have been composed; and so, because of its being unique in its way, it ought to be pardoned." Earlier we had reason to see how quickly Don Quixote was alerted to the clues needed to convey his illusions to Sancho, and we see here a similar quick-wittedness in the curate as he, in making his case for preserving Lofraso's work, echoes the barber's vocabulary. The great majority of critics do not accept the priest's opinion here as indicative of a correspondingly positive response from Cervantes. Some believe the comments to be sarcastic satire; most point to Cervantes' evident dislike for Lofraso, as revealed in the *Viaje del Parnaso*. A few have ventured other opinions.

In Chapter 1, I cited Aylward's opinion that only before the introduction of Cide Hamete in I, 9, does the priest represent Cervantes' views. This critic, therefore, discerns a difference between the priest at the beginning of the novel and as he is portrayed later (upon his reappearance in I, 26, and in subsequent chapters). But Aylward refers to the *introduction* of the priest and barber in I, 5 (our phase A), thereby excluding their function in I, 1 (our phase B). In other words, Aylward has perceived that a major figure of phase A, the priest, is unlike what he appears to be in phase C: "And so, while I agree that the Curate is generally portrayed as something less than a pillar of wisdom in most of Part One of the *Quijote*, I submit that a structural analysis of the text reveals that such is *not* the case in the first eight chapters."[7] Let us recall that it is in Chapter 1 (that is, in a portion of phase B, excluded from Aylward's judgment of the priest "in the first eight chapters") that the priest's enjoyment of chivalric romances is revealed as he is introduced as the protagonist's debating partner in the matter of who was the best knight, whereas in phase A (on which Aylward bases his analysis), *Amadís de Gaula* is spared because of the arguments of the barber, and only two others (*Palmerín de Ingalaterra* and *Tirante el Blanco*) are similarly spared. (*Belianís de Grecia* is preserved, but again because of the intervention of the barber, and not without harsh criticism by the priest.) In phase A, the priest is far more disposed to say favorable things about pastoral novels, among which is Lofraso's *Fortuna de amor*.

One of the reasons for praising Lofraso, suggests Aylward, is in accord with matters raised in our discussion of Cervantes' own pastoral, *La Galatea*. Aylward believes that Cervantes "is lauding Lofraso's work for taking a new road, for daring to be different from the pastoral models that had gone before it." What is more, Aylward surmises that "the favorable remarks of the Priest in the 1605 *Quijote* were probably penned many years before."[8] These remarks of the curate, I need scarcely emphasize, are found in phase A. In short, we find in the observations on Lofraso a favorable view of a pastoral novel that dared to be different, observations written at least a quarter century before Cervantes' negative comments about Lofraso (in the *Viaje del Parnaso*), and in a context that stresses pastoral works at least as much as, if not more than, romances of chivalry.

A decade and a half before Aylward's article, that is, without the benefit of the latter's findings, Hermann Iventosch expressed a similar reaction: "I think I discern in Cervantes a gesture of fondness for the extravagant Sardinian [Lofraso], a 'colleague' of his, whose book the curate 'set apart with a great deal of pleasure' in the scrutiny."[9] The belief that Cervantes had reason to view Lofraso's work favorably in the period in which phase A was written helps to clarify an important detail. A potential rejoinder to my argument regarding the existence of phase A is that Dulcinea is mentioned in this portion several times, that is, that a fundamental element of the ultimate version is already identified by the name allegedly invented in what I have called phase B. But the name "Dulcinea" is not something patterned after the names of ladies of chivalric romances. It is a name based on those of pastoral literature. More specifically, it was taken by Cervantes from Lofraso.

As long ago as 1907, Menéndez Pelayo pointed out that Cervantes took the name Dulcinea from the shepherd Dulcineo, a character in Lofraso's *Fortuna de amor*.[10] Iventosch observes that "the most important thing is not, of course, the fact of finding the great author imitating another author, but that of seeing him follow a well-known pastoral author."[11] Lofraso, says Iventosch, "is the master of all in onomastic matters. *Dulcineo* is his, and so is *Dulcino*, *Dulcina* and *Dulçanio*, every one of them with a sense of the 'sweet character' of pastoral man."[12] Moreover, "chivalric ladies are not 'sweet' [*dulces*], at least not in a representative series of books of chivalry: *Amadís de Gaula*, *Palmerín de Inglaterra*, *Lepolemo* and *Amadís de Grecia*."[13] Not only is the "chivalric world . . . totally absent from the name *Dulcinea*,"[14] but "*Dulcinea* in itself, as a name, resists any chivalric attribution."[15]

This argument strengthens my contention that Cervantes' original purpose was not confined to the depiction of an individual obsessed with romances of chivalry. That the latter were included in the original plan is not at issue. My point is that, as the library collection reveals, and as the hero's source for his lady's name confirms, the subject of phase A was a depiction of how imaginative literature affected, or could affect, readers. It was only later (phase B) that the matter was reduced to works of chivalry. The fact that pastoral creeps in again and again (and, as is now believed, by interpolation, such as in the Marcela episode) reinforces the suppostion that these were matters composed long before the version I have called phase B, and that their subsequent addition resulted in phase C.

What of the protagonist's own name? Given my perspective in this chapter, what is striking is that the name Quijana is used only in phase A. It is not found among the possibilities suggested in the opening chapter, nor is it the name the protagonist claims to have in the final chapter of Part II (although he does suggest it as a *feminine* variant for his niece). In Part I, we are told in Chapter 1 that his name might have been Quijada or Quesada or Quejana. If we use the spelling of Cervantes' time, we read, respectively, Quixada, Quesada, Quexana. Given that the pronunciation of the "x" in those times approximated our "sh," we can appreciate the confusion of the first two. Furthermore, it is the protagonist's own declaration in I, 49, that he is a direct descendant of Gutierre Quixada.

There really existed a Gutierre de Quixada. Still more interesting is the fact that there existed an Alonso Quixada, who lived in Esquivias during the first half of the sixteenth century and who had a reputation as an aficionado of romances of chivalry. All these details are well known to Cervantists; I bring them out here because I wish to emphasize the repeated use of forms based on this historical name, that is, *not* the name found in Chapter 5, which is to say, not the name offered in phase A.

By understanding how readily the "x" and "s" could be mistaken for one another (aurally, so that the corresponding spelling would be in doubt, which is in fact what the author claims), and how frequent was the confusion between the "i" and the "e" (the "mismo"/"mesmo" vacillation is perhaps the most familiar, sometimes occurring in the same sentence),[16] we can simplify much of the confusion by considering Quixada and Quesada variants of *one* name. Likewise, Quexana and Quixana are variants of *one* name. Throughout all of Part I, therefore, we are dealing with only *two* names (in addition, of course, to the assumed name, Don Quixote de la Mancha).

It is interesting to note in passing that Mancing, in a study devoted specifically to the function of names in *Don Quixote*, discusses the appending of the suffix "-ote" to the stem of *all five* surnames given the protagonist. Since this list includes Quesada and Quexana, his analysis may seem questionable until we recognize that he must have taken into account the "e"/"i" vacillation of Cervantes' time.[17]

Now all this makes sense. In phase B Cervantes begins his novel by giving us two variations in the spelling of the same name: Quixada. It matters little whether it is written with an "e" or an "i," with an "x" or an "s". (We may take literally the remark in that paragraph that all this does not matter so long as we do not violate the truth, that is, so long as we preserve verisimilitude; or we may appreciate the playfulness regarding the inaccuracy of historians.) In any event, it is this name, Quixada, that the protagonist claims as his patrimony in I, 49. And it is this name, Quixada, that Avellaneda uses, no doubt believing – another irony – that the narrator in Chapter 1 and the protagonist in Chapter 49 are more reliable than the farmer in Chapter 5. (Cervantes simply continues the game in Part II, changing the surname to Quixano and correcting Avellaneda's choice of Martín as a given name by having the protagonist "reveal" it on his deathbed as Alonso, thereby showing up Avellaneda's inaccuracy.)

The introduction in the opening paragraph presents three variants, but a close reading suggests two, followed by an afterthought: "They say that he had the surname of Quixada, or Quesada, for in this matter there is some difference among the authors who write about the matter; although likely conjecture allows it to be understood that he was called Quexana." I submit that the final clause is an interpolation placed there at the time when Cervantes incorporated phase A into phase B, in order to account for the name Quixana found in what we now call Chapter 5. This move not only corrected a discrepancy but fitted in well with his more mature handling of the possibilities inherent in equivocal reporting. The correction was made only on the first page, where its need was evident at a glance, and not toward the end of what is now Chapter 1, where there was no chapter break at that time and where he had probably forgotten its need. (The fact that phase B had neither chapter nor paragraph breaks explains the likelihood that only a painstaking reading would reveal such discrepancies, as well as the fact that most of the emendations are to be found either on the opening page or close to the points where I believe phase A began and ended, that is, at points requiring scrutiny.) Toward the end of what is now Chapter 1, the narrator explains the name Quixote as based on Quixada, specifying that it was not Quesada, "as others tried to say." Would this not have been a time to bring up Quixana or Quexana? It might be argued that Quixana could not be brought in here because it would disturb the neat "etymology" of Quixada > Quixote on the basis of the first syllable, since Quixana, too, begins with that syllable. But if my hypothesis is correct, at the time Cervantes wrote this passage toward the end of what is now the first chapter, he had immediate reference only to Quixada and Quesada, the two variants at the beginning of the chapter, which, I maintain, is part of the original phase B.

Moreover, when the narrator says, toward the end of Chapter 1, that the name is Quixada and not Quesada, he claims that the "authors" of the "true history" reached such a conclusion, "as has been said." But it has *not* been said. The phrase "as has been said" can refer to one of only three possibilites: (1) all three variants given in the opening passage, since that is what was said, as we read the book today; (2) that it was really Quexana, since that is what the "likely conjectures" supposedly led to, as also was said, but again in the version we read today and in total opposition to what we read later, in the sentence now under consideration; (3) that the *two* names under discussion here are the *same* two names mentioned in the opening paragraph, so that "as has been said" is consistent with what in fact was said. This third choice, requiring the excision of the reference to Quexana in the opening passage, is the only one that permits consistency. The discrepancy accordingly disappears if we accept the reference to Quexana as a later intercalation, following the decision to interpolate phase A, with its Quixana, into the text.

The statement in Chapter 5, that Quixana "must have been his name when he was in his right mind," is usually taken as a further development of the sentences in Chapter 1. Of course, such a conclusion follows from a reading of the chapters as they are found *now*. But if Chapter 5 is part of a primitive version (phase A) composed without reference to what we now read in Chapter 1 (phase B), the statement in Chapter 5 must be read for its own discrete value. That statement simply tells us that Quixana was the protagonist's name when he was in his right mind. We do not find a contrasting statement like "and not Quesada" because, of course, there was no other name during the writing of phase A with which to contrast Quixana. In Chapter 5, the contrast is between the assumed name and the real name, not between the "right" name and the "wrong" name, a subtlety that was not part of phase A. The unique use of Quixana in Chapter 5, compared with three instances of Quixada in the 1605 volume, adds weight to my proposition that Chapter 5 is part of a composition written independently of the portion I have labeled phase B.

If my hypothesis is correct, the original phrasing of Chapter 1 (that is, phase B, before the Quexana was interpolated) referred only to Quixada and Quesada. Not only were the "x" and "s" acoustically similar enough to permit a confusion to be considered plausible, but they presented a particular problem to speakers of Arabic descent: "The Moorish people found it hard to pronounce the voiceless dorso-alveolar sibilant 's'; consequently they changed its point of articulation so that it became a prepalatal 's' (*xenior* for *señor*, *xastre* for *sastre*)."[18] If today we need footnotes to bring this phonemic confusion to our attention, the reader of 1605 most likely recognized immediately that the difference between Quixada and Quesada corresponded to the Moorish inability to make the necessary phonological distinctions. The reader of 1605 could well ask whether the narrator was having difficulty with the spelling of the name because his source was perhaps Moorish. Or the reader might wonder whether the authors alluded to were Moorish: Our author might well question their accuracy in noting down the spelling, since the name Quixada, when pronounced, would be perceived by Moorish ears as either Quixada or Quesada. (An analogy may help. To the Spanish ear, there is little, if any, perceptible acoustic difference between our "footnote" and "food note." In the attempt to transcribe a lecture, a Spanish-speaking reporter might, given the appropriate context, mistake the one for the other and, ultimately, confess that it could have been either. But, he might add, this distinction matters little to the recounting of the event, for it concerned notes on food.) In short, the reader of 1605, alert to the possible Moorish accent of the narrator or the author (no awareness of a translator is possible in Chapter 1), could, in the opening paragraph, suspect the presence of what in Chapter 9 is revealed to be an Arabic historian. Needless to say, the insertion of the reference to Quexana, which I maintain is a later addition, clouds such a ready recognition. In his hurried effort to get his work ready for the printers (the research of Stagg and Flores confirms the hurry), Cervantes' retouching of details to make interpolations fit concurrently concealed some of the consistencies that, ironically, have been read as puzzling sources for exegetic explorations. His original plan for Chapter 1 may have been more ironic than we have suspected and less esoteric than we have imagined.

When Don Quixote wants the merchants to swear that Dulcinea is the most beautiful damsel in the world, he describes her as "the empress of La Mancha" (I, 4). Nowhere else in all of *Don Quixote* is she given this title. When hyperboles of this kind are bestowed on Dulcinea, the three most common terms are "queen," "princess," and "lady." (In fact, when pressed on the matter of her lineage, Don Quixote combines all three: "She must be at least a princess, for she is my queen and my lady" [I, 13].) It is only in phase A that she is called empress. Just a detail, perhaps, but it is another element in the mounting evidence that a discrete version, phase A, existed.[19]

An anomaly of a different order may be observed in the following description: "He had not ridden far when it seemed to him that on his right-hand side, from the denseness of some woods that were over there, some frail cries, like those of a person who was complaining, were coming forth" (I, 4).[20] To the casual reader, this sentence perhaps seems unremarkable. Two points need to be made, however. Such a description is atypical of *Don Quixote*. On the other hand, it is typical, as my analysis in Chapter 4 details, of *La Galatea*. Nothing in the passage permits us to date it, of course. Given the descriptive styles of the two works, however, this passage is more easily associated with the technique of the 1585 *Galatea* than with that of the 1605 *Don Quixote*.

For analogous reasons, I would argue that Eugenio's tale in Chapters 50–2 of the 1605 *Don Quixote* was orginally written separately. Flores says that it is "one more extraneous tale incorporated at the end of the novel, the goatherd's story about Leandra (Chapter 51), but it is only seven pages long . . . and, above all, it was well woven into the main plot."[21] Indeed, it was so well entwined that it is easy to forget that it is in fact longer than the original seven pages and that it is not confined to Chapter 51.[22] Not only does it spill over into Chapter 52; its beginning is to be found in the middle of Chapter 50, and it is there that we come upon the only description in *Don Quixote* that bears a likeness to the passage in I, 4: "And as they were eating, they suddenly heard a loud clatter and the sound of a little bell, and right away they saw coming out from among the underbrush a beautiful she-goat. . . . Behind her came a goatherd shouting to her."[23] Needless to say, we have here another episode of a pastoral nature. It is for this kind of literature, or during that time in Cervantes' career when he was concerned with this kind of literature, that such descriptions came readily from his pen.

The episode introduced by the description in Chapter 4 is not of a pastoral nature, to be sure. It need not be in order to support my proposition. It need only be, as indeed it is, written in a style unlike that found in *Don Quixote* generally in order to permit the inference that it was composed separately. It bears noting that in that episode, Don Quixote claims to be, among others, the Moor Abindarráez, answering his neighbor with "the same words and reasons as the captive member of the Abencerraje family used in replying to Rodrigo de Narváez, just as

he [Don Quixote] had read the story in *La Diana*, by Jorge de Monte-
mayor, where it is written." What is more, Don Quixote claims that
the "beautiful Jarifa that I have mentioned is now the lovely Dulcinea
del Toboso" (I, 5). The allusions are to yet another genre, the *novela
morisca*, but significantly included in *La Diana*, a pastoral novel. Furthermore, at this stage of his career – which for us means phase A – Don
Quixote unequivocally makes Dulcinea out to be a reincarnation of a
heroine from something *not* chivalric, a point reinforced by Iventosch's
study of the name Dulcinea. More anomalous still is the open admission
that she is derived from a book, not springing from the Aldonza Lorenzo
described in phase B. If his calling her empress is a mere detail, the
attribution of her origin here is nothing less than fundamental – fundamentally at odds with phases B and C.

Even more at variance with the remainder of the book are the multiple
identities claimed by Don Quixote here, which are unique to phase A.
He fancies himself the reincarnation of a hero of the ballads (Valdovinos),
of the *novela morisca* (Abindarráez), of the Carolingian ballads (Reinaldos
de Montalbán, in Chapter 7), and even of all the twelve Peers of France
and the nine Worthies of Fame. Only here, in Phase A, does he represent
himself as *being* characters of books. This is in sharp distinction to the
emulation of heroes in phase C. Not even in the 1615 volume, when he
is tempted to take up a pastoral existence, does he fancy himself to be
someone else: He will be the shepherd Quixotiz, an onomastic variation
of *himself*, not an impersonation of a literary character. Not only is the
impersonation in Chapter 4 unlike the more characteristic emulation in
the remainder of the novel, but it finds its contradiction in I, 20. There
Don Quixote explains that it is his function to *revive* the orders of the
Round Table, the Peers of France, and the Worthies of Fame. It is he,
he continues, who will consign to oblivion the Platirs, the Tablantes,
the Olivantes and Tirantes, the Febos and Belianises, by *outshining* them.
Similarly, when he once more mentions Valdovinos and the Marqués
de Mantua, he swears to "lead the life" ("hacer la vida") of the latter,
that is, to imitate him (I, 10). The contrast between these declarations
of emulation and surpassing of models in phase C and the delusions of
phase A is patent.

In a manner uncharacteristic of phase C, the protagonist of phase A
boasts a protean nature and seeks his inspiration not exclusively in books
of chivalry but in his reading generally. Such a broader range of literature
is just what we find in his library. And it is books – not books of chivalry
or books in any way qualified – that are described as his usual recourse
in Chapter 5. This essential point, although it has been spotted by Mancing as an inconsistency, is not fully appreciated in the following analysis:

As Don Quijote lies unable to move, he again resolves (I, 5 . . .) to take recourse to "su ordinario remedio, que era pensar en algún paso de sus libros" ("his usual remedy, which was to think of some passages in his books . . . "). This statement is somewhat misleading, however, as his inspiration throughout most of this chapter is not the books of chivalry but several traditional *romances* about Valdovinos and the popular short story of Abindarráez. Don Quijote's near delirious raving represents a height in his chivalric madness; it is ironic that his famous . . . "Yo sé quién soy" ("I know who I am . . . ") is uttered precisely at the moment when he assumes multiple identities.[24]

In a recent review, Thomas A. Lathrop cites the final point just quoted as one of Mancing's "one-liners of insight."[25] Indeed, there is insight in the entire paragraph, but the fundamental issue revealed by the substance of the passage under scrutiny is missed. What is in the long run ironic is that the oft-quoted "yo sé quién soy," when read in the context of the multiple identities that Don Quixote assumes *only* in this section of the novel, is *not* characteristic of his subsequent psychology and behavior. He will indeed know who he is, *after* phase B resumes. Never again will he do what he has been doing here in phase A, namely, impersonating literary characters.

Mancing's perception that something is amiss is accurate, but the reason lies elsewhere: not in Cervantes' capacity for irony, but in the intercalation of phase A into phase B. In point of fact, the only reason for reading the passage as misleading is our knowledge of the rest of the book. Had we read a story whose plot comprised only the second half of Chapter 4, plus Chapters 5 and 6, and the first half of Chapter 7, we could not view the reference to Don Quixote's books and their nonchivalric character as a misleading or anomalous feature. It is because we are indeed familiar with the protagonist's obsession as it is depicted in Chapter 1 and developed throughout the novel after Chapter 7 that the impersonation of characters from these books in Chapters 5 and 7 appears so uncharacteristic and inconsistent. The existence of phase A confirms the different worlds portrayed in that version and in the subsequently developed novel that we know as *Don Quixote*.

Although not all scholars agree with Menéndez Pidal's theory that the anonymous *Entremés de los romances* inspired *Don Quixote*, it is significant that in the former, the hero, Bartolo, performs in much the same way as does Don Quixote in phase A. Even the characters he chooses (Valdovinos, Abindarráez, the Marqués de Mantua) are identical. Whether one wishes to argue that Cervantes took these ideas from the play, or that the unknown author got his ideas from Cervantes (or even that

Cervantes was the author of the play), the similarity of Bartolo only to
the extent that we compare him with the Don Quixote of Chapters 4–
7 lends weight to the argument that an earlier conception of Don Quixote,
different in significant respects from the subsequently developed Don
Quixote, did exist. Raymond R. MacCurdy and Alfred Rodríguez have
noticed the difference in the nature of the obsessions exhibited by Don
Quixote in the two phases (to use my term). In contrast with previous
scholars, who have interpreted the difference as intentional variations for
aesthetic reasons, and unlike those who, like Menéndez Pidal, see the
difference as evidence of Cervantes' corrective measures to develop a
character worthy of the reader's sympathy, MacCurdy and Rodríguez
see a madness within a madness, the purpose of which is to dissociate
Don Quixote from Bartolo and other madmen by contrasting this momentary lapse into impersonation with the uniquely quixotic madness
with which we are now familiar.[26] This is an ingenious interpretation.
But I do not subscribe to it for the same reason that I do not accept
Menéndez Pidal's belief that the changes reflect an evolution within the
same manuscript: the numerous inconsistencies that point to the composition of separately composed phases.

The first discrepancy that I mentioned concerns the barber's favorite
book, the *Caballero del Febo*. That is, it is a discrepancy if we see that he
fails to mention it during the scrutiny, at which time he does praise in
superlative terms the very *Amadís de Gaula* whose hero, he maintains in
Chapter 1, cannot compare with that of the *Caballero del Febo*. For whatever reason, when Cervantes wrote phase A, the *Caballero del Febo* was
not a book he had in mind, and so it did not appear in the scrutiny of
the library. This investigation of the book collection was the central
episode in Phase A.

Stagg adduces some inconsistencies to point to a separate composition
of the scrutiny itself. One carries weight; another is suggestive; the third
is an a posteriori judgment. The most persuasive point is Stagg's observation that the library is walled up after the books have already been
burned.[27] Unless we are to argue that the library itself was considered a
cause of the protagonist's madness (since it presumably could be res-
tocked), we must agree that the discrepancy is patent. Suggestive but
less convincing is the description of Don Quixote in I, 6, as though he
has not slept. Stagg infers that he has not, a supposition reinforced by
the curate's declaration that he seems overly tired. This is certainly a
valid reading. Other interpretations are possible, however. In the first
place, the curate uses a typically Cervantine imprecision: "Me *parece* que
debe de estar demasiadamente cansado" ("It *seems* to me that you *must* be
overly tired"). The emphasis is mine, of course, and reveals the redoubled
conjecture uttered by the priest. Furthermore, the sentence concludes:

"si ya no es que está malferido" ("if. . . not badly wounded"). The priest uses the antiquated form *malferido* in place of *malherido*, and this effort to humor Don Quixote by using a form from the chivalric books suggests that he is seeking convincing arguments to get Don Quixote to return to bed so that the burning of the books (or the walling of the library), which has not yet been accomplished, can be seen to. Surely the best way to persuade someone to go to bed is to tell him how tired he looks. If this attempt fails, an allusion in chivalric terms to the wounds received may have the desired effect. (Don Quixote himself expresses a different need: something to eat, hardly the first requirement of an exhausted man, yet easily the desire of one who has indeed rested.) The imprecision of the priest's remark is sustained in the narrator's description, which is a model use of the subjunctive in a contrary-to-fact clause: "estando tan despierto como si nunca hubiera dormido" ("being as awake as if he had never slept"). What does this mean? It may be sarcasm: By "awake" we may be meant to understand its opposite, namely, drowsy. It may be irony: Don Quixote is as insane as before; that is, the sleep has not had a curative effect and he is therefore in a manic state, despite having slept. In the final analysis, however, the text does not say that he has not slept. It says that his condition is *as if* he had not slept. Finally, the text makes it unequivocal that after he has something to eat, he goes back to sleep *again* ("quedóse otra vez dormido"). In short, though Stagg's comment has validity, there is no unambiguous statement in the text to contradict the information that Don Quixote has in fact already slept.

Stagg's other observation has to do with a discrepancy we noted earlier, namely, that in Chapters 5 and 7 Don Quixote is inspired more by ballads than by chivalric romances. The scrutiny "seems to rectify this error," suggests Stagg, and in view of the return to the influence of the ballads in Chapter 7, he wonders whether we have another interpolation.[28] However, as we have seen, not only is the material that animates Don Quixote in Chapter 5 not confined to balladry, but, more significantly, the scrutiny in Chapter 6 does far more than "rectify" the absence of chivalric romances, including as it does epics, pastoral novels, and collections of poetry. The original purpose of the scrutiny, though clearly at variance with the rest of the novel, is consonant with the rest of phase A. Stagg is correct in his observation that something is amiss. As Mancing does with respect to Chapter 5, Stagg reads both the scrutiny and the chapters that frame it from the perspective of one who has read the novel that we all know as *Don Quixote de la Mancha*. But the search for corrective passages should not be circumscribed by the chivalric theme that motivates the final product. When we recognize that the original version – phase A – was concerned with the ludicrous reenactment of literature generally, its existence as a discrete entity, written before phase B, explains most if not all of the inconsistencies.

Earlier I mentioned the barber's redundant introduction in Chapter 5. Stagg has also remarked on the superfluous nature of that introduction, but he makes no comment on another oddity. In Chapter 5, just before the second revelation of the barber's name, the narrator gives the priest's name. Not only is it the first time, it is the *only* time in the entire novel that we are told the name of the priest. We might disregard this detail, were it not for a number of circumstances in which, were the priest's name known, it surely would have been used. One such instance occurs in II, 52. In Teresa Panza's letter to the duchess, she mentions that no one will believe Sancho's new status as governor, "principally the priest, and Maese Nicolás the barber, and Sansón Carrasco the bachelor." Conspicuous for its absence is the name of the priest.

If Teresa does not seem to know the priest's name, his old debating partner, Don Quixote, virtually confesses his ignorance of it. After the defeat by the Knight of the White Moon, Don Quixote and Sancho consider turning to the pastoral life. This step, of course, would require a new baptism in accordance with the names of that genre. In addition to their own Quixotiz and Pancino, Don Quixote suggests that Sansón Carrasco assume the name of Sansonino or Carrascón, and the barber that of Miculoso (a rustic version of Nicolás was Micolás). But, as for the curate, "I don't know what name to pin on him, unless it be some derivation of his name, calling him the shepherd *Curiambro*" (II, 67).[29] Would we not expect some variation on Pero or Pérez?

The fact that there really was a priest in Esquivias named Pero Pérez may have something to do with the use of that name in phase A, and it may also have something to do with Cervantes' decision not to use it later. What is confirmed for us here is its restriction to phase A. For whatever reason, Cervantes chooses not to use the name throughout his novel, leaving one of his major figures virtually anonymous. Only the interpolated passage of phase A, with so many other matters at odds with the subsequent phases, retains the name, a detail Cervantes forgot when he incorporated it into phase B.

In the foregoing pages I have shown that some of the inconsistencies of the early chapters of the 1605 *Don Quixote* find a coherence they do not appear to have even in the eyes of critics who have noted them. In addition, I have come upon inconsistencies not noticed by others, and here again, an explanation that links them all together provides the needed clarification. Although numerous theories have suggested primitive versions of *Don Quixote* antedating the version submitted to the printer in 1604, none has suggested the existence of a self-contained unit, centered around the scrutiny of the books and comprising as well the adventures of Andrés, the merchants, the return home with the neighbor who alone calls the protagonist Señor Quixana, and the early portion of what is now Chapter 7.

It might be objected that what I have called phase A could have been written after the other parts of the first eight chapters. If it had been, not only would we be more likely to find books published after 1591 in the library, as Stagg's research suggests, but we would expect the name Quixana, if it were a later development, to appear in, say, I, 49, where in fact Quixada appears. We would similarly expect the priest's name to be mentioned at several points. Most important of all, we would expect the characteristics of the hero's madness to be reflected in subsequent episodes, characteristics that are consistent throughout phase A but that never reappear in those chapters that precede or follow phase A. Since both the very first chapters and the chapters after phase A agree on the basic tenets, it stands to reason that phase A, though incorporated after the writing of phase B, was an earlier effort, superseded by the larger work rather than simply embedded in it.

It is not sufficient to enumerate the many clues that point to the existence of phase A. The literary archaeology of the preceding pages requires us to evaluate anew some judgments that have been made about *Don Quixote*. In the first place, we may no longer speak of onomastic playfulness regarding the protagonist's name. This restriction does not preclude our perceiving such linguistic perspectivism in Cervantes' use of other names. With respect to the protagonist, however, our understanding of his many names must be informed by the implications of our findings here.

If we were to consider both parts of *Don Quixote* as we now find them, and regard them as a coherent whole, dismissing the interpolations and revisions as drafts of the same work animated by a consistent plan, only then could we say that the protagonist has six names attributed to him: Don Quixote, Quixada, Quesada, Quexana, or Quixana and Alonso Quixano. To this list we could add the proposed Quixotiz, as well as the identities the protagonist claims for himself: Valdovinos, Abindarráez, Reinaldos, and, significantly for such an argument, whoever he chooses to be. We could cite as well the sobriquets Caballero de la Triste Figura and Caballero de los Leones. Small wonder that scholars have considered this aspect to be a rich field for investigation.

If we instead regard *Don Quixote* as the culmination of a number of discrete compositions, our conclusion must be a different one. In phase A Cervantes invented a character who called himself Don Quixote, and it is explained to the reader that Quixana must have been his name when he was in his right mind. When, years later, Cervantes developed a new and more ambitious plot, he again used the name Don Quixote, adding that the authors who write of the matter do not agree on whether the real name is Quixada or Quesada. Later in the chapter he again refers to these two names, settling on Quixada as the more likely one in view of the protagonist's assumption of a name with the same initial syllable. In contrast to phase A, here in phase B Cervantes is undeniably engaging in an important playfulness. Not only has he established the germ of the "true history" by alluding to other authors, but he has brought out the latter's unreliability as historians while going on to underscore the greater importance of poetic truths. The fact that in Cervantes' time the pronunciation of the two names as they were then spelled could be readily confused makes the inaccuracy of the historians a much more credible indictment. If we read the passage as a complaint by Cide Hamete (though the latter is not identified until much later), that is, by a writer whose research in the annals of La Mancha is hampered by his imperfect knowledge of Spanish, we may appreciate Cervantes' use of the Arabic chronicler, but we base such appreciation here on a prosaic fact: the difficulty, particularly in those times, of getting names straight in documents. There is further playfulness in the narrator's insistence on Quixada, because it is informed by a choice made by the protagonist at a time when the latter has already been declared to be mad: The correct name is determined not by the efforts of any historian but by the choice of an imaginative madman.

The playfulness to which I have referred is not a playing with or on names. Rather, it consists of a toying with the most elemental problem of a writer's substance: the inability to get the facts right. By confessing that he does not know the exact name of the central character of the book until the character suggests it amid a host of related acts that betray a confusion of reality and fiction, the author makes a number of important points. It is a question not of the relativity of truth but of the human limitations that circumscribe the apprehending of the truth. By representing the book as a true history, the author strips bare the fallibility of the historian. We have here *not* the Aristotelian dichotomy between the historian (who speaks of particulars) and the poet (who speaks more of universals). Instead, the historian stands exposed as no more knowledgeable, no more accurate, no better versed in factual detail, than the poet. It is the historian who must confess not only that he does not know the precise name of his major personage but that it does not matter! The poetic, universal truth, from which he vows not to depart, becomes, in the hands of Cervantes, the inevitable recourse of the historian.

Were the issue the Aristotelian opposition between universal and historical truth, the author would not, in the same breath, provide us with the minute details of the protagonist's daily menu and dismiss the accuracy with which his name is rendered as unimportant. What emerges alongside the historian's limitations is his desire to fill his pages with whatever documentation he can glean or conjecture. It is Cide Hamete's nature to be prolific. He is in need of restraint, to balance the material at his disposal so as not to clutter the text with irrelevancies, no matter how factual. This is why the translator refuses to include the details of Don Diego's house, counting them among the historian's "cold digressions" (II, 18). If the historian is at times tempted to crowd his pages with minutiae, a perceived dearth of factual material in other circumstances leads him to conjecture.

I venture to say that most readers, were they asked why the barber in I, 21, wore his shaving basin on his head, would reply that it was raining and he wanted to protect his new hat. But which was new, the basin or the hat or both? Let us listen to the narrator as he proposes to tell us the facts:

> The fact of the matter [regarding] the helmet, the horse, and the knight that Don Quixote saw was this: that in that part of the country there were two places, one of them so small that it had neither apothecary nor barber, and the other, which was close by, did; and so, the barber of the larger place served the smaller place, in which a sick man had need of a bleeding, and another of a shave, which is why the barber was coming, and he carried a brass basin. As luck would have it, as he was coming along it began to rain, and so that his hat, which must have been new, would not get stained, he put the basin on top of his head, and since it was clean, it gleamed from half a league away.

The narrator, presumably relaying the findings of the historian, appears at first to reflect authorial omniscience. Not only is he acquainted with the two towns in question, but he knows exactly why this barber is traveling from the one to the other on this particular day. He even knows why the barber put his shaving basin on his head: It had begun to rain. But he is forced to resort to conjecture when he tries to justify what in effect is the first step in the quixotic transformation of basin to helmet, namely, the use of the object as headgear. The barber's hat *must have been new*.

Very little is explained if we simply remark that this is typical of Cervantes' style. When next we meet this barber, he has nothing to say about the newness of his hat. This in itself is of little significance, inasmuch as the dispute does not concern his use of the basin but whether or not it really is a basin. The hat is not at issue. Nevertheless, we may legitimately wonder why the narrator, with so intimate a knowledge of the barber's affairs, can only speculate about the newness of the hat. It would have been so simple for the author to have written, "the hat, which *was* new." The inclusion of the conjectural verb invites our attention. Accordingly, we are alerted when, in I, 44, the barber reports his version of the event and claims that the shaving basin was brand new, never inaugurated. Back in I, 21, the narrator explained that the basin's gleam was caused by its being clean. Although he speculated that the hat was new, he evidently was not aware that the basin was new.

All of this opens the door for speculation of our own. We may appreciate the relative points of view, a subject explored by Allen.[30] The confusion would lead us to suppose that the newness of the basin is of little consequence to the narrator, whose primary interest lies in rationalizing the barber's use of the object as headgear. The barber's concern in I, 44, is to recover the basin, and his insistence on its newness explains his tenacity in pursuing the matter and serves as a bargaining point when the curate ultimately settles the issue by compensating him for it. But in view of the parallel procedure in the matter of the protagonist's name, what warrants emphasis here is the limitation of the narrator's knowledge (he must speculate about the hero's name and the barber's hat) and the need to rely on the characters for information (the hero will name himself and thereby confirm a speculation, and the barber will inform us that the basin was brand new).

A different work by Allen aids us here. The most interesting aspect of the style we are considering is "not simply the existence of alternatives at different points in the narrative, but the way in which these alternatives are proposed in certain cases. The author does not say: 'His name was either Quijada, Quejana, Quijana, Quesada, or Quijano.' [What he does say] is obviously not the simple presentation of a list of alternatives, but . . . part of a calculated campaign to keep the reader unsure and off balance, and is only fully exploited in Part II."[31] Although my own conclusion does not agree in all respects with Allen's, his point of departure complements mine. It is indeed important to note that we are not given a list of the alternatives in the initial paragraph of *Don Quixote*. But the implication of Allen's thesis is that Cervantes had in mind, during the writing of page 1 of the 1605 *Don Quixote*, all the variants of the hero's name, down to the Quijano revealed in the final pages of the 1615 volume.

We are not given the complete list in I, 1, for reasons evident to the reader of the present chapter. Quijano (Quixano) in particular (and with a given name for the first time) owes its existence to the need to give the lie to Avellaneda. Had the other four variants been given in the initial paragraph, then we would have been treated to the kind of linguistic perspectivism that Cervantes does engage in elsewhere (for example, the variations on "codfish" in I, 2).[32] The existence of phase A requires us to remove from Allen's list Quijana and its variant, Quejana, leaving only Quijada and its variant, Quesada (always bearing in mind the original spelling and pronunciation of Quixada). The irony lies in the fact that the opening sentence of phase B is a typically Cervantine reshaping of a commonplace: The "I do not wish to recall" is a variation on the conventional "I do not recall" of folklore.[33] This is no insignificant detail, despite Riquer's dismissal of the "no quiero" ("I do not wish") as a mere auxiliary, the phrase presumably meaning simply "I do not recall." Riley, in contrast, underlines the *quiero* and labels this "artistic licence of the most mischievous kind."[34] By allowing the historian to express volition, Cervantes permits him to portray himself as being in control of which elements he will *wish* to recall. But in the same paragraph, the historian evidently wishes to recall the variants of the hero's name, limiting himself to conjecture regarding the correct version and thereby confessing that he does not know: He is *not* in control and must await the hero's assumption of Quixote before he can settle on Quixada. It is not a matter of perspective calculated to disorient the reader but a depiction of the fallibility of the writer of true histories.

This same purpose informs the resumption of the narrative in I, 9, when Cide Hamete's manuscript is described as reporting Sancho's surname alternately as Panza and Zancas. It is a question not of perspective but of authorial insufficiency. By telling us openly that this is the sort of thing to be found in the historian's pages, Cervantes is not betraying "a calculated campaign to keep the reader unsure and off balance" but exposing the fallacy in the claim that the historian sets forth "every detail of [the history], without leaving anything, however minute it may be, from being made distinctly clear. [He] clarifies doubts, resolves objections; in short, he brings out the elements of the most inquisitive desire" (II, 40). By revealing the unreliability of Cide Hamete's history, Cervantes at once calls into question the accuracy of the book he is presenting himself. Although he claims that the translator agreed to render the Arabic manuscript into Spanish without adding or deleting anything (an agreement that is overtly violated in Part II), we do not find, in the book we are given to read, instances of Zancas. Someone – Cervantes? the translator? Sancho's own utterances? – has corrected Cide Hamete's "true history" and settled on Panza.

Allen contends that although "many readers will take the obfuscations . . . as evidence of impaired omniscience on the part of the author, the more perceptive are apt to count them against authorial reliability."[35] Rather than serving as a measure of the reader's perspicacity, the two responses suggested here correspond to two valid and not contradictory levels of interpretation. Beginning with the invitation in the prologue to Part I, in which the reader is encouraged to "say about the history whatever might seem fitting to you," an exhortation echoed in II, 24, by none other than Cide Hamete himself ("You, reader, since you are so prudent, judge [it to be] whatever may seem fitting to you"), it is suggested that the reader supply what the author fails to concretize. (We recall the plea in the *Persiles*, cited in Chapter 3, that the eloquent description of Lisbon should refrain from providing all the details, preserving something for the listeners' vision. Moreover, remarks praising authors or narrators for what they have not said are to be found in *La Galatea* and the *Novelas ejemplares*, as well as in *Don Quixote*.) The unreliability of the author is, accordingly, an opportunity for the reader to participate in the literary process.

On a different plane, we may appreciate what Allen calls the author's "impaired omniscience." Viewing the historian's vacillations from this standpoint is what Leo Spitzer has in mind when he observes that, rather than an indictment of the romances of chivalry in particular, Cervantes' purpose reveals "a recognition of the potential danger of 'the book.' [Books and their words] are no longer . . . depositories of truths [but] sources of hesitation, error, deception – 'dreams.'"[36] It is the ironic truth of this view that Michel Foucault brings out when he writes: "Don Quixote must also furnish proof and provide the indubitable sign that [the books] are telling the truth, that they really are the language of the world . . . His adventures will be . . . a diligent search . . . for the forms that will prove that what the books say is true . . . Don Quixote reads the world in order to prove his books."[37] It is not the historian but the protagonist who reveals the correct name. The problem of that name not as a calculated series of perspectivistic manifestations but as an indictment of the fallibility of books of "true history" is placed in relief by the revelation of discrete phases of composition (as opposed to an evolving continuum).

The existence of phases A and B as separately composed narratives allows the appreciation of Dulcinea insofar as phase A highlights aspects of phase B, even though the substance is well known. That is, we know that when Don Quixote creates Dulcinea in Chapter 1 (phase B), he engages in a characteristic process: the poeticization of the prosaic. By choosing a peasant and elevating her to the role of his lady, a process symbolized by the change of name from Aldonza Lorenzo to Dulcinea del Toboso, Don Quixote gives us the first example of that world view which makes damsels of prostitutes, castellans of innkeepers, castles of inns, helmets of shaving basins, and so forth. We know all this. But our appreciation is heightened by the knowledge that in an earlier composition (phase A), Dulcinea was not an idealized poeticization of a real wench but simply a recasting of a character already poeticized: the beautiful Jarifa of the Moorish novella.

It would have been easy for Cervantes to have followed that trajectory in phase B. He could have made reference to the protagonist's usual recourse to his books, from among which he might have chosen not only Jarifa but any one or a combination of heroines. But Don Quixote chooses instead to superimpose the noble qualities of those ladies upon a coarse peasant of El Toboso. Our reading of Chapter 5 of *Don Quixote* permits us to underscore that he, in phase B, chooses so *instead*. That is, in writing Chapter 1, Cervantes does not follow the course reported in Chapter 5. Instead of depicting Dulcinea as a literary reincarnation of Jarifa, and Don Quixote as a reincarnation of Abindarráez, as he does do in Chapter 5, Cervantes reveals a new conception, of the lady as well as of the hero. The difference between Dulcinea as Jarifa in a new guise and Aldonza-turned-lady is the distinction between delusion and illusion. The contrast, corresponding respectively to phase A and phase B, reinforces the difference between burlesque and parody. Moreover, unlike the Dulcinea of phase A, who owes her existence to a literary character, the Dulcinea of phase B is created by Don Quixote (which may explain as well why there is no confusion regarding her name: It is a question not of documents but of the hero's declaration).

Revision in the 1615 *Don Quixote* has not provided literary sleuths with the fascinating puzzles offered by Part I. The most intriguing speculation revolves around the time when Cervantes first became aware of Avellaneda's spurious continuation. Although textual evidence confirms that he knew of it by the time he penned Chapter 59 (in which he himself mentions it), there is nothing to prevent his having been apprised of Avellaneda's book, or even having read it, at some earlier point. There has been speculation that a number of earlier episodes were in fact inspired in one way or another by Avellaneda's work.[38] To what extent some of Cervantes' playfulness regarding equivocal reporting by the narrator, intervention by the translator, credibility of the Moorish historian, and the like is part of the original plan, and to what extent it is the result of preparing the way for the discrediting of a very real personification of those "other authors" Cervantes himself had claimed existed, is only one of the issues raised by the clues that possibly point to Cervantes' acquaintance with the Avellaneda book at a date earlier than we may now substantiate.

A revision on a smaller scale has been noted by some scholars. It occurs in Chapter 45 of Part II and deals with the judgment that Sancho, in his role as governor, must render regarding the dispute between the tailor and the farmer. It is the first of three legal cases, yet it is reported as a cause for laughter in comparison with a "past" case that, however, turns out to be the last of the three in the order of their published presentation. It goes without saying that the discrepancy is the result of a revision, and as such it has been accepted (although a few editors have tried to intercalate a word or phrase to emend the evident erratum). In what follows I should like to describe the circumstances and postulate the intent.

Having been welcomed as the new "governor" of Barataria, Sancho Panza is informed by the majordomo that it is customary to have the new governor "respond to a question put to him, one which will be somewhat intricate and difficult." There follows a brief digression in which it is Sancho, not the majordomo, who twice asks a question and the majordomo, not Sancho, who is the one to answer. Following this interchange, Sancho returns to the previous subject and asks the major-domo to proceed with the question, which he, Sancho, promises to answer to the best of his ability. But there is a new interruption, and we have the first of the three lawsuits.

Two men – a farmer and a tailor – present their case. The farmer had asked the tailor to fashion a hood from a piece of cloth; when the tailor agreed, the farmer asked whether he could make two hoods from the same cloth, a process that continued until five hoods from the cloth were agreed upon. The tailor now complains that he has not been paid, and the farmer replies that the hoods are only big enough to cover the five tips of one's fingers. Sancho rules that the farmer must lose his cloth and the tailor his labor.

With respect to the earlier question that is apparently never formulated, Rodríguez Marín has suggested that it is the matter of the bridge and those who must pass across it, a litigation that is presented to Sancho for his resolution farther on in the book (Chapter 51).[39] A comparison of the two passages in question lends weight to Rodríguez Marín's supposition:

> It is an old custom on this island, Mr. Governor, that he who comes to take possession of this famous island is obligated to respond to a question put to him, one that will be somewhat intricate and difficult. [II, 45]

> The first thing presented to him was a question that a stranger put to him. . . . And . . . the matter is somewhat difficult. . . . And [it is asked that the governor give] his opinion on such an intricate and dubious case. [II, 51][40]

The coincidence of the phraseology supports the view that the two pas-sages refer to the same "question" (*una pregunta*). Cervantes evidently broke off the presentation of the riddle in Chapter 45 and, for reasons unknown to us, either resumed or, unmindful of the earlier start, began anew the brainteaser he had planned.

I am making a distinction between "a question" and the three – ultimately several more – lawsuits. Not only do I take literally the numerical limitation imposed by the Spanish quantifier *una*, but I accept the definition of *pregunta* given by Riquer, who sees it "in the sense of difficult-to-solve problem."[41] Cervantes himself gives what amounts to a definition in *La Galatea*, when Aurelio suggests that each of those present display the keenness of his *ingenio*, by posing "some question or riddle" ("alguna pregunta o enigma") (Book VI).

The riddle is interrupted twice. The first break is the result of Sancho's own question (an inquiry, not a riddle); the second is that of the interpolation of the case of the farmer and the tailor. Following the narration of this lawsuit, the narrator declares: "If the past sentence of the drover's purse moved those present to *admiratio*, this one provoked them to laughter" (II, 45). This declaration is confusing unless we accept the obvious, namely, that it was originally written following what is, in the final version, the last of the three lawsuits. Attempts to amend the sentence (or to remove the reference to a past judgment, as Cohen does in his translation) fail to take into account an earlier sentence. Just before Sancho's resolution of the case we are discussing, the narrator describes the general reaction to the revelation of the five little hoods: "All those present laughed at the multitude of hoods and at the new lawsuit" (II, 45). The qualification of this litigation as a new case, that is, another one,[42] complements the reference to that of the drover's purse as a past case. Accordingly, the case of the tailor and the farmer was not originally written first, and its position as first is the result of an interpolation. This interpolation, let us recall, constitutes the second interruption in the truncated discussion of the riddle.

The first interruption is Sancho's inquiry about the meaning of some writing painted on the wall facing the gubernatorial chair. The question, as well as the ensuing discussion about the abuse of the title "Don" – Sancho not only emphasizes his illiteracy but boasts that no one in his family has ever held that title – serves to place in relief Sancho's background as a *labrador*, that is, as a farmer. There is no need to document here how frequently Sancho has flaunted his inability to read or write and his belief that his status as an Old Christian is sufficient to enable him to become a count. Cervantes depicts this attitude in other circumstances, notably in the one-act play *La elección de los alcaldes de Daganzo*, in which Humillos boasts of his own and his family's illiteracy: sufficient, Humillos believes, for him to be chosen alderman. In the episode from *Don Quixote* under consideration here, the riddle to be put to Sancho is postponed so that we may be reminded of a pervasive satire: Our "governor" is an illiterate Old Christian, a farmer who considers it his function to be "mortal enemy, as I am, of the Jews" (II, 8). Having made the point that he is illiterate and not a Don, Sancho returns the thread of the story to the riddle: "Proceed with your question, Mr. Majordomo" (II, 45). It is at this point that the second interruption occurs as the farmer and the tailor burst in and present their case.

Thanks to the efforts of Fred Abrams, we may be reasonably certain that the source for this dispute is the novella of the fourteenth-century Italian storyteller Francho Sacchetti:

> A Florentine cloth dealer is visited by a man named Soccebonel who is anxious to purchase cloth in order to make a gentleman's cloak. Having chosen the color, Soccebonel agreed to pay the cloth dealer for eight meters of cloth. He then took the cloth dealer's measuring stick and began to measure out the cloth in such a way that he would get more than the eight meters agreed upon. The cloth dealer, cognizant of the trick, moved the stick behind him as he helped Soccebonel with the measuring. The result was that for every four arms length the trickster was only getting three and one half. In order to hide the reversed deception, the cloth dealer advised Soccebonel to soak the cloth overnight in water to improve its quality. He did this and dried the cloth before taking it to a shearer who informed him that it measured only about nine arms length. Soccebonel was astonished since he had paid the Florentine for eight meters and had cheated in addition.

Abrams goes on to enumerate those elements that the two episodes have in common and concludes: "Cervantes goes a step further and has both parties come out losing. The customer not only fails to receive a hood but loses the five hoodlets as well. The tailor loses payment for his services. . . . This judgment is an excellent example of Cervantes' sense of equity and a reflection of his belief that two wrongs do not make a right."[43]

I submit that a reading of the Cervantine refashioning leads to some other conclusions. The original novella states its moral explicitly: "A man who intended to defraud was himself defrauded."[44] This concept is frequently expressed by Cervantes in other passages (most recently in II, 33, with reference to Sancho's "enchantment" of Dulcinea), and so it bears noting that Cervantes chooses not to adopt it along with his appropriation of the basic ingredients of Sacchetti's tale. One logical explanation is that Cervantes has changed the substance of the plot. In the Italian model, Soccebonel attempts to get more than he is paying for and the dealer sees to it that he gets less: The deceiver is deceived by his own cupidity. In the Cervantine version, the farmer distrusts the integrity of tailors and is given what he asks for, in accordance with the letter, but not the spirit, of his agreement: The bigot is outwitted by his own stupidity. By changing these elements, Cervantes has altered the essence of the argument. The original moral, accordingly, no longer applies. Yet we find it expressed four chapters later: "Jests turn into truths and mockers find themselves mocked" (II, 49).

The allusion is to those who have thought Sancho a buffoon, a point I shall discuss again later in this chapter. What prompts the remark is of interest to us now. Sancho has just enumerated the groups he intends to favor: farmers, *hidalgos*, the clergy. Although the farmer here does receive a punishment (he loses the material), in comparison with his counterpart in the Italian tale he gains some sense of justice (what Abrams sees as Cervantes' sense of equity) in the knowledge that the tailor loses his payment (the dealer of Sacchetti's tale evidently receives payment). By this light, Cervantes has allowed Sancho to treat the farmer comparatively favorably (the latter loses the useless hoods and need pay no money). Given this denoument of the lawsuit, Sancho's remark about favoring farmers, which in turn prompts the majordomo's articulation of the moral of the Italian tale, appears to have a relationship with the case of the farmer and the tailor. I think it not unwarranted to see here additional clues that support the relocation of the lawsuit. I conjecture that its original place was in Chapter 49, where it would have prompted Sancho's remark that he sees it as his duty to favor, among others, the peasant class, and would have led immediately to the majordomo's voicing of the moral. In typical Cervantine fashion, as we explored in Chapter 2, the restatement of the moral is now part of a larger scheme, applicable not only to an incident at Barataria but to the delusion of the duke, the duchess, the majordomo, and those who have misunderstood Cervantes' Sancho. When Cervantes decided to shift the lawsuit to Chapter 45, he probably made many of the changes in the plot that we have noted, thereby requiring the moral to be separated from the argument. By placing the story in Chapter 45, he gave a sense of unity to the series of lawsuits depicted there, added the element of laughter to balance the *admiratio* (as I shall elaborate shortly), and prefixed another interruption of the riddle that sets up the real theme of the lawsuit, namely, the issue of the New and Old Christian.

In the Sacchetti tale, both individuals cheat. The client initiates the fraud by measuring out more cloth than he is paying for. In retaliation, the dealer cheats in reverse, so to speak, and we may even sympathize with his clever way of obviating his loss, though we are forced to admit that his conduct is no less dishonest. In the dispute brought before Sancho, the issue is not really dishonesty. The farmer has not attempted to get more material than that which he is prepared to pay for. In point of fact, he already owns the material and it is the labor for which he engages the tailor. His desire may be termed puerile, closefisted, even absurd, but it is not a question of cheating. It is a matter of a different order, as I shall point out shortly. As for the tailor, he has taken his instructions literally and can be faulted only for insolence. We may further call the farmer to account for stupidity and the tailor for guile. And it is at this level that we may find the dispute's relevance to Sancho Panza. It is at this level as well that the argument has its beginning, namely, the level of stereotypical behavior. If we readily accept the narrator's identification of the farmer as a farmer because he is dressed like one, the parallel reference to the tailor requires the qualification "because he carried scissors in his hand," an almost caricaturish, stereotypical representation.

When the transaction began, the tailor already suspected that the farmer believed he could be cheated: "He must have imagined, I imagine, and I imagined well, that I undoubtedly wanted to steal some portion of the cloth, basing himself on his own maliciousness and on the bad reputation of tailors." (When Sancho asks the farmer to confirm the tailor's account in all its details, the farmer concurs.) It is made clear, accordingly, that the point of departure was the farmer's conviction that tailors were dishonest, and the outcome was the result of the tailor's cunning. Moreover, the farmer's belief that tailors were not to be trusted was based on a generally accepted view about tailors.

To document here the low esteem in which tailors were held would require an inordinate amount of space for a matter that, I think, is well known. Suffice it to say that their poor reputation was proverbial and that "of all the mechanical trades, none has been satirized more than that of tailor."[45] While some "New Christians . . . became apothecaries and doctors, [others] were reduced to the trades of tailor or old clothes dealer." Those of Jewish descent were "invariably financier, supply-master, merchant, usurer, pawnbroker, doctor, artisan, tailor, weaver."[46] Tailors could be of Moorish descent: "Certain occupations were 'impure': blacksmiths, tailors, cobblers, innkeepers, muleteers, for example, were 'Moorish.'"[47] Or, as Américo Castro points out, "tailors were very often Jewish."[48] Aylward, thinking of the aversion to having a tailor touch his wife that is expressed by the old man in Cervantes' *Celoso extremeño*, sees their New Christian status as a factor in that tale: "Many, perhaps even most, of the tailors in sixteenth-century Spain were of *converso* or *morisco* ancestry, and here Carrizales' paranoia is representative of the ruling caste's intense dread of contamination of their Gothic bloodlines by mixture with the 'inferior' Semitic stock."[49]

With respect to our farmer and tailor, my purpose is not to engage in an inconclusive discussion about characters twice fictive: Not only are they creatures of Cervantes' fiction but they are enacting a farce directed by the duke and duchess. It is, rather, the conditioned response of Sancho

Panza that I wish to bring out. It is reasonable to assume that Sancho associates the tailor with a class other than those he thinks it proper to uphold.

Those whom Sancho wants to favor he unequivocally identifies shortly afterward: "I intend to favor the farmers, protect the privileges of the *hidalgos*, reward the virtuous, and, above all, respect religion and the honor of the clergy" (II, 49). Now, in addition to the other matters in which Cervantes' story differs from that of Sacchetti, the clients of the two versions are socially opposed. Sacchetti's customer is either a gentleman or someone desirous of appearing as one. He specifically wants "a cloak worthy of a baron." In either case, he is depicted as pretentious: Having chosen a sky color, he "imagined from the name that there would be upon it the sun and the moon and the stars and perchance a great part of Paradise."[50] In contrast to the presumptuous customer of the Italian story, the tailor's client at Barataria is a farmer, a member of that down-to-earth class with pretentions of a different order, namely, pure blood.

What Cervantes found in the Italian novella was the tale of a pretentious gentleman whose avarice led to his comeuppance, a bit of poetic justice enhanced by the irony of his ignorance of the effects of water on the material. Cervantes has converted the original opposition between the gentleman and the tradesman – a matter of social levels – into the polarity of the Old Christian peasant and the New Christian artisan – a matter of social castes. At the same time, he has reduced the gentleman's cheating to the farmer's mistrust of the Jews, setting up a self-fulfilling prophecy as the tailor responds in the same coin, that is, by reacting as he is expected to. The tailor is incited by the farmer's prejudicial opinion and responds in accordance with that bias (though in a way that leads not to the expected appropriation of leftover cloth but to a mockery of the farmer's fears); his reduction of the material to five small hoods produces laughter among the spectators.

Unlike the Italian model, Cervantes' tale does not end here. Sancho next passes judgment. The peasant loses the material and the tailor receives no payment. In a symbolic way, the farmer loses property and the Jew loses money. Sancho's wisdom reflects a stereotypical response. As for the little hoods, they are to be sent to the inmates of the jails.

It is at this point that the narrator tells us that Sancho's judgment provokes laughter among the onlookers. If the first laughter, provoked by the revelation of the little hoods, is easily accounted for, the laughter occasioned by the adjudication is, in my opinion, difficult to justify. There is not much that is funny about punishing the peasant's stupidity by having him lose a small bit of material he ordered made into five hoods, for which he refused to pay. There is nothing funny about punishing the tailor's insolence by denying him payment for having produced something other than what was intended by his client, as he well knew. And there is little humor in sending the hoods to the prisoners. Although some critics have assumed this last point to be no more than a sarcastic reference to the poor conditions of prisons generally, I think Cervantes here recalls the particular discomfort of the writer in such circumstances: numb fingers that will not serve their purpose. We may appreciate the irony of letting the illiterate Sancho pass this sentence. But it is not funny.

We have come full circle, and this is why I have selected this episode with which to close the main body of the text. The narrator reports laughter and there seems precious little to laugh about. As I pointed out in Chapter 1, we are promised two bushels of laughs throughout Sancho's governorship. In Vladimir Nabokov's recent *Lectures on Don Quixote* we read: "Scholars who speak of sidesplitting episodes in [*Don Quixote*] do not reveal injury to their ribs ... The Don is certainly not funny. His squire, with all his prodigious memory for old saws, is even less funny than his master."[51] Not only have I found very little in the Barataria chapters that is truly worthy of provoking bushels of laughter, but the only time anyone is reported as laughing during any of these chapters is here, in the case of the farmer, the tailor, and the five little hoods. I think we may clarify the interpolation as well as the matter of humor by recalling some points raised in Chapter 1.

Cervantes made frequent reference to humor in the 1615 *Don Quixote* because he had come to understand that this was why the 1605 volume was well received and that this was what the reader expected to find in a continuation. Although Part II indisputably has far less risibility than Part I, it is in Part II that Cervantes makes a repeated point of the humor and his talent for it. The laughter of those who witness Sancho's judgment of the farmer and tailor is the laughter of those who expect him to be funny. But if we wonder what they are laughing at, perhaps we should rather ask why, if they find Sancho's judgments funny, they do not laugh at the case of the drover's purse and the woman who claims to have been raped. (As readers will recall, she avers that she was unable to defend her virtue but has little trouble defending the purse of money awarded to her.)

The case of the drover's purse, however, was written first. Cervantes subsequently realized that he had better temper the *admiratio* of that case with some laughter in another. He accordingly made sure to have the narrator specifically point out that this time, in contrast with the previous case, those present were moved to laughter. When he then inserted the episode before the case of the drover's purse (and before the case of the cane), he failed to make some of the necessary amendments and thereby produced the inconsistencies we have noted.

The significance of the case we have been examining is to be found in the consistent characterization of Sancho Panza. From our first acquaintance with him in Part I, we have recognized in him a culturally imposed attitude regarding the Old Christian–New Christian controversy. Of course, he has given no serious thought to the matter. Cervantes depicts him as a good-natured peasant, informed by the prejudices of his class, never doubting that his pure blood is sufficient to make him a count or a governor.

In Chapter 1 we saw why Cervantes feels a need to turn much of Sancho's rational conduct into something risible, and in Chapter 2 we noted that many of Sancho's intelligent responses are explained away as not original. We should perceive a related characterization in the episode we are considering here. The matter of the laughter is made emphatically clear by the narrator's insistence on it. One purpose of that assertion complements what Riley identifies as the function of an audience's expressing *admiratio*, namely, an opportunity for the reader to identify with an attitude of appreciative listeners.[52] By reporting laughter from an audience, Cervantes accomplishes the same thing: Even if it is not an inherently funny matter, readers looking for humor may believe that they have found it if they are told that others laughed. (The canned laughter of television programs billed as comedies serves the same purpose.)

The judgment of the case is not just an example of Sancho's innate good sense or of Cervantes' sense of equity. Faced with the classic confrontation of castes personified in the farmer and the tailor, Sancho behaves exactly as *we* should expect, provided not only that we know Sancho better than the duke and duchess but that we recognize how Cervantes reshapes the Italian tale. If Cervantes were to remain faithful to the original, he would have to let the tailor get the last laugh. By representing him as a stereotypical Jew (complete with formulas of humility), Cervantes sets up Sancho's conditioned response: The tailor will be punished as well. To make the point less subtle, Cervantes inserts a preamble. Preceding the lawsuit, he injects a brief tirade by Sancho on his illiteracy and the family's lack of the title "Don." The majordomo expresses the viewpoint of those who believe Sancho's attitude and conduct to be at odds with the burlesque figure they have been led to expect. Conversely, Cervantes allows us to see a consistent characterization that is at variance only with the buffoon perceived by those who fail to understand *Don Quixote*.

By interrupting the riddle, Cervantes has, no doubt unwittingly, alerted us to an interpolation. His failure to make some adjustments in the text confirms the revision, and the location of the Italian model's moral later in the text suggests the original location. What may have been a more faithful restatement of Sacchetti's tale in a primitive Cervantine version turns out, as usual, to be a masterful reshaping that gives apposite significance to the lawsuit as it reinforces characteristic traits of the Sancho Panza created by Cervantes. By leaving the moral at the point where the majordomo refers to Sancho's having been misunderstood, Cervantes not only shows his recognition of how he has altered the essence of the tale but accommodates the tale's original motto to a purpose of his own on a different level. We have indeed come full circle.

Chapter 8
Sum and substance

The eighteenth-century *Diccionario de Autoridades* defines *conclusión* as "the sum and substance of what one has treated, aired, and pondered regarding some matter."[1] The dictionary goes on to speak of resolution and accord, (expert) opinion and judgment. I do not presume to bring such decisive and unequivocal findings to the fore in this final chapter, and therefore I have evaded "conclusion" as a title for it, preferring instead that portion of the definition excerpted here. I shall not pretend that the matters treated, aired, and pondered in the preceding seven chapters have been brought to a conclusive end. Nor will I abuse these final pages with a restatement of theses advanced in those earlier chapters. Rather, I should like to approach the sum and substance of those pages from altogether different perspectives.

Were I to attempt a comparison between *Don Quixote* and El Greco's *Burial of the Count of Orgaz*, I would scarcely be the first to do so.[2] But it is not a comparison of the works that I wish to draw; rather, the painting suggests to me an analogy with the concerns of my opening chapter. The perspective I have in mind is sharpened as one passes through Toledo's Church of Santo Tomé, where the masterpiece is still positioned as it has been since El Greco's time. The visitors of today, having paid a few pesetas for the privilege of viewing the large canvas, find themselves surrounded by fellow tourists, by art students, and by teachers and guides elucidating what the untrained eye does not wholly apprehend. Permitted just a touch of cynicism, one may perceive in this configuration of picture and beholder a Velázquez-like phenomenon: The spectators are unwittingly aping the behavior of the gentlemen in the painting!

The explanations for the evident lack of excitement on the faces of the Spaniards portrayed in the painting are many, and it is not in my province to offer interpretations of El Greco's art. It is clear, however, that the observers of the miraculous descent of Saints Stephen and Augustine remain unperturbed, whether that dispassion be the reflection of boredom with life in this world (as contrasted with the dynamism displayed in the upper, heavenly scene of the painting) or the product of an indoctrinated belief in the association of the miraculous with death and beyond. In either case, there is a conspicuous lack of marvel at an event that is scarcely an everyday experience. The nonchalance displayed by the Spanish gentlemen in the presence of the prodigious occurrence is, in my view, a reflection of incomprehension. Although they understand the facts of the matter, they fail to grasp its spectacular substance. The miracle does not arouse *admiratio*.

It goes without saying that such need not have been El Greco's intention, especially if one subscribes to the general consensus that he included himself among the observers portrayed, a touch not only prefiguring Velázquez but analogous to the multiple-author device as well as to Cervantes' allowing himself and his works to be discussed in his fiction. (It is no longer believed that Cervantes was also one of those portrayed in the painting, a fanciful notion that would compound the irony of the parallel drawn here to an incredible degree.) The equation I wish to draw is one not of intentions but of responses.

The people depicted by El Greco as observers of the miraculous interment are not unlike those who come in contact with Don Quixote (both novel and character). They include a doctor (though not a barber), a nephew (though not a niece), a town official, and the village priest, who not only officiates and directs but whose robes – appropriately, to be sure – are the only ones that approximate the dramatic finery of the two saints. All this notwithstanding, the onlookers do not seem to appreciate the wonder of the spectacle before them. Even so would Cervantes portray, in the 1615 *Don Quixote*, the readers of his book of 1605. Those readers, too, understood that they were in the presence of a work that represented the contrast of two worlds, namely, the fictitious one of the romances and the down-to-earth world of La Mancha. That anyone should confuse the two was evidently funny. Indeed, so it was and so it remains. But there was much more, and like El Greco's spectators, Cervantes' readers failed to transcend the expected and the conventional. As did the spectators in the painting, who appreciated the significance of the miracle while failing to marvel at its drama, so the readers of *Don Quixote* appreciated the humor of the episodes while failing to perceive the drama that, from ethical, aesthetic, and sociological perspectives, Cervantes explored.

In my second chapter, I considered originality in Cervantes and his works. I was concerned less with the identification of original material than with the study of Cervantes' attitude toward the concept. Indeed, it proved more interesting to probe the handling of refashioned material, and in the process, our appreciation of Cervantes' treatment of sources was enhanced. Of course, it is common knowledge that Cervantes availed himself of models, and his use of them has been widely studied. What Chapter 2 brought out was not that he appropriated earlier works but that such a procedure was the substance of his craft. The art of Cervantes was the result of that craft, and the notion of fabricating original material was not central to his approach. His claim of *invención* notwithstanding, I venture to say that if we take literally, and in the narrowest sense, the meaning of "invent," "create," "originate," and the like, precious little will be found in Cervantes' works to justify such labels. Chapter 2 explored how Cervantes' ingenuity lay in the reshaping rather than in the origination of both form and content. I should like to suggest here a different way of seeing this aspect of his art.

As is well known, the criticism applied to the most conspicuous models, the romances of chivalry, is that they are lies. Words like *disparate*, particularly when modified by pejorative adjectives, describe the nonsensical, absurd, and illogical composition of the romances, but the substance of such books is characterized by words that portray them as false, lying, and fabricated. At the same time, as a few sensitive critics have observed, Don Quixote's entire existence – not merely the point of departure but his whole being – depends on these same romances. Don Quixote, Cervantes' creature, could not perform a single deed, could not name himself or his lady – let alone have a lady to name, no matter how irrational the process – or set up his creed, pursue his goals, or even speak Spanish as he does, without continuous dependence on the books that Cervantes labels false and fabricated.[3]

Herein is found the crux of the perennial debate about the meaning of *Don Quixote*: If it is a parody or a burlesque, the essence of such an approach demands adherence to identifiable characteristics of the source material. On the other hand, if the humor, though important, is only incidental to the central purpose, then it is the vitalizing force with which literature – or art generally – is seen to imbue the individual that forces us to take that art more seriously than parody or even satire might require.[4] The degree to which one reads this motivation by literature as comical determines the interpretation of the author's intention. The conclusions reached in Chapter 1 led me to the scrutiny that is Chapter 2, namely, the examination of the variegated ways in which Cervantes surpasses his models. But how does a writer surpass sources that he condemns as false?

With the truth, one is quick to reply; or with truthful sources. And here we meet a fundamental element of Cervantes' approach to his *Don Quixote*. The question whether it is story or history is but one aspect.[5] That its underlying theme is the exploration of truth – relative, absolute, historical, poetic – is but another. The aesthetic concern for verisimilitude is yet a third of several ramifications of setting out to take the art of the narrative beyond that of untruthful, implausible, and unreliable accounts of chivalric heroism. But as so often when one seeks the substance of Cervantes, there is a more elemental question that must be posed: Why denounce works of narrative fiction for their fictitiousness?

It is true that the three aspects just mentioned, especially the problem of verisimilitude, address the question, but only to a degree. Cervantes does condemn the implausible, and he does play with the concept of storyteller and historian – a game that will come back to plague him when Avellaneda "consults" other "archives" in an attempt to continue the "true history" – but one point remains unclarified. It is one thing to criticize the romances for violations of aesthetic principles; it is a different sort of criticism when works of fiction are censured because they are fabricated or because they are "feigned" or "pretended," which is what the adjective frequently used – *fingido* – means. Now this word, the past participle of *fingir*, "to pretend," comes from the Latin *fingere*, meaning "to fashion," "shape," "form," "mold"; also "to represent," "imagine," "conceive"; and as well "to feign," "fabricate," "devise." The Latin past participle – *fictus* – meaning "feigned," corresponds to the Spanish *fingido*, and, of course, words like "fiction" and "fictive" are derived therefrom. Covarrubias, in his dictionary published midway between the publication of the two parts of *Don Quixote*, defines *ficción* as a well-composed ruse or lie, done with artifice,[6] but Cervantes invokes the basic Latin meaning of fashioning, fabricating, molding, or, as it were, creating. For Cervantes, this meaning has a pejorative connotation: The romances of chivalry are wholly "compostura y ficción de ingenios ociosos" ("composition and fabrication of idle minds" [*Don Quixote*, I, 32]).

Cervantes does on occasion use *ficción* in the more familiar, figurative sense.[7] That is to say, what is "fabricated" or "made up" is called fiction by virtue of its lack of historical reality. The example cited in the preceding paragraph, although its purpose is also to differentiate the fictitious content of the romances from historical truth, betrays a more elemental nuance. Cervantes' conviction that the romances are untruths stems not from negative judgments about the results – they are unrealistic, implausible, inaccurate figments – but from the fundamental ingredient inherent in the process of their creation – they are invented. When we describe something as made up or thought up or fabricated, we tend to think of the outcome, which is to say that such labels are adjectival. By reading them as past participles, that is, as verbs, we may better focus on the moment of their invention. It is from this perspective that Cervantes' understanding of originality must be studied.

William Nelson quotes Lactantius as follows: "The poet's function consists in this, that those things which were actually performed he may transfer with some graceful converse into other appearances by means of figurative language. But to feign the whole account which you relate – that is to be a fool and a liar instead of a poet."[8] For Lactantius' fool and liar we may substitute Cervantes' idle minds of those who fabricate the romances. In Lactantius' declaration we find the sum and substance of Cervantes' position regarding originality. When Cervantes denounces the romances as the composition and fiction of idle minds, he is condemning the facet of the creative process that "feigns the whole account which you relate." His own art is centered on matter already created, which he "may transfer with some graceful converse into other appearances." One notes with no little appreciation for his art that Cervantes includes among those subjects fit for "some graceful converse" the fabricated romances of chivalry.

To some extent, then, Cervantes' criticism of the romances is a denunciation of their authors' "idly" sitting down to fabricate a plot. (At the other extreme is the canon's complaint: They are all the same thing, which is to say that copying is equally to be reproved.) Although much of the foregoing analysis bears on the Aristotelian principle of poetic truth, the aspect I have been examining here does not contrast historical truth with poetic truth. We are dealing here not with the universalization of the particular (although this is unquestionably a major concern for Cervantes) but with the artist's urge to surpass what has gone before. In this respect, the quixotic model is the Cervantine model. No matter how badly or how well composed, how false or how truthful, how ugly or how beautiful, the purpose of a model is to lead one to surpass it.

When Avellaneda took up Cervantes' proposition that the adventures of Don Quixote and Sancho were historical, garnered from the annals of La Mancha, Cervantes responded in a number of ingenious ways, one of which is but a variant of the principle just discussed. I need not restate here the details of the incorporation into Cervantes' 1615 *Don Quixote* of characters created by Avellaneda. It bears underscoring, however, that Cervantes was, at bottom, simply resorting to the approach of which he was past master, namely, the appropriation of another's material and the subsequent surpassing, in artistic dexterity, of the source. To be sure, what is "original" here is in reality a poor imitation of Cervantes' own subject matter, but the twist given by Cervantes is an exemplary stroke of his gift for irony. The Cervantine *Don Quixote* is presented as a "true history." In contrast, Avellaneda's false, fabricated version is labeled a "new history" (II, 59). Stated in terms of our focus here, Cervantes condemns Avellaneda's work for its newness; for its being not a clumsy imitation but an original invention inapposite to the prototype it presumes to elaborate; for its having been fabricated out of whole cloth, so to speak, whereas Cervantes' legitimate continuation of 1615 is pointedly identified as cut "del mismo paño que la primera" ("from the same cloth as the first [part]" [II, prologue]). It would be immaterial to argue here that the difference in the two works is one of artistic merit and not of originality. What is to the point is the perspective Cervantes imposes:

The falsity of Avellaneda's work lies in the invention of characters fundamentally unlike those of the original. Inasmuch as proper imitation, including parody, requires the skillful use of recognizable characteristics of the model, Cervantes aims at making Avellaneda's character confess that the spurious Don Quixote and Sancho do not conform to the essential characteristics of the 1605 prototypes. By means of a peculiarly Cervantine kind of logic, Avellaneda is condemned for originality.

What is one to conclude, then, about Cervantes' insistence on his own inventive gifts? Though he clearly flaunts his *invención*, scholars continue to demonstrate that plot invention is not an attribute of any significant frequency in his works. His oft-expressed belief that the manner of a narrative compensates for defects in the content does lend weight to something other than plot origination as the principal aim of the writer. (The even-handed declaration in the *Coloquio de los perros* to the effect that some stories have their merit in their content whereas others find it in the manner of the telling does not deal with the issue before us here, inasmuch as the question of the invention of the content is not raised there.) What must be addressed is the meaning of *invención* when Cervantes boasts of exceeding many others in this quality.

The *Princeton Encyclopedia of Poetry and Poetics*, after summarizing the complexity of the concept, brings out the following: "In one large group of theories, in which essentially rhetorical principles and doctrines are predominant but are combined in various ways with ideas found originally in the 'mimetic' poetic theories of Plato, Aristotle, and Democritus, poetic invention of the proper sort is a matter primarily of the proper imitation of nature (in one or another of several senses)."[9] Students of poetic theory will not find in this statement the contradiction that is otherwise implicit in the terms "invention" and "imitation."[10] The key, of course, lies in the word "proper." When the imitation is in the appropriate manner, one may speak of poetic invention. What that manner is may itself be a matter of controversy. What bears emphasizing here is Cervantes' conviction that his manner – the subject of Chapter 2 – is indeed appropriate and that in this way he has realized poetic invention. Sanford Shepard has noted that El Pinciano's reading of Aristotle's definition of imitation would have the poet "traverse all of nature, animate or inanimate, and create a new world."[11] It is in this sense that Cervantes, strongly influenced by El Pinciano, as we have noted, invents. Having properly imitated, he surpasses his models and creates a new world.

If a painting by El Greco helped us to put Chapter 1 in perspective, another will aid in our review of the focus of Chapter 3. This canvas is a part of the collection of New York's Metropolitan Museum of Art, but one needs to visit Toledo – or at least to see a photograph – in order to observe what becomes evident when we compare the painting to the reality. Whereas El Greco's painting the *Vista de Toledo* unmistakably shows the city's cathedral to be to the left of the Alcázar as viewed from the Alcántara Bridge, any traveler will confirm that from that vantage point the positions are reversed: The cathedral is to the *right* of the Alcázar.

I begin with the assumption that all artists endeavor to represent – literally re-present – reality. What reality is and how it is best represented are matters of no little controversy. I have in mind not a photographic likeness but the artist's sense of the spiritual, philosophical, psychological, metaphysical, metaphorical, sociological, political – the list is endless – reality. Let us grant that the artist's perspective, whatever its premise, is some facet of the essence of the reality of the painting's subject. The subject of the El Greco painting under discussion is the city of Toledo. The spectator is to behold a view of Toledo.

A proper and perhaps obvious qualification is that the painting offers only a partial view of Toledo. Or, put another way, we have a full view of only a part of Toledo. In any event, we do not have the opportunity to apprehend the total reality known as Toledo, despite the painting's title, which suggests not a partitive but a general representation. At best, it is a slice of Toledo, viewed with the limitations of one individual's perspective in space at one given time. Representative as it may be, it is no more the reality of Toledo than a scene of Times Square conveys the reality of New York.

Needless to say, El Greco must have been aware of this problem. His elongated figures in other paintings attest to his desire to convey something beyond the limitations of the corporal eye, extending instead to the mind's eye. Using that mind's eye, one does not need to do what I did: Walking around the city of Toledo, one reaches a vantage point from which the cathedral indeed is to the left of the Alcázar. I need scarcely add that this "view of Toledo" is from the other side. What El Greco depicts on his canvas – whether or not that is what he intended to do – is a representation of two simultaneous views of Toledo.

Ortega y Gasset has taught us that "each individual is a point of view. Juxtaposing the partial visions of everyone, you would succeed in weaving the all-embracing and absolute truth. Now, this sum total of individual perspectives, this knowledge of what each and every one has seen and knows, this omniscience, this real 'absolute truth' is the sublime function that we once attributed to God."[12] If El Greco has not quite reached this "sublime function," his efforts, antedating Picasso's by more than three centuries, call attention to the inability of our sense of vision to provide us with more than a fraction of reality. Seeing may be believing, but what it is that we allow ourselves to believe in the light of what we see needs to be tempered by the realization that the "whole truth" is beyond our apprehension. Of course, when one stands at the

Alcántara Bridge, one does *see* the cathedral and Alcázar in a spatial relationship. However, since that reality is only a partial reality, we must confess that from the standpoint of one who wishes to gauge the totality, what we see is a kind of illusion inasmuch as its partiality is not manifest – until we study El Greco's representation of that phenomenon. In order to place in relief that it is indeed only an illusion of reality, El Greco's inversion of right and left superimposes a mind's-eye perspective. How Cervantes confronts this same question is the concern of Chapter 3.

In the third act of Lopé de Vega's *La moza de cántaro*, Doña María wants to relate an occurrence to Leonor, Doña Ana's maid. "Let's go," says Doña María, "and from here to your house I'll tell you what happened by the river." It requires no fewer than eleven stanzas of *octavas reales* (strophes of eight hendecasyllabic lines with a specific rhyme scheme) to relate the events, and at the end Leonor declares, "We have arrived at my house."

It takes approximately three or four minutes to recite eleven *octavas reales*. It is a reasonable amount of time to permit the illusion of a stroll from one street to another. It is, of course, only an illusion. The characters remain on the same stage in view of the audience throughout the recitation, and the farthest they can travel is from one side of the stage to the other. The scenery available to the playwright, though minimal in those days, could help to enhance the illusion, but even elaborate sets would not cloak the make-believe nature of a three- to four-minute walk from one location to another. In the final analysis, the illusion is dependent not on what the spectators see but on what the audience hears. The Spanish drama of the period was, as I have argued elsewhere, an auditory art form.[13] The audience accepts the illusion principally because of the *words* just quoted. Although the visual evidence helps, the belief that we are "seeing" Doña María and Leonor walk from one street to another is based on our having received the verbal clues that send messages to the inner eye.

If the dramatist had to rely on words to compensate for the primitive sound effects, stage designs, and limited physical movement of the actors, in order to project the illusion of certain events, the novelist faced an even greater challenge. Bereft of all but words, the writer of imaginative literature faced the formidable task of conveying to the reader not only the facts of the plot but also the picture of the setting and the action – in a word, an image.

The illusion of reality is, in the context that Chapter 4 explores, not a matter of make-believe in the theatrical sense. No actor plays a role; no sounds mimic peripheral activity; no colors differentiate objects; no spatial relationships are self-evident – in short, nothing aids the writer but the words and the way in which they are put to use.

> We want to see the life of the figures in a novel, not to be told it,
> [writes Ortega y Gasset.] When I read in a novel "John was peevish"
> it is as though the writer invited me to visualize, on the strength
> of his definition, John's peevishness in my own imagination. That
> is to say, he expects me to be the novelist. What is required, I
> should think, is exactly the opposite: that he furnish the visible facts
> so that I obligingly discover and define John to be peevish.[14]

Cervantes was experimenting with this technique when he wrote his first
major work, *La Galatea*.

What was common about the commonplace that the soul consisted of
three faculties was that a given soul was thought to be informed by all
three jointly. It was a comforting notion that the balance of the faculties
reflected the equilibrium of the human condition. A disturbance of that
balance, therefore, betokened a disorder. Just as drama depends on the
rupture of order and harmony, so conflict could be depicted metaphorically as an imbalance among the soul's faculties. In Chapter 5 we examined a number of such instances and found it possible to conclude
that the use of the commonplace underlies a large part of Cervantes' plot
structure, from *La Galatea* to *Persiles y Sigismunda*. Although not every
reference to memory, will, or intellect automatically signifies an allusion
to the metaphor (particularly if all three are not invoked together), the
recurrence of the triad led us to look at the contexts in which it appeared,
and it became evident that Cervantes made use of the symbolic harmony
of the evenly balanced soul. An imbalance in the faculties and the subsequent struggle to regain equilibrium through the orderly control of
one's behavior are elements not unlike the order disrupted–order restored
paradigm typical of the *comedia* and a number of other types of fictive
conflict.

Our familiarity with Cervantes' accommodation of the metaphor enables us to appreciate a passage in the *Viaje del Parnaso*. During the battle
between the "good" and "bad" poets, the distinction becomes blurred:
"So mingled are they that there is no one who can / discern which is
bad or which is good" ("Tan mezclados están, que no hay quien pueda
/ discernir cuál es malo o cuál es bueno"). But then "a young man alien
to ignorance" ("un mancebo de ignorancia ajeno") appears:

> llegó tan rica el alma de memoria,
> de sana voluntad y entendimiento,
> que fue de Febo y de las musas gloria. [Chapter 7]
> [he arrived, his soul so rich with *memoria*,
> wholesome *voluntad* and *entendimiento*,
> that he was the glory of Phoebus and the muses.]

The poem goes on to stress how this man (Pedro Mantuano) was able to distinguish the two groups and clear up the confusion that had existed. I think it not unreasonable to say that had we not in Chapter 5 explored in some detail Cervantes' handling of the metaphorical triad, the most that we could say of this passage is that it includes a cliché, the function of which most likely is to praise Mantuano in hyperbolic terms. Our study of Cervantes' application of the commonplace allows us to say a bit more.

Although we found *entendimiento* to be the most important of the faculties, in accordance with the primacy assigned to it by Thomas Aquinas, many of the dramatic situations we considered were animated by the particular kind of *voluntad* involved. The difference between self-centered desire and a morally commendable volition was frequently at the center of the conflict. We appreciate here, therefore, Cervantes' making a point of identifying Mantuano's *voluntad* as *sana*, literally "healthy" or, as I have rendered it here, "wholesome." The soul, motivated by *sana voluntad*, informed by *memoria*, and directed by *entendimiento* – in all of which Mantuano's soul is "rich" – is therefore able to distinguish good from bad, clear up confusion and chaos, and restore order. This passage in the *Parnaso*, more than the typical laudatory verses regarding a poet, conforms to a metaphorical pattern that pervades Cervantes' writings.

If Cervantes believed Spain's Golden Age to have arrived with the poets enumerated in *La Galatea*, that is, in the years leading up to 1584 or 1585, Agustín de Rojas thought it to have flourished some two decades later. In his *Loa en alabanza de la comedia* (*Loa in Praise of the Comedia*), Rojas gives a brief history of the Spanish theater, including a one-line reference to Cervantes. The *loa*, published in 1603, baldly declares:

> our time arrived, which could
> be called the golden time,
> in accordance with the point reached
> by *comedias* . . .
> and, finally, matters so diverse
> that we see them at a point today
> that it seems incredible
> that more than what has been said be said
> by those who have been, are, and may yet be.
> What will those yet to come do
> that is not already an accomplished thing?
> What will they invent that is not
> already invented? That's for sure.

Rojas, as did Cervantes in *La Galatea*, apologizes that there is not enough time to mention the endless number of *ingenios* who contributed and continue to contribute to the *comedia*. But the *loa* ultimately becomes an unequivocal testimonial to Lope de Vega, "phoenix of our time / and and Apollo of poets" ("fénix de nuestros tiempos / y Apolo de los poetas").[15]

We do not know whether this poem of 1603 reached Cervantes' attention before the completion of the first *Don Quixote* in 1604. When the discussion between the canon and the curate turns from the romances to the theater, there is repeated emphasis on the kind of play that *now* is in vogue. Five times in that exchange, reference is made to this temporal identification. Despite the many points for which *comedias* and romances of chivalry are both criticized, the emphasis on the kind of play that *now* is performed injects a singular element into the discussion of the *comedia*. The contrast with Rojas' *loa* is patent: Whereas the latter had acclaimed the Lopean *comedia* as the ultimate stage in the theater's evolution, Cervantes allows his characters to disparage specifically those plays that are now in fashion and now being performed. The criticism is aimed at the chronological degeneration of the genre. Moreover, the two verbs chosen for these references are indicative of Cervantes' thinking: *se usan* and *se representan*, plays that are "used" and "performed" now. There is no reference to the plays being written or composed. In short, it is again a question of those who permit their staging, be they the impresarios or the poets, the latter criticized not for their artistic ineptitude but for going along with the demands of the box office.[16]

Today Cervantes and Lope de Vega flank one of the portals of Madrid's Biblioteca Nacional. One wonders what either of the two would have thought of this tribute. Lope considered himself a serious poet and frequently boasted of his familiarity with the classics. But his triumph was fundamentally a popular one, not calculated to gain him enduring prominence at the entrance to the library, alongside the likes of Nebrija and Vives. Cervantes, for his part, most likely would have considered it fitting that he should balance the quartet of writers as he does: Lope and Vives are framed by Cervantes and Nebrija. If the latter's claim to fame is his dictionary and grammar of the Spanish language, Cervantes claimed to have opened the way for writers to make appropriate use of that language. The irony, once more, would be that it was to be Cervantes, not the popular Lope, who would find himself and his literary creations the subject of monuments throughout Spain. That this phenomenon should be extended to other nations is a reflection of the irony described in Chapter 6. Cervantes, who had aspired to being part of Spain's literary grandeur, gradually came to believe that the force of popular taste had reduced poetic productivity to that of a handful of writers. If he could speak in 1615 of only three and a half poets and earlier of so small a number that they were not worth counting, in 1605 he had pointed to a reason: Those who were able to understand works written according to artistic principles were only four in number.[17] Yet it is as the creator of a popular genre, of popular characters, and of a funny book that Cervantes is generally remembered.

Standing in front of the Biblioteca Nacional, alongside Lope, Vives, and Nebrija (behind Alfonso el Sabio and San Isidoro), or seated in the Plaza de España (behind Don Quixote and Sancho), Cervantes remains on a pedestal. Perhaps the monument that best epitomizes many of the questions raised in this book is found on Guillén de Castro Avenue in Valencia. On this long street named for the poet who was the first to dramatize episodes from *Don Quixote*, across from a grammar school bearing Cervantes' name, a bust of Cervantes can be seen, supported by Don Quixote. In Madrid, Cervantes holds *Don Quixote*; in Valencia, Don Quixote holds up Cervantes, and it is Don Quixote, not Cervantes, who treads on *Amadís de Gaula* and other romances. If at first glance we seem to see Cervantes' creation triumphantly trampling the chivalric romances, a reconsideration leads us to interpret the romances as a stepping-stone for Don Quixote, whose own vitality, animated by the books from which he springs, enables him to bring renown to the biographer he holds aloft. This perspective, which would give an Unamuno-like interpretation to the relationship between Don Quixote and Cervantes, returns us to our starting point, for it is nearly impossible to view this monument without smiling. "Ful ofte in game a sooth I have herd seye."

When Franz Schubert composed his Opus 114, a quintet for piano and strings, he included as its fourth movement a theme and variations. Although it is only one of five movements, this theme gave its name to the entire quintet, which is known to this day as the *Trout* Quintet. The theme is the tune of a song by that name, *Die Forelle* in German, which Schubert composed several years earlier than the quintet. The song is written in D-flat but is introduced in the quintet in the key of D, with subsequent variations in B-flat major and B-flat minor.

The interpolation of one work into another is not a rarity in the arts. The example of the Schubert composition is of particular relevance to the matters studied in Chapter 7 because, unlike other interpolations in *Don Quixote* (substantiated and postulated), the seminal chapters that I have labeled phase A present the basic theme – the substance – whose subsequent elaboration has become the magnum opus that we acknowledge today. The variations or clues left for us range from the incidental minutiae that permit us only to guess to the evident inconsistencies and outright contradictions that require us to clarify.

Just as Schubert began with a simple melody and later enveloped it in a composition of greater intricacy and with a different purpose and a new beginning and end, so Cervantes started out with the comparatively simple idea of the effects of confusing history and story, a malady sardonically attributed to the variegated, not unidimensional, collection in the library of a certain Señor Quixana, who did not confine his delusion to chivalric matters but considered himself the reincarnation of other types of literary heroes as well. "I am I, Don Quixote," may be what a recent musical comedy has the protagonist asserting, but in the earliest phase of Cervantes' composition, the hero, though called Don Quixote by the narrator and Señor Quixana by his neighbor, insisted only that he was Abindarráez or Valdovinos, or Reinaldos de Montalbán, and that he could take whatever identity he chose.

It was an interesting idea, and it matters relatively little to us today whether it originated with Cervantes or he reshaped it. Given his penchant for parading authors and their works before us from *La Galatea* to the *Viaje del Parnaso*, it is not unreasonable to suspect that the initial purpose in phase A was the examination and criticism of some books, for which he devised the pretext for an invasion of the gentleman's library. What does matter for us is the ultimate result, *Don Quixote de la Mancha*. What does matter is how small ideas germinate in the mind of a great artist. What matters is what the creative imagination of Cervantes fashioned from the material at his disposal. If it is in the ultimate arrangement of the notes, chords, and phrases that we appreciate the music of a composer, so it is in the disposition of the plot, the refashioning of models, the projection of images, and the coherence of the design that we appreciate the totality of a literary opus. By probing matters of this kind, we explore the substance of Cervantes.

To write, as I have written, of the substance of Cervantes implies that his work is to be taken seriously. No one questions such an approach to the *Persiles*, *La Galatea*, or the *Novelas ejemplares*. Even the one-act *entremeses*, so evidently intended to amuse, are the subject of much research for their serious elements of ethical, sociological, and psychological significance.[18] (Needless to say, no one objects to studies that concentrate on their humor.) It is only *Don Quixote* that is the source of heated debate in this regard. In my opinion, the polarized nature of the polemic diverts us from the substance. Consider the recent essay by Daniel Eisenberg, "Teaching *Don Quixote* as a Funny Book." The opening statement is unequivocal: "Cervantes wrote *Don Quixote* to make us laugh at the amusing misadventures of a burlesque knight-errant."[19] At bit later Eisenberg adds:

> Cervantes certainly had secondary purposes, as well as secondary sources, and I do not mean to imply that the study of sources or

of humor is anything like a comprehensive approach to *Don Qui-xote*. Yet to claim that *Don Quixote* is not primarily a work of humor is to claim that it is a failure. As Russell has shown, Spanish as well as foreign readers of the time unanimously considered *Don Quixote* a funny book.[19]

My readers will appreciate that I disagree with Eisenberg's understanding of Cervantes' priorities. No one can deny the humor in *Don Quixote*. It is a funny book. But to maintain that it was intended to be so *primarily* is debatable. Eisenberg's error, in my view, lies in his assumption that Russell's research, which indeed documents what Eisenberg says it does (the reception of the book by seventeenth-century readers), is tantamount to a revelation of the intention of the author. Not only do I insist upon the distinction, but I maintain that, given Cervantes' depiction of his readers, even of his admirers, as detailed in my opening chapter, the identification of his contemporaries' reaction with his purpose is the product of fallacious syllogistic reasoning. It is sometimes suggested that Cervantes makes his intention known in the 1605 prologue. But the irony of that passage is multiple: In the first place, the words are placed in the mouth not of the author but of a fictive friend. This friend gives advice about the writing of the prologue but also advises the author regarding the writing of the text! In other words, he is giving advice about the writing of what he has presumably already read and judged. Finally, the prologue is addressed to the "idle reader," that is, the very sort of mind that composes romances of chivalry (according to the priest in I, 32) and reads them (Don Quixote is introduced as being idle most of the year in I, 1). And despite the friend's conclusion, the author asks the reader to make of the book what he or she deems fitting.

One of the unique characteristics of *Don Quixote* is that its meaning has been and remains elusive. Eisenberg oberves, "If Cervantes had a 'true' purpose, it eludes even modern critics, who cannot agree on any alternative interpretation."[20] In this he echoes Mark Van Doren (although the intent is clearly different): "The sign of [*Don Quixote*'s] simplicity is that it can be summarized in a few sentences. The sign of its mysteriousness is that it can be talked about forever. . . . For a strange thing happens to its readers. They do not read the same book. Or if they do, they have different theories about it."[21] The claim that the book was intended to be primarily a funny book is one of those theories. At least as valid is my position, namely, that the intention was a serious one or, more likely, a number of serious ones and that the humor served as a vehicle for the presentation of serious matters. But this is scarcely to imply that the *book* was a failure. Rather, as my first chapter illustrates,

Cervantes repeatedly depicted the failure of *readers* to comprehend his work.

My thesis in no way suggests a return to the position of the Romantics. In fact, it bears stressing that a position that opposes the funny-book thesis is not ipso facto a Romantic interpretation in disguise. Close refers to Manuel Durán's reading of the dinner-table conversation between Don Quixote and the duke and duchess and concludes:

> Durán identifies in the hero an ambiguous mixture of sublime romanticism, grotesque ineptitude, intelligence, risibility, and humanity, all of which evokes from the reader mixed responses of pathos, admiration, and mirth. Take away the references to "ambiguity," which betray the voice of the twentieth-century critic; and Durán's interpretation is essentially akin to those of Doré and Victor Hugo.[22]

There are two fallacies in Close's argument. In the first place, it is Cervantes himself who, precisely during the episode at the ducal estate, informs the reader that Don Quixote's adventures are to be received either with *admiratio* or with laughter. In point of fact, Cervantes' fictive friend of the prologue to Part I advises him to traverse from laughter for the melancholy reader to *admiratio* for the reader of good sense. Durán is engaging not in Romantic interpretation but in a reading of Cervantes' words. That the words of the imaginary friend and Cide Hamete are themselves charged with ambiguity only reinforces Durán's approach. Moreover, there is a suggestion in Close's judgment that the twentieth-century critic is "betrayed" by a reading that sees in the protagonist not a unidimensional character but a many-sided personality. We need to recall that Cervantes depicts Don Diego de Miranda, whose opinion of Don Quixote is not colored by a reading of Part I, as one who must make his judgment based on observation of the protagonist's behavior. That judgment necessarily vacillates between believing that Don Quixote is mad and thinking that he is sane. Durán, unlike a critic conditioned by the shackles of the Romantic vision, and indeed very much like a twentieth-century critic alert to nuances of the text, reads that text and finds it complex. It is, in fact, in the very multiplicity of interpretations made by readers that Durán finds the point of departure for his study of *Don Quixote*'s ambiguity.[23]

Virtually all of Cervantes' works reveal a desire to experiment. I do not believe that he ever looked upon a work in the way that academic scholars habitually do in order to classify and label it. When he did look back, it was to boast of having opened the way and of having been inventive. To argue whether *Don Quixote* is a novel or a romance, a "true history" or a comedy, is to confess the difficulty of fitting it into a pigeonhole. It is all of those and none of those. Cervantes was experimenting with the very essence of writing imaginative literature, and the topics discussed in this book and others – the illusion of reality conveyed by words; the question of originality; the perspective of readers, authors, narrators, and characters; the use of parody and humor as vehicles – reflect that experimental nature. It is impertinent for us to say what *Don Quixote* "is," presumptuous to claim to know what Cervantes intended by virtue of what people reading the work for the first time took it to be, and simplistic to polarize his readers as "hard" or "soft" interpreters.

To conclude that the Romantics misinterpreted Cervantes is to take a valid position. To assert that they differed from the readers of Cervantes' time is to state a documented fact. To claim that Cervantes' contemporaries understood his purpose is to leap to a conclusion that not only belies his remarks about his readers but is also contradicted by our own reading of Avellaneda's inability to capture the essence of *Don Quixote*. Therefore, to conclude that our interpretation resolves the question is to accommodate the text to our own priorities. Cervantes himself urged the reader to say whatever seemed appropriate. The irony of this invitation is that what seems appropriate to one reader may be inappropriate to another, a fate that pursues us still.

The substance of *Don Quixote*, like the substance of most of Cervantes' writings, is replete with profound questions. To consider matters like the nature of fiction, the relationship between art and reality, the functions of authors and readers, the elusive nature of truth, the social fabric of a society comprising Old and New Christians, the significance of the individual, communication between individuals, and so on as secondary matters is to miss the substance of Cervantes. That substance, and not merely its undeniable humor, is the source of the never-ending investigation that, after nearly four centuries, continues to be stimulated in the minds of successive generations.

Notes

Chapter 1. Don Quixote: *the comedy in spite of itself*

1 Cited from *Chaucer's Major Poetry*, ed. A. C. Baugh (New York: Appleton-Century-Crofts, 1963), p. 354.

2 "... las burlas se vuelven en veras y los burladores se hallan burlados."

3 "'Don Quixote' as a Funny Book," *Modern Language Review*, 64 (1969), 319. Cervantes' words are "Decir gracias y escribir donaires es de grandes ingenios" (II, 3).

4 *The Romantic Approach to "Don Quixote"* (Cambridge: Cambridge University Press, 1978).

5 "... no quiere ser manoseada, ni traída por las calles, ni publicada por las esquinas de las plazas ni por los rincones de los palacios."

6 "Los niños la manosean, los mozos la leen, los hombres la entienden y los viejos la celebran; y finalmente, es tan trillada y tan leída y tan sabida de todo género de gentes.... Y los que más se han dado a su lectura son los pajes: no hay antecámara de señor donde no se halle un *Don Quijote*: unos le toman si otros le dejan; éstos le embisten y aquéllos le piden."

7 "En su esencia [la poesía] misma es idealización: ella misma es hecha alegoría – forma esencialmente poética y ajena a la novela –. La Poesía puede representar los más finos conceptos y aspiraciones humanos, pero flota encima del mundo actual de la contingencia histórica, que es el dominio de la novela y, hasta cierto punto, del drama" (cited from *Suma Cervantina*, ed. J. B. Avalle-Arce and E. C. Riley [London: Tamesis, 1973], p. 302). Cf. Helena Percas de Ponseti, *Cervantes y su concepto del arte: Estudio crítico de algunos aspectos y episodios del "Quijote"* (Madrid: Gredos, 1975), II, 373: "Es la exaltación de la literatura *antivulgar*, de la *superliteratura* que logra elevar todo lo rastrero y pedestre del vivir y el pensar del hombre a un nivel de pureza estética."

8 "La Historia, la Poesía y la Pintura simbolizan entre sí y se parecen tanto, que cuando escribes historia, pintas, y cuando pintas, compones. No siempre va en un mismo peso la historia, ni la pintura pinta cosas grandes y magníficas, ni la poesía conversa siempre de los cielos. Bajezas admite la Historia; la Pintura, hierbas y retamas en sus cuadros, y la Poesía tal vez se realza cantando cosas humildes."

9 For an examination of the priest and his role in *Don Quixote*, see my "Cervantes's Curious Curate," *Kentucky Romance Quarterly*, 30 (1983), 87–106.

10 "Cervantes' *Arte Nuevo de Hazer Fábulas Cómicas en este Tiempo*," *Cervantes*, 2 (1982), 17.

11 "Cervantes on Lofraso: Love or Hate?" *Revista de Estudios Hispánicos*, 13 (1979), 163–4. R. M. Flores warns of "the characteristic inconsistencies of this sort of criticism – a character acts or speaks for its author whenever it says something that supports the critic's theory, but it conveniently does not when what it does or says does not fit the proposed critical frame" (*Sancho Panza through Three Hundred Seventy-five Years of Continuations, Imitations, and Criticisms, 1605–1980* [Newark, Del.: Juan de la Cuesta, 1982], p. 91).

12 "... se queman varios libros sin haber sido examinados... los cuales sin duda se hubieran salvado si el cura los hubiese visto" (Riquer, in his 1975 edition of *Don Quijote de la Mancha* [Barcelona: Planeta], p. 69n).

13 *Cervantes's Theory of the Novel* (Oxford: Clarendon Press, 1962), p. 20.

14 *Tesoro de la lengua castellana, o española* (Madrid, 1611), s.v. *disparate*: "lo mesmo que dislate, como acabamos de dezir, cosa despropositada, la qual no se hizo, o dixo con el modo deuido, y con cierto fin."

15 Aylward, "Cervantes on Lofraso," p. 15, mentions the standard definition of the dictionary of the Real Academia Española and then observes that that of Covarrubias "is even more interesting."

16 "Disparate, la qual se dixo de dispar por no tener paridad, ni igualdad con la razon. Iuan de el Enzina, a lo que yo entendi fue vn hombre muy docto, y que leyó y escrivio en Salamanca, y... compuso vnas coplas ingeniosissimas, y de grande artificio, fundado en disparates, y dieron tan en gusto, que todos los demas trabajos suyos hechos en acuerdo se perdieron, y solo quedaron en prouerbio los disparates de Iuan del Enzina, quando alguno dize cosa despropositada. Yendo camino oyó vna vieja mesonera a sus criados que dezian[:] Iuan del Enzina, mi señor, y llegose a el mirandole de hito en hito, y dixole[:] Señor, es su merce el que hizo los dislates, y fue tan grande su corrimiento que le respondio con alguna colera diziendole el nombre de las Pascuas. A este peligro se ponen los hombres graues, quando por desenfado escriuen algunas cosas liuianas, aunque sean ingeniosas y de mucho gusto." Cf. Quevedo's *El sueño de la muerte*: "Toda la vida andáis, en haciéndose un disparate o en diciéndole vosotros, diciendo: 'No hiciera más Juan del Encina; daca los disparates de Juan del Encina'" (cited by J. P. W. Crawford, in *Spanish Drama before Lope de Vega* [Philadelphia: University of Pennsylvania Press, 1967], p. 30). Crawford adds: "*Los disparates de Juan del Encina* is listed in Correas' *Vocabulario* of proverbial phrases. It is the irony of fate that the founder of the Spanish drama... should be known a hundred years later chiefly as the author of the first nonsense verses in Spain." *Disparates* were among a number of calculated incongruities produced by poets in the sixteenth and seventeenth centuries, analogous in intent to medieval carnival offerings. See Blanca Periñán, *Poeta ludens: "Disparate," "perqué" y "chiste" en los siglos XVI y XVII* (Pisa: Giardini, 1979).

17 *Cervantes's Theory of the Novel*, pp. 21–2. For a reading of *desatino con propiedad* as "absurdity with propriety," that is, with appropriate decorum, as distinguished from the low esteem in which the novella was held previously, see Alban K. Forcione, *Cervantes and the Humanist Vision: A Study of Four "Ex-*

emplary Novels" (Princeton, N.J.: Princeton University Press, 1982), pp. 3–
9.

18 *Cervantes's Theory of the Novel*, p. 20.

19 See Bruce W. Wardropper, "Cervantes' Theory of the Drama," *Modern Philology*, 52 (1955), 218–9. Cf. Stanislav Zimic, "Cervantes frente a Lope y a la comedia nueva," *Anales Cervantinos*, 15 (1976), 22.

20 *Cervantes, Aristotle, and the "Persiles"* (Princeton, N.J.: Princeton University Press, 1970), p. 111; *Cervantes and the Humanist Vision*, p. 347.

21 Close believes the concessive clause "puesto que [= aunque] conocí ser temeridad esorbitante" to reflect an "artificial and implausible characterization on Cervantes's part; it is as though he wants to make quite sure that the reader grasps the rights and wrongs of the case, and assigns his hero a 'lucid interval' in order to point them out" ("Don Quixote's Sophistry and Wisdom," *Bulletin of Hispanic Studies*, 55 [1978], 111). But Don Quixote has already said that he knew what he was doing, and further, the use of the preterite tense (*conocí*) rather than the present (which would suggest that he is now conceding that it was a rash thing to do) betrays not an alternation of lucid and irrational moments but a consistent purpose throughout this episode.

22 *Cervantes y su concepto del arte*, II, 450–2.

23 Ibid., p. 592: "Las impropiedades e intromisiones del trujumán son impertinentes porque rompen el hilo de la ficción. Son, por tanto, inadmisibles en la creación poética. Las impropiedades del autor de la cueva de Montesinos ... están puestas 'de industria' para crear ciertos efectos grotescos y humorísticos, cuyo fin es el de imitar a perfección las incongruencias del sueño. Y así estas impropiedades cumplen un papel artístico necesario para la creación de verosimilitud."

24 "Concerning Change, Continuity and Other Critical Matters: A Reading of John J. Allen's *Don Quixote: Hero or Fool* Part II," *Journal of Hispanic Philology*, 4 (1980), 253. El Saffar objects in particular to Allen's unhesitating assessment of the priest as "undeniably" taking on "total literary authority in Chapter VI" of *Don Quixote*, Part I.

25 *Don Quixote: Hero or Fool?* (Gainesville: University Presses of Florida, 1979), Part II, p. 59.

26 "Cervantes on Lofraso," p. 165.

27 *Cervantes's Theory of the Novel*, p. 25. On this point, see Daniel Eisenberg, "Pero Pérez the Priest and His Comment on *Tirant lo Blanch*," *MLN*, 88 (1973), 321–30, republished in Eisenberg, *Romances of Chivalry in the Spanish Golden Age* (Newark, Del.: Juan de la Cuesta, 1982), pp. 147–58.

28 I use the word "underlying" in the sense in which I employ "substance" in this book. I do not mean to imply that *Don Quixote* is nothing other than a parody. But I do mean to convey that the premise – the foundation on which Cervantes builds whatever we, as interpreters, think he has built – is a parodic imitation of a number of models. I shall expand on this contention in Chapter 2.

29 The original reads *entendimiento*, but most editors amend it to read *entreten-*

imiento. See the cogent argument by Daniel Eisenberg, "On Editing *Don Quixote,*" *Cervantes,* 3 (1983), 32–4.

30   "Y no penséis, señor, que yo llamo aquí vulgo solamente a la gente plebeya y humilde; que *todo aquel que no sabe,* aunque sea señor y príncipe, puede y debe entrar en número de vulgo" (II, 16; emphasis mine).

31   An analogous reception was given to the *Novelas ejemplares:* "Lope [de Vega] and, presumably, numerous readers who shared his expectations concerning the form and proper subject matter of the novella were inclined to discount the exemplarity of Cervantes's tales" (Forcione, *Cervantes and the Humanist Vision,* p. 6).

32   E.g.: "... cuán encajados tenía en la fantasía los mesmos disparates que su amo..." (I, 29); "¿Quién no había de reír de los circunstantes, viendo la locura del amo y la simplicidad del criado?" (I, 30).

33   As R. M. Flores notes, "Charles Lamb misunderstood [Sancho's] character-development and attributed Sancho's rising importance in *Don Quijote,* Part II, to Cervantes's wish to profit by making people laugh" ("Sancho's Fabrications: A Mirror of the Development of His Imagination," *Hispanic Review,* 38 [1970], 175 n.4).

34   Aristotle, *Poetics,* 1454a26. Cf. the comment by O. B. Hardison, Jr.: "The traits revealed by the speeches at the end of the play should be the same sort as those revealed by the speeches at the beginning.... Once [the writer] has chosen the type traits appropriate to a specific agent, these traits remain constant throughout the drama. A young man remains 'youthful'; a warrior remains 'military'; a woman remains 'feminine'" (pp. 204, 125, cited from the commentary accompanying Leon Golden's translation of the *Poetics* [Englewood Cliffs, N.J.: Prentice-Hall, 1968]). R. M. Flores remarks that "Cervantes constantly protects his back to avoid being accused of distorting reality and goes to great pains to meet and outwit his critics.... At times, however, Cervantes cannot refrain from taking sides... once he has made it perfectly clear that the objections did not originate with him"; among the examples Flores cites for this second point are the translator's objections of II, 5 ("The Rôle of Cide Hamete in *Don Quixote,*" *Bulletin of Hispanic Studies,* 59 [1982], 6–7). The translator thus becomes a sort of devil's advocate, voicing what Cervantes knew or anticipated (no doubt from the response to Part I) to be the objections of his readers with respect to plausibility, credibility and consistency. The device obviates the accusation that Cervantes was ignorant of a given aesthetic principle and emphasizes his purposiveness.

35   Approximately one hundred years later, Diego de Torres Villarroel saw Sancho as too acute for his circumstances, in comparison with the supposedly spontaneous humor of Avellaneda's Sancho: "El Sancho cervantino resulta demasiado agudo para su condición y a veces se nota que es el autor quien habla por su boca. El Sancho de Avellaneda es espontáneamente gracioso, sin proponérselo mientras que el de Cervantes se propone serlo y no lo consigue. Don Quijote peca también de desigual. En general, Cervantes se ha apartado del modelo homérico, en el que 'todos los caracteres se mantienen hasta el fin'" (cited from Luis López Molina, "Una visión dieciochesca del *Quijote,*" *Anales Cervantinos,* 16 [1977], 102).

36 *Cervantes's Theory of the Novel*, pp. 92–3.

37 Wardropper, "Cervantes' Theory of the Drama," p. 219.

38 "... como sean de honesto entretenimiento, que deleiten con el lenguaje y admiren y suspendan con la invención."

39 It is significant that Cervantes stresses that the *admiratio* would have disappeared if Don Diego had *read* the 1605 *Don Quixote*, for it supports my contention that in 1615 Cervantes wishes to say something specifically about *readers* of his work. Back in 1605, his concern was of a different order, of course. Not by reading but by observation of the protagonist's behavior were people able to conclude that he had lost his mind, "de lo cual recibieron la mesma admiración que recibían todos aquellos que de nuevo [= por primera vez] venían en conocimiento della [i.e., de la locura]" (I, 13).

40 Maureen Ihrie, in *Skepticism in Cervantes* (London: Tamesis, 1982), p. 68, describes them as "operating according to a limited (dogmatic) evaluation of Don Quijote and Sancho as two highly amusing jesters."

41 *Perspectives by Incongruity* (Bloomington: Indiana University Press, 1964), pp. 96–9. Calderón used virtually the same phrase in *Las visiones de la muerte*: "disparatar adrede" ("to talk nonsense on purpose").

42 *La lengua del "Quijote"* (Madrid: Gredos, 1971), p. 59.

43 *Sancho Panza*, pp. ix, 21. In his earlier article "Sancho's Fabrications," Flores pointed out: "Seventeenth-century writers considered Sancho a buffoon, suited only for making people laugh, and failed to see the character-development that he undergoes in *Don Quixote*" (p. 175 n. 3).

44 *Sancho Panza*, pp. 119, 127; emphases mine. For Flores' research, see ibid., especially pp. 117–21. Daniel Eisenberg, in a recent review of Flores' book (*Bulletin of Hispanic Studies*, 61 [1984], 507–8), attacks what he thinks is "the Romantic approach to Sancho: he is to be admired, not laughed at, unless he is trying to be funny." Eisenberg's misreading of Flores' conclusion is, by his own admission, grounded in his inability to consider a view that departs from his own: "*Cervantistas* who do not share [Flores'] view of Sancho ... can have little use for this book." Flores does not suggest that Sancho is not to be laughed at. Rather, he is pointing out that in addition to their humor, Sancho's sayings have a purpose, as in the example of the fulling mills, in which Sancho's drawing out of his story (silly as it is) achieves the desired effect of retaining his master's attention until dawn: "En esto, parece ser, o que el frío de la mañana, que ya venía ... " (I, 20). Howard Mancing, in *The Chivalric World of "Don Quijote": Style, Structure, and Narrative Technique* (Columbia: University of Missouri Press, 1982), p. 79, notes that "Sancho fails to impress as genuinely stupid."

45 It bears recalling that Cervantes does not allow this notion to come from his own mouth. In the prologue to Part I, it is his fictive friend who declares this to be his purpose, and at the end of Part II it is Cide Hamete who directs these comments to his pen.

46 Cited by William Byron, *Cervantes: A Biography* (Garden City, N.Y.: Doubleday, 1978), p. 420.

47 "'Don Quixote,'" p. 318.

48 For a discussion of the representation of other contemporary imitations and their comical perspective, see Flores, *Sancho Panza*, pp. 2–23. It bears remarking that authors of imaginative literature retain their freedom to create characters adapted from other works in accordance with their own intentions. If Cervantists dismiss Dale Wasserman's *Man of La Mancha* because it does not reflect their conception of the original characterization, why should we equate the comical – even farcical – creations of Cervantes' contemporaries with the original intentions of Cervantes? That they, unlike Wassserman, were of Cervantes' own time and culture is not sufficient reason to conclude that they were as well capable of understanding a genius's intention. Even learned readers like the Licentiate Francisco Márquez Torres, in his *aprobación* of the 1615 *Don Quixote*, believed (or pretended to believe, since there is some reason to believe that here again Cervantes puts words into the mouth of another) that the book's purpose was the downfall of the romances of chivalry. James A. Parr, in "Extrafictional Point of View in *Don Quijote*," in *Studies on "Don Quijote" and Other Cervantine Works*, ed. D. W. Bleznick (York, S.C.: Spanish Literature Publications, 1984), p. 25, comments on the remarks of Márquez Torres and similar words by another censor: "I would hope that these learned gentlemen are not representative of the best readers of that day."

49 *The Romantic Approach*, pp. 24–7.

50 "Algunas observaciones introductivas a la teoría dramática de los siglos XVI y XVII," in *Preceptiva dramática española*, ed. F. Sánchez Escribano and A. Porqueras Mayo (Madrid: Gredos, 1972), p. 30: "El adjetivo *suave*... está cargado de intensidad estética y beneficia a la comedia, hasta cierto punto. Ya desde el siglo XVI... se señala para la bondad del estilo... su suavidad y dulzura."

51 "The Chronology of the *Comedias* of Guillén de Castro," *Hispanic Review*, 12 (1944), 96–7. Rennert's reasoning is found in his edition of Castro's *Ingratitud por amor* (Philadelphia: University of Pennsylvania Publications, 1899), p. 22.

52 "Guillén de Castro: Apostilla cronológica," *Segismundo*, 27–32 (1978–80), 103–20.

53 Gregory G. LaGrone, in *The Imitations of "Don Quixote" in the Spanish Drama* (Philadelphia: University of Pennsylvania Publications, 1937), p. 13, summarily notes: "The first act is almost entirely of Castro's own invention. The idea of the 'two friends' is about all that is taken from Cervantes."

54 After the date of the *aprobación* an author could not again touch his work. I wish to thank Dr. Theodore S. Beardsley, Jr., Director of the Hispanic Society of America, for his advice on this matter. In a letter to me Dr. Beardsley expresses his belief that "the prologue was almost always in on the *aprobación*" and adds: "Generally, you can probably fix the *terminus ad quem* for prologue and text some days prior to the earliest date on almost any of the printed official documents preceding the work." This information becomes even more important for Part II of *Don Quixote*, as we shall see in a moment. The earliest of such documents there is the Márquez Torres *aprobación* dated 27 February 1615.

55 *Cervantes*, p. 505.

56 Bruerton, "The Chronology," p. 97.

57 *The Chivalric World*, pp. 77–8; emphasis mine.

58 *The History and Adventures of the Renowned Don Quixote*, trans. Tobias George Smollett, 2 vols. (London: Millar, Osborne, Rivington, 1755); *The Ingenious Gentleman Don Quixote de la Mancha*, trans. Samuel Putnam, 2 vols. (New York: Viking Press, 1949); *Don Quixote of La Mancha*, trans. Walter Starkie (New York: New American Library, 1964); *The Adventures of Don Quixote*, trans. J. M. Cohen (Harmondsworth: Penguin, 1950).

59 It is of interest to note that Close, whose *The Romantic Approach* has been so instrumental in clarifying the difference between the reception given *Don Quixote* before and after the advent of the Romantics, cites the dialogue of the *Persiles* prologue but skips the portion that contains Cervantes' response regarding the error of identifying him as *escritor alegre*. To judge by Close's condensed citation in "Cervantes' *Arte Nuevo de Hazer Fábulas Cómicas*," p. 4 n.4, Cervantes is first greeted as a merry writer and then bids farewell to life, jests, and friends.

60 Victoriano Ugalde, "La risa de Don Quijote," *Anales Cervantinos*, 15 (1976), 158.

61 Forcione (*Cervantes and the Humanist Vision*, p. 269) observes: "Modern readers occasionally admit with a trace of embarrassment that they have failed to respond to many of the flourishes of the licentiate's wit. . . . Part of the problem, of course, lies in the topical quality of satirical humor in general and specifically in the remoteness of the preoccupations and activities of seventeenth-century Spanish society from the twentieth-century reader. However, when one scrutinizes closely the spectacle of wit, that is, its pronouncement and reception, in *El Licenciado Vidriera*, one senses that a reader's exclusion from the participating audience within it has as much to do with the nature of the humor as with its content and that it may in fact be an effect that Cervantes carefully attempted to achieve."

62 Ruth S. El Saffar, *Novel to Romance: A Study of Cervantes's "Novelas ejemplares"* (Baltimore: Johns Hopkins University Press, 1974), pp. 59–61. For an opposing view, see Forcione, *Cervantes and the Humanist Vision*, pp. 225–316.

63 See R. D. F. Pring-Mill, "Sententiousness in *Fuente Ovejuna*," *Tulane Drama Review*, 7 (1962), 5–37.

64 Lavonne C. Poteet-Bussard, "*La ingratitud vengada* and *La Dorotea*: Cervantes and *La ingratitud*," *Hispanic Review*, 48 (1980), 348–9.

65 In his "Narrative 'Errors' in *Rinconete y Cortadillo*," *Bulletin of Hispanic Studies*, 58 (1981), 16, Aden W. Hayes observes that Cortado uses "nonsensical language as his ruse." Cervantes himself describes Cortado's use of language as saying "tantos disparates."

66 With the *Novelas ejemplares* in mind, Forcione remarks: "The disorienting *desatinos* – the 'swerves from the destined mark – are clearly intended." If we substitute "expected" for "destined," as indeed Forcione puts it in his previous sentence, we may appreciate the divergence between what Cer-

vantes intended and what his readers expected, a perspective I have tried to delineate in this chapter but with regard to *Don Quixote*: "Indeed there is hardly a tale that fails to deviate in some radical way from the expectations that its traditional ingredients would arouse in its audience" (*Cervantes and the Humanist Vision*, p. 28).

67 *Madness and Lust: A Psychoanalytical Approach to Don Quixote* (Berkeley: University of California Press, 1983), pp. 48-9.

68 Ibid., pp. 172-3; emphasis mine. I might add that on another point maintained in this chapter, Johnson also confirms an argument of mine, and again from a perspective unrelated to my concerns here. The characters of the 1615 *Don Quixote* "relate to our hero according to whether they have or have not read Part I" (ibid., p. 139). Clearly, then, the depiction of characters in accordance with this criterion reveals that Cervantes had one opinion of readers of Part I and another of those who were not preconditioned by that reading. In short, such differences aid us in extrapolating Cervantes' attitude toward his readers.

69 Michael Bell, "Sancho's Governorship and the 'Vanitas' Theme in 'Don Quixote' Part II," *Modern Language Review*, 77 (1982), 332.

70 L. A. Murillo, "*Don Quixote* as a Renaissance Epic," in *Cervantes and the Renaissance*, ed. M. D. McGaha (Easton, Pa.: Juan de la Cuesta, 1980), p. 55.

Chapter 2. Gilt o'erdusted: the problem of originality

1 Harry Levin, "The Tradition of Tradition," in Levin, *Contexts of Criticism* (Cambridge, Mass.: Harvard University Press, 1957), p. 63. Cf. Ramón Menéndez Pidal, "Un aspecto en la elaboración del *Quijote*," in Menéndez Pidal, *De Cervantes y Lope de Vega* (Madrid: Espasa-Calpe, 1940), pp. 26-7: "El estudio de las fuentes literarias de un autor, que es siempre capital para comprender la cultura humana como un conjunto de que el poeta forma parte, no ha de servir, cuando se trata de una obra superior, para ver lo que ésta copia y descontarlo de la originalidad; eso puede sólo hacerlo quien no comprende lo que verdaderamente constituye la invención artística. El examen de las fuentes ha de servir precisamente para lo contrario, para ver cómo el pensamiento del poeta se eleva por cima de sus fuentes, cómo se emancipa de ellas, las valoriza y las supera. Cervantes, justamente en los momentos en que sigue más de cerca al *Entremés [de los Romances]*, aparece más original que nunca."

2 *Main Currents of Spanish Literature* (New York: Holt, 1919), p. 92.

3 *Novel to Romance*, p. xv. The reference is to G. Hainsworth, *Les "Novelas ejemplares" de Cervantes en France au XVIIᵉ siècle* (Paris: Champion, 1933). Cf. the praise bestowed on Cervantes by Tirso de Molina: "nuestro español Boccaccio, quiero decir, Miguel de Cervantes" (*Los Cigarrales de Toledo* [Madrid: Aguilar, 1954], p. 172).

4 "Why so much emphasis on their originality?" asks E. T. Aylward in his recent *Cervantes: Pioneer and Plagiarist* (London: Tamesis, 1982), adding:

"What is especially irritating is [Cervantes'] repeated insistence upon the originality of his invention. One cannot help but sense that Cervantes might be protesting too strongly on this point and that indeed one or more of the tales contained in this volume could be less than original" (pp. 30–1). On Aylward's thesis – "the myth of Cervantes' authorship" (p. 15) of *Riconete y Cortadillo, El celoso extremeño*, and *La tía fingida* – see my review in *Kentucky Romance Quarterly*, forthcoming.

5 María Moliner, *Diccionario de uso del español* (Madrid: Gredos, 1966), s.v. *darse a entender*. See John G. Weiger, "A Clue to Cervantine Ambiguity: *Darse a entender*," *Hispanic Journal*, 3 (1982), 83–9. For *darse a*, Moliner gives, among other definitions, "ser en una reunión de personas un elemento discordante" ("to be a discordant element in a gathering of people"). In my article, I give numerous examples from Cervantes' works to show that *darse a entender* is found primarily in situations in which the individual who "gives himself to understand" is mistaken, deluded, or referring to the delusion of someone else.

6 One variation may serve to illustrate the possibilities that inhere in a bilateral assertion of a "truth." When Don Quixote sets out on his first sally, he can already envision his exploits' being written down by some future historian, and he proceeds to recite a flowery beginning for such an account. As he reaches the conclusion of the lengthy opening sentence that he has parodically imagined, he mentions that he has been traveling along the ancient and well-known plain of Montiel. Before he can continue, the narrator interrupts to say, "And it was true that he was traveling along it," whereupon Don Quixote resumes his monologue. The authorial intrusion seems to project a disinterested confirmation of the truth of Don Quixote's statement. That the interjection may serve to confirm only the truth of Don Quixote's comment that he is in Montiel (as opposed to the truth of his self-described heroic initiation of his adventures) does not negate the effect of providing a verification by the simple assertion that "it was true." For a compilation and analysis of the juxtaposition of the "must be-doubtless is" type of construction, see Rosenblat, *La lengua del "Quijote,"* pp. 302–5. Rosenblat ultimately reaches the conclusion that the real significance varies in each passage, for Cervantes deliberately plays with all the possibilities among what is certain, what is doubtful, and what is possible. See also Richard L. Predmore, *The World of Don Quixote* (Cambridge, Mass.: Harvard University Press, 1967), pp. 69–83. John T. Cull, in his "Cervantes y el engaño de las apariencias," *Anales Cervantinos*, 19 (1981), 77, notes an instance from the *Persiles* that illustrates the other side of the coin: "'Conoció, sin duda alguna, ser el herido el duque de Nemurs; . . . El duque herido, o a lo menos el que parecía ser el duque, sin abrir los ojos . . . ' (IV, 2). La declaración absoluta (sin duda alguna), basada únicamente en lo aparente, cede a una frase concesiva, dejando lugar para dudas, que es l[a] actitud más mesurada en todo lo que toque al conocimiento humano."

7 Cited from the translation by William T. Brewster, in *Papers on Playmaking*, ed. Brander Matthews (New York: Hill & Wang, 1957), p. 16. I have

substituted *comedia* for Brewster's "comedy" for the well-known reason that the Spanish term embraces more than what in English we understand by the label "comedy."

8   Although the play was not published until 1609 – the year when Lope first published his *Arte nuevo*, in which he supports Virués' claim – the work was probably composed in the early 1580s. See my book *Cristóbal de Virués* (Boston: Twayne, 1978), pp. 23–5.

9   *Spanish Drama*, p. 183.

10 Cited from Vich's *Breve discurso en favor de las comedias* (1650) by Vicente Ximeno, *Escritores del reyno de Valencia*, I (Valencia: Dolz, 1747), 247. Artieda's only extant play, *Los amantes*, is in four acts.

11 E. C. Riley, "The *pensamientos escondidos* and *figuras morales* of Cervantes," in *Homenaje a W. L. Fichter: Estudios sobre el teatro antiguo hispánico y otros ensayos*, ed. A. D. Kossoff and J. Amor y Vázquez (Madrid: Castalia, 1971), p. 624.

12 *European Literature and the Latin Middle Ages*, trans. W. R. Trask (Princeton, N.J.: Princeton University Press, 1973), pp. 35–89.

13 *El prólogo como género literario* (Madrid: CSIC, 1957), p. 141.

14 Richard L. Predmore, in his biography, *Cervantes* (New York: Dodd, Mead, 1973), p. 140, summarizes an incident that occurred some two dozen years before the publication of Cervantes' *comedias* and the prologue we have been discussing: "A curious document, dated 5 September 1592, testifies to his continuing (or renewed) inclination to write for the theater. On that date, he signed with the successful impresario Rodrigo Osorio an agreement to compose six plays at a price of fifty ducats each. One of the conditions of the agreement was that Osorio was required to put each play on the stage within twenty days of receiving it. Another condition stipulated that Osorio was obliged to pay nothing at all for any of the plays that did not turn out to be among the best ever represented in Spain. The price was very good by the standards of the day. . . . That he should now offer to waive payment for any of the plays not well received says something about his self-confidence as a writer. So far as is known, he never delivered any of the plays to Osorio. No doubt he was prevented from doing so by the endless distractions of the life of a commissary, beginning with his arrest in Castro del Río only about two weeks after he signed the agreement."

Predmore's hypothesis is a plausible one, but there is room for further speculation. Cervantes' acquiescence to the stipulations, especially since the price was very good, may reflect not so much his self-confidence as the plain fact that the contract would not be offered without the condition of a successful reception. (This type of requirement may account in part for the almost inevitable label of *famosa* attached by the poets to their *comedias*.) The situation seems analogous to that of any present-day agreement that guarantees royalties only after a minimum number of copies has been sold. That the plays were not even delivered to Osorio, much less staged, may reasonably be explained by Predmore's conjecture. On the other hand, in the 1615 prologue to his *comedias*, Cervantes tells us that "some years ago" he composed some *comedias*, but he could not find any impresario who would ask him for any, "although they knew that I had them, and so I put them away in a chest and consigned them to perpetual silence." The 1592 document and the 1615 prologue appear to refer to the same group of plays (or at least some of them, for a number can be dated well into the seventeenth century), yet Cervantes claims that no one wanted them. If we take him literally, it was not a question of their not being successful, for the plays were never put on stage, let alone requested. Since the contract indicates that they were indeed commissioned, it follows that it was Cervantes himself who decided to condemn them to "perpetual silence."

Given Cervantes' own statement in the prologue that he could have sold them if an impresario had not told a bookseller that "of my prose much could be expected, but of my poetry nothing," and given that this statement follows upon his well-known declaration that "the monster of nature, the great Lope de Vega, ran off with the monarchy of comedy," and given also the fact that it was in the 1590s that Lope's dominance began to make itself felt, it is not difficult to envision a Cervantes in late 1592 not only beset by financial and legal problems but painfully aware that his plays would not be well received, would not be judged – by standards then in vogue – "to be among the best ever represented in Spain," in short, a Cervantes who consequently preferred not to have them performed. (Perhaps, like Don Quixote with his visor, he preferred not to put his work to the test. Agustín G. Amezúa even conjectures that Cervantes never wrote the plays at all. See his *Cervantes: Creador de la novela corta española*, I [Madrid: CSIC, 1956], 29.) The self-confidence was therefore revealed not in the 1592 agreement but in the 1615 prologue (at which time he found the plays worthy of publication, expressing the hope that "they be the best in the world, or at least, reasonable"). He by then possessed enough self-confidence not only to poke fun at himself by revealing that his works had been judged wanting but also to hint that "firsts" in the *comedia* are trivia.

15 The original, *No le ha de valer al hijo la bondad del padre*, is rendered by Putnam as "The father's merits are not to be set down to the credit of his offspring"; by Starkie as "The goodness of the father is not going to help the son"; by Cohen as "The father's goodness shall not help the son."

16 I have intentionally used the word "sequel" in order to differentiate the automatic father–son type of reflected fame that Cervantes eschews from the concept of imitation, to which I shall return shortly. Cf. Russell Fraser, *The Dark Ages and the Age of Gold* (Princeton, N.J.: Princeton University Press, 1973), p. 30: "Originality is the proud possession of Thomas Nashe, who [in 1592] boasts that 'the vein which I have . . . is of my own begetting, and calls no man father in England but myself.'"

17 "Cervantes' Theory of the Drama," p. 218. Wardropper's next sentence suggests that the canon's "self-confessed ignorance of the genre might be supposed to disqualify him as a critic." It is more accurate to say that the canon's limited acquaintance is revealed but not confessed, for it is his contention that he does indeed know them well, even better than the theological

text mentioned earlier. That the canon's knowledge of his theology books may be even more superficial should not pass unobserved, for it is more than a sardonic commentary on the clergy and permits what Wardropper calls "a fine inconsistency [in] the canon's views." My point, therefore, is not to quibble but to distinguish what we may properly infer (the canon's superficial erudition generally) from what he most emphatically does *not* confess (any limits to his self-image as a literary critic).

18 Not his approval, as Wardropper suggests (p. 219). Again, my intention is not to split hairs, for as my quotations reveal, I find Wardropper's article an insightful study. As much for Wardropper's subsequent points as for my own, however, I find it necessary to insist on a closer reading of the canon's reaction – "no poco se rió el canónigo" ("the canon laughed not a little," i.e., he laughed a good deal) – for it is the account of the book burning that instantly gives rise to the canon's reversing his stand and finding something good to say about the books of chivalry.

19 "Cervantes' Theory of the Drama," p. 219.

20 *Cervantes's Theory of the Novel*, p. 49.

21 Ibid. The last point is, of course, a particular reference to Cervantes' declaration that the epic may be written in prose as well as in verse. For an explication of the passage under discussion as a "purification" of the older romances on the road to the newer romance as exemplified by the *Persiles*, see Forcione, *Cervantes, Aristotle, and the "Persiles,"* pp. 91–104.

22 Rollo May, in *The Courage to Create* (New York: Norton, 1975), p. 73, declares that "the poet is a menace to conformity." Cf. Fraser, who in *The Dark Ages*, pp. 62–3, suggests that when Roger Ascham (in 1570) "attacks medieval romances, he does so because, as they were 'made in monasteries by idle monks or wanton canons,' they breathe the spirit of the indolent past."

23 I repeat this point because the curate's interruption is what prompts the canon to turn from his previous position and find the *one good thing*, which in turn produces what Wardropper calls the "flood of other *good things*." Forcione, in *Cervantes, Aristotle, and the "Persiles,"* p. 95, sees an earlier change: "At this point the canon's argument takes an important turn from the negativism that marks his initial statements on the romances." The point to which Forcione refers is the canon's insistence on balancing the pleasure of imaginative literature and the observation of the principle of verisimilitude. This, it seems to me, is a reflection of the canon's views on literature generally. It is only after the curate's account of the mindless destruction of Don Quixote's books that the canon purposefully contradicts himself: *Despite all the bad things he has said about such books, he finds in them one good thing.*

24 *Cervantes's Theory of the Novel*, p. 54.

25 See, for example, Jorge Luis Borges, *Other Inquisitions*, trans. Ruth L. C. Simms (Austin: University of Texas Press, 1964), p. 53: "The adventures of the *Quixote* are not so well planned, the slow and antithetical dialogues ... offend us by their improbability, but there is no doubt that Cervantes

knew Don Quixote well and could believe in him. Our belief in the novelist's belief makes up for any negligence or defect in the work. What does it matter if the episodes are unbelievable or awkward when we realize that *the author planned, not to challenge our credibility, but to define his characters?"* (emphasis mine). See also, among many other examples of this assessment by both Borges and Salvador de Madariaga, the latter's *Don Quixote: An Introductory Essay in Psychology* (London: Oxford University Press, 1961), pp. 92–3: "These are but abundant proofs of negligence, not merely of style but as to the very facts of the narrative. [We recall that these are the very charges Cervantes levels at Avellaneda's *Quixote.*] Yet they do but enhance the value of the chapter as a significant example of marvellous accuracy in character-drawing even under this distracted attention toward externals. We catch a glimpse of that unswerving subconscious attention which remains attached to the characters despite the wanderings of the conscious intellect. With all its negligence in style and story, this is one of the chapters in *Don Quixote* [I, 36] in which Cervantes' psychological insight is at its best, and there is not one word, look, gesture in it which does not fit perfectly with the character to which it is attributed."

26   This point is made in a number of ways by Close, "Cervantes' *Arte Nuevo.*"

27   See my article "Lo nunca visto en Cervantes," *Anales Cervantinos*, 17 (1978), 111–22.

28   *Sentido y forma de las Novelas ejemplares* (Madrid: Gredos, 1962), pp. 185–6, 188. Cf. Dorotea's description of her seduction by Fernando as the "new event" (*nuevo acaecimiento*), i.e., the recent – hardly novel – occurrence (*Don Quixote*, I, 28), and the closer parallel in *El curioso impertinente*: "Rindióse Camila; Camila se rindió. . . . Sólo supo Leonela la flaqueza de su señora, porque no se la pudieron encubrir los dos malos amigos y nuevos amantes" (I, 34). Cf. also the description of the newly arrived travelers at the inn as *los nuevos caminantes* (I, 44); the label *mozo y nuevo ermitaño* for the young Silerio recently turned hermit in *La Galatea* (Book II); and the reference in *Persiles* to *nuevos huéspedes* (II, 5) and to *nuevos peregrinos* (passim). See also the description of the Clavileño episode as *vuestro nuevo viaje* (*Don Quixote*, II, 41) and the mention of the *nueva, aunque vieja peregrina* of *Persiles* (III, 6).

29   *Troilus and Cressida*, III, 3.

30   *European Literature*, p. 141.

31   "Art as Knowledge," in Levin, *Contexts of Criticism*, p. 24.

32   *The Adversary Literature: The English Novel in the Eighteenth Century: A Study in Genre* (New York: Farrar, Strauss & Giroux, 1974), pp. 147, 206.

33   Larry D. Benson, "The Originality of *Beowulf*," in *The Intepretation of Narrative*, ed. M. W. Bloomfield (Cambridge, Mass.: Harvard University Press, 1970), p. 30.

34   The translation is by Peter Russell in his "Arms versus Letters: Towards a Definition of Spanish Fifteenth-Century Humanism," in *Aspects of the Renaissance: A Symposium*, ed. A. R. Lewis (Austin: University of Texas Press, 1967), p. 58.

35   Ibid. Cf. the similar declaration and parallel reaction by the modern scholar

who brings it to the fore: "The Elizabethan critic William Webbe knows of 'no memorable worke written by any Poete in our English speeche until twenty yeeres past.' That eliminates Chaucer, whose talent is generally conceded but who is thought to have been unlucky in his birth" (Fraser, *The Dark Ages*, p. 3).

36   Michael Rosenblum, "Smollett and the Old Conventions," *Philological Quarterly*, 55 (1976), 390; emphasis in the original. I would not concur with the implications inherent in Rosenblum's word "attack," but the thrust of his sentence generally is in accord with the thoughts I present here.

37   *The Discarded Image: An Introduction to Medieval and Renaissance Literature* (1964; rpt. Cambridge: Cambridge University Press, 1967), p. 210. See also his remark on p. 211: "I doubt if [medieval writers] would have understood our demand for originality or valued those works in their own age which were original any the more on that account. If you had asked Layamon or Chaucer 'Why do you not make up a brand-new story of your own?' I think they might have replied (in effect) 'Surely we are not yet reduced to that?'"

38   See n.1 to this chapter.

39   Peter N. Dunn, "Las *Novelas ejemplares*," in *Suma Cervantina*, ed. Juan Bautista Avalle-Arce and E. C. Riley (London: Tamesis, 1973), p. 83: "En el Prólogo, Cervantes proclama que sus novelas son entretenidas, morales y originales."

40   "La intención del *Quijote*," *Revista de Occidente*, 18 (1967), 152: "el discutible concepto romántico de la originalidad."

41   Benson, "The Originality of *Beowulf*," p. 1.

42   *Princeton Encyclopedia of Poetry and Poetics*, ed. Alex Preminger (Princeton, N.J.: Princeton University Press, 1974), p. 379, points out that "creation" and "imitation" were nearly synonymous.

43   Dunn in "Las *Novelas ejemplares*," p. 88, includes other reasons, but they do not pertain to priority: "Los volúmenes de narraciones recogidas por Timoneda apenas son originales y carecen de unidad imaginativa, muchas no pasan de ser anécdotas o *facetiae*, muchas se sitúan en tiempos y espacios remotos."

44   Quoted from *Spanish Ballads*, ed. C. Colin Smith (Oxford: Pergamon Press, 1964), p. 188.

45   Francisco Rodríguez Marín, in his edition of 1948 (*El ingenioso hidalgo Don Quixote de la Mancha*, VI [Madrid: Ediciones Atlas, 1948], 11) comments: "Sancho apaña a su propósito el romance, como don Quijote lo había acomodado al suyo." Cervantes himself uses similar words to describe Teolinda's verses: "acomodando a su propósito una copla antigua . . . " (*Galatea*, Book I). I do not share the judgment expressed by Conchita Herdman Marianella in her exhaustive study, *"Dueñas" and "Doncellas": A Study of the "Doña Rodríguez" Episode in "Don Quijote"* (Chapel Hill: North Carolina Studies in the Romance Languages and Literatures, 1979), p. 104: "In 1615 Sancho, and not Don Quijote, actively projects himself into the chivalric situation, in a humorous usurpation of the knight's domain, and inappropriate to the squire."

46 Johnson, in *Madness and Lust*, pp. 68–72, reminds us that the original ballad
    goes on to deal with "the illicit sexual relationship between Lancelot and
    Guinevere. . . . What Don Quixote accommodates to his needs here is a story
    about illicit sex and violence and not merely a fanciful description of a
    knight's arrival at a castle" (p. 69). L. A. Murillo, in his essay "*Lanzarote*
    and *Don Quijote*," *Folio*, 10 (1977), 58, points out that "the adulterous and
    even scandalous affair between the Queen and Lanzarote does not play any
    part in Cervantes' story . . . and . . . Cervantes does not cite nor allude any-
    where to this portion of the ballad." Johnson objects that the ballads, being
    a popular, oral tradition, were so well known that the reader (and Don
    Quixote himself) knew very well the subsequent part of the ballad's content.
    Whether we insist on the text and consider the breaking-off point as reason
    to exclude all matter not cited, or whether we accept Johnson's thesis that
    the automatic response would be to call forth one's knowledge of the con-
    tinuation, the purposeful accommodation of the ballad is indisputable. I shall
    shortly deal with another *romance*, suggesting much as Johnson does here
    that what is not articulated is significant for its absence. My own case,
    however, depends on Don Quixote's articulation of the ballad earlier in the
    text.
47 *Spanish Ballads*, p. 109.
48 *Cervantes's Theory of the Novel*, p. 57.
49 Ibid., p. 61.
50 *Madness and Lust*, pp. 19, 22.
51 Putnam translation. The last word quoted reads *invención* in the Spanish.
52 Putnam translation.
53 "Sólo tiene que aprovecharse de la imitación en lo que fuere escribiendo."
    Putnam's rendition of *aprovecharse* ("to take advantage of" or "to make use
    of") is perhaps enhanced by the addition of the word "proper," as in the
    passage I have cited. Riley similarly translates it as "make proper use of"
    (*Cervantes's Theory of the Novel*, p. 58). Starkie's translation reads "make
    best use of," but his version is marred by the erroneous beginning: "All
    you claim to do is to make best use of imitation in your writing." Only
    Cohen leaves it intact: "In what you are writing you have only to make use
    of imitation." It is true that the Spanish *aprovecharse* connotes *beneficial* use
    (which might be the most exact translation in the sentence in question), but
    I wonder if "proper" does not reflect the translator's awareness of the precept
    rather than the simpler statement of the original. On the other hand, these
    interpolations may well reflect keen intuition because of an ambiguity in-
    herent not in the word *aprovecharse* but in the word *sólo*. This word (literally,
    "only") is accurately rendered in the version cited to reflect that this is all
    the author needs to do. If, however, we take the Cohen translation – "you
    have only to make use of imitation" – and transpose it – "you have to make
    use of imitation only" – we approach the reading given to this passage by
    Américo Castro ("Los prólogos al *Quijote*," in Castro, *Hacia Cervantes* [Mad-
    rid: Taurus, 1957], pp. 212–13), who, to be sure, leaps ahead a number of
    lines and relates imitation to intention. Although Castro's vault is somewhat

greater than his phraseology implies ("viene a continuación esta sentencia esencial"), his inference that imitation should be limited to the extent that it serves the intention and conception of the artist ("pintando... vuestra intención; dando a entender vuestros conceptos," advises Cervantes' "friend") is consistent with the attitude of Don Quixote in the Sierra Morena when he affirms that he will imitate Roland (Orlando) not in every detail but only in those things that to him appear to be most essential (I, 25). This reading is also consistent with the reshaping principle under discussion in my text. In view of these considerations, a more accurate translation of *aprovecharse* in the sentence just examined might be "to make *appropriate* use of imitation."

54 *Cervantes's Theory of the Novel*, p. 58.
55 *The Old and the New: From Don Quixote to Kafka*, trans. C. Cosman (Berkeley: University of California Press, 1977), pp. 28, 30.
56 The original does in fact read "unseen" (*no vista*). Although it may be thought of as "extraordinary," i.e., never before seen, its use has ironic significance in Cervantes' works. See my "Lo nunca visto en Cervantes."
57 *Cervantes's Theory of the Novel*, p. 67.
58 Juan Bautista Avalle-Arce, *Nuevos deslindes cervantinos* (Barcelona: Ariel, 1975), pp. 347, 348. Cf. Dominick L. Finello, "En la Sierra Morena: *Quijote* I, 23–26," in *Actas del Sexto Congreso Internacional de Hispanistas*, ed. A. M. Gordon and E. Rugg (Toronto: University of Toronto, 1980), p. 244 n.11. Finello disagrees with those who see no relevance in Don Quixote's penance and considers the behavior in Sierra Morena to be in perfect accord with the Aristotelian principle of *mimesis*. Compare these interpretations, particularly Avalle's emphasis on pure will, with that of Francisco Márquez Villanueva in *Personajes y temas del "Quijote"* (Madrid: Taurus, 1975), p. 45. Márquez Villanueva sees the humor of the episode and then points out that Don Quixote's arguments concerning his lack of motivation "representa el triunfo de la razón pura dentro de un terreno por definición y desde siempre muy cerebral" ("represent the triumph of pure reason within a field [that] by definition has always been cerebral"). He also makes the sensible remark that Don Quixote's decision to imitate Amadís rather than Orlando has a very practical motivation: It is a rather difficult task to uproot trees and somewhat simpler to imitate lamentation (p. 46).
59 The number eleven is "symbolic of transition, excess and peril and of conflict and martyrdom. According to Schneider [*El origen musical de los animales-símbolos en la mitología y la escultura antiguas* (Barcelona, 1946)], there is an infernal character about it...; but at the same time it corresponds... to the focal point of symbolic Inversion and antithesis" (J. E. Cirlot, *A Dictionary of Symbols*, trans. Jack Sage [New York: Philosophical Library, 1962], pp. 223–4). In this respect there is interest in the change made in the second edition of *Don Quixote* by Juan de la Cuesta, which omits this passage and substitutes for the shirttail rosary of eleven knots "a rosary of corktree nuts which he strung together and of which he made a decade." The change, occasioned by the disrespect implicit in the shirttail version, necessarily eliminates the originality inherent in the choice of number as well. The fact

that Don Quixote is naked from the waist down adds to the indecorous effect ("en carnes y en pañales" means "naked and in shirttails"), an image that will be corrected, as we shall see, when Sancho claims to have reported to Dulcinea that his master was naked from the waist *up*.

60 *The Old and the New*, p. 31.

61 P. 600. Cf. Rafael Osuna, "Una parodia cervantina de un romance de Lope," *Hispanic Review*, 49 (1981), 102: "La ambigüedad que toda parodia contiene: se trivializa lo serio y lo cómico se solemniza." Mancing, in *The Chivalric World*, p. 20, makes a similar argument: "Parody [is] not to be confused with burlesque."

62 Margaret A. Rose, *Parody/Meta-Fiction* (London: Croon Helm, 1979), pp. 17, 21, 22, 34.

63 Forcione, *Cervantes and the Humanist Vision*, p. 343 n. 41 (Forcione bases this remark on L. P. May's *Cervantes, un fondateur de la libre-pensée* [Paris, 1947]).

64 Lowry Nelson, Jr., "Chaos and Parody: Reflections on Anthony Close's *The Romantic Approach to 'Don Quixote*,'" *Cervantes*, 2 (1982), 93.

65 L. A. Murillo, *The Golden Dial: Temporal Configuration in "Don Quijote"* (Oxford: Dolphin, 1975), pp. 32 n. 11, 67 n. 3. Murillo refers us to Avalle-Arce's note in the latter's edition of the *Persiles* (*Los trabajos de Persiles y Sigismunda* [Madrid: Castalia, 1969]), p. 222, but that entry simply deals with the confusion between *verano* and *primavera*. A more germane example is found later in the text of the *Persiles* itself (p. 241 of Avalle-Arce's edition), in which Periandro narrates a visit to an island *locus amoenus*, where all known fruits are in season the year round, the year consisting of *primavera, verano, estío*, and *otoño*; winter or *invierno* is of course nonexistent in such a mythical environment. It is noteworthy that this episode is later revealed to have been a dream.

66 "El uso de los números en el *Quijote*," in Gordon and Rugg, *Actas del Sexto Congreso Internacional de Hispanistas*, p. 826.

67 Augustín Redondo, "Tradición carnavalesca y creación literaria, del personaje de Sancho Panza al episodio de la Insula Barataria en el *Quijote*," *Bulletin Hispanique*, 80 (1978), 39–70; J. M. Sobré, "Don Quixote, the Hero Upside-Down," *Hispanic Review*, 44 (1978), 127–41.

68 *Don Quixote: Hero or Fool?* Part I, pp. 58–63. Allen summarizes comments on similar passages by Diego Clemencín and E. C. Riley. See also ibid., Part II, pp. 32–3.

69 *Sentido y forma del "Quijote"* (Madrid: Insula, 1949), p. 325.

70 In his Planeta edition of 1975, p. 984: "Es posible, como me sugiere el prof. Juan Vernet, que aquí *estío* equivalga a *sama'un* (período de veinte días antes del 12 de julio y veinte después, o sea, más largo que la canícula) que se emplea en el Norte de Africa. Cervantes pudo conocer este período en Argel, que debería hacer creer a algunos cristianos que era una estación más, y así lo hace decir a Cide Hamete Benengeli."

71 In his edition of *Don Quixote de la Mancha*, IV (Madrid: V. Suárez, 1941), 436. Mancing, in *The Chivalric World*, p. 207, similarly remarks: "That Cide Hamete Benengeli is now a Mohammedan philosopher and that he has

everything backward can be considered a synthesis of his role in part II of
Don Quijote."

72 Johnson, in *Madness and Lust*, p. 39, reminds us of Don Quixote's first sally,
in which the narrator refers to July as *verano*, "in accord with literary tradition
– when *estío* – a reflection of real seasons and their characteristics – would
clearly be more appropriate." Johnson concludes: "For Cervantes, then,
there is an element of parody." The parody there (Don Quixote's age contrasted with the mythical spring) is of a different order but based on analogous elements.

73 Cf. Flores, "Sancho's Fabrications," p. 180 n. 13, with reference to Sancho's
description of the earth and its people as seen from Clavileño: "a patent
mixture of the sublime (the Biblical reminiscences of 'grano de mostaza')
and the common ('avellana')."

74 Patrick Cullen, "Imitation and Metamorphosis: The Golden-Age Eclogue
in Spenser, Milton, and Marvell," *PMLA*, 84 (1969), 1562.

75 *Creative Intuition in Art and Poetry* (New York: Pantheon, 1953), p. 23.

76 Aubrey F. G. Bell, *Cervantes* (Norman: University of Oklahoma Press,
1947), p. 111.

77 "You, Me, and the Novel," *Saturday Review/World*, 29 June 1974, p. 9.

78 *Sentido y forma del "Quijote,"* p. 309. The original includes a pertinent citation
from Baltasar Gracián, although Casalduero's generalization about the age
is debatable: "Cervantes, como exige su época (Gracián lo subrayará: 'Pro-
póngase en cada predicamento los primeros, no tanto a la imitación cuanto
a la emulación; no para seguirles, sí para adelantárseles'), no trata de imitar
a los antiguos; lo que quiere es entrar en competencia con ellos."

79 Leicester Bradner, "From Petrarch to Shakespeare," in *The Renaissance* (New
York: Harper & Row, 1962), p. 117; emphasis mine.

80 Avalle-Arce, introduction to his edition of the *Persiles*, p. 10: "La misma
actitud de valerosa confianza en sí mismo le llevará a declarar, años más
tarde, que el *Persiles* será el mejor libro de entretenimiento escrito en español,
y esto en la dedicatoria del segundo *Quijote*, nada menos." The reference to
the "same attitude" is to Avalle's interpretation of the 1592 contract as
illustrative of Cervantes' self-confidence. As I have indicated, I suspect that
the fact that he did not submit the plays at that time may illustrate precisely
the contrary feeling. I suspect as well that despite the evident confidence
that is revealed in the prologue to *Don Quixote*, Part II, Cervantes continues
to need to have his works judged to be good. This in itself is hardly surprising, for nearly every artist shares such a desire. Nonetheless, something
less than the arrogance that Castro attributes to Cervantes ("Los prólogos
al *Quijote*," p. 205) comes through when, in the midst of ridiculing Avellaneda, Cervantes cannot help but announce that Avellaneda found the *Novelas ejemplares* to be good. Might it not be supposed that Cervantes selects
this particular sentence to cite – Avellaneda criticized the *Novelas* for being
less exemplary than satirical although not a little *ingeniosas* – not only to
ridicule Avellaneda's inability to appreciate the tales but also to seize upon
the opportunity to reproduce a favorable assessment? My conjecture is given

added weight by Cervantes' conversion of the charged *ingeniosas* employed by Avellaneda to the unequivocal *buenas*. It is in this same vein, I suggest, that Cervantes allows Sansón Carrasco to repeat the criticisms made by readers of *Don Quixote*, Part I, with respect to the alleged irrelevance of *El curioso impertinente*, for it is nonetheless judged good: "no por mala ni por mal razonada, sino por no ser de aquel lugar" (II, 3). Whether it is a rival like Avellaneda or the reading public generally, Cervantes does not mind putting in print the criticism made of his works, so long as he has an opportunity to bring out the fact that what remains after all other criticism is dealt with is that the works are deemed good.

81 "Querría que fuesen las mejores del mundo, o, a lo menos, razonables." The same word, *razonable*, is applied to the collection as a whole in the dedication, the quality being ascribed to their unperformed state: unperformed, that is, because they have not been handled by actors, who delude themselves by performing instead works of "serious authors." The sarcasm is evidently intended to refer to the greater popularity accorded to the Lope de Vega style of play, and so "reasonable" presumably means devoid of the excesses of such works. It is this connotation that the statement quoted in my text is meant to convey, rather than any possible ironic antonym of "best." Cf. the reaction of Schevill and Bonilla in their edition of the *Comedias y entremeses*, VI (Madrid: Gráficas Reunidas, 1922), p. 67: "No podrá menos de sonreír el lector moderno al tropezar con semejante frase y al pensar en que fue Cervantes quien la escribió. Y no es fácil de explicar lo que este último entendió por 'razonable,' porque poco de ello tienen las páginas del tomo [de comedias] de 1615." See also the *Viaje del Parnaso*, Chapter IV: "Yo con estilo en parte razonable / he compuesto *Comedias* . . . " Cf. Don Quixote's approval of Cardenio's sonnet (I, 23) as he judges its author to be a *razonable poeta*.

82 *La Galatea*, Book III:

> que no está en la elegancia
> y modo de decir el fundamento
> y principal sustancia
> del verdadero cuento,
> que en la pura verdad tiene su asiento.

"This passage is most often read as confirmation of Cervantes' campaign against affectation," writes Mary Gaylord Randel in "The Language of Limits and the Limits of Language: The Crisis of Poetry in *La Galatea*," *MLN*, 97 (1982), 259. She goes on to say that "'truth' may give words a foundation; but only words, trembling in their incapacity, can provide evidence of that truth."

83 On the "legitimate marvelous," see Forcione, *Cervantes, Aristotle, and the "Persiles,"* esp. pp. 95–104.

84 *Cervantes' Christian Romance* (Princeton, N.J.: Princeton University Press, 1972), p. 62.

85 *Experience and Artistic Expression in Lope de Vega: The Making of "La Dorotea"*
    (Cambridge, Mass.: Harvard University Press, 1974), pp. 431, 733.
86 Ibid., p. 733.

Chapter 3. The reality of illusion

1 *Cervantes's Theory of the Novel*, p. 195.
2 Forcione, in *Cervantes and the Humanist Vision*, p. 251, citing a popular
   sixteenth-century Spanish translation of Erasmus' *Enchiridion* (*Enquiridion*),
   recalls the latter's wish "to impress on his reader the necessity of learning
   to see with the 'ojos del corazón,' or, as he puts it elsewhere, with the 'ojos
   del ánimo y del entendimiento,' beyond the surfaces that the physical eye
   beholds."
3 Barry Lydgate, "Mortgaging One's Work to the World: Publication and
   the Structure of Montaigne's *Essais*," *PMLA*, 96 (1981), 213.
4 Flores, in "Sancho's Fabrications," p. 179 n. 12, writes: "Under the suggestion of his master – presumably after the knight had made his usual
   chivalric remarks about who[m] and why he was fighting – in the darkness
   and with the promised earldom in mind, the squire sees rather than imagines
   the blood and the giant's head."
5 For instance, "there are persons who can recall having seen Dame Quintañona [Guinevere's lady-in-waiting]. . . . So true is this that I can remember
   how my grandmother . . . used to say to me, when she saw a lady in a
   venerable hood, 'That one, my grandson, looks just like Dame Quintañona.'
   From which I infer that she must have known her or at least seen a picture
   of her" (I, 49). The principle was applied to his own book: "No sooner do
   people see some skinny nag than they immediately shout, 'There goes Rocinante!'" (II, 3). Perhaps closer to Don Quixote's manner of apprehending
   visually what he reads is Campuzano's repeated reference to having *seen* the
   dogs' colloquy: "In the hospital, when I saw what I shall now tell. . . . You
   must also have seen or heard what is told about [the dogs]. And the fact is
   that I heard and almost saw with my own eyes." Cervantes himself refers
   to Campuzano's "telling what he had seen." As every reader knows, Campuzano did not physically see any of the colloquy, which he claims to have
   overheard in the hospital. Cf. Américo Castro, "La palabra escrita y el
   Quijote," in *Hacia Cervantes*, p. 281: "Supuesto esencial de tan extraño fe-
   nómeno es que la palabra escrita sea sentida como realidad animada, vital-
   izada, y no como simple expresión de fantasías o conocimientos distanciados
   del lector."
6 A secondary aspect is the sense of sound in the same passage: "What must
   it be to hear the music which is played while he eats, without knowing who
   is singing or where it comes from?" For an aesthetic analysis, see Forcione,
   Cervantes, Aristotle, and the "Persiles," pp. 113–16.
7 *Aprehensión*: "Aunque en su sentido literal y recto se entiende por esta voz
   el acto de aprehender, o retener alguna cosa, cogiéndola y asiéndola: en el
   común y usual se ciñe esta voz a explicar la vehemente y tenaz imaginación

con que el entendimiento concibe, piensa y está cabilando sobre alguna cosa, que por lo regular le assusta y desazona." *Aprehender*: "Tomar y asir las cosas, retenerlas, y traherlas a sí: lo que con propriedad se entiende de lo que el entendimiento concibe, piensa, imagina y retiene con vehemencia."

8 Cited by Joel Snyder, "Picturing Vision," in *The Language of Images*, ed. W. J. T. Mitchell (Chicago: University of Chicago Press, 1980), p. 221.

9 *Meditaciones del Quijote* (Madrid: Revista de Occidente, 1966), pp. 152–3: "Bien que estos gigantes no lo sean, pero . . . ¿y los otros?; quiero decir, ¿y los gigantes en general? ¿De dónde ha sacado el hombre los gigantes? Porque ni los hubo ni los hay *en realidad*. Fuere cuando fuere, la ocasión en que el hombre pensó por vez primera los gigantes no se diferencia en nada esencial de esta escena cervantina." Ramón Saldívar, in "Don Quijote's Metaphors and the Grammar of Proper Language," *MLN*, 95 (1980), 260, observes: "The sense of the word 'gigante,' instead of designating the thing which the word should normally designate (a sense which for this particular word is *already in the realm of metaphor*), goes elsewhere" (emphasis mine). I cannot answer Ortega's question, but I can offer a possible source for Cervantes' use of giants and windmills. Dante describes it:

> I had not long kept my head turned in that direction when I seemed to see many lofty towers, whereon I, "Master, say, what city is this?" And he told me, "It is because you pierce the darkness from too far off that you stray in your imagining; and when you reach the place you will see plainly how much the sense is deceived by distance; therefore, spur yourself on somewhat more." Then lovingly he took me by the hand and said, "Before we go further forward, in order that the fact may seem less strange to you, know that these are not towers, but giants, and every one of them is in the pit, round about the bank from the navel downward."
>
> As when a mist is vanishing, the sight little by little shapes out that which the vapor hides that fills the air; so, as I pierced the thick and murky atmosphere and came on nearer and nearer to the brink, error fled from me and fear grew upon me; for, as on its round wall Montereggione crowns itself with towers, so here the horrible giants, whom Jove still threatens from heaven when he thunders, betowered with half their bodies the bank that encompasses the pit.

The translation is by Charles S. Singleton (Princeton, N.J.: Princeton University Press, 1970), from *Inferno*, XXXI, vv. 19–45. See also the following from *Inferno*, XXXIV, vv. 4–9, 28–51:

> As, when a thick fog breathes, or when our hemisphere darkens to night, a mill which the wind turns appears from afar, such an edifice did I now seem to see; then, because of the wind, I drew back behind my leader, for there was no other shelter there. . . .
>
> The emperor of the woeful realm stood forth from mid-breast out of the ice; and I in size compare better with a giant than giants with his arms. . . . Oh how great a marvel it was to me when I saw three

faces on his head. . . . From under each there came forth two mighty wings, of size befitting such a bird – sails at sea I never saw so broad. They had no feathers, but were like a bat's. And he was flapping them, so that three winds went forth from him.

Commenting on these passages, Singleton observes: "We may pause to reflect that this is a curious windmill indeed if it 'blows' – gives forth a wind – instead of being turned by the wind: a grotesque reversal in itself." Grotesque indeed, but the "windmill" is *not* a windmill; it is a giant (Lucifer)! Also see Francisco Márquez Villanueva, *Fuentes literarias cervantinas* (Madrid: Gredos, 1973), pp. 297–311.

10   *The Old and the New*, p. 160.
11   *Art and Illusion* (Princeton, N.J.: Princeton University Press, 1969), p. 204. Close ("Cervantes' *Arte nuevo*," p. 8) describes Cervantes' "ironic strategy of presenting the phenomena misinterpreted by Don Quixote in an initially ambivalent way so that they seem for a time to contain marvellous potentialities. Don Quixote is deluded about the strange clanking of the *batanes*; yet is not the dark wood in which he hears it a genuinely awe-inspiring place?"
12   Robert refers to Don Quixote's "habit of creating optical illusions" (*The Old and the New*, p. 139).
13   "Sancho's Governorship," p. 330. Murillo, in *"Don Quixote"*, p. 57, calls it "an audio-visual fallacy."
14   The instance cited here is notable for its deviation from a pattern generally (but, evidently, not invariably) characteristic of "Cervantes' way of presenting things: first what is seen, then its interpretation" (Predmore, *The World of Don Quixote*, p. 72n).
15   "Porque te desengañes y veas ser verdad lo que te digo: sube a tu asno y síguelos bonitamente, y verás cómo, en alejándose de aquí algún poco, se vuelven en su ser primero, y, dejando de ser carneros, son hombres hechos y derechos, como yo te los pinté primero." The reference to "them" is in the masculine ("síguelos"), despite the most recent allusion to the animals as the feminine "manadas de ovejas." We might look ahead to the masculine "carneros" as reflecting what was in the narrator's mind, but if it is Don Quixote's state of mind that interests us, a more intriguing aspect is his insistence on what he considers their *original* shape, even while he grants that they *now* appear as sheep.
16   Karl-Ludwig Selig, in "The Battle of the Sheep (*Don Quixote*, I, xviii)," *Revista Hispánica Moderna*, 38 (1974–5), 65, observes that "the 'object' to be transformed may move toward them, since one must always keep in mind that direction of movement is an essential structural element of the *Quixote*."
17   *De Anima*, 2.7.
18   "Y así, eso que a ti te parece bacía de barbero, me parece a mí el yelmo de Mambrino, y a otro le parecerá otra cosa" (I, 25). I suspect that the source here is Juan Huarte de San Juan, whose *Examen de ingenios* (1575) influenced Cervantes in many ways: "What happened to those four men who, upon seeing a blue cloth, one swore it was red, one swore it was white, one said

yellow, and the other said black, and none of them hit the mark, due to the peculiar aberration of each man's vision" (cited by Ihrie, *Skepticism in Cervantes*, p. 25). Allen, in *Don Quixote: Hero or Fool?* Part I, p. 22, sees the matter differently: "The author explains Don Quixote's self-deception before the helmet is even won, and every reader and all other characters assent, though some of the latter may agree with Don Quixote in jest." The assent of the reader, to my way of thinking, is to the plausibility of mistaking the one for the other, precisely because of the painstaking description of the circumstances. Don Quixote's "self-deception" is limited to the chivalric interpretation of the perception, i.e., that it is a helmet, specifically Mambrino's helmet. That it is headgear is not self-deception but a likely interpretation of the visual evidence, reinforced for us particularly because it is so perceived "before the helmet is even won."

19 *Tesoro*, s.v. *columbrar*: "Divisar alguna cosa de lejos, que apenas se puede distinguir y conocer lo que es." In Cervantes' play *El gallardo español*, the phrase is presented the other way around – "columbro y veo" (*Obras*, p. 216) – although it is true that the rhyme requires the line to end in *-eo*.

20 That this portion of his account is wholly fabricated is clear from its utter rupture with any semblance of reality. In this it may be differentiated from the earlier description of what he saw, thought he saw, or expected to see as a person viewing the earth from on high. At least one commentator is convinced that Sancho steadfastly believes every moment of the events described to have occurred: "We have noted that Sancho holds no doubts whatsoever about the ascent. His conviction that the transcendent journey took place is evident in his adamant refusal to withdraw his assertions or to give way to confusion when confronted by the Duke, the Duchess, and Don Quijote who question him skeptically" (Franklin O. Brantley, "Sancho's Ascent into the Spheres," *Hispania*, 53 [1970], 42).

21 Brantley, in ibid., p. 42, remarks, "The Duchess's question as to his ability to see the entire earth through only a small opening is of course an absurd question, one that can be readily answered by anyone with the simplest notion of the laws of perspective which since the Renaissance were commonly known." Indeed. If this "anyone" includes Sancho Panza, what needs to be emphasized here is that such simple notions were apparently not at his disposal in earlier adventures.

22 Ibid., pp. 41, 42.

23 Sancho subsequently tells the duke, "Ever since I came back down from the sky and since from its high peak I looked at the earth and saw it to be so small, the great desire I had to be governor has been somewhat tempered in me" (II, 42).

24 To some extent this inversion in itself is part of another well-known topos, the world upside down, and its corollary, the stringing together of impossibilities. See Curtius, *European Literature*, pp. 94–8. For a specific linking of this topos to Sancho's governorship, see Redondo, "Tradición carnavalesca."

25 *El pensamiento de Cervantes* (Barcelona: Noguer, 1973), p. 333: "El engaño a los ojos tiene una vertiente artística y otra ética."

26 Flores, in "Sancho's Fabrications," p. 180, writes, "The use of words such as *grano de mostaza* and *avellana* is faintly reminiscent of his past life, but it also serves a more important purpose, making tangible to his public the fantasies of a dreamer."

27 The original, including the poem alluded to (from the *Proverbios* of the Marqués de Santillana) reads: "Cosas y casos suceden en el mundo, que si la imaginación, antes de suceder pudiera hacer que así sucedieran, no acertara a trazarlos; y así muchos por la raridad con que acontecen, pasan plaza de apócrifos, y no son tenidos por tan verdaderos como lo son; y así es menester que les ayuden juramentos, o a lo menos el buen crédito de quien los cuenta; aunque yo digo que mejor sería no contarlos, según lo aconsejan aquellos antiguos versos castellanos, que dicen: 'Las cosas de admiración / no digas ni las cuentes; / que no saben todas gentes / cómo son.'" See the lengthy note by Avalle-Arce in his edition of the *Persiles*, p. 381.

28 "Cosa posible sin ser milagro." On this type of rationalization, see Riley, *Cervantes's Theory of the Novel*, pp. 187–9. Stephen Harrison, in his "Magic in the Spanish Golden Age: Cervantes's Second Thoughts," *Renaissance and Reformation*, 4 (1980), 47–64, sees such corrective remarks as interpolations following upon Cervantes' rereading and consequent uneasiness about some of the irrational elements. The intrusions of the translator and Cide Hamete in *Don Quixote*, however, perform a similar function.

29 "Era la hora de mediodía, herían los rayos del sol derechamente a la tierra, entraba el calor, y la sombra de una gran torre de la casa les convidó que allí esperasen a pasar la siesta, que con calor riguroso amenazaba.... Bartolomé [hizo] su repuesto [de los manjares y] satisfacieron la hambre, que ya comenzaba a fatigarles. Pero apenas habían alzado las manos para llevarlo a la boca, cuando alzando Bartolomé los ojos, dijo a grandes voces: 'Apartaos, señores, que no sé quién baja volando del cielo, y no será bien que os coja debajo.'

    "Alzaron todos la vista, y vieron bajar por el aire una figura, que antes que distinguiesen lo que era, ya estaba en el suelo junto casi a los pies de Periandro.... Dejóla el suceso atónita y espantada, como lo quedaron los que volar la habían visto."

30 Examples: *Don Quixote*: "esta terrible sed que nos fatiga" (I, 20), "fatiga de estómago" and "no hay cosa que más fatigue el corazón de los pobres que la hambre, y la carestía" (II, 51), "por ser la hora de la mañana y herirles a soslayo los rayos del sol, no les fatigaban" (I, 7); *Persiles*: "el frío que comenzaba a fatigarles" (I, 4); *Galatea*: "el deseo que le fatigaba de volver a su ermita" (Book II), "fatigar al deseo por alcanzar [las cosas que están imposibilitadas de alcanzarse]" (Book III). Ihrie, in *Skepticism in Cervantes*, p. 35, notes: "Situations are not always readily apparent at first glimpse, as distance, darkness, dust, etc., impede immediate perception in a manner consistent with the skeptical emphasis upon the limitations of human senses." As we have seen, the physical state of the observer may be another contributing factor in perception. On a number of occasions, Don Quixote himself suggests that fear distorts perception: "El miedo que tienes... te

hace, Sancho, que ni veas ni oyas a derechas; porque uno de los efectos del miedo es turbar los sentidos y hacer que las cosas no parezcan lo que son" (I, 18). Flores agrees with Don Quixote from another perspective: Sancho's lies, which is to say, his own illusory creations, are set in motion by fear ("Sancho's Fabrications," p. 177). Ihrie sees a perspective consistent with classical skeptical modes and attitudes: "The power of emotions and physical condition to alter perceptions and behavior is explored at length" (*Skepticism in Cervantes*, pp. 48–9).

31   "The Metaphorical Process as Cognition, Imagination, and Feeling," *Critical Inquiry*, 5 (1978), 153.

32   S. K. Heninger, Jr., *A Handbook of Renaissance Meteorology* (1960; rpt. New York: Greenwood Press, 1968), p. 48.

33   Ibid., p. 150. The first reference is to William Fulke, *A Goodly Gallery . . . into the Garden of Naturall Contemplation, to Beholde the Naturall Causes of All Kinds of Meteors* (London: William Griffith, 1571), fol. 45–45ᵛ. The quotation from *Antony and Cleopatra* is from Act IV, Scene xiv.

34   Shakespeare, *The Tempest*, IV, i.

Chapter 4. The illusion of reality

1   *Don Quixote's Profession* (New York: Columbia University Press, 1958), p. 19.

2   "Al anochecer, su rocín y él se hallaron cansados y muertos de hambre; y . . . mirando a todas partes por ver si descubriría algún castillo o alguna majada de pastores . . . vio, no lejos del camino por donde iba, una venta, que fue como si viera una estrella que, no a los portales, sino a los alcázares de su redención le encaminaba."

3   "Y como a nuestro aventurero todo cuanto pensaba veía o imaginaba le parecía ser hecho y pasar al modo de lo que había leído, luego que vio la venta se le representó que era un castillo con sus cuatro torres y chapiteles de luciente plata, sin faltarle su puente levadiza y honda cava, con todos aquellos adherentes que semejantes castillos se pintan."

4   Angel Sánchez Rivero, "Las ventas del 'Quijote,'" in *El concepto contemporáneo de España*, ed. A. del Río and M. J. Benardete (Buenos Aires: Losada, 1946), p. 663, observes: "Sus pensamientos no necesitan regirse por el ser de las cosas; eran las cosas quienes debían conformarse a los *a prioris* de su mente."

5   Ibid.

6   Renée Sieburth, in "Metamorphosis: The Key to an Interpretation of Don Quixote's Adventure in the Cave of Montesinos," *Revista de Estudios Hispánicos*, 15 (1981), 3, points out that the Montesinos episode "is the only adventure [aside from those manipulated by the ducal pair] in Part II not shared by Sancho, thus giving us only Don Quixote's interpretation." When Sancho refuses to believe what supposedly happened, Don Quixote insists that "what I have related I saw with my own eyes and touched with my own hands. *But what will you say when I tell you that . . . ?*" The remainder

of this lengthy sentence describes the "Dulcinea" that Sancho has "enchanted." Of course, if it is all a dream, he will dream of her as he has recently seen her – a different kind of illusion based on a physical reality – but the portion I have italicized here goes hand in hand with episodes like that of the sheep: It is important to convey the illusion, and he selects, purposely or intuitively, the "proof" most likely to convince Sancho.

7   See Forcione, *Cervantes, Aristotle, and the "Persiles."*
8   "The Language of Limits," p. 271.
9   Cf. Arthur F. Kinney, "Rhetoric and Fiction in Elizabethan England," in *Renaissance Eloquence: Studies in the Theory and Practice of Renaissance Rhetoric,* ed. J. J. Murphy (Berkeley: University of California Press, 1983), p. 393: "Nor does *Arcadia* – new or old – ever come to a conclusion: Sidney, in promising more to come, suggests that a plot grounded either in fortune or in providence . . . is not all there is to tell. Sidney's conclusion is inconclusive, enigmatic because it brings us back to the beginning of *Arcadia* and to a sense of promise rather than of completion." In "Cervantes' *Arte nuevo,*" p. 17, Close makes the intriguing suggestion that Cervantes has "as it were, 'pastoralised' the comic fable; *La Galatea* Part II is already in print, implicit in *Don Quixote* Part II."
10   *Dictionary of the History of Ideas,* ed. P. P. Wiener (New York: Scribner, 1968), IV, 168–71.
11   The translation is mine, in turn from a translation of the Latin by Antonio Martí, *La preceptiva retórica española en el siglo de oro* (Madrid: Gredos, 1972), p. 79.
12   *Diccionario de Autoridades,* s.v. *disposición.*
13   Bernard Weinberg, "Robortello on the *Poetics,*" in *Critics and Criticism,* ed. R. S. Crane (Chicago: University of Chicago Press, 1975), p. 325.
14   See Chapter 1, n. 29.
15   See Jennifer Lowe, "The *cuestión de amor* and the Structure of Cervantes' *La Galatea,*" *Bulletin of Hispanic Studies,* 43 (1966), 98–108.
16   Biblioteca Nacional de Madrid, document 2856.
17   Johnson, *Madness and Lust,* p. 68.
18   El Saffar, *Novel to Romance,* p. 60.
19   " . . . por la [ventaja] que Tirsi le hacía en la edad y en la experiencia, y en los acostumbrados estudios, y asimismo les aseguraba esto porque deseaban que la opinión desamorada de Lenio no prevaleciese."
20   " . . . pareciéndoles que lo que Lenio había dicho, de más caudal que de pastoril ingenio parecía . . . "
21   "Ahora puedes, famoso pastor, tomar justa venganza del atrevimiento que tuve de competir contigo" (Book V).
22   This aspect of Rodaja's character is lucidly brought out by Forcione in *Cervantes and the Humanist Vision,* pp. 272–5.
23   *Poetics,* 1455a21–5.
24   *Poetics* (Ann Arbor: University of Michigan Press, 1970), p. 101.
25   *Poetics,* p. 29.
26   *Poética de Aristóteles* (Madrid: Gredos, 1974), p. 302: "Lo que aquí se recom-

ienda al poeta trágico es que, al estructurar la fábula, se ponga en el lugar del espectador." Heinrich F. Plett, in "The Place and Function of Style in Renaissance Poetics," in Murphy, *Renaissance Eloquence*, pp. 362–3, notes that Scaliger lists four poetic qualities: "*Prudentia* demands of the poet a rich and well-ordered invention, *efficacia* vivid and effective depiction, *varietas* a varied arrangement of ideas and words, *suavitas* a pleasant and winning tone. ... The *Poetices libri septem* presents a poetics of representation, not a rhetorical poetics, even though the adoption of various rhetorical concepts suggests the latter."

27   "Y así, un día... hallándose en medio de un deleitoso prado, convidado de la soledad y del murmullo de un deleitoso arroyuelo que por el llano corría, sacando de su zurrón un pulido rabel... "

28   "... si no sonaran a su derecha mano las voces de Erastro, que con el rebaño de sus cabras hacia el lugar donde él estaba se venía."

29   "Ya se aparejaba Erastro para seguir adelante en su canto cuando sintieron por un espeso montecillo que a sus espaldas estaba, un no pequeño estruendo y ruido; y levantándose los dos en pie por ver lo que era, vieron que del monte salía un pastor corriendo a la mayor prisa del mundo, con un cuchillo en la mano, y la color del rostro demudada; y que tras él venía otro ligero pastor, que a pocos pasos alcanzó al primero, y, asiéndole por el cabezón del pellico, levantó el brazo en el aire cuanto pudo, y un agudo puñal que sin vaina traía, se le escondió dos veces en el cuerpo... Y esto fue con tanta presteza hecho que no tuvieron lugar Elicio y Erastro de estorbárselo, porque llegaron a tiempo que ya el herido pastor daba el último aliento."

30   "Cervantes y el engaño de las apariencias," p. 76: "El cambio abrupto del enfoque de la acción está anunciado con un ruido. La diferencia entre lejos y cerca se sugiere estilísticamente por el uso de un diminutivo (montecillo) y la litote (no pequeño) para indicar el empequeñecimiento de lo distante, y la retardación del ritmo narrativo, enfocando en detalles concretos (agudo puñal sin vaina) para evocar presencia inmediata. No obstante, el uso del eufemismo 'escondió' plantea una duda sobre la verdadera naturaleza de la acción, aunque sea una fiel representación, dad[a] la perspectiva de los observadores."

31   "... viniendo los tres pastores con el manso rebaño de sus ovejas por una cañada abajo, al subir de una ladera oyeron el zumbido de una suave zampoña que luego por Elicio y Erastro fue conocido que era Galatea quien la sonaba. Y no tardó mucho que por la cumbre de la cuesta se comenzaron a descubrir algunas ovejas, y luego, tras ellas, Galatea.... Cuando Galatea vio que el rebaño de Elicio y Erastro con el suyo se juntaba... llamó a la borrega mansa de su manada, a la cual siguieron las demás, y encaminóla a otra parte diferente de la que los pastores llevaban.... A esta sazón llegó Erastro, y viendo que Galatea se iba y los dejaba, la dijo: '¿Adónde vas, o de quién huyes, hermosa Galatea? Si de nosotros, que te adoramos, te alejas...'"

32   "'¿Ríeste de lo que digo, Galatea? Pues yo lloro de lo que tú haces.' No pudo Galatea responder a Erastro, porque andaba guiando su ganado hacia el arroyo de las Palmas, y bajando desde lejos la cabeza en señal de despedirse

los dejó, y como se vio sola, en tanto que llegaba adonde su amiga Florisa creyó que estaría... fue cantando.... El acabar el canto Galatea y llegar adonde Florisa estaba fue todo uno.... En este ejercicio andaban ocupadas las dos hermosas pastoras, cuando por el arroyo abajo vieron al improviso venir una pastora... y vieron que venía poco a poco hacia donde ellas estaban; y aunque estaban bien cerca, ella venía tan embebida y transportada en sus pensamientos, que nunca las vio hasta que ellas quisieron mostrarse."

33 "Adelante pasara con su cuento Silerio si no lo estorbara el son de muchas zampoñas y acordados caramillos que a sus espaldas se oía; y volviendo la cabeza, vieron venir hacia ellos hasta una docena de gallardos pastores puestos en dos hileras, y en medio venía un dispuesto pastor.... Traía un bastón en la una mano, y con grave paso poco a poco se movía, y los demás pastores, andando con el mismo aplauso y tocando todos sus instrumentos.... Luego que Elicio los vio, conoció ser Daranio el pastor que en medio traían, y los demás ser todos circunvecinos que a sus bodas querían hallarse [y] de aquella manera hacia la aldea se encaminaban.... Y a esta sazón llegó el montón alegre de pastores... y renovando la música y renovando el contento, tornaron a proseguir el comenzado camino, y ya que llegaban juntos a la aldea, llegó a sus oídos el son de la zampoña del desamorado Lenio.... Y así como Lenio los vio y conoció, sin interrumpir el suave canto, de esta manera cantando hacia ellos se vino."

34 "No quedara Lenio sin respuesta si no vieran venir hacia donde ellos estaban a la hermosa Galatea con las discretas pastoras Florisa y Teolinda.... Llegaron y fueron de los pastores con alegre acogimiento recibidas.... Aquí acabó su canto Erastro, y se acabó el camino de llegar a la aldea."

35 "Al tiempo que ya querían volverse y dejarla, vieron atravesar por una quebrada que poco desviada de ellas estaba cuatro hombres de a caballo y algunos de a pie, que luego conocieron ser cazadores en el hábito y en los halcones y perros que llevaban; y estándolos con atención mirando por ver si los conocían, vieron salir de entre unas espesas matas que cerca de la quebrada estaban dos pastoras.... Traían los rostros rebozados con los blancos lienzos, y alzando la una de ellas la voz pidió a los cazadores que se detuviesen, los cuales así lo hicieron, y llegándose entrambas a uno de ellos, que en su talle y postura el principal de todos parecía, le asieron las riendas del caballo y estuvieron un poco hablando con él sin que las tres pastoras pudiesen oír palabra de las que decían por la distancia del lugar que lo estorbaba. Solamente vieron que, a poco espacio que con él hablaron, el caballero se apeó, y habiendo, a lo que juzgarse pudo, mandado a los que le acompañaban que se volviesen..., trabó a las dos pastoras de las manos y poco a poco comenzó a entrar con ellas por medio de un cerrado bosque que allí estaba, lo cual visto por... Galatea, Florisa y Teolinda, determinaron de ver, si pudiesen, quién eran las disfrazadas pastoras y el caballero que las llevaba." The reader familiar with the language of Cervantes' time will have noticed that in this and other passages in this chapter, I have regularly translated *luego* as "then," which is what it means in modern Spanish, though in the Golden Age it was equivalent to "right away." My rendition is not

incognizant of that connotation, for the concept of "right away" or "immediately" differs from "then" only in its suggestion of the rapidity with which one thing follows another. The fundamental aspect, which I have tried to stress, is that even immediately, it did follow afterward.

36 "*Don Quixote* and the Origins of the Novel," in *Cervantes and the Renaissance*, ed. M. D. McGaha (Easton, Pa.: Juan de la Cuesta, 1980), p. 137.

37 Ibid., pp. 138–9.

Chapter 5. The faculties of the soul

1 "El profeta David, por Spíritu Santo fablando, a cada uno de nos dize en el psalmo triçesimo primo del verso dezeno [*sic*]. . . . En el qual verso entiendo yo tres cosas, las quales dizen algunos doctores philósophos que son en el alma é propiamente suyas; son estas: entendimiento, voluntad é memoria" (cited from the edition of Julio Cejador y Frauca [Madrid: Espasa-Calpe, 1951], I, 6).

2 Ibid., p. 8: "E desque el alma con el buen entendimiento é la buena voluntad, con buena rremenbrança escoge é ama el buen amor, que es el de Dios, é pónelo en la çela de la memoria, porque se acuerde dello trae al cuerpo á fazer buenas obras, por las quales se salva el ome."

3 *Spain and the Western Tradition*, I (Madison: University of Wisconsin Press, 1963), 48. For a detailed analysis, see Janet A. Chapman, "Juan Ruiz's 'Learned Sermon,'" in *'Libro de buen amor' Studies*, ed. G. B. Gybbon-Monypenny (London: Tamesis, 1970), pp. 29–51, esp. pp. 32–6. See also Brian Dutton's article in the same volume, "'Buen amor': Its Meaning and Uses in Some Medieval Texts," pp. 109–10.

4 *Spain and the Western Tradition*, I, 48–9. The reference is to Palencia's *Universal vocabulario*: "Voluntas voluntad . . . es . . . deseo . . . de lo que avn no alcançamos. Et voluntad es delectacion buena o mala de lo que conseguimos."

5 Alonso López Pinciano, *Philosophía antigua poética*, ed. A. Carballo Picazo (Madrid: CSIC, 1953), I, 70.

6 In addition to the cited books by Riley and Forcione, consult Sanford Shepard, *El Pinciano y las teorías literarias del siglo de oro* (Madrid: Gredos, 1962); and William C. Atkinson, "Cervantes, El Pinciano, and the *Novelas ejemplares*," *Hispanic Review*, 16 (1948), 189–208.

7 Avalle-Arce, in his editions of Cervantes' *La Galatea* (Madrid: Espasa-Calpe, 1961), *Persiles y Sigismunda* and *Ocho entremeses* (Englewood Cliffs, N.J.: Prentice-Hall, 1970), and Eugenio Asensio, in his edition of the *Entremeses* (Madrid: Castalia, 1970), explain in brief footnotes that the faculties of the soul are the three mentioned here, but they do not elaborate.

8 Aristotle, *Nicomachean Ethics*, 6.2.1, 2 (cited from the Loeb Classical Library edition, trans. H. Rackham [Cambridge, Mass.: Harvard University Press, 1934]).

9 Ibid., p. 328n.

10 Ibid., 6.2.2.

11 Ibid., 1.13.18.

12 A. Mark Smith, "Getting the Big Picture in Perspectivist Optics," *Isis*, 72 (1981), 571–2.

13 *Republic*, 4.436a.

14 George Boas, in *Dictionary of the History of Ideas*, II, 127, s.v. *macrocosm and microcosm*. I have transposed the words in brackets in order to correspond to the citation from Plato.

15 Ciriaco Morón Arroyo, in a review of D. Rössler's *Voluntad bei Cervantes*, *Hispanic Review*, 39 (1971), 325, maintains that memory was not considered a faculty in the scholastic scheme, it being merely a repository that served the intellect: "La teoría escolástica de la voluntad, que es la reflejada en el autor del *Quijote*, se puede esquematizar así: la voluntad es una potencia espiritual del alma – la otra es el entendimiento; la memoria es el 'thesaurus intelectus' pero no potencia distinta." The many examples that constitute the basis of this chapter do not support Morón's argument. It is, of course, possible to consider only one or two of the faculties as befits the circumstances. Trueblood speaks of the "necessary concomitant of memory, understanding – *entendimiento* – [as] the truly decisive faculty for Lope's characters [in *La Dorotea*]." He goes on to say: "The prizing of *entendimiento* in *La Dorotea* is consistent with the importance Lope regularly gives this quality of *mind and spirit*" (*Experience and Artistic Expression*, pp. 415–16; emphasis mine). Lope, of course, was familiar with the tripartite topos: " ... de donde se colige que la sangre dan los hombres y Dios las almas, cuyas potençias no se heredan ni están vinculadas en la ascendençia para los suçesores, y asi el entendimiento discurre, la memoria se acuerda y la voluntad apeteçe" (cited from *Epistolario de Lope de Vega Carpio*, ed. Agustín G. de Amezúa, III [Madrid: Artes Gráficas "Aldus," 1941], 18).

16 Anthony A. Long, in *Dictionary of the History of Ideas*, IV, 9.

17 Cited by Green, *Spain and the Western Tradition*, II, 160.

18 Saint Augustine, *The Trinity*, trans. Stephen McKenna (Washington, D.C.: Catholic University of America Press, 1963), p. 311. Cf. Will Durant, *The Age of Faith*, Vol. IV of *The Story of Civilization* (New York: Simon & Schuster, 1950), p. 985: "The attribution of magic powers to certain numbers came down from Pythagoras through the Christian Fathers: three, the number of the Trinity, was the holiest number, and stood for the soul."

19 Cited from the edition by E. Cotarelo y Mori, Nueva Biblioteca de Autores Españoles, XVII (Madrid, 1911), 47.

20 "Si voluntades se toman en cuenta, treinta y nueve días hace hoy que ... di yo a Cristina la mía, con todos los anejos a mis tres potencias" (cited from the Asensio edition, p. 144). The subsequent references to Cervantes' *entremeses* that are given parenthetically in the text are to this edition.

21 "Este amanerado discurrir lo parecía menos a los contemporáneos que, desde el catecismo, sabían las tres potencias del alma."

22 "Que tanta memoria tengo como entendimiento, a quien se junta una voluntad de acertar a satisfacerte, que excede a las demás potencias."

23 Damián de Vegas, *Coloquio entre un alma y sus tres potencias, donde se introduce irse dellas, amotinada por el mal servicio que le hacen*, in *Romancero y cancionero*

sagrados, ed. J. de Sancha, Biblioteca de Autores Españoles, Vol. XXXV (Madrid: Atlas, 1950), 530a: "Ves mi carne ir desfrenada / Tras del bestial apetito, / Ves llena de amor maldito / La voluntad desbocada / ¿Y tú, que eras suficiente / A reducirlos al quicio / De la razón, tras el vicio / Te despeñas juntamente?"

24 Ibid., p. 532a: "Mal pueden seguirte ellas / Si tú no las vas guiando, / Pues no tienen otra luz / Que aquella que tú les dieres, / Con que han de ir donde tú fueres / Al deleite o a la cruz."

25 Ibid., p. 532b: "Pues de cuanto él entendió / Que le dio gusto, aunque sea / Cosa vana, torpe y fea, / Hace que me acuerde yo; / Tan sujeto a novedades, / Que, a mi pesar y despecho / Desván y almacén me ha hecho / De todas sus vanidades."

26 Ibid., p. 533a: "¿Hay cosa más inhumana / Que gustes tú y que permitas / Que estén en mí siempre escritas / Las culpas de nuestra hermana?"

27 Ibid.: "Di, ¿cuántas veces seguimos / Al cuerpo en sus torpedades, / Y cuántas a mil maldades / Tras el apetito fuimos?"

28 Ibid.: "Bien sé cuándo sigo el bien / Y también cuándo el mal sigo; / Mas para medrar contigo / Han de me llevar por bien."

29 Frederick Copleston, *A History of Philosophy*, Vol. II, Part II (Garden City, N.Y.: Doubleday, 1962), 95–6.

30 *The Age of Faith*, pp. 977, 972.

31 On this matter, see the relevant bibliography in El Saffar's *Novel to Romance*, p. 128n. Also see Forcione, *Cervantes and the Humanist Vision*, pp. 317–97. Forcione makes a convincing case for seeing the novella as a secularized miracle narrative.

32 Forcione's accurate translation of *entendimiento* here as "reason" (*Cervantes and the Humanist Vision*, p. 356), rather than as "intellect," is but one more example of why I have chosen to leave these words in Spanish. David M. Gitlitz, in his "Symmetry and Lust in Cervantes' *La fuerza de la sangre*," in *Studies in Honor of Everett W. Hesse*, ed. W. C. McCrary and J. A. Madrigal (Lincoln, Nebr.: Society of Spanish and Spanish-American Studies, 1981), p. 116, renders it "understanding."

33 "La función de lo visual en *La fuerza de la sangre*," *Hispanófila*, 49 (1973), 64: "Psicológicamente [la prueba] revela en Rodolfo la misma pasión por la belleza que había aplicado antes para el mal."

34 *Novel to Romance*, p. 136.

35 *Sentido y forma de las Novelas ejemplares*, p. 161.

36 Ibid.: ". . . el pecado de la carne purificado y redimido por el sacramento del matrimonio." This view is shared by Robert V. Piluso: See his article "*La fuerza de la sangre*: Un análisis estructural," *Hispania*, 47 (1964), 487–8.

37 *El pensamiento de Cervantes*, pp. 376–8.

38 See Levisi, "La función," p. 65: "Rodolfo es presentado así como un ser que vive de lo que deleita la vista."

39 *Novel to Romance*, p. 129. Cf. Thomas Pabon, "Secular Resurrection through Marriage in Cervantes' *La Señora Cornelia, Las dos doncellas* and *La fuerza de la sangre*," *Anales Cervantinos*, 16 (1977), 112: "Cervantes establishes here his

most idealized vision – he links beauty and the virtuous soul, thereby giving preference to nobility of intention over those experiences which run counter to social standards." See also *Persiles y Sigismunda*, II, 6, where beauty and virtue are treated together as if they were a single noun: ". . . ni imagines que a tu incomparable virtud y belleza otra alguna se anteponga." A similar treatment is accorded to beauty and *entendimiento* later in the work: ". . . confirmaron . . . ser sobrenatural el entendimiento y belleza de mi hermana" (II, 11).

40   "Structure, Symbol and Meaning in Cervantes's *La fuerza de la sangre,*" *Bulletin of Hispanic Studies*, 58 (1981), 200–1; emphases mine.

41   El Saffar, in *Novel to Romance*, pp. 62–82, repeatedly stresses the understanding achieved by Campuzano as a result of his having heard the colloquy. See also Luis A. Murillo, "Cervantes' *Coloquio de los perros*, a Novel-Dialogue," *Modern Philology*, 58 (1961), 174–85, particularly p. 178: "The *Coloquio* . . . is, in fact, a story of apprenticeship in life, a pedagogy, in action" (cited by El Saffar, *Novel to Romance*, p. 65n).

42   Quoted from the translation by C. A. Jones: *Exemplary Stories* (Harmondsworth: Penguin, 1972), pp. 238–9.

43   Calderón, some two decades later, would restate the principle that even in dreams it is good to conduct oneself well (*La vida es sueño*).

44   *Cervantes's Theory of the Novel*, p. 196.

45   *Novel to Romance*, p. 64.

46   "Lo que yo he oído alabar y encarecer es nuestra mucha memoria, el agradecimiento y gran fidelidad nuestra" (p. 998).

47   *Novel to Romance*, p. 63.

48   Jones translation, p. 234.

49   E. M. W. Tillyard, *The Elizabethan World Picture* (New York: Random House, n.d.), p. 73.

50   *Republic*, 9.571c–572b.

51   Quoted in Lewis, *The Discarded Image*, p. 23.

52   Cf. *Don Quixote*, II, 59: "De las cosas obscenas y torpes los pensamientos se han de apartar, cuanto más los ojos." On a later occasion in the *Persiles*, Cervantes reminds us of "la torpe y viciosa Rosamunda" (II, 5). In his edition of the *Persiles*, Avalle-Arce states that he considers Rosamunda the personification of "la lascivia" (p. 27).

53   "Yo, desde el punto que tuve uso de razón, no la tuve, porque siempre fui mala. Con los años verdes, y con la hermosura mucha, con la libertad demasiada y con la riqueza abundante, se fueron apoderando de mí los vicios de tal manera, que han sido y son en mí como accidentes inseparables. Ya sabéis . . . que he querido las voluntades de los hombres; pero el tiempo, salteador y robador de la humana belleza de las mujeres, se entró por la mía tan sin yo pensarlo, que primero me he visto fea que desengañada. Mas como los vicios tienen asiento en el alma, que no envejece, no quieren dejarme; y, como yo no les hago resistencia, sino que me dejo ir con la corriente de mis gustos . . . "

54   "Hasta veintidós tendría un caballero de aquella ciudad a quien la riqueza,

la sangre ilustre, la inclinación torcida, la libertad demasiada y las compañías libres le hacían hacer cosas."
55 *Novel to Romance*, p. 129.
56 C. S. Lewis, *The Allegory of Love* (London: Oxford University Press, 1958), pp. 16–17.
57 See Francisco López Estrada, *"La Galatea" de Cervantes: Estudio crítico* (Tenerife: Universidad de La Laguna, 1948), pp. 39–45.
58 "No todos los amores son precipitados ni atrevidos, ni todos los amantes han puesto la mira de su gusto en gozar a sus amadas, sino con las potencias de su alma."
59 "¿Hay, por ventura, entendimiento tan agudo en el mundo que, estando mirando una de estas hermosas que pinto, dejando a una parte las de su belleza, se ponga a discurrir las de su humilde trato? La hermosura, en parte ciega, y en parte alumbra: tras la que ciega, corre el gusto; tras la que alumbra, el pensar en la enmienda."
60 "Una de las tres potencias del alma, que (según San Agustín) es aquella virtud que entiende las cosas que no ve."
61 El Saffar on separate occasions identifies equanimity as the characteristic of Isabela and of Recaredo (*Novel to Romance*, pp. 153, 157).
62 "Y esto, a lo que creo, con intención que la mucha belleza de esta doncella borre de mi alma la tuya, que en ella estampada tengo; yo, Isabela, desde el punto que te quise fue con otro amor de aquel que tiene su fin y paradero en el cumplimiento del sensual apetito, que puesto que tu corporal hermosura me cautivó los sentidos, tus infinitas virtudes me aprisionaron el alma, de manera que si hermosa te quise, fea te adoro."
63 *Sentido y forma del "Quijote,"* pp. 241, 243.
64 *Cervantes y su concepto del arte*, II, 363. More perceptive in this regard is Flores, who in *Sancho Panza*, p. 125, notes that the Sancho of I, 26, "with his weak and failing memory, is the exact opposite of the Sancho who *at other times and when necessary* shows that he has an excellent memory." The portion I have emphasized shows that, in keeping with Flores' arguments elsewhere to the effect that it is inaccurate to speak of "two Sanchos," there is but one Sancho and his memory is purposefully selective.

Chapter 6. From happy age of gold to detestable age of iron

1 Jorge de Sena, "Hispanismo: Archipiélago de glorias y vanidades en el maroceáno de la ignorancia universal," in *Actas del Sexto Congreso Internacional de Hispanistas*, ed. A. M. Gordon and E. Rugg (Toronto: University of Toronto, 1980), pp. 19–25.
2 The words are Garcilaso's. See p. 59.
3 For a good summary and bibliography, see Gilbert Highet, *The Classical Tradition* (London: Oxford University Press, 1957), pp. 261–88 and the corresponding notes, pp. 640–6. The argument is marred – typically, one is forced to say – by Highet's assertion that "as a test of the vitality of taste in various European nations during the baroque age it is worth observing

that the battle started in Italy, or rather that the early frontier encounters occurred there; that the real fighting took place in France; that an interesting but secondary struggle went on in England; and that no other European or American country played any part except that of spectator" (pp. 261–2).

4   "Queja de siempre de los poetas de España, y a menudo, y por desgracia, no retórica" (in his edition of *La Galatea*, I, 5).

5   "Y no penséis que es pequeño el gusto que he recibido en saber por tan verdadera relación cuán grande es el número de los divinos ingenios que en nuestra España hoy viven, porque siempre ha estado y está en opinión de todas las naciones extranjeras que no son muchos, sino pocos, los espíritus que en la ciencia de la poesía en ella muestran que le tienen levantado, siendo tan al revés como se parece, pues cada uno de los que la ninfa ha nombrado al más agudo extranjero se aventaja, y darían claras muestras de ello, si en esta nuestra España se estimase en tanto la poesía como en otras provincias se estima. Y así, por esta causa, los insignes y claros ingenios que en ella se aventajan, con la poca estimación que de ellos los príncipes y el vulgo hace, con solos sus entendimientos comunican sus altos y extraños conceptos, sin osar publicarlos al mundo, y tengo para mí que el Cielo debe de ordenarlo de esta manera, porque no merece el mundo ni el mal considerado siglo nuestro gozar de manjares al alma tan gustosos."

6   *On Style*, trans. W. Rhys Roberts, Loeb Classical Library, Vol. CXCIX (Cambridge, Mass.: Harvard University Press, 1932), pp. 313–15.

7   Avalle-Arce speaks of the "problema de España" in his edition of *La Galatea* (II, 226n). See also Green, *Spain and the Western Tradition*, IV, 250–79.

8   Quoted in *Spain and the Western Tradition*, IV, 250. The translations are by Green.

9   Cited from *Poetas dramáticos valencianos*, ed. E. Juliá Martínez (Madrid: Real Academia Española, 1929), I, xxvi.

10   Ibid., p. xxxv.

11   *Historia de las ideas estéticas en España* (Madrid: CSIC, 1947), II, 280: "Era, por consiguiente, Artieda, del mismo modo que Cervantes, uno de los dramaturgos rezagados y vencidos y, por tanto, uno de los descontentos contra Lope, contra Tárrega y Aguilar, que en su propia ciudad de Valencia le habían sustituido en el teatro."

12   Rinaldo Froldi, *Lope de Vega y la formación de la comedia*, rev. ed., trans. Franco Gabriele (Salamanca: Ediciones Anaya, 1968), p. 101. Entrambasaguas' words are paraphrased by Alfredo Hermenegildo in his *La tragedia en el renacimiento español* (Barcelona: Planeta, 1973), p. 197. The quotation from Hermenegildo (the translation is my own) comes from pp. 197–8 of this work.

13   For an exploration of this matter, see my article "Lope's Role in the Lope de Vega Myth," *Hispania*, 63 (1980), 658–65.

14   "Este siglo en que andamos / es como los passados que alabamos" (cited from Cecilia Vennard Sargent, *A Study of the Dramatic Works of Cristóbal de Virués* [New York: Instituto de las Españas, 1930], p. 41).

15 The original may be found in *Obras trágicas y líricas del Capitán Cristóval de Virués* (Madrid: Alonso Martín, 1609), pp. 278–9.

16 *Lope de Vega*, p. 114; translation mine.

17 *La tragedia*, p. 262. Cf. p. 261: "This work [*La infelice Marcela*] is the author's last degree of evolution toward the modern theater." Translations mine.

18 *El laurel de Apolo*, silva IV: "¡Oh ingenio singular! en paz reposa, / A quien las musas cómicas debieron / Los mejores principios que tuvieron" (cited from *Biblioteca de Autores Españoles* [Madrid: Atlas, 1950], XXXVIII, 202).

19 "Séneca, Virués, Lope de Vega," in *Homenatge a Antoni Rubió i Lluch* (Barcelona: Estudis Universitaris Catalans, 1936), I, 115.

20 *Ejemplar poético* (cited from the edition by F. Sánchez Escribano and A. Porqueras Mayo, *Preceptiva dramática española* [Madrid: Gredos, 1972], p. 142).

21 "Comedias," in *Suma Cervantina*, ed. Avalle-Arce and E. C. Riley (London: Tamesis, 1973), p. 154; translation mine.

22 *Sentido y forma del teatro de Cervantes* (Madrid: Gredos, 1966), p. 26; translation mine.

23 "Teoría literaria," in Avalle-Arce and Riley, *Suma Cervantina*, p. 308; translation mine.

24 On this matter see Percas, *Cervantes y su concepto del arte*, pp. 350–1.

25 "Teoría literaria," p. 300; translation mine.

26 Julio Cejador y Frauca, *La lengua de Cervantes* (Madrid, 1906), II, 620: "*Poeta intonso* equivale a poeta *de primera tonsura* (Quevedo), a quien todavía no se ha cortado el pelo, novel, inexperto, principiante." Cf. *Diccionario de Autoridades*, s.v. *intonso*: "Significa también ignorante, necio o rústico."

27 See Martín de Riquer, "La technique parodique du roman médiéval dans le *Quichotte*," in *La Littérature narrative d'imitation, des genres littéraires aux techniques d'expression* (Paris: Presses Universitaires de France, 1961), pp. 59–69; Riquer, "Cervantes y la caballeresca," in Avalle-Arce and Riley, *Suma Cervantina*, pp. 273–92; Daniel Eisenberg, "*Don Quijote* and the Romances of Chivalry: The Need for a Reexamination," *Hispanic Review*, 41 (1973), 511–23; and Mancing, *The Chivalric World*.

28 "Cervantes and the Question of Language," in *Cervantes and the Renaissance*, ed. M. D. McGaha (Easton, Pa.: Juan de la Cuesta, 1980), pp. 32, 28.

29 See Chapter 2, n. 15.

30 In his edition of the *Viaje del Parnaso* (Madrid: Bermejo, 1935), p. 416.

31 "Lope's Conservative *Arte de hacer comedias en este tiempo*," in *Studies in Honor of Everett W. Hesse*, ed. W. C. McCrary and J. A. Madrigal (Lincoln, Nebr.: Society of Spanish and Spanish-American Studies, 1981), pp. 187–98; "Lope de Vega según Lope: ¿Creador de la comedia?" *Cuadernos de Filología*, 3 (1981), 225–45.

32 Cited and translated by Trueblood, *Experience and Artistic Expression*, p. 127.

33 "El arte viejo de hacer teatro: Lope de Rueda, Lope de Vega y Cervantes," *Cuadernos de Filología*, 3 (1981), 257.

34 ". . . de la sangre podrida de los malos poetas que en aquel sitio habían

sido muertos comenzaban a nacer, del tamaño de ratones, otros poetillas rateros . . . ''

Chapter 7. Phases of substance

1 Geoffrey Stagg, "Revision in *Don Quixote*, Part I," in *Hispanic Studies in Honour of I. González Llubera*, ed. F. Pierce (Oxford: Dolphin, 1959), pp. 347–66; Stagg, "Sobre el plan primitivo del 'Quijote,'" in *Actas del Primer Congreso Internacional de Hispanistas* (Oxford: Dolphin, 1964), pp. 1–9; R. M. Flores, "Cervantes at Work: The Writing of *Don Quixote*, Part I," *Journal of Hispanic Philology*, 3 (1979), 135–60; Flores, "The Rôle of Cide Hamete in *Don Quixote*," *Bulletin of Hispanic Studies*, 59 (1982), 3–14. See also Erwin Koppen, "Gab es einen '*Ur-Quijote*'? Zu einer Hypothese der Cervantes-Philologie," *Romanistisches Jahrbuch*, 27 (1976), 330–46; and Luis Andrés Murillo, "El *Ur-Quijote*: Nueva Hipótesis," *Cervantes*, 1 (1981), 43–50.
2 "Revision in *Don Quixote*," p. 19; "Sobre el plan primitivo del 'Quijote,'" p. 5.
3 "Cervantes at Work," p. 136
4 I think it reasonable to include the sentence immediately following as part of the first portion of the chapter, that is, as part of what I shall label phase B in the next paragraph of my text. The process has parallels elsewhere, for instance, in the intercalation of the reference to Cide Hamete at the beginning of I, 22, framed by "Y alzando [don Quijote] los ojos vio lo que se dirá en el siguiente capítulo" (I, 21) and " . . . don Quijote alzó los ojos y vio que . . . " (I, 22).
5 Of the books mentioned during the scrutiny, none has a first publication date later than 1591.
6 "Sobre el plan primitivo del 'Quijote,'" p. 6.
7 "Cervantes on Lofraso," p. 164.
8 Ibid., pp. 166, 172.
9 "Dulcinea, nombre pastoril," *Nueva Revista de Filología Hispánica*, 17 (1963–64), 69: "Creo discernir en Cervantes un gesto de cariño para el extravagante sardo, 'colega' suyo, cuyo libro 'puso aparte' el Cura 'con grandísimo gusto' en el escrutinio."
10 Iventosch cites Marcelino Menéndez Pelayo's *Orígenes de la novela* (Buenos Aires, 1945), II, 308. The work was first published in 1907.
11 "Pero lo más importante no es, claro está, el hecho de hallar al gran autor imitando a otro escritor, sino el de verle seguir a un autor pastoril y conocido" ("Dulcinea," p. 69).
12 "Y resulta que el sardo es el maestro de todos en materia onomástica. *Dulcineo* es suyo, y también *Dulcino, Dulcina*, y *Dulçanio*, todos con un sentido del 'carácter dulce' del hombre pastoril" (ibid., p. 68).
13 "Las damas caballerescas no son 'dulces,' al menos en una serie representativa de libros de caballerías: *Amadís de Gaula, Palmerín de Inglaterra, Lepolemo* y *Amadís de Grecia* . . . " (ibid., p. 68 n. 16).
14 "Ese mundo caballeresco . . . está del todo ausente del nombre *Dulcinea* (ibid., p. 67).

15 *"Dulcinea* en sí, como nombre, se resiste a toda atribución caballeresca" (ibid., p. 72).

16 In addition to numerous examples of the "e"/"i" confusion, Rafael Lapesa lists for the "s"/"x" confusion (in modern spelling, with "j" and "g" for the "x"), *vigitar* for *visitar, relisión* for *religión, colesio* for *colegio,* and, most interesting for us here, *quijo* for *quiso (Historia de la lengua española* [Madrid: Escelicer, 1959], p. 244).

17 "The Comic Function of Chivalric Names in *Don Quijote," NAMES,* 21 (1973), 221.

18 A. Julián Valbuena, "Verbal Strategies, Images, and Symbolic Roles in the Use of a Conventional Language by a Spanish Golden Age Playwright," in *The First Delaware Symposium on Language Studies: Selected Papers,* ed. R. J. Di Pietro, W. Frawley, and A. Wedel (Newark, Del.: University of Delaware Press, 1983), p. 69. Cf. Robert K. Spaulding, *How Spanish Grew* (Berkeley: University of California Press, 1948), p. 159: "The presence formerly of the unvoiced palatal fricative, that is, *sh,* is sufficiently indicated by its equivalence with Arabic *shîn* and by loan words like *Quichotte* (French) and *Chisciotte* (Italian) < *Quixote, Chimène* < *Ximena,* sherry < *Xerez."* Moreover: "The nature of Castilian *s* . . . makes it sound somewhat like the English *sh* or like *ch* in French . . . The stock Moor of the Spanish stage of the Golden Age is represented as always mistaking Castilian *s* for his *shîn,* the *sh* sound formerly written *x* in Spanish" (ibid., p. 161).

19 Another detail, one that I relegate to these notes because it is quite circumstantial (though no less curious), has to do with Rocinante. In the encounter with Andrés and Haldudo, Don Quixote leaves the two as he "spurred his Rocinante" ("picó a su Rocinante"). Nowhere else in the novel is the horse referred to as *his Rocinante.* There are six references to the horse in phase A, including this one. One of the others refers to "Rocinante, his horse" ("Rocinante, su caballo" [I, 5]). If my hypothesis about the existence of phase A is correct, it is reasonable to expect of Cervantes some intercalations in order to smooth the transition or avoid those inconsistencies that he spotted. The use of the horse's name, of course, may be used for any argument: to wit, that it disproves my hypothesis, that it reflects revision, or that it is immaterial, Cervantes having access to the name at any time. Nevertheless, the parenthetical clarification of the name ("his horse") in Chapter 5 is as superfluous as the similar identification of the barber's name in the same chapter. More interesting is the use of the word *su* ("his") in Chapter 4. Since this modifier is never again used with the name Rocinante – it is, of course, used when modifying a common noun used for the animal (*rocín* or *caballo,* that is, "nag" or "horse") – it appears that the original sentence in phase A may well have read *su rocín,* as indeed we find it elsewhere. I think it likely that Cervantes, in an attempt to make phase A fit in well with phase B, made a cursory inspection of phase A, inserting a word here, deleting one there, very much in the manner suggested by both Stagg and Flores, failing to notice the inconsistency of "Quixana" (or perhaps appreciating at this last stage its irony and interpolating "Quexana" into the opening passage

of phase B), but adding the name Rocinante in addition to or instead of the simple word for a nag. When in what is now Chapter 4 he spotted *su rocín* (spelled *rozin*, without the accent mark, in the 1605 edition), he simply inserted the suffix to make it *su Rocinante* (*su Rozinante* in the original).

20 "No había andado mucho, cuando le pareció que a su diestra mano, de la espesura de un bosque que allí estaba, salían unas voces delicadas, como de persona que se quejaba."

21 "Cervantes at Work," p. 157.

22 On the difference between the Leandra episode and its narration by Eugenio, see my article "The Curious Pertinence of Eugenio's Tale in *Don Quijote*,"*MLN*, 96 (1981), 261–85.

23 "Y estando comiendo, a deshora oyeron un recio estruendo y un son de esquila, que por entre unas zarzas y espesas matas que allí junto estaban sonaba, y al mismo instante vieron salir de entre aquellas malezas una hermosa cabra."

24 *The Chivalric World*, p. 44.

25 Review of *The Chivalric World of "Don Quijote," Cervantes*, 2 (1982), 189.

26 "Las dos locuras de don Quijote," *Anales Cervantinos*, 17 (1978), 3–10. Others who have dealt with the. matter include Riley, in "Who's Who in *Don Quixote*? or an Approach to the Problem of Identity," *MLN*, 81 (1966), 113–30; and Avalle-Arce, in his *Don Quixote como forma de vida* (Valencia: Castalia, 1976), especially p. 94.

27 "Sobre el plan primitivo del 'Quijote,'" p. 5.

28 Ibid., p. 4.

29 In II, 73, the name is Curambro, no doubt an erratum.

30 "*Don Quixote* and the Origins," p. 137.

31 *Don Quixote: Hero or Fool?* Part I, pp. 18–19.

32 For an analysis of the lexical variants for the fish in question, see my "Cervantes's Curious Curate," pp. 89, 103–4.

33 See María Rosa Lida, "De cuyo nombre no quiero acordarme," *Revista de Filología Hispánica*, 1 (1939), 167–71.

34 Riquer makes the comment in his Planeta edition, p. 32 n.1. Riley's observation is found in his "Three Versions of Don Quixote," *Modern Language Review*, 68 (1973), 810.

35 *Don Quixote: Hero or Fool?* Part I, p. 23.

36 "Linguistic Perspectivism in the *Don Quijote*," in Spitzer, *Linguistics and Literary History* (Princeton, N.J.: Princeton University Press, 1967), p. 52.

37 *The Order of Things: An Archaeology of the Human Sciences*: (New York: Random House, Vintage Books, 1973), p. 47.

38 See F. García Salinero's edition of Fernández de Avellaneda's *El ingenioso hidalgo Don Quijote de la Mancha* (Madrid: Castalia, 1971), p. 23.

39 In his edition of 1948, VII, 12n: "la de la cuestión del puente y los que habían de pasar por él, dificultad litigiosa que más adelante (cap. LI) se propone a Sancho para que la resuelva."

40 "Es costumbre antigua en esta ínsula, señor gobernador, que el que viene a tomar posesión desta famosa ínsula está obligado a responder a una pregunta

que se le hiciere, que sea algo intricada y dificultosa" (II, 45); "Lo primero que se le ofreció fue una pregunta que un forastero le hizo. . . . Y . . . el caso es algo dificultoso. . . . Y [suplico que el señor gobernador dé] su parecer en tan intricado y dudoso caso" (II, 51).

41 In his Planeta edition, p. 968n: "en el sentido de problema de difícil solución."
42 See Chapter 2, n. 9.
43 "A Possible Italian Source of Sancho Panza's First Judgment at Barataria," *Italica*, 41 (1964), 439–40.
44 *Tales from Sacchetti*, trans. M. G. Steegmann (London: Dent, 1908), p. 73.
45 Rodríguez Marín, in his edition of *Don Quixote*, VII, 13n: "de todos los oficios mecánicos, ninguno ha sido más satirizado que el de alfayate."
46 Fernand Braudel, *The Mediterranean and the Mediterranean World in the Age of Philip II*, trans. Siân Reynolds (New York: Harper & Row, 1973), II, 807–8, 814. I wish to thank Professor Joseph Silverman for providing me with an exhaustive list of documents to confirm the *converso* status of most tailors.
47 Byron, *Cervantes*, p. 18.
48 *La realidad histórica de España* (Mexico: Porrúa, 1962), p. 213: "los sastres eran muy a menudo judíos."
49 *Cervantes: Pioneer and Plagiarist*, p. 85.
50 *Tales from Sacchetti*, p. 71.
51 Ed. Fredson Bowers (New York: Harcourt Brace Jovanovich, 1983), p. 24.
52 *Cervantes's Theory of the Novel*, pp. 90–1.

Chapter 8. Sum and substance

1 "La suma y substancia de lo que se ha tratado, ventilado y discurrido sobre alguna materia."
2 See especially the many works of Manuel Bartolomé Cossío.
3 See Mancing, *The Chivalric World*, pp. 25–6. Cf. Foucault, *The Order of Things*, pp. 46–7: "The book is not so much his existence as his duty. He is constantly obliged to consult it in order to know what to do or say, and what signs he should give himself and others in order to show that he really is of the same nature as the text from which he springs. The chivalric romances have provided once and for all a written prescription for his adventures. . . . Don Quixote reads the world in order to prove his books." My statement in the text is predicated on *Don Quixote* as we now find it. To account for the imitative rather than emulative aspects in I, 5, we have to make a few changes, but the ultimate dependence on books remains constant.
4 Mancing, in *The Chivalric World*, p. 26, writes: "In order to comprehend what is happening in *Don Quijote*, the protagonist's book-inspired existence must be acknowledged. Twentieth-century readers who learn to recognize Don Quijote's chivalric archaism gain more than an ability to appreciate a seemingly incidental comic level of parody. Their awareness of the archaic element in his speech allows them to appreciate the very essence of his concept of himself as a knight-errant." Mancing's wording – "a seemingly

incidental comic level of parody" – is essential. The archaisms are indisputably part of the humor, particularly a part of the comic level of parody, but, and I believe this is Mancing's point here, their function as a lifeline raises that level beyond the risible. Cf. *Princeton Encyclopedia of Poetry*, p. 488: "The humor of *Don Quixote*, *as well as its tragedy*, depends on a recognition of romance conventions" (emphasis mine).

5 See Bruce W. Wardropper, "*Don Quixote*: Story or History?" *Modern Philology*, 63 (1965), 1–11.

6 *Tesoro*, s.v. *fingir*: "Ficcion[:] la maraña o mētira bien cōpuesta, y cō artificio."

7 E.g., *Don Quixote*, II, 1: "Imagino que todo es ficción, fábula y mentira, y sueños contados por hombres despiertos, o, por mejor decir, medio dormidos" ("I imagine that it's all fiction, fable, and lie, and dreams related by men who are wide awake or, rather, half asleep").

8 *Fact or Fiction: The Dilemma of the Renaissance Storyteller* (Cambridge, Mass.: Harvard University Press, 1973), p. 13.

9 S.v. *invention*, p. 401.

10 Forcione, in *Cervantes, Aristotle, and the "Persiles,"* p. 327, gives a succinct history of the term *ingenio* and its significance in literary and oratorical tradition: "From Quintilian to Tesauro *ingenium* was used to describe the inventive faculty of the poet . . . which takes delight in producing new and startling creations." He even goes so far as to translate *ingenio agudo* as "creative faculty . . . so quick" (in a passage from *Pedro de Urdemalas*). I am inclined to share the qualification offered in a recent study: "However, invention and imitation are closely connected concepts and both refer to the process of encountering and selecting materials to utilize. It seems probable that, among other things, Cervantes is referring here [in the prologue to the *Novelas ejemplares*] to a unique reworking and recombining of existing literary models" (Robert M. Johnston, "Picaresque and Pastoral in *La ilustre fregona*," in *Cervantes and the Renaissance*, ed. M. D. McGaha [Easton, Pa.: Juan de la Cuesta, 1980], p. 175).

11 "El concepto que Pinciano tiene de la literatura obliga al poeta a recorrer toda la naturaleza, animada o inanimada, y a crear un mundo nuevo" (*El Pinciano*, p. 51).

12 "Cada individuo es un punto de vista esencial. Yuxtaponiendo las visiones parciales de todos se lograría tejer la verdad omnímoda y absoluta. Ahora bien: esta suma de las perspectivas individuales, este conocimiento de lo que todos y cada uno han visto y saben, esta omnisciencia, esta verdadera 'razón absoluta' es el sublime oficio que atribuíamos a Dios" (*El tema de nuestro tiempo* [Madrid: Revista de Occidente, 1956], p. 100).

13 *Hacia la comedia: De los valencianos a Lope* (Madrid: Cupsa, 1978).

14 "Notes on the Novel," in Ortega y Gasset, *The Dehumanization of Art* (Garden City, N.Y.: Doubleday Anchor, 1956), p. 59.

15 Cited from *Preceptiva dramática española*, ed. F. Sánchez Escribano and A. Porqueras Mayo (Madrid: Gredos, 1972), pp. 126–7.

16 On this point, see Sturgis E. Leavitt, "Spanish *Comedias* as Potboilers," *PMLA*, 82 (1967), 178–84.

17 *Don Quixote*, I, 48: "Las [comedias] que llevan traza y siguen la fábula como el arte pide, no sirven sino para cuatro discretos que las entienden."

18 Bruce W. Wardropper, in "Ambiguity in *El viejo celoso*," *Cervantes*, 1 (1981), 19, writes: "Unlike the prose fictions, the *entremeses* present a world of farce, in which nothing, not even marriage is sacred. Nevertheless, serious concerns protrude from these playlets. . . . This is not to say that all the *entremeses* are satires, . . . [but] in them an insistent probing of man and his society takes cover behind the frivolity."

19 In *Approaches to Teaching Cervantes' "Don Quixote*," ed. Richard Bjornson (New York: Modern Language Association of America, 1984), pp. 62, 63. Eisenberg repeats here his insistence on "accepting the book as a work of humor – no more, no less – written without further pretensions." ("Cervantes' *Don Quijote* Once Again: An Answer to J. J. Allen," in *Estudios literarios de hispanistas norteamericanos dedicados a Helmut Hatzfeld con motivo de su 80 aniversario*, ed. J. M. Solà-Solé, A. Crisafulli, and B. Damiani [Barcelona: Hispam, 1974], p. 110.)

20 "Teaching *Don Quixote*," p. 63.

21 *Don Quixote's Profession*, p. 3.

22 *The Romantic Approach*, p. 55. The reference is to the work identified in the following note.

23 *La ambigüedad en el Quijote* (Xalapa: Universidad Veracruzana, 1960), p. 77.

Bibliography

Abrams, Fred.   "A Possible Italian Source of Sancho Panza's First Judgment at Barataria." *Italica*, 41 (1964), 438–42.

Allen, John J.   *"Don Quixote* and the Origins of the Novel." In *Cervantes and the Renaissance*, ed. M. D. McGaha. Easton, Pa.: Juan de la Cuesta, 1980, pp. 125–40.

Don Quixote: Hero or Fool? Gainesville: University Presses of Florida, 1969.

Don Quixote: Hero or Fool? Part II. Gainesville: University Presses of Florida, 1979.

Amezúa, Agustín G.   *Cervantes: Creador de la novela corta española.* 2 vols. Madrid: CSIC, 1956–8.

Aristotle.   *The Nicomachean Ethics.* Trans. H. Rackham. Loeb Classical Library. Cambridge, Mass.: Harvard University Press, 1934.

Poética de Aristóteles. Ed. V. García Yebra. Madrid: Gredos, 1974.

Poetics. Trans. Gerald F. Else. Ann Arbor: University of Michigan Press, 1970.

Poetics. Trans. Leon Golden. Commentary by O. B. Hardison, Jr. Englewood Cliffs, N.J.: Prentice-Hall, 1968.

Atkinson, William C.   "Cervantes, El Pinciano, and the *Novelas ejemplares.*" *Hispanic Review*, 16 (1948), 189–208.

"Séneca, Virués, Lope de Vega." In *Homenatge a Antoni Rubió i Lluch.* Barcelona. Estudis Universitaris Catalans, 1936, I, 111–31.

Augustine, Saint.   *The Trinity.* Trans. Stephen McKenna. Washington, D.C.: Catholic University of America Press, 1963.

Avalle-Arce, Juan Bautista.   *Nuevos deslindes cervantinos.* Barcelona: Ariel, 1975.

Aylward, Edward T.   "Cervantes on Lofraso: Love or Hate?" *Revista de Estudios Hispánicos*, 13 (1979), 163–4.

Cervantes: Pioneer and Plagiarist. London: Tamesis, 1982.

Bell, Aubrey F. G.   *Cervantes.* Norman: University of Oklahoma Press, 1947.

Bell, Michael.   "Sancho's Governorship and the 'Vanitas' Theme in 'Don Quixote' Part II." *Modern Language Review*, 77 (1982), 325–38.

Benson, Larry D.   "The Originality of *Beowulf.*" In *The Interpretation of Narrative*, ed. M. W. Bloomfield. Cambridge, Mass.: Harvard University Press, 1970, pp. 1–43.

Borges, Jorge Luis.   *Other Inquisitions.* Trans. Ruth L. C. Sims. Austin: University of Texas Press, 1964.

Bradner, Leicester. "From Petrarch to Shakespeare." In *The Renaissance*. New York: Harper & Row, 1962, pp. 97–119.

Brantley, Franklin O. "Sancho's Ascent into the Spheres." *Hispania*, 53 (1970), 37–45.

Braudel, Fernand. *The Mediterranean and the Mediterranean World in the Age of Philip II*. Trans. Siân Reynolds. 2 vols. New York: Harper & Row, 1973.

Bruerton, Courtney. "The Chronology of the *Comedias* of Guillén de Castro." *Hispanic Review*, 12 (1944), 89–151.

Burke, Kenneth. *Perspectives by Incongruity*. Bloomington: Indiana University Press, 1964.

Byron, William. *Cervantes: A Biography*. Garden City, N.Y.: Doubleday, 1978.

Calcraft, R. P. "Structure, Symbol and Meaning in Cervantes' *La fuerza de la sangre*." *Bulletin of Hispanic Studies*, 58 (1981), 197–204.

Casalduero, Joaquín. *Sentido y forma de las Novelas ejemplares*. Madrid: Gredos, 1962.

Sentido y forma del "Quijote." Madrid: Insula, 1949.

Sentido y forma del teatro de Cervantes. Madrid: Gredos, 1966.

Castro, Américo. *Hacia Cervantes*. Madrid: Taurus, 1957.

El pensamiento de Cervantes. Barcelona: Noguer, 1973.

"Los prólogos al *Quijote*." In Castro, *Hacia Cervantes*, pp. 205–40.

La realidad histórica de España. Mexico: Porrúa, 1962.

Cejador y Frauca, Julio. *La lengua de Cervantes*. 2 vols. Madrid, 1906.

Cervantes Saavedra, Miguel de. *The Adventures of Don Quixote*. Trans. J. M. Cohen. Harmondsworth: Penguin, 1950.

Comedias y entremeses. Ed. R. Schevill and A. Bonilla. 6 vols. Madrid: Gráficas Reunidas, 1915–22.

Don Quijote de la Mancha. Ed. Martín de Riquer. Barcelona: Juventud, 1950.

Don Quijote de la Mancha. Ed. Martín de Riquer. Barcelona: Planeta, 1975.

Don Quixote de la Mancha. Ed. Rudolph Schevill. 4 vols. Madrid: V. Suárez, 1928–41.

Don Quixote of La Mancha. Trans. Walter Starkie. New York: New American Library, 1964.

Entremeses. Ed. Eugenio Asensio. Madrid: Castalia, 1970.

Exemplary Stories. Trans. C. A. Jones. Harmondsworth: Penguin, 1972.

La Galatea. Ed. Juan Bautista Avalle-Arce. 2 vols. Clásicos Castellanos. Madrid: Espasa-Calpe, 1961.

The History and Adventures of the Renowned Don Quixote. Trans. Tobias George Smollett. 2 vols. London: Millar, Osborne, Rivington, 1755.

El ingenioso hidalgo Don Quijote de la Mancha. Ed. Francisco Rodríguez Marín. 10 vols. Madrid: Ediciones Atlas, 1947–9.

The Ingenious Gentleman Don Quixote de la Mancha. Trans. Samuel Putnam. 2 vols. New York: Viking Press, 1949.

Obras completas. Ed. Angel Valbuena Prat. Madrid: Aguilar, 1965.

Ocho entremeses. Ed. Juan Bautista Avalle-Arce. Englewood Cliffs, N.J.: Prentice-Hall, 1970.

Los trabajos de Persiles y Sigismunda. Ed. Juan Bautista Avalle-Arce. Madrid: Castalia, 1969.

Viaje del Parnaso. Ed. Francisco Rodríguez Marín. Madrid: Bermejo, 1935.

Chapman, Janet A.   "Juan Ruiz's 'Learned Sermon.'" In *"Libro de buen amor"*
  Studies, ed. G. B. Gybbon-Monypenny. London: Tamesis, 1970, pp. 29–
  51.

Chaucer's Major Poetry. Ed. A. C. Baugh. New York: Appleton-Century-Crofts,
  1963.

Cirlot, J. E.   *A Dictionary of Symbols*. Trans. from the Spanish, *Diccionario de
  símbolos tradicionales*, by Jack Sage. New York: Philosophical Library, 1962.

Close, Anthony.   "Cervantes' *Arte Nuevo de Hazer Fábulas Cómicas en este Tiempo*."
  Cervantes, 2 (1982), 3–22.

"Don Quixote's Sophistry and Wisdom." *Bulletin of Hispanic Studies*, 55 (1978),
  103–14.

The Romantic Approach to "Don Quixote." Cambridge: Cambridge University
  Press, 1978.

Copleston, Frederick.   *A History of Philosophy*. 9 vols. Garden City, N.Y.: Doubleday, 1962–3.

Covarrubias [H]orozco, Sebastián de.   *Tesoro de la lengua castellana, o española*.
  Madrid: Luis Sánchez, 1611.

Crawford, J. P. Wickersham.   *Spanish Drama before Lope de Vega*. 2d rev. ed.,
  1937; rpt. with corrections and bibliographical supplement by Warren T.
  McCready. Philadelphia: University of Pennsylvania Press, 1967.

Cull, John T.   "Cervantes y el engaño de las apariencias." *Anales Cervantinos*,
  19 (1981), 69–92.

Cullen, Patrick.   "Imitation and Metamorphosis: The Golden-Age Eclogue in
  Spenser, Milton, and Marvell." *PMLA*, 84 (1969), 1559–70.

Curtius, Ernst Robert.   *European Literature and the Latin Middle Ages*. Trans. W.
  R. Trask. Princeton, N.J.: Princeton University Press, 1973.

Demetrius.   *On Style*. Trans. W. Rhys Roberts. Loeb Classical Library. Cambridge, Mass.: Harvard University Press, 1932.

Diccionario de Autoridades. Facsimile ed. 3 vols. Madrid: Gredos, 1969.

Dictionary of the History of Ideas. Ed. P. P. Wiener. 5 vols. New York: Scribner,
  1968.

Dunn, Peter N.   "Las *Novelas ejemplares*." In *Suma Cervantina*, ed. Juan Bautista
  Avalle-Arce and E. C. Riley. London: Tamesis, 1973, pp. 81–118.

Durán, Manuel.   *La ambigüedad en el Quijote*. Xalapa: Universidad Veracruzana,
  1960.

Durant, Will.   *The Age of Faith*. Vol. IV of *The Story of Civilization*. New York:
  Simon & Schuster, 1950.

Eisenberg, Daniel.   "Cervantes' *Don Quijote* Once Again: An Answer to J. J.
  Allen." In *Estudios literarios de hispanistas norteamericanos dedicados a Helmut
  Hatzfeld con motivo de su 80 aniversario*, ed. J. Solà-Solé, A. Crisafulli, and
  B. Damiani. Barcelona: Hispam, 1974, pp. 103–10.

"*Don Quijote* and the Romances of Chivalry: The Need for a Reexamination."
  Hispanic Review, 41 (1973), 511–23.

"On Editing *Don Quixote*." *Cervantes*, 3 (1983), 3–34.

"Pero Pérez the Priest and His Comment on *Tirant lo Blanch*." *MLN*, 88

(1973), 321–30. Republished in Eisenberg, *Romances of Chivalry in the Spanish Golden Age*. Newark, Del.: Juan de la Cuesta, 1982, pp. 147–58.

Review of *Sancho Panza through Three Hundred Seventy-five Years of Continuations, Imitations, and Criticism, 1605–1980*, by R. M. Flores. *Bulletin of Hispanic Studies*, 61 (1984), 507–8.

"Teaching *Don Quixote* as a Funny Book." In *Approaches to Teaching Cervantes' "Don Quixote,"* ed. Richard Bjornson. New York: Modern Language Association of America, 1984, pp. 62–8.

El Saffar, Ruth.   "Concerning Change, Continuity and Other Critical Matters: A Reading of John J. Allen's *Don Quixote: Hero or Fool* Part II." *Journal of Hispanic Philology*, 4 (1980), 237–54.

Novel to Romance: A Study of Cervantes's "Novelas ejemplares." Baltimore: Johns Hopkins University Press, 1974.

Fernández de Avellaneda, Alonso.   *El ingenioso hidalgo Don Quijote de la Mancha.* Ed. F. García Salinero. Madrid: Castalia, 1971.

Finello, Dominick L.   "En la Sierra Morena: *Quijote* I, 23–26." In *Actas del Sexto Congreso Internacional de Hispanistas*, ed. A. M. Gordon and E. Rugg. Toronto: University of Toronto, 1980, pp. 242–4.

Flores, R[obert] M.   "Cervantes at Work: The Writing of *Don Quixote*, Part I." *Journal of Hispanic Philology*, 3 (1979), 135–60.

"The Rôle of Cide Hamete in *Don Quixote*." *Bulletin of Hispanic Studies*, 59 (1982), 3–14.

Sancho Panza through Three Hundred Seventy-five Years of Continuations, Imitations and Criticism, 1605–1980. Newark, Del.: Juan de la Cuesta, 1982.

"Sancho's Fabrications: A Mirror of the Development of His Imagination." *Hispanic Review*, 38 (1970), 174–82.

Forcione, Alban K.   *Cervantes and the Humanist Vision: A Study of Four "Exemplary Novels."* Princeton, N.J.: Princeton University Press, 1982.

Cervantes, Aristotle, and the "Persiles." Princeton, N.J.: Princeton University Press, 1970.

Cervantes' Christian Romance. Princeton, N.J.: Princeton University Press, 1972.

Ford, J[eremiah] D. M.   *Main Currents of Spanish Literature.* New York: Holt, 1919.

Foucault, Michel.   *The Order of Things: An Archaeology of the Human Sciences.* New York: Random House, Vintage Books, 1973.

Fraser, Russell.   *The Dark Ages and the Age of Gold.* Princeton, N.J.: Princeton University Press, 1973.

Froldi, Rinaldo.   *Lope de Vega y la formación de la comedia.* Rev. ed. Trans. Franco Gabriele. Salamanca: Ediciones Anaya, 1968. Originally published as *El teatro valenzano e l'origine della commedia barocca.* Pisa: Editrice Tecnico-Scientifica, 1962.

Gitlitz, David M.   "Symmetry and Lust in Cervantes' *La fuerza de la sangre*." In *Studies in Honor of Everett W. Hesse*, ed. W. C. McCrary and J. A. Madrigal. Lincoln, Nebr.: Society of Spanish and Spanish-American Studies, 1981, pp. 113–22.

Green, Otis H.   *Spain and the Western Tradition*. 4 vols. Madison: University of Wisconsin Press, 1963–6.

Harrison, Stephen.   "Magic in the Spanish Golden Age: Cervantes's Second Thoughts." *Renaissance and Reformation*, 4 (1980), 47–64.

Hayes, Aden W.   "Narrative 'Errors' in *Rinconete y Cortadillo*." *Bulletin of Hispanic Studies*, 58 (1981), 13–20.

Heninger, S. K., Jr.   *A Handbook of Renaissance Meteorology*. 1960; rpt. New York: Greenwood Press, 1968.

Hermenegildo, Alfredo.   *La tragedia en el renacimiento español*. Barcelona: Planeta, 1973.

Highet, Gilbert.   *The Classical Tradition: Greek and Roman Influences on Western Literature*. 1949; rpt. London: Oxford University Press, 1957.

Ihrie, Maureen.   *Skepticism in Cervantes*. London: Tamesis, 1982.

Iventosch, Hermann.   "Dulcinea, nombre pastoril." *Nueva Revista de Filología Hispánica*, 17 (1963–4), 60–81.

Johnson, Carroll B.   "El arte viejo de hacer teatro: Lope de Rueda, Lope de Vega y Cervantes." *Cuadernos de Filología*, 3 (1981), 247–59.

Madness and Lust: A Psychoanalytical Approach to Don Quixote. Berkeley: University of California Press, 1983.

Johnston, Robert M.   "Picaresque and Pastoral in *La ilustre fregona*." In *Cervantes and the Renaissance*, ed. M. D. McGaha. Easton, Pa.: Juan de la Cuesta, 1980, pp. 167–77.

Karl, Frederick R.   *The Adversary Literature: The English Novel in the Eighteenth Century: A Study in Genre*. New York: Farrar, Strauss & Giroux, 1974.

Kinney, Arthur F.   "Rhetoric and Fiction in Elizabethan England." In *Renaissance Eloquence: Studies in the Theory and Practice of Renaissance Rhetoric*, ed. J. J. Murphy. Berkeley: University of California Press, 1983, pp. 385–93.

Koppen, Erwin.   "Gab es einen '*Ur-Quijote*'? Zu einer Hypothese der Cervantes-Philologie." *Romanistisches Jahrbuch*, 27 (1976), 330–46.

LaGrone, Gregory G.   *The Imitations of "Don Quixote" in the Spanish Drama*. Philadelphia: University of Pennsylvania Publications, 1937.

Lapesa, Rafael.   *Historia de la lengua española*. Madrid: Escelicer, 1959.

Lathrop, Thomas A.   Review of *The Chivalric World of "Don Quijote*," by Howard Mancing. *Cervantes*, 2 (1982), 189–90.

Levin, Harry.   "Art as Knowledge." In Levin, *Contexts of Criticism*. Cambridge, Mass.: Harvard University Press, 1957, pp. 15–37.

"The Tradition of Tradition." In Levin, *Contexts of Criticism*. Cambridge, Mass.: Harvard University Press, 1957, pp. 55–66.

Levisi, Margarita.   "La función de lo visual en *La fuerza de la sangre*." *Hispanófila*, 49 (1973), 59–67.

Lewis, C. S.   *The Allegory of Love*. London: Oxford University Press, 1958.

The Discarded Image: An Introduction to Medieval and Renaissance Literature. 1964; rpt. Cambridge: Cambridge University Press, 1967.

Lida, María Rosa.   "De cuyo nombre no quiero acordarme." *Revista de Filología Hispánica*, 1 (1939), 167–71.

Llorens, Vicente.   "La intención del *Quijote*." *Revista de Occidente*, 18 (1967), 143–58.

López Estrada, Francisco. *"La Galatea" de Cervantes: Estudio crítico.* Tenerife: Universidad de la Laguna, 1948.

López Molina, Luis. "Una visión dieciochesca del *Quijote.*" *Anales Cervantinos,* 16 (1977), 97–107.

López Pinciano, Alonso. *Philosophía antigua poética.* Ed. A. Carballo Picazo. Madrid: CSIC, 1953.

Lowe, Jennifer. "The *cuestión de amor* and the Structure of Cervantes' *La Galatea.*" *Bulletin of Hispanic Studies,* 43 (1966), 98–108.

Lydgate, Barry. "Mortgaging One's Work to the World: Publication and the Structure of Montaigne's *Essais.*" *PMLA,* 96 (1981), 210–23.

MacCurdy, Raymond R., and Rodríguez, Alfred. "Las dos locuras de don Quijote." *Anales Cervantinos,* 17 (1978), 3–10.

Madariaga, Salvador de. *Don Quixote: An Introductory Essay in Psychology.* London: Oxford University Press, 1961.

Mancing, Howard. *The Chivalric World of "Don Quijote": Style, Structure, and Narrative Technique.* Columbia: University of Missouri Press, 1982.

——— "The Comic Function of Chivalric Names in *Don Quijote.*" *NAMES,* 21 (1973), 220–35.

Marianella, Conchita Herdman. *"Dueñas" and "Doncellas": A Study of the "Doña Rodríguez" Episode in "Don Quijote."* Chapel Hill: North Carolina Studies in the Romance Languages and Literatures, 1979.

Maritain, Jacques. *Creative Intuition in Art and Poetry.* New York: Pantheon, 1953.

Márquez Villanueva, Francisco. *Fuentes literarias cervantinas.* Madrid: Gredos, 1973.

——— *Personajes y temas del "Quijote."* Madrid: Taurus, 1975.

Martí, Antonio. *La preceptiva retórica española en el siglo de oro.* Madrid: Gredos, 1972.

May, Rollo. *The Courage to Create.* New York: Norton, 1975.

Menéndez Pelayo, Marcelino. *Historia de las ideas estéticas en España.* Madrid: CSIC, 1947.

Menéndez Pidal, Ramón. "Un aspecto en la elaboración del *Quijote.*" In Menéndez Pidal, *De Cervantes y Lope de Vega.* Madrid: Espasa-Calpe, 1940, pp. 9–51.

Moliner, María. *Diccionario de uso del español.* Madrid: Gredos, 1966.

Murillo, L[uis] A[ndrés]. "Cervantes' *Coloquio de los perros,* a Novel-Dialogue." *Modern Philology,* 58 (1961), 174–85.

——— "*Don Quixote* as a Renaissance Epic." In *Cervantes and the Renaissance,* ed. M. D. McGaha. Easton, Pa.: Juan de la Cuesta, 1980, pp. 51–70.

——— *The Golden Dial: Temporal Configuration in "Don Quijote."* Oxford: Dolphin, 1975.

——— "*Lanzarote* and *Don Quijote.*" *Folio,* 10 (1977), 55–68.

——— "El *Ur-Quijote*: Nueva hipótesis." *Cervantes,* 1 (1981), 43–50.

Nabokov, Vladimir. *Lectures on Don Quixote.* Ed. Fredson Bowers. New York: Harcourt Brace Jovanovich, 1983.

Nelson, Lowry, Jr. "Chaos and Parody: Reflections on Anthony Close's *The Romantic Approach to 'Don Quixote.'*" *Cervantes,* 2 (1982), 89–95.

Nelson, William. *Fact or Fiction: The Dilemma of the Renaissance Storyteller.* Cambridge, Mass.: Harvard University Press, 1973.

Ortega y Gasset, José. *The Dehumanization of Art.* Garden City, N.Y.: Doubleday Anchor, 1956.

Meditaciones del Quijote. Madrid: Revista de Occidente, 1966.

El tema de nuestro tiempo. Madrid: Revista de Occidente, 1956.

Osuna, Rafael. "Una parodia cervantina de un romance de Lope." *Hispanic Review,* 49 (1981), 87–105.

Pabon, Thomas. "Secular Resurrection through Marriage in Cervantes' *La Señora Cornelia, Las dos doncellas* and *La fuerza de la sangre.*" *Anales Cervantinos,* 16 (1977), 109–24.

Parr, James A. "Extrafictional Point of View in *Don Quijote.*" In *Studies on "Don Quijote" and Other Cervantine Works,* ed. D. W. Bleznick. York, S.C.: Spanish Literature Publications, 1984, pp. 20–30.

Percas de Ponseti, Helena. *Cervantes y su concepto del arte: Estudio crítico de algunos aspectos y episodios del "Quijote."* 2 vols. Madrid: Gredos, 1975.

Periñán, Blanca. *Poeta ludens: "Disparate," "perqué" y "chiste" en los siglos XVI y XVII.* Pisa: Giardini, 1979.

Piluso, Robert V. "*La fuerza de la sangre*: Un análisis estructural." *Hispania,* 47 (1964), 485–90.

Plato. *The Collected Dialogues of Plato.* Ed. E. Hamilton and H. Cairns. Princeton, N.J.: Princeton University Press, 1963.

Plett, Heinrich F. "The Place and Function of Style in Renaissance Poetics." In *Renaissance Eloquence: Studies in the Theory and Practice of Renaissance Rhetoric,* ed. J. J. Murphy. Berkeley: University of California Press, 1983, pp. 356–75.

Porqueras Mayo, Alberto. "Algunas observaciones introductivas a la teoría dramática de los siglos XVI y XVII." In *Preceptiva dramática española,* ed. F. Sánchez Escribano and A. Porqueras Mayo. Madrid: Gredos, 1972, pp. 16–38.

El prólogo como género literario. Madrid: CSIC, 1957.

Poteet-Bussard, Lavonne C. "*La ingratitud vengada* and *La Dorotea*: Cervantes and *La ingratitud.*" *Hispanic Review,* 48 (1980), 347–60.

Predmore, Richard L. *Cervantes.* New York: Dodd, Mead, 1973.

The World of Don Quixote. Cambridge, Mass.: Harvard University Press, 1967.

Princeton Encyclopedia of Poetry and Poetics. Ed. A. Preminger. Princeton, N.J.: Princeton University Press, 1974.

Pring-Mill, R. D. F. "Sententiousness in *Fuente Ovejuna.*" *Tulane Drama Review,* 7 (1962), 5–37.

Randel, Mary Gaylord. "The Language of Limits and the Limits of Language: The Crisis of Poetry in *La Galatea.*" *MLN,* 97 (1982), 254–71.

Redondo, Augustín. "Tradición carnavalesca y creación literaria, del personaje de Sancho Panza al episodio de la Insula Barataria en el *Quijote.*" *Bulletin Hispanique,* 80 (1978), 39–70.

Ricoeur, Paul. "The Metaphorical Process as Cognition, Imagination, and Feeling." *Critical Inquiry,* 5 (1978), 143–59.

Riley, E[dward] C.   *Cervantes's Theory of the Novel*. Oxford: Oxford University Press, Clarendon Press, 1962.

"The *pensamientos escondidos* and *figuras morales* of Cervantes." In *Homenaje a W. L. Fichter: Estudios sobre el teatro antiguo hispánico y otros ensayos*, ed. A. D. Kossoff and J. Amor y Vázquez. Madrid: Castalia, 1971, pp. 623–31.

"Teoría literaria." In *Suma Cervantina*, ed. J. B. Avalle-Arce and E. C. Riley. London: Tamesis, 1973, pp. 293–322.

"Three Versions of Don Quixote." *Modern Language Review*, 68 (1973), 807–19.

"Who's Who in *Don Quixote*? or an Approach to the Problem of Identity." *MLN*, 81 (1966), 113–30.

Rivers, Elias L.   "Cervantes and the Question of Language." In *Cervantes and the Renaissance*, ed. M. D. McGaha. Easton, Pa.: Juan de la Cuesta, 1980, pp. 23–33.

Robert, Marthe.   *The Old and the New: From Don Quixote to Kafka*. Trans. C. Cosman. Berkeley: University of California Press, 1977.

Rose, Margaret A.   *Parody/Meta-Fiction*. London: Croon Helm, 1979.

Rosenblat, Angel.   *La lengua del "Quijote."* Madrid: Gredos, 1971.

Rosenblum, Michael.   "Smollett and the Old Conventions." *Philological Quarterly*, 55 (1976), 389–402.

Russell, Peter E.   "Arms versus Letters: Towards a Definition of Spanish Fifteenth-Century Humanism." In *Aspects of the Renaissance: A Symposium*, ed. A. R. Lewis. Austin: University of Texas Press, 1967, pp. 47–58.

"'Don Quixote' as a Funny Book." *Modern Language Review*, 64 (1969), 312–26.

Saldívar, Ramón.   "Don Quijote's Metaphors and the Grammar of Proper Language." *MLN*, 95 (1980), 252–78.

Sánchez Rivero, Angel.   "Las ventas del 'Quijote.'" In *El concepto contemporáneo de España*, ed. A. del Río and M. J. Benardete. Buenos Aires: Losada, 1946, pp. 662–72.

Sargent, Cecilia Vennard.   *The Dramatic Works of Cristóbal de Virués*. New York: Instituto de las Españas, 1930.

Selig, Karl-Ludwig.   "The Battle of the Sheep (*Don Quixote*, I, xviii)." *Revista Hispánica Moderna*, 38 (1974–75), 64–72.

Sena, Jorge de.   "Hispanismo: Archipiélago de glorias y vanidades en el mar-océano de la ignorancia universal." In *Actas del Sexto Congreso Internacional de Hispanistas*, ed. A. M. Gordon and E. Rugg. Toronto: University of Toronto, 1980, pp. 19–25.

Shepard, Sanford.   *El Pinciano y las teorías literarias del siglo de oro*. Madrid: Gredos, 1962.

Sieburth, Renée.   "Metamorphosis: The Key to an Interpretation of Don Quixote's Adventure in the Cave of Montesinos." *Revista de Estudios Hispánicos*, 15 (1981), 3–15.

Smith, A. Mark.   "Getting the Big Picture in Perspectivist Optics." *Isis*, 72 (1981), 568–89.

Snyder, Joel.   "Picturing Vision." In *The Language of Images*, ed. W. J. T. Mitchell. Chicago: University of Chicago Press, 1980, pp. 219–46.

Sobré, J. M. "Don Quixote, the Hero Upside-Down." *Hispanic Review*, 44 (1978), 127–41.

Spanish Ballads. Ed. C. Colin Smith. Oxford: Pergamon Press, 1964.

Spaulding, Robert K. *How Spanish Grew*. Berkeley: University of California Press, 1948.

Spitzer, Leo. "Linguistic Perspectivism in the *Don Quijote*." In Spitzer, *Linguistics and Literary History*. Princeton, N.J.: Princeton University Press, 1967, pp. 41–85.

Stagg, Geoffrey. "Revision in *Don Quixote*, Part I." In *Hispanic Studies in Honour of Ignasi González Llubera*, ed. F. Pierce. Oxford: Dolphin, 1959, pp. 347–66.

"Sobre el plan primitivo del 'Quijote.'" In *Actas del Primer Congreso Internacional de Hispanistas*. Oxford: Dolphin, 1964, pp. 1–9.

Suma Cervantina. Ed. Juan Bautista Avalle-Arce and E. C. Riley. London: Tamesis, 1973.

Tales from Sacchetti. Trans. Mary G. Steegmann. London: Dent, 1908.

Tillyard, E. M. W. *The Elizabethan World Picture*. New York: Random House, n.d.

Trueblood, Alan S. *Experience and Artistic Expression in Lope de Vega: The Making of "La Dorotea."* Cambridge, Mass.: Harvard University Press, 1974.

Ugalde, Victoriano. "La risa de Don Quijote." *Anales Cervantinos*, 15 (1976), 157–70.

Valbuena, A. Julián. "Verbal Strategies, Images, and Symbolic Roles in the Use of a Conventional Language by a Spanish Golden Age Playwright." In *The First Delaware Symposium on Language Studies: Selected Papers*, ed. R. J. Di Pietro, W. Frawley, and A. Wedel. Newark, Del.: University of Delaware Press, 1983, pp. 59–72.

Van Doren, Mark. *Don Quixote's Profession*. New York: Columbia University Press, 1958.

Vega Carpio, Lope de. *Epistolario de Lope de Vega Carpio*. Ed. Agustín G. de Amezúa. Vols. III–IV. Madrid: Artes Gráficas "Aldus," 1941–3.

"The New Art of Writing Plays." Trans. W. T. Brewster. In *Papers on Playmaking*, ed. Brander Matthews. New York: Hill & Wang, 1957, pp. 1–19.

Vegas, Damián de. *Coloquio entre un alma y sus tres potencias, donde se introduce irse dellas, amotinada por el mal servicio que le hacen*. In *Romancero y cancionero sagrados*, ed. J. de Sancha. Biblioteca de Autores Españoles, vol. XXXV. Madrid: Atlas, 1950, pp. 530–4.

Wardropper, Bruce W. "Ambiguity in *El viejo celoso*." *Cervantes*, 1 (1981), 19–27.

"Cervantes' Theory of the Drama." *Modern Philology*, 52 (1955), 218–19.

"Comedias." In *Suma Cervantina*, ed. J. B. Avalle-Arce and E. C. Riley. London: Tamesis, 1973, pp. 147–69.

"*Don Quixote*: Story or History?" *Modern Philology*, 63 (1965), 1–11.

Weiger, John G. "Cervantes's Curious Curate." *Kentucky Romance Quarterly*, 30 (1983), 87–106.

"A Clue to Cervantine Ambiguity: *Darse a entender.*" *Hispanic Journal*, 3 (1982), 83–9.

Cristóbal de Virués. Boston: Twayne, 1978.

"The Curious Pertinence of Eugenio's Tale in *Don Quijote.*" *MLN*, 96 (1981), 261–85.

"*Don Quixote*: The Comedy in Spite of Itself." *Bulletin of Hispanic Studies*, 60 (1983), 283–92.

"Guillén de Castro: Apostilla cronológica." *Segismundo*, 27–32 (1978–80), 103–20.

Hacia la comedia: De los valencianos a Lope. Madrid: Cupsa, 1978.

"Lo nunca visto en Cervantes." *Anales Cervantinos*, 17 (1978), 111–22.

"Lope de Vega según Lope: ¿Creador de la comedia?" *Cuadernos de Filología*, 3 (1981), 225–45.

"Lope's Conservative *Arte de hacer comedias en este tiempo.*" In *Studies in Honor of Everett W. Hesse*, ed. W. C. McCrary and J. A. Madrigal. Lincoln, Nebr.: Society of Spanish and Spanish-American Studies, 1981, pp. 187–98.

"Lope's Role in the Lope de Vega Myth." *Hispania*, 63 (1980), 658–65.

Weinberg, Bernard. "Robortello on the *Poetics.*" In *Critics and Criticism*, ed. R. S. Crane. Chicago: University of Chicago Press, 1975, pp. 319–48.

Wouk, Herman. "You, Me, and the Novel." *Saturday Review/World*, 29 June 1974, pp. 8–13.

Ximeno, Vicente. *Escritores del reyno de Valencia.* 2 vols. Valencia: Dolz, 1747–9.

Zimic, Stanislav. "Cervantes frente a Lope y a la comedia nueva." *Anales Cervantinos*, 15 (1976), 19–119.

Ziomek, Henryk. "El uso de los números en el *Quijote.*" In *Actas del Sexto Congreso Internacional de Hispanistas*, ed. A. M. Gordon and E. Rugg. Toronto: University of Toronto, 1980, pp. 825–7.

Index